534

Prairie Women

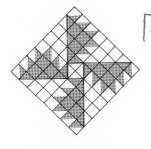

Prairie Women

Images in American and Canadian Fiction

CAROL FAIRBANKS

Yale University Press

NEW HAVEN AND LONDON

Designed by James J. Johnson and set in Goudy Old Style type.
Printed in the United States of America by Halliday Lithograph, West Hanover, Massachusetts.

Library of Congress Cataloging-in-Publication Data

Fairbanks, Carol, 1935–
    Prairie women.

    Bibliography: p.
    Includes index.
    1. American fiction—Middle West—History and criticism.   2. Canadian fiction—Prairie Provinces—History and criticism.   3. Rural women in literature.   4. Women pioneers in literature.   5. Women in literature.   6. Prairies in literature.   7. Frontier and pioneer life in literature.   8. American fiction—Women authors—History and criticism.   9. Canadian fiction—Women authors—History and criticism.   10. Feminism and literature.   I.   Title.
    PS273.F34   1986   813'.009'352042   85–22616

ISBN 0–300–03374–5

10 9 8 7 6 5 4 3 2 1

For T. A. Browne

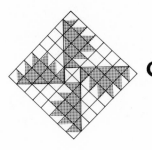

Contents

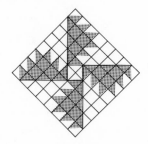 **Illustrations**

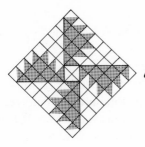 **Acknowledgments**

Although I grew up in the Finger Lakes region of upstate New York, I was familiar with such names as Blue Earth and Winnebago and Mankato— my father had grown up in Minnesota. When I was seven years old he gave me a book called *Prairie Children,* but it was many years before I made the connection between the book and his childhood, that those southern Minnesota towns were in the midst of the tallgrass prairies. My great-grandparents, the Hills, had emigrated from Vermont to Minnesota in the 1850s. Both Cynthia Hill and her daughter (my grandmother) Eva Hill Fairbanks left reminiscences of their Minnesota years. So in a sense, this book began with my family and is a tribute to my own prairie forebears. It is also a tribute to my mother, Clara Hunt Fairbanks.

My interest in researching Canadian materials evolved from a National Endowment for the Humanities seminar on Canadian history and literature held at Michigan State University, in 1978, under the direction of Dr. Russel B. Nye. Dr. Nye continued to guide my research over the next several years and served on my doctoral committee at the University of Minnesota.

I am indebted to the American Studies Program at the University of Minnesota and several faculty members in particular for their direction and encouragement as I wrote the first version of this study for my dissertation: Clark Chambers; Arthur Geffen; Roland DeLattre, my program advisor; and Chester Anderson, my thesis advisor.

I deeply appreciate the guidance provided by Ellen Graham, editor for Yale University Press, during the revision process. In addition, Elizabeth Casey's editing of the manuscript contributed immensely to accuracy, clarity, and style; her interest in the writings of prairie women and in this study was personal as well as academic—she grew up on a Kansas farm.

Funding from a variety of sources facilitated the research process. The Canadian Embassy in Washington, D.C., and the Canadian Consulate in Chicago provided funds for attending Canadian Studies conferences and researching materials in libraries and archives in Manitoba, Saskatchewan, Alberta, and British Columbia. The University of Wisconsin–Eau Claire provided several curriculum development grants for research in Canada and study at the University of Minnesota. This past year Douglas A. Pearson, Chair of the English Department, and the department's Advisory Committee approved a grant which provided release-time for preparing the manuscript for publication.

Research has been facilitated by a variety of people. Kay Henning, supervisor of Inter-Library Loans, McIntyre Library, University of Wisconsin–Eau Claire, processed hundreds of requests over the years, always with perseverance, enthusiasm, and good will. Debra Maben, a graduate assistant in the English Department, painstakingly checked footnotes. Bob Fuller and Jim Christopherson of the UW–EC Media Development Center contributed their expertise in the preparation of illustrations. The English Department secretarial staff and Caryl Laubach, supervisor, frequently assisted me by typing and xeroxing materials.

Minnie Lyon Avery not only contributed a photograph of her family but brought the pioneer experience to life through her vivid descriptions of life in a Nebraska soddie. I am grateful to several other people for illustrations of their work: T. A. Browne, Michael Hilger, Eleanor Jones, Hazel Litzgus, and Joan Stradinger. I am indebted also to the following for permission to reprint illustrations: Alberta Photograph Library; Glenbow Museum; The Minneapolis Institute of Arts; The Glass Negative, Ponca City, Oklahoma; Public Archives Canada; South Dakota Memorial Art Center; Topeka, Kansas, State Archives; National Museum of American Art, Smithsonian Institution. The poets Martha Mihalyi and Roberta Hill Whiteman each kindly gave permission to quote a complete poem.

In a less direct way, numerous studies on prairie women's history and literature provided invaluable background and insights for my own research. I would like to thank two scholars in particular, Glenda Riley and John Mack Faragher, for their interest in my work. In addition, Sara Brooks Sundberg has been a treasured colleague and friend over a six-year period as we both researched and shared materials; there is no other scholar south of the forty-ninth parallel more knowledgeable about Canadian prairie women's history.

In the process of preparing this manuscript, I crossed the threshold into the computer age and the mysterious technology related to word processing. I am grateful to James Olson for giving unsparingly of his time to teach me how to use the computer.

As I rewrote the dissertation and added new sections, Helen X. Sampson, one of my professors at the University of Wisconsin–Eau Claire, stepped forward to serve as sounding board, grammarian, shaper of style, and cheering gallery. She brought several aptitudes to my subject: the objectivity and regimentation of her training in English literature, a long-term commitment to humanist feminism, and the memories of a small-town Iowa girlhood. Our long afternoons of reading, talking, editing, and proofreading are a precious part of this work.

Finally, I want to thank Thomas A. Browne for his unwavering support. He read some third-rate prairie novels, shook up the dust in secondhand bookstores in a search for out-of-print books, and, most importantly, read innumerable versions of the manuscript. At every stage of my research—even when the trout streams were calling him—he remained my steadfast advocate and friend.

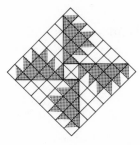

CHAPTER ONE

Introduction

A weathered gambrel-roofed barn stands silhouetted against a bronze wheat field in Alberta. Somewhere between Regina and Winnipeg, the one-room schoolhouse gazes empty-windowed at an unused crossroads; a few feet away eighteen-wheelers and Fords speed by on the Trans Canada Highway. Near the town of Tolstoi in southern Manitoba, a miniature, onion-domed church competes for attention on the flat horizon with rock piles stacked four feet high in a cleared field nearby. Just south of Fargo, North Dakota, a lush shelterbelt no longer protects the old homestead; it now encloses an aluminum-sided tri-level. In April, man-set fires burn across the prairies at Crex Meadows in northwestern Wisconsin; shortly thereafter the sandhill cranes arrive and prairie flowers—pasqueflower, crowfoot violet, and lupine—emerge from the crumbly, sooty soil. In Blue Earth, Minnesota, some of the oldest tombstones read Orthondt, Hill, Felzer, and Chittenden. On Route 80 west of Chicago some of the signs point to Kankakee, Kewanee, Oskaloosa, Omaha, and Wahoo.

These names, these birds and plants, these pioneer-era barns, schoolhouses, churches, and shelterbelts have their counterparts throughout the prairie provinces of Canada and the prairies of the midwestern states. They serve as reminders of a vital past that has stirred the curiosity and imagination of the environmentalist, the historian, and the creative writer. In the mind's eye the prairie suddenly comes to life again: a carpenter constructs a gambrel-roofed barn reminiscent of his father's farm in the Ukraine; a young schoolteacher arrives from eastern Ontario and meets her first class, her Christian zeal no less than that of the itinerant preacher; while a prairie fire burns out of control, a farmer plows

1

a fireguard around his buildings and the wife and children beat at flames with wet blankets; an Indian woman watches a covered wagon on the horizon.

Envisioning the prairie past is more difficult and complex for those reconstructing the pasts of women on the prairie. In fact, a process must be initiated that Adrienne Rich appropriately calls re-visioning:

> Re-vision—the act of looking back, of seeing with fresh eyes, of entering an old text from a new critical direction—is for women more than a chapter in cultural history: it is an act of survival. . . . A radical critique of literature, feminist in its impulse, would take the work first of all as a clue to how we live, how we have been living, how we have been led to imagine ourselves, how our language has trapped as well as liberated us, how the very act of naming has been till now a male prerogative, and how we begin to see and name—and therefore live—afresh. . . . We need to know the writing of the past, and know it differently than we have ever known it; not to pass on a tradition but to break its hold over us. [35]

The present study is committed to this act of revisioning the lives of prairie women in Canada and the United States—looking back, seeing with new eyes, and entering old texts from a feminist critical perspective. I hope to discover the ways women writers have described the experiences of pioneer prairie women and how they have named the "new" land—the land that was new to the pioneers but old and familiar to the native peoples.

But what are the prairies? One novelist, Dora Aydelotte, describes an eastern Oklahoma prairie which is typical of most prairies: "Straight to the sky-line swept great waves of prairie land, lifting in one grassy swell after another. In every direction it was the same—miles of bare, rolling country, with trees keeping close to the stream-beds along the winding draws" (*Trumpets Calling* 58). In *North American Prairie*, the geographer J. E. Weaver identifies the prairies as level areas that also consist of "knolls, steep bluffs, rolling hilly land, valleys, and extensive alluvial flood plains" (quoted in Duncan, *Tallgrass Prairie* 5). The climate is characterized by extremes with highs in summer of 100°F and lows in winter of −50°F in some portions. Because there are no major physical barriers, air masses move freely, causing rapid changes in temperature. Frosts, droughts, heat waves, hailstorms, and dust storms create havoc with crops (Watson 380).

The Canadian works included in this study are set in southern Manitoba, southern Saskatchewan, and southern Alberta east of the Rockies. This area was originally "tall grass" or "mixed grass," which includes big bluestem, little bluestem, and Indian grasses. Excluded are works located in the "short grass" regions judged too arid for agricultural settlements, particularly those set in the area known as Palliser's Triangle in southeastern Alberta and southwestern Saskatchewan. However, geographical criteria for including or excluding works are complicated by the fact that during two periods in the early twentieth century there were unusually heavy rainfalls in portions of Palliser's Triangle in western Saskatchewan and eastern Alberta. Greatly encouraged, settlers rushed in and attempted to create a way of life that would eventually become typical of prairie farms and towns. Each of these periods, unfortunately, was followed by unusually dry times; many settlers struggled to survive while others who had the resources left.

Most of the American[1] prairie works are located in the central lowlands (once covering 400,000 acres) east of the 98th meridian in the Dakotas, Nebraska, and Kansas; southern and western Minnesota; northern Texas; Iowa; and large portions of Illinois, including the Grand Prairie of central Illinois. The emphasis is on areas that were originally covered by tall grass and that equate closely to present land-use zones classified as over sixty percent arable. Excluded from the study are ranch country and irrigation communities of the short grass; these semiarid prairies are usually designated by geographers as high plains rather than prairies.

The works emphasize the prairie itself—soil, crops, flowers, trees, animals, birds, wind, rain, and temperatures, as well as the distance of the horizon, the flatness or rolling qualities of the landscape, and the intensity of the sky.[2] The works emphasize other qualities as well. Prairie people describe the territory as the Garden of the World or as the Next Year Land, according to how well crops are doing. They share specific historical events and political movements. Therefore, works by Nellie L. McClung have been included in the study although she was not particularly interested in the landscape per se and its effects on character and life-style. Her collection of short stories, *The Black Creek Stopping-House*, has been included because individual characters and clusters of settlers

---

1. "America" or "American" is used in this study to refer to the United States. Canadians rarely refer to themselves as "Americans."

2. These criteria are similar to Laurence Ricou's in his selection of poets for *Twelve Prairie Poets*. He included works that "both create and depend upon a sense of the locale and history of the Canadian prairie. . . . In each case the prairie is a prominent, and often persistent, focus of the poet's work" (6, 7).

represent the human types and aspirations of prairie province pioneers during the 1880s. An American novel by Loula Grace Erdman, *The Edge of Time,* is geographically on the fringe of the "true" prairie, but its account of experiences of "nesters" in the Texas Panhandle illuminates the lives of individuals trying to maintain a prairie-farm way of life in a country dominated by ranchers.[3]

It becomes apparent, then, that an obtrusive prairie setting is not the only ingredient for a prairie novel, but it *is* an important one in most analyses. As Arthur Adamson reminds us in "Identity through Metaphor," a description of a prairie setting provides a starting point in the task of identifying, categorizing, and analyzing works by prairie writers. Not all the writers in this study have what Adamson calls "the ability to translate descriptive elements into metaphor, to reveal the reality of the confrontation of nature and civilization" (93); nevertheless, even the less skilled and perceptive writers, in their revisioning of women's lives on the prairie, record objects, events, places, moods, and human characteristics and actions that help us to reconstruct portions of our past history.

Over 120 works make up the tradition of prairie women writers— thirty-two Americans and thirty-four Canadians—beginning with the short fiction of Mary Hartwell Catherwood in the 1870s and extending into the 1980s with such works as Louise Erdrich's *Love Medicine* (1984) and Barbara Sapergia's *Foreigners* (1984).

A number of generalizations can be made about the writers working within the tradition of prairie women's fiction. All of them were either born on the prairie or lived significant portions of their lives on prairie farms or in prairie towns. Nellie L. McClung, for example, immigrated to the prairie in 1880, at the age of seven, with her parents. She participated in each of the major stages of frontier life in Manitoba, making the transitions from isolated life on a homestead to participation in small-town life and finally to active social and political life throughout the prairie provinces (Zieman 62). As a result of these experiences, McClung and others like her (including those from second and third generations who had heard about but had not lived the experiences) were

---

3. Erdman makes this distinction between "farm" and "ranch": "Farms were founded on the basic fact of the presence of water. Cattle country needed it too, but it could exist without wells. If a rancher had four or five hundred sections, or even less, he would be sure to have water running naturally somewhere on it—a stream, or a spring, or even a river. But when you had only one section, it was a matter of chance" (175).

compelled to write about the frontier experience; there was a sense of having a story to tell that had not been told before.

Willa Cather said that she " 'had searched for books telling about the beauty of the country . . . its romance, the heroism and strength and courage of its people that had been plowed into the very furrows of its soil.' She said: 'I did not find them.' " She then proceeded to write *O Pioneers!* in an attempt to provide the missing perspective (Bennett, "Willa Cather" 231–32).[4] In fact, Cather and most prairie women writers seemed to feel that women like Alexandra, the hero of *O Pioneers!*, had been excluded from historical and literary accounts of pioneer women. Certainly heroic images of frontier women were missing from most books.

Alexis de Tocqueville's *Democracy in America*, based on his 1832 travels in America, has impressed generations of Americans and Europeans with his observations of people and institutions; his impressions of the frontier woman would have been noted by many. "I find the following passage in my travel diary," he writes, "and it will serve to show what trials are faced by those American women who follow their husbands into the wilds":

> A woman was sitting on the other side of the hearth, rocking a small child on her knees. She nodded to us without disturbing herself. Like [her husband], this woman was in the prime of life; her appearance seemed superior to her condition, and her apparel even betrayed a lingering taste for dress; but her delicate limbs were wasted, her features worn, and her eyes gentle and serious; her whole physiognomy bore marks of religious resignation, a deep peace free from passions, and some sort of natural, quiet determination which would face all the ills of life without fear and without defiance. [732]

This image of the frontier woman—worn and resigned, but determined—pervades frontier letters, journals, diaries, memoirs, poems, paintings, popular songs, fiction, travel books, and illustrations. There is no reason to doubt its accuracy. Many writers like Cather, however, insist that there were other images. They want to juxtapose the images of women like Alexandra—energetic, strong, self-sufficient, inventive, far-sighted—against de Tocqueville's description.

The attempts of these writers have been largely overlooked. Wal-

---

4. Eleanor Gates's *Plow-Woman* had been published in 1906. Surely Cather would have approved of its portrayal of the prairie landscape and women's heroism, strength, and courage.

ter Prescott Webb, the respected historian, devoted less than two pages of his book *The Great Plains* (1931) to the topic "What has been the Spiritual Effect of the American Adventure in the Great Plains on Women?" He observed that men who settled on the prairie found "zest to the life, adventure in the air, freedom from restraint; men developed a hardihood which made them insensible to the hardships and lack of refinements." He claims that women, on the other hand, experienced fear and distrust of the land; they were lonely and missed the comforts of former homes and the cultural activities of former communities (505). This attitude persists. For example, in the 1970s a Canadian literary critic, Eric Callum Thompson, affirms the opinion of a 1930s novelist, John Beames, who wrote this in his novel *An Army without Banners*: "It is not in women that the pioneer spirit stirs; the horizon does not beckon them; hills and rivers are to them a barrier, not an invitation to explore. It was the men only who pressed on across the great plains; the women had little more to say than the horses who drew the wagons in which they sat. Where women had the deciding word no move was made" (quoted in Thompson 216). Thompson responded thus: "Beames makes an astute comment on the different attitudes held by the sexes." He accepts the myth of the female as reluctant pioneer.[5]

What would critics like Webb and Beames and Thompson have made of a woman like Letitia McCurdy Mooney who talked her husband

---

5. Many other historians and critics have taken a position similar to Thompson's, but they show the complexities involved in arriving at this particular generalization. In *Women and Men on the Overland Trail*, Faragher concluded, on the basis of trail diaries and letters, that "not one wife initiated the idea" of emigration. "Less than a quarter of the women writers recorded agreeing with their restless husbands." (163). See his discussion of the reluctant female emigrant, 163–73. Sara Sundberg's study of Minnesota prairie farm women cites several women who take an active role in the decision (26–31). Sometimes women's statements are ambiguous; for example, Sundberg cites Cynthia York Hill, my great-grandmother, who commented on the events following her marriage and subsequent plans to emigrate from Vermont to Minnesota: "As we were agreed to go west we started next Dec." (Sundberg 31). The subject of the reluctant emigrant is also analyzed in Fairbanks and Sundberg 39–43, 74–79. In *Frontier Women: The Trans-Mississippi West, 1840–1880*, Julie Roy Jeffrey raises the question "Were they just dragged unwillingly by their men or did they participate in the decision?" She notes that resources are "meager," but that some answers are available: economic factors were, of course, of primary consideration; secondary reasons related to health and climate (see 25–36). Susan H. Armitage's "Reluctant Pioneers" is a recent analysis that explores the difficulties in assessing women's roles in the decision to emigrate. The notion that women were "afraid of the wilderness, afraid of the Indians, homesick, and often physically or mentally sick" is a male myth; on the other hand, there were many reasons why women were reluctant to emigrate, so the stereotype cannot be discounted as completely false (40).

into emigrating? Her daughter, Nellie McClung, recreates the scene in her autobiography, *Clearing in the West*:

> "We'll have to go some place, John," she said one night to my father. "There's nothing here for our three boys. What can we do with one-hundred-and-fifty stony acres? The boys will be hired men all their lives, or clerks in a store. That's not good enough!"
>
> Father was fearful! There were Indians to consider, not only Indians but mosquitoes. He had seen on the Ottawa what mosquitoes could do to horses; and to people, too. No! It was better to leave well enough alone. [32]

But Letitia McCurdy Mooney was determined to emigrate, and emigrate she and her family did. According to her daughter's account, she walked every foot of the way from the train depot in Saint Boniface to the homestead 180 miles away: "She liked to have her eye on the whole procession and she could only do this from the rear" (57).

While the images of women portrayed by de Tocqueville, Beames, and Webb have received a great deal of attention, fictional versions of women like Mrs. Mooney have been given very little visibility by the critics or, sometimes, by the authors themselves. Nevertheless, such women have been present in prairie literature from the first, as a brief survey of works by male writers will reveal. These works include James Fenimore Cooper's *Prairie*; Joseph Kirkland's *Zury: The Meanest Man in Spring County*; several of Hamlin Garland's Middle Border works—*A Son of the Middle Border, A Daughter of the Middle Border, A Pioneer Mother, Trail-makers of the Middle Border*; Ole Rölvaag's *Giants in the Earth* and *Peder Victorious*; Wright Morris's *Plains Song: For Female Voices*. Relevant Canadian works include Frederick Philip Grove's *Fruits of the Earth*; Sinclair Ross's *Sawbones Memorial*; and Robert Kroetsch's short story "The Harvester."

James Fenimore Cooper concluded in *The Prairie* (1827) that the prairie, then called "the Great American Desert," was not hospitable to the farmer and his plow. As Natty Bumppo says to Ishmael Bush, the prospective squatter, "If you have come in search of land, you have journeyed hundreds of miles too far, or as many leagues too little" (78). One of Bush's sons is of a similar mind: "The rifle is better than the hoe in such a place as this." (77). The story takes place in 1805, shortly after the Louisiana Purchase. Ishmael Bush represents the settlers on the border who, feeling the pressure of encroaching civilization, move on before being restricted by either the law or the church bell (69). At the end of the novel, however, Bush is portrayed with his back to the setting sun: settlement of the prairie, according to Cooper, has to be left for the next generation; the Bush family is forced to move back toward the East primarily because Indians still occupy the territory.

The Prairie is a story of a failed pioneering venture, but the problem is not due to the timidity of the emigrants, male or female. As Cooper observes in the first chapter, "there was no visible sign of uneasiness, uncertainty, or alarm among them," and he was including women with the men in his description of the party (12). As the story develops, the fearlessness of the women is tested and proven repeatedly. Esther Bush is a born trailmaker, supervising the tasks of her many children in a "spirited" manner, a favorite word of Cooper's in reference to the pioneers. She assigns tasks with such an assured voice of authority that even her husband complies rather than risk losing an argument in a debate over procedures. When the eldest Bush son disappears, Esther organizes the search. When Ishmael tells her she might find some hostile Sioux, she is unperturbed. "I will shoulder a rifle myself," Esther says, "and woe betide the redskin that crosses my path! I have pulled a trigger before today; aye, and heard an Indian yell too, to my sorrow" (127, 135). The search party leaves the camp. Esther, "attired in a dress half masculine and bearing a weapon like the rest, seemed no unfit leader for the group of wildly clad frontiersmen that followed in her rear" (136). "Follow me!" Esther shouts. "I am leader today, and I will be followed. Who so proper, let me know, as a mother to head a search for her own lost child?" (137).

The two eldest daughters, like their mother, show "insensibility to danger" (153) and, in a threatening situation, keep their fingers poised on the triggers of their guns, refusing to surrender (161). "Reared in the hardihood of a migrating life on the skirts of society, where they had become familiarized to the sights and dangers of the wilderness, these girls promised fairly to become at some future day no less distinguished than their mother for daring and for that singular mixture of good and evil which in a wider sphere of action would probably have enabled the wife of the squatter to enroll her name among the remarkable females of her time" (153). Their cousin, Ellen Wade, though educated and refined, is also "spirited" and self-reliant. She commands the camp while Esther and the Bush men search for a lost son. When she and the other girls see Indians in the distance, she tries to remember all the stories she had read and heard about female heroism. Remembering a story of a "solitary female" who had killed her captor and, in addition, set free "a brood of helpless young," she has a sufficient model of female heroism to sustain her through an attack (153). In this and other scenes in the novel, Ellen demonstrates that a woman can be both feminine and fearless. In this first major novel of the prairie, there is no suggestion of the reluctant, long-suffering female emigrant.

Cooper was living in Paris at the time that he put the finishing touches on his story about the prairies, a territory he had never visited.[6] In contrast, Joseph Kirkland spent his years between ages five and thirteen on the frontier in Michigan and, at the age of twenty-eight, settled in the small town of Tilton, Illinois. Three decades later, in 1887, he published his first novel about the Grand Prairie of Illinois—*Zury: The Meanest Man in Spring County.*

The significance of this novel in terms of its female images cannot be overstated.[7] Kirkland had as a model of a frontierswoman his own mother, Caroline Kirkland, who described the Michigan wilderness settlements in *A New Home—Who'll Follow?* It is no wonder, therefore, that the main female character of *Zury* is an educated easterner who adapts well to prairie life. At the same time, however, Kirkland provides other portraits of women: some were reluctant emigrants who complied with their husbands' decisions and hesitated to demand attention to their own needs on the homesteads for which they had sacrificed so much.

The opening paragraph of *Zury* describes the way the prairies tested the first settlers:

> Great are the toils and terrible the hardships that go to the building up of a frontier farm; inconceivable to those who have not done the task or watched its doing. In the prairies, Nature has stored, and preserved thus far through the ages, more life-materials than she ever before amassed in the same space. It is all for man, but only for such men as can take it by courage and hold it by endurance. Many assailants are slain, many give up and fly,

6. Cooper was immensely popular in Europe and contributed much to the European's impressions of the midwestern prairies. Van Wyck Brooks points out that Cooper's "fame was already vast and universal, and as early as 1833 every new novel by Cooper was published simultaneously in thirty-four cities of Europe. . . . The 'American novels' rivalled the Waverly novels. There renown was far greater on the continent than it was in England. . . . He had castles placed at his disposal, while his books were not only praised by the greatest novelists and critics in Europe but had begun to influence generations of writers" (329).

7. In his critical study of Joseph Kirkland, Clyde E. Henson observes that "*Zury* sets down the life of the Middle West in all its crudeness—the constriction of pioneer life with its harshness and waste of finer values, the crude surroundings which limit the characters, and the struggle for survival are clearly set forth. Yet Kirkland has given the final triumph to man, for the very struggle in which his people engage gives dignity to them and reality to his fiction" (117).

but he who is sufficiently brave, and strong, and faithful, and fortunate, to
maintain the fight to the end, has his ample reward. [1]

At the beginning of the novel (which certainly plays out these opening
generalizations), Zury is still a boy. His family has emigrated from the
mountains of southern Pennsylvania; their new homestead includes 640
acres of some of the choicest land in Illinois, consisting of both timber
and prairie. The family's first sight of the land is presented from the point
of view of the mother, Selena. Kirkland chooses this perspective to
demonstrate a woman's involvement in the settlement experience:
"With haste Selena scrambled out to the wagonseat, where she sat and
feasted her eyes on the long-wished-for sight." She sees what looks like
"an undulating ocean of grass and flowers"—including blue gentian,
rosinweed, goldenrod, lady slippers—"weeds and flowers of a thousand
descriptions and as many shades of color and varieties of form and tex-
ture. Among, between, and around them was the persistent, peculiar
prairie grass." (9–10).

The first years of homesteading, however, take their toll. Zury's
little sister dies: "The little girl, who might have lived, and even
thriven, in a warm, rich and comfortable city home, could not bear the
cruelty of her environment, and died after long, quiet suffering" (28).
Pioneer life alone is not to blame, as this passage makes clear; money,
which provides for physical necessities, is the key factor in the health of
a child, and money is scarce for this pioneer family. The mother too
gradually weakens.

Zury's compulsion to succeed on his prairie homestead stems from
the suffering of his mother and his small sister. Zury gradually "subdues"
the farm, clears it, plants it, pays off his father's mortgages, and begins
making a profit. Then he buys up the mortgages of other farmers who fail
(65), thus earning the name "the meanest man in Spring County." By
the 1850s Zury has become a prosperous farmer, a prototypical prairie
farmer whose image appears, in slightly varying forms, in the novels of
Rölvaag and Grove. When he marries it is because he needs someone to
do the woman's work. He picks Mary Prouder, from a family of women
who have worked hard without appreciation or rewards; these women are
spiritless, undemanding victims of male aspirations.

Later in the novel, Kirkland describes an equally hardworking
woman but one with spirit—Mrs. Peddicomb. Zury says, "When o' man
Peddicomb come to his land, shortly after we come to ours, she was wuth
more onto th' place than what he was. She—why she was one of these

'come gals' kind of women" (416). She is the kind, apparently, who can do twice as much work as a woman should and thus saves the homestead.

The most important woman in the story, however, is Annie Sparrow, who arrives from Massachusetts "with all the reckless and splendid courage of New England youth, self-reliance and inexperience." As Kirkland says, she "had taken her life in her hand and journeyed into the unknown wild" (89). Annie had helped her widowed mother edit a small newspaper in Massachusetts; in the process she had been introduced to some of the ideas of the New England socialist movement. Her involvement in politics increased after her mother's death, and these activities eventually resulted in the disapproval of her acquaintances, hence the necessity for leaving the East. Clearly, "her theories, her independence, her pride, her strength, her weakness, had led her far out into the West—to Wayback in Spring County, Illinois" (92). Here she eventually gains the approval of a suspicious, ignorant school board after Zury prepares her for the kind of questions the board members are apt to ask.

Annie gets caught in a terrifying storm and because of a special fear of loneliness, she becomes too intimate with her rescuer: the rescuer is Zury and the baby is Zury's. When she realizes that she is pregnant, she examines her life and asks this question:

> Was the horizon opening out, or was it closing in? Her life had had a world of dreams; some very bright. She was to have been a writer; she was to have been the priestess of a coming revelation: even as late as her westward journey she was to have become a little queen among the rough people she was to meet in the wilds. *Now,* what was she to be after all her little attainments and fond hopes of greater? "Poor Mrs. John McVey!" [294]

In this dilemma she thinks of the man who has been courting her, John Endicott McVey, another New Englander. He is described as "slender in body and mind—too soft in head and heart" (124). If he had stayed in Boston, he might have succeeded at something, but, the narrator notes, "a palm is out of place in a prairie" (125).

Up to this point McVey has had very little confidence that Annie would marry him. When she reveals her predicament, he decides that she is "as blameless as a woman can be" and proposes to her again. After the marriage, they move to Springville, where John becomes an accountant. The first few years he "kept up a fair show of service; then his laziness allowed the accounts to get into arrears, and he used to bring home the books for Anne to work at. . . . It was mere child's play to her, and she fell into doing more and more of it, at home and at the warehouse" (320–

21). Eventually John, like a lot of his contemporaries, decides to take a look at California, where he dies of ague. Annie is hired to replace him as an accountant and balances her time between work and raising her twins, whom she treasures. Over the years Annie sees Zury on a few accidental occasions when he comes to town on business; she refuses to maintain any kind of friendship, although she eventually becomes his anonymous speech writer when he runs for office. She enjoys watching him use her ideas and words to win the support of voters.

The novel ends, in the author's words, "a whole generation later . . . well on in the Fifties." Zury, having become a widower, courts Annie with trepidation and persistence. Annie, finally convinced that he is *not* the meanest man of Spring County, marries him. Zury's home-stead, once "the abode of toil and hardship—poor in money, comfort, grace, gaiety, leisure, cultivation, refinement, liberality"—now has all these qualities: Zury provided the money, the comforts, and the leisure; Annie contributed the grace, cultivation, and refinement. Both gave the farm an air of gaiety and liberality (509).[8]

The acknowledged authority on midwestern life and literature, Hamlin Garland, reviewed *Zury* when it first came out. He praised the book as "the best picture of pioneer Illinois life yet written" (quoted in Henson 95). A short time later, the two authors met. Kirkland urged Garland, as "the first actual farmer in literature," to write fiction as well as nonfiction about the Midwest" (Henson 96).

Garland, like Kirkland, sympathized with the woman pioneer and her unselfish devotion to creating a new home in the West. Those familiar with Garland's works recognize, however, that none of Garland's women in fiction or nonfiction is as independent and self-sufficient as Annie Sparrow. Garland wrote A *Pioneer Mother* (1922) as a tribute to his own mother, Isabelle Garland. He provides additional portraits of Belle Garland in the autobiographies, A *Son of the Middle Border* (1917) and A *Daughter of the Middle Border* (1921); her fictional counterpart (Isabel Graham) appears in the novel, *Trail-makers of the Middle Border* (1926). In each of these works, Belle Garland symbolizes all prairie women who married men whose dreams were always focused on the western prairies; no matter how many times they moved, David Garland imagined another, more sumptuous, prairie Eden just beyond.

8. Henry Nash Smith calls the marriage of Zury and Annie Sparrow "one of the strangest matings in all literature . . . a transaction as odd as would have been the marriage of Davy Crockett to Miss Alcott's Jo March" (243).

Belle recognizes that emigration would result in a better economic situation for the family, but at the same time she deeply regrets being uprooted. According to Garland, each new homestead required enormous sacrifices and physical work nearly beyond even a strong woman's endurance; nevertheless, Belle dedicates her life to being an uncomplaining helpmate to her husband and a model of heroism to her son.

In *A Son of the Middle Border* Garland begins his account of midwestern pioneers with his father's emigration stories. One episode in particular impressed Garland: his aunt, then a young girl, came down with smallpox and the family had a desperate and critical time until one family took pity on them and helped. Garland writes: "What it all must have seemed to my gentle New England grandmother I grieve to think about. Beautiful as the land undoubtedly was, such an experience should have shaken her faith in western men and western hospitality" (10). Why does Garland believe that only a woman could be disillusioned? Perhaps he reasons this way: because she was reluctant to emigrate she would naturally be more easily disappointed; on the other hand, a man like his grandfather—hardy and independent—would not be easily disheartened.[9]

Garland reinforces this view of a woman who is temperamentally ill-equipped for the frontier in a portrait of his Grandmother McClintock who had seven sons and six daughters. Garland reports that "she made frequent pathetic attempts to open her Bible or glance at a newspaper— all to little purpose, for her days were filled from dawn to dark with household duties" (*Son of the Middle Border* 18). When she died, he says, "she fell like a soldier in the ranks" (26). Certainly her days *were* busy, leaving her little time to relax. Yet in another passage he mentions playing under his mother's quilting frame, noting that "quilting bees of an afternoon were still recognized social functions" (34). He fails, however, to contemplate the satisfactions felt by women who sat around the quilt, talking and sewing. This activity was surely no "pathetic attempt"

---

9. In *Trail-makers of the Middle Border*, Garland describes the reluctant emigrant: "Like thousands of other wives, she was a forced emigrant. Her childhood had been spent in Portland, and her youth in Oxford County. Her life-history was interwoven with the religious and literary traditions of New England and the pain of breaking with familiar scenes and parting with lifelong friends had been especially bitter in her case. Nothing but the conviction that her husband and sons would enjoy the larger life and share in the greater prosperity of a new state, sustained her.

"What an almost mortal agony that parting with her friends had been! We of today can not measure the sense of loss, the passionate grief, the agony, the despair which accompanied such an uprooting. It had in it something of the solemnity of death" (59).

but a true pleasure, and it seems unlikely that his Grandmother McClintock never participated in such common gatherings. In fact, a few pages
later he admits that "life on a Wisconsin farm, even for women, had its
compensations. There were times when the daily routine of lonely and
monotonous housework gave place to an agreeable bustle, and human
intercourse lightened the toil" (50).

After describing the frontier home in the Wisconsin coulee,
Garland turns to his mother's experiences as an emigrant: "She was not
by nature an emigrant,—few women are" (43). He describes moving
day: "It was February, and she very properly resented leaving her home
for a long, cold ride into an unknown world" (71). Garland recalls that
the night before the departure, when family and friends gathered, his
father's face shone "with the light of the explorer, the pioneer." His
mother's expression, however, was "wistful" as she joined in singing
"O'er the Hills in Legions, Boys!"—"She sang it submissively, not exul-
tantly, and I think the other women were of the same mood though their
faces were less expressive to me. To all of the pioneer wives of the past the
song had meant deprivation, suffering, loneliness, heartache" (63).

After a few years on the isolated Iowa prairie, the Garlands moved
to Ordway, South Dakota. In A *Pioneer Mother* Garland describes this
move:

> I don't know what her feelings were about these constant removals to the
> border. . . . My father's adventurous and restless spirit was never satisfied.
> The sunset land always allured him, and my mother, being one of those who
> follow their husbands' feet without a complaining word, seemed always ready
> to take up the trail. . . . I now see that she must have suffered each time the
> bitter pangs of doubt and unrest which strike every woman's heart when
> called to leave her snug, safe fire for a ruder cabin in strange lands. [9]

Late in *Son of the Middle Border*, Garland raises a fundamental
question about the Ordway years: "I resented the conditions under which
my mother lived and worked. . . . Was it for this she had left her home
in Iowa? Was she never to enjoy a roomy and comfortable dwelling?"
(312–13). The answer is an emphatic *yes*—and, significantly, it is a
house the son, not the father, provides. At the conclusion of *Son of the
Middle Border*, Garland recounts his victory over his father: he had arranged a purchase of a farm in West Salem, Wisconsin, so that his
mother could spend her last years among kinfolk. A *Daughter of the Middle
Border* opens at this point in the Garland family history. In the foreword,
Garland writes that his father was not enthusiastic about the return to

Wisconsin, but his mother "enfeebled by the hardships of a farmer's life, and grateful for my care, was glad of the arrangement I had brought about. . . . That I had rescued her from a premature grave on the barren Dakota plain was certain (xii).[10]

Again and again, in Garland's descriptions of pioneer women, certain negative words occur: *agony, pain, weariness, dread, confusion, despair, loss, grief, bitterness, weakness, frailness.* Indeed, Garland seems blind to any contrasting possibilities. The following passage reveals his very limited understanding of the pioneer woman. He is spending some time with his mother in West Salem shortly after the move from Ordway, South Dakota, to Wisconsin. The two have gone into the garden to inspect the new growths of pieplant leaves and asparagus spears.

> "This is the life!" I exultantly proclaimed. "Work is just what I need. I shall set to it at once. Aren't you glad you are here in this lovely valley and not out on the bleak Dakota plain?"
>
> Mother's face sobered. "Yes, I like it here—it seems more like home than any other place—and yet I miss the prairie and my Ordway friends."
>
> As I went about the village I came to a partial understanding of her feeling. The small dark shops, the uneven sidewalks, the rickety wooden awnings were closely in character with the easy-going citizens who moved leisurely and contentedly about their small affairs. It came to me (with some sense of amusement) that these coatless shopkeepers who dealt out sugar and kerosene while wearing their derby hats on the backs of their heads, were not only my neighbors, but members of the Board of Education. Though still primitive to my city eyes, they no longer appeared remote. Something in their names and voices touched me nearly. They were American. [*Daughter* 14]

I have quoted this passage at length to point out that Garland hears and sees—and records—only what conforms to his view of midwestern life. He asks his mother if she is glad to be back in Wisconsin. He wants, of course, to hear her praise him for being a thoughtful son. He contrasts the "bleak Dakota plain" with the "lovely valley," obviously expecting his mother to agree. There is no indication that he heeded what she clearly said—that she misses the prairie and she misses her friends. The only word to which he responds is "friends"—not *her* friends, but friends

10. Roger E. Carp analyzes Garland's ambivalence about women's gender roles and feminism. He notes that Garland's early works seemed in favor of women acquiring "education, careers, and culture. When they married they should do so as equals with their husbands. By the turn of the twentieth century, however, Garland appeared to have abandoned these sentiments, for his female characters became submissive and domestic" (83).

in the abstract, the fellow Americans, whom he condescendingly describes as "primitive" to his "city eyes."

Belle Garland said she missed the prairie and her friends. Hundreds of women in fact and fiction have said the same thing. But for some reason historians and critics, until recently, have not listened to their words or recognized that some women developed strong attachments to the prairie landscape and to the people.

In an article entitled "Hamlin Garland's Feminism," Frances W. Kaye provides invaluable insight into Garland and his interpretations of women's personalities and experiences. She describes the first Thanksgiving dinner after having bought "The Homestead" in West Salem:

> Having purchased for his mother the house in Wisconsin . . . and having claimed her from his father in Dakota, he placed her at the foot of the family table and himself at the head. This marvelously Oedipal scene represents the triumph of the man of culture, the woman's man, over the farmer, the man's man, but it reduces the woman to a mere object of desire, not an actor in her own right. . . . He can empathize with the struggling woman, but the finally triumphant figure must be a man, himself, superior to men and women alike. [156]

This convincing interpretation of Garland's motives helps us to understand why he ignored the fact that his mother missed her Dakota home and friends.

Garland provides one glimpse of a triumphant female figure—his great-aunt Patty—and he has absolutely no empathy with her. Aunt Patty makes her appearance in *Trail-makers of the Middle Border*, Garland's fictionalized version of his family's migrations West. Aunt Patty is introduced as the "robust young wife" of Nate, but "less imaginative" than her husband. It is difficult to accept this characterization as sound because Uncle Nate has been described in terms that could apply to any one of thousands of men who were tired of farming poor land. Nate says, "'All my life I've crawled up and down these hills. . . . Right here I quit the job of watching for rocks to hop out of the ground. I sold my farm for just about what the barn cost me, but no matter. I'm going where land is not only good, but cheap'" (55).

In this novel Garland contradicts statements made in the three works noted above and acknowledges that there are some women (admittedly "few in number") "who are natural pioneers." Patty was "by temperament a joyous adventurer. Handsome, strong as a man, and of confident temper, the plan for going West was the promise of a grand excursion to her, whereas to Harriet [Garland's grandmother] . . . it was an appalling break-up, a tragic necessity" (55). The term "grand excursion," however, minimizes Aunt Patty's image as a pioneer, making it seem more like a lark than a serious undertaking. Garland says that Aunt Patty sounds "happy as a bobolink," whereas his grandmother's voice contained "a plaintive note": "She was so frail of body, so sensitive of mind to be starting on a journey whose vicissitudes would try the most robust, and at the end of the long, wearisome journey, her resting-place could be, at its best, only a rough cabin in a strange community. That she failed of Patty's exultation her sons perceived, but her glance was steady and her words confident. Her own desires were wholly subordinate to those of her sons. Like thousands of other wives, she was a forced emigrant" (58–59). In this passage Garland lingers over his grandmother's frailty and reluctance; he is not at all interested in exploring the reasons for Aunt Patty's enthusiasm.

At the end of the journey from New England to Wisconsin, a young man describes Nate and Patty: "Your aunt and uncle are trumps! We came up to Galena together. Patty never whimpered at any hardship. In fact, she stood it better than most of the men. She's a born pioneeress, that woman!" (121). Again, note Garland's choice of words. By repeating the young man's phrase—"Aunt Patty never *whimpered*"—he diminishes her image as a born pioneer. On the other hand, he never would have said of his mother, "she never whimpered." As Kaye has observed, Garland can empathize only with a "struggling female."

While Harriet and Isabelle Garland suffered and endured many trials, they never approached the edge of insanity and never achieved the archetypal status that has been most unfortunately awarded to Beret Hansa, Ole Rölvaag's female hero in *Giants in the Earth*. Scholars from a variety of disciplines have pointed to Beret as the prototypical female immigrant. Vernon Parrington, in his introduction to the 1929 edition of *Giants*, says that Beret is "the child of an old folk civilization who hungers for the home ways and in whose heart the terror of loneliness gathers" (quoted in Reigstad 117). In a *Landscape* article on Canadian prairie pioneers, Ronald Rees points to Beret as "the classic victim": she "escaped from a prairie storm by climbing into a chest inside her cabin. In extremis she was comforted by the memory of the churchyard in which she had played as a little girl" ("In a Strange Land" 4). Another geographer, David Lowenthal, observes that pioneer women, as symbolized by Beret, were "less engaged than men in the process of transformation [of the land and] often found the solitude unbearable" ("Pioneer Landscape" 10).

These three interpretations describe Beret during the first stages of settlement. Fortunately, other critics who have looked at Beret's prairie experience over a longer period of time interpret Beret as a hero, not as a victim. Paul Reigstad traces Beret's descent into madness and, with the help of her pastor, her return to health; he than concludes that "Beret, who lives on long after Per Hansa's death, herself becomes a daughter of the prairie, experiencing at times satisfaction—even joy—in accepting the challenge of the frontier" (124–25). Paul Olson insists that the strong person of the book is Beret, not Per Hansa, and he draws on the interpretation of another critic, Steven Hahn, to make his point: "It is Beret who emerges as the survivor of this story, for she retains the means to order her life, to create a knowable world for herself" while Per Hansa's response to the pioneer venture was one of "courageous but foolish Romanticism" (quoted in Olson 270). Einar Haugen also points out a significant flaw in Per—significant because it shows that the female value system may be more mature and less competitively greedy: "Per's concern with his material success has left his wife behind, unhappy and misunderstood. She says, 'You know what our life has been: land and houses, and then more land, and cattle'" (Haugen 91). Haugen emphasizes the fact that Beret *sent* Per Hansa into the blizzard; however, Per chose to go "to his sacrifice . . . in an angry, unforgiving mood, an act that one critic has suggested is in effect suicide" (92). One more critical reaction to Beret and Per Hansa rounds out what I believe to be necessary corrective criticism on the novel. Catherine D. Farmer provides this summary:

> Beret was an intrinsically joyful person, never overly concerned with Judeo-Christian sinfulness or its consequences; . . . she loses her joy in herself and in her relationship with Per Hansa, and becomes obsessed with sin and its resulting punishment. . . . She comes to conceive of herself not as a wife or even as a helpmate but as "a hindrance to him, like chains around his feet"; she believes that her presence has "burdened and impeded" her husband. [185]

Beret—a powerful fictional character, multifaceted, subtle in her reactions, and believable in the changes she undergoes—deserves full status as a pioneer hero. She clearly demonstrates heroic qualities in *Peder Victorious* (1929), in which Rölvaag resumes the story begun in *Giants*. It is a distortion of Rölvaag's intentions to call Beret an archetyp-

pose it represents her willingness not only to live *in* America, but to take a place *among* Americans; it also represents a willingness to let the forces of life and love take precedence over religious and cultural beliefs that ⌐.⌐ ⌐e and isolate individuals and communities.

⌐. ⌐ ⌐ readers might have preferred a plot line showing her movement towa⌐ ⌐conciliation resulting entirely from a rational analysis of her relationship to her children and community. Nevertheless, Rölvaag has convincingly portrayed Beret as head of a family, a leader who avoids making the mistakes that Per Hansa and many other prairie patriarchs have made. Thus she emerges as a heroic prairie matriarch who speaks for "hope, for the future, for the west." Ironically, this is the way Robert Scholes describes Per Hansa: "Per Hansa speaks for hope, for the future, for the west. And Beret speaks for fear, for the past, for the values of the old country" (2). This interpretation is, I believe, untenable.

The themes, plots, and characters explored in *Giants in the Earth* persist in a major Canadian novel of the prairie frontier, Frederick Philip Grove's *Fruits of the Earth.* As Dick Harrison has noted, "both novels are accepted as among the best fictional accounts of pioneering in their regions" (252). Both explore the physical, mental, emotional, and spiritual rigors of pioneering (253).

In *Giants in the Earth,* Per Hansa envisioned "a royal mansion" and clings to the belief that he is "both prince and king, the sole possessor of countless treasures." He believes he is going to do something remarkable "which should become known far and wide" (5). The hero of Grove's novel, Abe Spalding, is equally committed to a grand vision, but his notions of pioneering are much less romantic than Per Hansa's. Although he knows that his nearest neighbor on the Manitoba prairie has become "half-crazed with work and isolation" (22), Abe believes that hard work gets results: "He would conquer this wilderness; he would change it; he would set his seal upon it" (22). And one day he would raise a white mansion as symbol of his conquest over nature.

His wife, Ruth, fails to share her husband's optimism. The daughter of a small merchant in Brantford, Ontario, she yearns for a finer and easier way of life than the new settlement can offer. Abe admits that "he had been in love with a face and a figure rather than a mind or soul" (20), yet he hopes that she will rise to the challenge and patiently work by his side. When the children are born, she becomes absorbed in their growth and development, ignoring Abe's accomplishments. Abe, exhausted by the farm work, has no energy left for his wife or children. Paul

Olson's evaluation of Per Hansa applies also the Abe Spalding: he, too, is guilty of "a series of acts of neglect of love" (270). Abe rationalizes his behavior in this way: "The 'kids' were still small; he would take them in hand later; let him build up the farm first, an empire ever growing in his plans" (45).

One day Ruth asks him, "What is it all for?" Abe is puzzled, because the reasons seem so obvious to him: money, prestige, eventual comfort. Ruth says, "To me it seems senseless, useless, a mere waste. Work, work, work! What for?" (48). When she tells him that the country isn't fit to live in, he says: "I'm making it into a country fit to live in. This is my task. The task of a pioneer. Can't you see that I need time, time, time? In six years I've built a farm which produces wealth. Give me another six years, and I'll double it. Then I'll build you a house such as you've never dreamt of calling you own" (48). Such single-minded devotion to wealth is not, in the final analysis, a sign of strength.

Many years later, Abe realizes that he may have built a great estate, he may have had the school district named for him as the first settler in the area, he may have brought law and order to the community during a period in office as reeve; but he has lost his children in the process, although not, strangely enough, Ruth.

In an article entitled "Rölvaag, Grove and Pioneering on the American and Canadian Plains," Dick Harrison observes that "Abe and Per have brought to the prairies reluctant wives, temperamentally unsuited to pioneering and to the plains environment, who deteriorate physically or mentally as their husbands forge the material parts of their visions" (253). This is an exaggeration of their condition, as I have already demonstrated. It does not do justice to Beret Hansa or to Ruth Spalding. By the end of the novel Ruth has accepted Abe's goals and even admires his accomplishments: he had succeeded where so many others had failed in establishing homesteads. Perhaps the comfort and status of the new house did help. Perhaps the bank account which he established in her name gave her a sense of security and made her feel more like a partner in the farm.[11]

---

11. Isobel McKenna points out that Grove, in *In Search of Myself*, says that his sympathies were always on the side of pioneer women, not on the side of the men. McKenna says that "the women in the prairie novels had been condemned to lives completely lacking in any other purpose than running the home, and for this Grove pitied them" (115). Another critic says that "Grove's depiction of Abe's wife Ruth also serves to dramatize his thesis about pioneer life. In a pioneer society, he remarks in his autobiography, woman is perforce a slave, a mere helper of man.

It is important to note that there is no happy ending in *Fruits of the Earth*. Abe Spalding realizes that "his life had been wrong. . . . He had lived to himself and had had to learn that it could not be done" (264). His son Charlie was killed because Abe needed a driver to haul grain to town and gave Charlie permission to take on a task that should have been done by a man. His other son, Jim, chooses to become a mechanic rather than to manage the farm. One daughter marries a lawyer and assumes an entirely different way of life in town. The final crisis is brought about by the younger daughter, Frances: "Like so many others, she had grown out of hand. She did not rebel or disobey; but she lived a life of her own, admitting no one into her confidence" (231). Abe and Ruth are disturbed by her style of dress, by her friends, by her inattentiveness to schoolwork, by her attitudes and activities; yet it is not until she becomes pregnant that both the father and mother are forced to recognize the degree of Frances's alienation.

Abe Spalding has successfully used mind and body to conquer nature. He had enjoyed a rich harvest of fruits from the earth; however—to extend Grove's metaphor—the fruits of his marriage have not been given enough time and attention and he must pay the consequences. Earlier Ruth had asked him, "What is it all for?" At the time, Abe had an answer. Now he viewed his situation differently: "He had worked and slaved; what for? His great house was useless: the three people left in it would have had ample room in the patchwork shack. Soon he and Ruth would be alone, lost in that structure which, from behind the rustling wind-breaks, looked out over that prairie which it had been built to dominate" (227).

Some biographical criticism becomes useful at this point. Grove's vignettes in *Over Prairie Trails* and other autobiographical writings show that there is much of Frederick Grove in Abe Spalding: both the writer and the fictional character are exhilarated by matching intellect and physical endurance against blizzards and flooded rivers and runaway horses. However, Grove's affection and respect for his wife and his grief over the early death of their only child, a daughter, are in sharp contrast with Abe Spalding's feelings about family. Grove ends the novel without

---

Unfortunately for pioneer women, the qualities in their husbands which make them successful pioneers are 'incompatible with that tender devotion which alone can turn the relation of the sexes into a thing of beauty.' . . . Ruth, in fact, is a woman 'fitted for the life in towns or cities rather than for the life on the open prairies'" (Parks ix). These interpretations discount the fact that Ruth and Abe are quite compatible at the end of the novel.

providing for a reconciliation between Spalding and his daughter; in this way Grove may imply that a man who has invested everything in material success and prestige rather than in a child deserves rejection. The tragedy is that the children become so alienated from the father that they never develop a sense of belonging to the land at a time and a place when life on a prairie farm could have brought both material and emotional rewards.

This review of prairie novels by men demonstrates the limited significance of the image of the reluctant female immigrant who sacrifices health and happiness on the homestead for the sake of her husband and children. From the first, male prairie writers have recognized the existence of multiple images. Why, then, does the negative image persist? The feminist historian Annette Atkins places the responsibility firmly on the shoulders of the historians. In the following passage she traces the image found in the works of a number of historians publishing between 1930 and 1980:

> Historians have portrayed pioneer women as stereotypes, almost all in virtual imitation of Beret Hansa. According to the commonly accepted view, women did not want to go west, but if familial responsibilities forced them to move, they carried in their hearts the eastern notions of culture, religion, and education. Upon their arrival in the forsaken West, they found themselves outnumbered by men. They craved the company of women, but could find few. Facing hard times, women urged giving up. Unable to persuade their men to turn back, women faced a prairie existence that broke them in spirit and body. This stereotype of women implies a completely contrary and equally distorted view of pioneer men. The two images provide foils for each other: Men wanted to go west; they cared nothing for civilization and culture; they were not lonely; they did not get discouraged; they did not die of overwork; and they certainly did not go mad. What women faced with dread, men looked to with hope and enthusiasm. While women slaved, men had fun. Men stood by and callously watched the femininity of their women destroyed by wretched surroundings and hard work. Most important, men made all of the decisions while women stood by helplessly and passively. Thus the stereotyped view of pioneer women has produced an equally stereotyped view of pioneer men. [1]

Basing her conclusions on fiction by Willa Cather, Mari Sandoz, and Bess Streeter Aldrich, Atkins demonstrates the flaws in the traditional stereotype.

The persistence of the stereotyped view of pioneer women can be explained in part by the ideas of two political scientists. In *Mediated Political Realities*, Dan Nimmo and James E. Combs explain that "for any situation there is no single reality. . . . There are several, frequently contradictory ones" (3–4). Thus the images people carry around in their heads are *mediated realities*. The fantasy of an individual or of a group becomes accepted and then persists "when it conforms to what one expects or desires" (9). For example, at the same time that people in eastern Canada, the United States, and Europe were being bombarded with descriptions of unfamiliar prairie landscapes, Indians, prairie fires, sod huts, and droughts, they were also absorbing information about gender roles. Such analyses insisted on the public domain for males and the private one for females. Is it any wonder, then, that the fantasy of the dominant culture, made up of Anglo males, perpetuated the image of the stalwart, competent, far-sighted, and ambitious male settler who must necessarily uproot his family for the sake of its future prosperity? And because the risks were great in developing the New World gardens of Canada and the United States—someone would suffer, someone would fail—it became most convenient to balance the glowing optimism of males with the conservativism, hardship, and suffering of females to produce a picture of the prairie venture that bore some semblance to "reality."

I would argue, therefore, that in the last quarter of the nineteenth century when prairie women began to publish their own stories about the frontier, they wanted to undermine or, at a minimum, modify the public's image of the lives of women on the frontier. They were challenged by what Rachel Blau Du Plessis has called the "construction of the other side" of a well-known plot in order to "reinsert women into myth"; in this way women writers have been able to "rescue culture from its own unexamined premises" (quoted in Lauter 12). These stories, when placed beside those of men, have produced a different, more widely based "mediated reality" which incorporates the images of both men and women. Although women used male characters as foils in much the same manner that the male novelists and historians used female characters, they consistently presented a more extensive range of images, both male and female, than their male counterparts; they also developed this variety in greater depth.

Before turning to these mediated realities of prairie women writers, however, I want to acknowledge that the cultural text of the frontier is still being written, and that at least three contemporary male writers have made significant contributions—two Canadians, Robert Kroetsch and Sinclair Ross, and the midwesterner Wright Morris.

In Robert Kroetsch's story "The Harvester" (1956) Maggie is an elderly widow who supports herself by cooking in a truck stop. One day she serves an old man who is hitchhiking to the bush country. While he eats, he reminisces about the golden age of harvesting when he worked as a field pitcher. As a tribute to the man and the times, Maggie bakes an apple pie for him. She tells him that those days were a time of contentment and fulfillment for her, too: "Fun cooking then," she said. "You cooked meals, not pig feed. And you fed men" (80). After the old harvester leaves, one of the young waitresses finds Maggie "smiling softly and her eyes were bright and two tears clung to the cheeks of her tired, careworn, sweaty red face. 'He remembered,' Maggie said. She caught her rough stained hands together in front of her apron like a woman recalling a lover. 'After 25 years he still remembered. . . . He called me Mrs. Rinehart. . . . He remembered my Dutch apple pie!'"

In this story Kroetsch captures the pride and dignity in hard work that many women and men derived from their routine responsibilities. Kroetsch said in an interview that "the fiction makes us real" (*Creation* 63). This quotation has been repeated so frequently by Canadian prairie literary critics that assent appears to be unanimous. Certainly portraits of women like Maggie Rinehart Winters enable female readers to identify with a hardworking farm woman in a positive way and, although fiction may indeed present a mediated account, it cannot be brushed off as "unreal." The central stereotypes have been shown to be unreal.

In *Sawbones Memorial* (1974), Sinclair Ross tells the story of a rural prairie doctor in Saskatchewan who is being honored for several decades of service. Yet Ross develops not only a portrait of Doc Hunter but also portraits of several types of pioneer women who were significant in the frontier doctor's life.[12] His wife Edith represents the "lady" type. She came from Ontario to teach in the prairie town, married the doctor, and stayed—but never fundamentally adjusted. Ida Robinson provides a contrast: she too came from a proper middle-class Ontario home, but, at least

---

12. Two of Ross's earlier works, *The Lamp at Noon and Other Stories* and *As for Me and My House*, describe women in negative situations on prairie farms and in a prairie town. See Paul Comeau's discussion of Ross's pioneer fiction: "The tragedy of the short stories and the irony that characterizes Mrs. Bentley's journal [in *As for Me and My House*] are replaced by the wry humour inherent in the mature perspective of a man [Doc Hunter] who has lived a full and useful life in the service of his fellow men. The vagaries of fortune, the hardships of life as a frontier doctor are behind him, but his enduring interest in people, the hallmark of his character and profession, remain" (181). Comeau concludes that Ross "pays tribute through his subject-matter to the pioneers and unsung heroes of Canada's past" (183). In this respect Ross's goals are very similar to those of prairie women writers.

in Doc Hunter's mind, she stood out among all the women who had had a hard time during those early years: "She didn't just survive, she came through with her head up, telling a joke on herself, ready for more. When she had to, busy times when Nat was out in the field twelve and fourteen hours a day, she'd put on a pair of old overalls and smock and go out slopping around the stable, feeding pigs, milking cows—I've seen her—but she never slopped inside. Always dressed. It might be an old dress, patched and faded, but it was always clean and it always hung like a dress should hang" (30). In a third portrait Ross presents Big Anna, a Ukrainian who finds work, supports an invalid husband, and raises a boy who is, in fact, Doc Hunter's son. With the exception of Doc's support, Anna is alone in a hostile, prejudiced community; yet she is an uncomplaining human being who survives with dignity.

Ross's *Sawbones Memorial* is an exceptionally fine work in its sensitive and unsentimental portrayal of women. The same can be said of Wright Morris's novel about women on the Nebraska prairie in *Plains Song: For Female Voices* (1980) which thoughtfully considers changes in female roles and attitudes toward sexuality from the late nineteenth to mid twentieth century. Morris's hero, Cora, was a first-generation pioneer, six feet tall and thus ineligible for the marriage market in Boston. She was sent to her uncle's home in Ohio with the hope that a western male would appreciate her strength and talents. Mr. Emerson, from Madison County, Nebraska, marries her and takes her home. When he "moved on her" the first time, Cora bit into the flesh on her hand, leaving, for the rest of her life, "a scar blue as gun metal between the first and second knuckles" (2). Morris's characterization of Cora reflects a man's admiration for women who, though they are unconscionably deprived of information about sex and marriage yet, despite trauma, completely accepted responsibility for husband and wife's mutual existence. Morris's point is that the heroism of pioneer women like Cora helped to establish prosperous farms where subsequent generations of females were born and given the luxury of choosing between careers and marriage, celibacy and sexual relationships. Wright Morris's contribution to western American literature has been acknowledged by Joseph J. Wydeven: "*Plains Song: For Female Voices* is a moving and compassionate study of American life and of the women whose lives have been silenced as a result of the peculiarities of American history and of the failures of the male-oriented system to provide emotional meanings which are necessary for the attainment of human fulfillment" (227).

Fortunately the voices of prairie women writers have not been silenced—fiction has recorded many of their stories. At no time, I hope, do I confuse fiction with so-called fact, but I am in very good company when I argue that fiction provides important clues to the ways women reacted to the frontier experience. As Russel B. Nye has pointed out in his essay "History and Literature: Branches of the Same Tree," literature is a genuine source of knowledge: "Both historian and literary artist begin with the 'fact' (however we define that term), with the raw material from which the creative process starts and out of which it shapes something new. . . . A literary fact is an imaginative event; but it is no less usable or real for all of that" (145–46). Yi-Fu Tuan, in an essay urging geographers to turn to literature for insights into people and places, says that "an aim of literary art is to present possible modes of experience." The novelist, he argues, with "accuracy and subtlety . . . has drawn the intricate web of feelings, actions, and interactions of [a] particular world. Such accuracy is one of relationships in context rather than isolated facts" ("Literature and Geography" 200).

Our confidence in the "facts" presented by prairie women writers increases when we examine their method of writing. For example, Mary Hartwell Catherwood's fictional town of Whoopertown (or Whooper City, as it was called in some of her stories) was based on Hoopeston, Indiana, one of the many prairie towns in which she lived throughout her life. According to Robert Price's study of Catherwood's realistic fiction, her setting not only seems real "but almost every detail of it is verifiable now by reference to histories of Hoopeston published in later years" ("Early Experiments" 143). Bess Streeter Aldrich, writing about her mother's era, "obtained information regarding the early days in Nebraska either from settlers themselves or from their first generation descendants" (Meier 77). Margaret Lynn acknowledges some of her sources in the dedication to Stepdaughter of the Prairie: "To Prairie Lovers Everywhere and Especially to Those Whose Happy Reminiscences Have Furnished Material for These Sketches." Edna Ferber, in her foreword to Cimarron, a novel about settling Oklahoma, points out that "in many cases material entirely true was discarded as unfit for use because it was so melodramatic, so absurd as to be too strange for the realm of fiction" (ix).

A devotion to authenticity has been noted also in Gabrielle Roy's work:

> So lifelike are Roy's portraits, so accurate her impressions of the land itself that the reader is not surprised to learn of her continuing concern with the authenticity of her "reporting," her desire to make sure that she has not

somehow warped the truth. Indeed, Roy admits to her preoccupation with accuracy in her essay, "Le Manitoba," when she mentions going back to review the scene of *La Petite Poule d'eau* "as a criminal returns to the scene of his crimes!" [Mitcham 163]

The best writers change dates, characters, and circumstances for the sake of artistic unity, but without interfering with the "truth" of the work.

The North Dakota writer Louise Erdrich discussed the process she goes through in transforming facts to fiction. A woman accused her of having used her life story in a work of fiction. Erdrich says, "I vaguely take bits and pieces here and there. . . . I write about my life, places I've worked, visited and lived. It all filters in, somehow. I can't say anything actually happened. Things *like* that happened" (quoted in Hand 4).

These are examples from respected writers, but the works of popular writers may also contain truths. In fact, the contemporary historian Alan Brinkley goes one step further. He argues that "a popular novel can be more revealing than a major work of literature. . . . The 'structures of everyday life,' to use Fernand Braudel's phrase, are as important as, perhaps more important than, the great public events and the major intellectual achievements that we commonly consider 'history'" (37). Some novels have been "lost" because critics have called them sentimental romances or potboilers. Many such works included in this study have redeeming qualities, primarily because they are rooted in the author's historical research and personal experiences, family histories, and interviews. We would do well to remember Northrop Frye's advice about rejecting all but the "best" Canadian writings: "To study Canadian literature properly, one must outgrow the view that evaluation is the end of criticism, instead of its incidental by-product. If evaluation is one's guiding principle, criticism of Canadian literature would become only a debunking project, leaving it a poor naked *alouette* plucked of every feather of decency and dignity" (*Bush Garden* 213). The same could be said of prairie fiction.

Prairie women writers, certainly, have had to concern themselves with "truth." An example is provided by Laura Goodman Salverson in her autobiography, *Confessions of an Immigrant's Daughter;* she comments that she alienated readers whose history she was recording when she created her own version of the Icelandic landscape in the opening lines of her novel *The Viking Heart:*

> I knew, as well as any one, the exact year of the last volcanic eruption, which had, for its aftermath, the misery and hardship which drove so many

to emigrate. I certainly knew that the great volcanoes were inland—how should I not, when my father had once lived under the shadow of Mount Hecla! But I did not see that such specific detail was necessary to an introduction that was obviously nothing but symbolism.

However, the Icelandic people were so indignant that I should have played fast and loose with their landscape, shrinking it, so to speak, until the volcano came down to the sea, that the story itself had no merit. That I had tried, to the best of my ability, to represent those spiritual qualities of the people themselves . . . was completely discounted. [513]

The example demonstrates that a certain amount of responsibility rests with the reader to recognize the artistic truth in a work, even when it differs from literal fact.

Giles Gunn observes that a work may "*not* be 'true' in the sense that it makes no pretense to conform to the shape of our (or anyone else's) past experience." However, he goes on to say that a work may be true "not because it reflects what we already know, but because, by adding to the store of our knowledge about what is at least possible if not actual, it thereby extends the realm of the known, of what we are prepared to accept as part of the potential field of our experience" (81). Because most of the prairie women writers present multiple images of prairie women, women writers have indeed added to the store of knowledge about American and Canadian culture. The time has come to recognize their considerable contributions and commitment to getting their truths published.

While many women writers did succeed in getting their works published and in attracting a large audience, some—particularly in the United States—have not been able to gain the approval of the male literary establishment. Nina Baym recently observed that the American canon of major fiction writers includes, before 1940, only men, and that even feminist critics frequently accepted this canon. Pointing to Lionel Trilling's statement that literature provides the "documents which are in some respects the most suggestive testimony to what America was and is," Baym notes the irony that the canon established by Trilling and other leading critics, because it ignores women writers, cannot in fact be considered truly representative of what America was and is (128–29).[13]

13. See also Annette Kolodny's important discussion of the canon in "Dancing through the Minefield: Some Observations on the Theory, Practice, and Politics of a Feminist Literary Criticism," *Feminist Studies* 6 (1980): 8–9; Lillian S. Robinson's "Treason Our Text: Feminist Challenges to the Literary Canon," *Tulsa Studies in Women's Literature* 2.1 (1983): 83–98; and Paul Lauter's introduction to *Reconstructing American Literature* (Old Westbury, N.Y.: Feminist Press, 1983), xi–xxv.

The Canadian canon, on the other hand, has included women writers from the first. As Russell Brown notes, "there has always been something receptive in the Canadian environment to the female voice. Women authors have figured in the Canadian literary scene in a way unparalleled elsewhere" (89).[14]

Many novels and collections of short fiction by women quickly receded into the obscurity of storage stacks in libraries and second-hand bookstores. These works are, however, retrievable and can be included in what anthropologist Clifford Geertz has referred to as "the consultable record of what man has said" (26). In *The Interpretation of Cultures*, Geertz insists that the goal of anthropology is to make available answers that others have given—to recover the "said" of social discourse (27). The present study retrieves the "said" of social discourse as recorded by a significant number of prairie women writers. Geertz also tells students of culture to look at what the "practitioners" are doing; in this study the practitioners are the writers of prairie fiction. This involves sorting out what Geertz calls "the structures of signification" in an attempt to understand what the subject (writer) is up to or thinks she is up to (9). Then, by "descending into detail," we can gather "piled up structures of inference and implication" (7). Next comes a three-part process: "guessing at meanings; assessing the guesses; and drawing explanatory conclusions from the better guesses" (20). This process should result in more balanced and richer "mediated realities" that will provide a springboard for future analysis of prairie fiction by women and by men.

Important structures of signification emerge throughout the hundred-year tradition of prairie women's fiction. Familiarity with the structures of signification enables critics to recognize and to look for what is being communicated by the writer, both consciously and unconsciously. Moreover, the *absence* of a particular structure signifies something—perhaps ignorance, embarrassment, prejudice, or different values. The structures of signification facilitate comparisons of works over a long period of time and of female characters representing diverse economic, ethnic, religious, and national groups.

14. A recent survey of educators, book reviewers, and literary critics produced a list of important Canadian novels. The first two books on the "top ten" were by prairie-born writers— Margaret Laurence's *Stone Angel* and Gabrielle Roy's novel about Quebec, *The Tin Flute*; Laurence's *Diviners* placed tenth on the list (see Steele 139). In fact, Frances Brooke's *History of Emily Montague* (1769) was "the first Canadian novel and first novel emanating from any part of North America" (Waterston 187).

"Small facts," notes Clifford Geertz, "speak to large issues" (23). The small facts of women's versions of experience, when analyzed and interpreted as structures of signification, lead to a new vision of women's roles in the cultures of Canada and the United States.

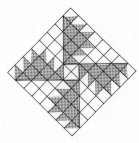

CHAPTER TWO

Women and the Prairie Landscape

Margaret Fuller, traveling through the prairies of Illinois and Wisconsin in 1843, described a process which many travelers, settlers, artists, and writers went through when first encountering the prairies: initial rejection of the landscape followed slowly and in varying degrees by exuberant acceptance. At first the prairie seemed monotonous; she writes: "to walk, and walk, and run, but never climb, oh! it was too dreary for any but a Hollander to bear" (26). As Fuller becomes better acquainted with the scenery, she begins to see subtle details—the "heavy swells" and the "varied coloring"; the prairie becomes, she thinks, not just a vast ocean, but a mirage. Gradually she experiences what she calls "a sort of fairyland exultation never felt before":

> After I had ridden out and seen the flowers, and observed the sunset with that calmness seen only in the prairies, and the cattle winding slowly to their homes in the "island groves"—most peaceful of sights—I began to love because I began to know the scene, and shrank no longer from the encircling vastness.
>
> It is always thus with the new form of life; we must learn to look at it by its own standard. At first, no doubt, my accustomed eye kept saying, if the mind did not, "What! no distant mountains? What! no valleys?" [27]

Fiction by prairie women writers repeatedly demonstrates the fact that many female characters went through this same process. The prairie at first felt like a limitless vastness, but gradually it became familiar, friendly, and even intimate. There were exceptions, of course. Some loved the prairie on first sight; others never became reconciled to a landscape so

33

unlike the one they had left behind. This latter group, however, represents a minority perspective in prairie women's fiction.[1]

A survey of the images of the prairie projected in books, magazines, and newspapers over two hundred years reveals a confusing range. Initially, the prairies of both Canada and the United States were described in negative terms, which continue to be reinforced by several contemporary critics. For example, in a 1982 *Landscape* article, Ronald Rees argues that there was little in the landscape with which pioneers could identify. "In most eyes the prairie was vacant, not merely spacious" (1). His illustrations are gleaned from the diaries of male immigrants. Although he has qualified the statement with the phrase "in most eyes," he makes no attempt to describe the perspectives of those who were attracted to the prairies. The literary critic Laurence Ricou entitled a 1973 essay "Empty as Nightmare: Man and Landscape in Recent Canadian Prairie Fiction." As his title suggests, Ricou found that wasteland images predominate in fiction from the 1950s and 1960s. The prairie is "flat," "bleak," "inscrutable and unsmiling," "dreary," "unchanging," "without point or meaning," "godless," "blighted and withered," "barren," and "debilitating"—these are a few of the words and phrases he finds in novels by male writers.

Ricou found an exception in Margaret Laurence's novels: "Among these visions of an increasingly dreary, life-denying landscape a consideration of Margaret Laurence's prairie settings is apt to seem disruptive" ("Empty" 145). Laurence's descriptions are disruptive only in the context of writings by men. In women's fiction, female characters often see the landscape as "fruitful," "new," "beautiful," and "lush." When they do use words like "level," "vast," and "solitary," they are used neutrally rather than negatively. In *The Diviners*, one of Laurence's characters remarks, "People who'd never lived hereabouts always imagined it was dull, bleak, hundreds of miles of nothing. They didn't know. They didn't know the renewal that came out of the dead cold" (282). Clearly, fiction by women writers poses a strong challenge to male interpretations of the prairie landscape.

---

1. R. Douglas Francis provides an overview of images of the Canadian West in "Changing Images in the West," which analyzes numerous works published over the last twenty years. For a comparison of Canadian and American attitudes toward nature, see Marcia B. Kline, *Beyond the Land Itself: Views of Nature in Canada and the United States* (Cambridge: Harvard Univ. Press, 1970).

This study, therefore, raises an important question: Why is love of the prairie landscape a dominant structure of signification in stories about prairie women? From the early nineteenth century Red River settlement to contemporary life in works by writers like Byrna Barclay, Sharon Butala, and Aritha Van Herk, the prairies are predominantly described as a positive force in women's lives.

To evaluate women's responses to the landscape as described in fiction, we need to consider the factors affecting those responses. A mode of analysis is provided by the internationally known geographer, Yi-Fu Tuan, in *Topophilia: A Study of Environmental Perception, Attitudes, and Values*. Tuan notes that attitude "is primarily a cultural stance, a position one takes vis-à-vis the world. It has greater stability than perception and is formed of a long succession of perceptions, that is, of experience. . . . Attitudes imply experience and a certain firmness of interest and value" (4). Before analyzing why a woman writer describes a character's attitude toward the new landscape in a particular way, we need to examine the cultural stance vis-à-vis the prairie from the early 1800s to the present.

According to Cooper's *Prairie*, the midwestern prairies of the United States in the first decade of the 1800s were inhospitable. Clearly it was a wilderness that needed someday to be tamed and civilized, but the time had not yet come. This view of the prairie as potentially inhabitable replaced an earlier view of the West as the devil's den or at least as a land better left to the Indians. By 1800, however, the situation had become analogous to that of the Puritan forefathers in New England: the West was a new heaven and a new earth where, to use Sacvan Bercovitch's terminology, the ritual of American consensus was extended into new territories. Nineteenth-century pioneers, like the Puritans before them, justified their conquest of Indian territories by calling it a "mission" into the wilderness, a movement away from the corruptions already spreading through the Atlantic seaboard. The lands of the West represented a new millennium. The Canadians, however, according to Bercovitch, had no comparable calling: "To a Canadian sceptic, a gentile in God's Country, it made for a breathtaking scene: a pluralistic pragmatic people openly living in a dream, bound together by an ideological consensus unmatched by that of any other modern society. . . . Migration as a mission, and the mission a rationale for greed" (272–73). The Canadians' rationale for expansion appears to have been quite different: according to a recent essay by Ramsay Cook, eastern Canadians emigrated West because of "economic imperatives," which are not to be confused with "greed"; expanding populations in both England and eastern Canada required more space.

No one would deny that the fur-trading companies had one goal, to make money. Many of those who worked for Hudson's Bay Company or the North West Company, especially the Scots and French-Canadian trappers and voyageurs, stayed in the West after retiring, but they were considered exceptions to the rule. In addition, they were more apt to adopt the values of the Indians than to try to transport their own cultures to the West. In 1807 George Heriot, deputy post master general of British North America, published his account of *Travels through the Canadas*. His lengthy subtitle suggests the ambitious scope of the journey: "A Description of the Picturesque Scenery on Some of the Rivers and Lakes; With an Account of the Productions, Commerce, and Inhabitants of those Provinces to which is Subjoined a Comparative View of the Manners and Customs of Several of the Indian Nations of North and South America." His descriptions of life in Rupert's Land clearly indicate that he had no visions of the western Canadian settlements that would develop in the future; instead, he was astonished to find such a large population at Grand Portage: "The number of persons encamped in tents and in huts, on the outside of the fort was, at certain periods, very great, and tended to excite surprise that so considerable an assemblage of men, under no military restraint, should be retained in obedience, and in a state of tolerable regularity, so far beyond the limits of all jurisdiction" (204). The deputy post master assumed that trade and settlements, rather than extending westward, would follow a line along the St. Lawrence River, through the Great Lakes, then southward into the Mississippi valley.

This territory, the eastern portion of the midwestern prairies, was described in *The Western Gazetteer; or Emigrant's Directory* just ten years after the Canadian deputy post master's report. In this 1817 guide, Samuel R. Brown commented on the "delightful plantations" which line the Illinois rivers running into the Mississippi. He carefully describes the "bottoms" as land that is "inexhaustible in fecundity; as is proved by its present fertility, where it has been annually cultivated without manure, for more than a century" (22). He goes on to describe the prairies east of the Mississippi, which, he estimates, cover 1,200,000 acres and are equal to, and perhaps even superior to, the bottoms (23). An early nineteenth-century reader of this guide would have a very good idea of where the best farm lands could be found in the states of Ohio and Indiana and in the territories of Illinois and the Northwest.

This rich land was not without its problems, according to Brown. The Indians posed a threat to settlement in many places, and Brown blames the British for most of these problems. He argues that the United States government, "with a commendable zeal for the preservation of the primitive inhabitants, afford every aid and encouragement on their part to prevent the unexampled destruction which has attended the natives of this continent, from the first arrival of the Europeans down to the present time." The Indians, he says, can be "civilized"; he cites the effective work of the Society of Friends as evidence. The British, however, are identified as troublemakers, having "warned the Indians from receiving instruction from us; [they] have misrepresented our views, by attributing them to selfish, corrupt, and improper motives, and by encouraging the Indians in their thirst of war and bloodshed; by inculcating on their minds at all times that the Americans are their natural enemies" (288–89).

In this guidebook, Brown convincingly argued that good farmlands were available while at the same time he conveyed a clear warning to the potential emigrant that Indian tribes in some areas were hostile to whites. A similar situation existed in reference to the farm settlements in southern Manitoba. In spite of propaganda discouraging settlement of the prairies, Lord Selkirk established a colony on the Red River in 1812.[2] A Toronto clergyman, writing in 1816 in an attempt to dissuade others from emigrating, said that Selkirk's attempt to establish a colony was "one of the most gross impositions that was ever perpetrated on the British public" (quoted in Owram 7). Certainly the fur-trade companies were opposed to the settlement: the settlers—immigrants from Scotland and Ireland—would transform the wilderness into plowed and planted fields. Indian, Métis,[3] and white trappers would suffer from the scarcity of wildlife, especially of buffalo upon which they relied for their major winter staple, pemmican. In addition, the powerful fur-trading com-

2. Accounts of the Red River settlement are provided in a variety of sources: C. Martin's *Lord Selkirk's Work in Canada* (Toronto: Oxford Univ. Press, 1916); A. Ross, *The Red River Settlement* (London, 1856); W. J. Healy, *Women of Red River*; Van Kirk's *Many Tender Ties: Women in Fur-Trade Society, 1670–1870.*

3. In *American Indian Women: Telling Their Lives*, Bataille and Sands provide the following information about the word *Métis*: "*Métis*, *mixed-blood*, and the more pejorative term *half-breed* have been used in the United States and Canada to define an individual of mixed Indian and white ancestry. During the nineteenth century and into the twentieth century the label *half-breed* was applied most often to those Indian males suspected of being particularly evil" (117). Thomas Flanagan points out that *Métis* "is a French word meaning mixed blood. . . . Until around 1940, people of mixed Indian-white ancestry in Canada were usually called, and called themselves, half-breed when English was spoken and Métis when French was spoken.

panies were not about to tolerate agricultural settlements which would interfere with their profitable business. One of the most dramatic efforts of the fur-trading companies to disrupt the Red River settlement resulted in the Seven Oaks massacre of 1816.

The Hudson's Bay Company had granted the lands to Lord Selkirk in return for "a certain supply of provisions at a moderate price" to the fur-trading company (*The Beaver* 44). The first settlers arrived in the fall of 1812 and, over the next two years, conflicts increased between settlers allied with the Hudson's Bay Company and the Nor'Westers (traders representing the North West Company), who were aligned with the Métis in the fur-trading business. In June 1816, twenty-two settlers were killed in an attack by the Métis; the remaining settlers immediately departed. The settlement was rebuilt after Lord Selkirk arrived with a regiment of De Meuron soldiers (Swiss and Germans) in 1817; they recaptured the Hudson's Bay fort, Fort Douglas, which marked the decline in the power of the Nor-Westers.[4]

Thus the Red River settlement eventually survived. At the same time that these events were going on in western Canada, intrepid settlers were pouring into the prairies of the American Midwest. At this point we need to ask why settlers continued to immigrate to the prairies despite the persistence of negative images associated with the prairie landscape and frontier settlements in both Canada and the United States. In Canada antiexpansionists could argue that the Canadian shield, stretching across western Ontario, was itself inhospitable to settlement and difficult to cross, thus prohibiting easy access to the prairies. In addition, the southern portions of what are now Alberta, Saskatchewan, and Manitoba were identified as an extension of "the Great American Desert" which supposedly reached northward from Texas, covering a vast portion of middle America and reaching into southern Canada. The successful agricultural ventures of the Red River settlers were considered atypical; therefore, potential immigrants were discouraged from experimenting elsewhere.

The desert image also interfered with expansion into the American prairies. In the nineteenth century the word *desert* was used interchangeably with *wilderness* to refer to any unoccupied land. As late as 1892 *Lippincott's Magazine* published an article in which the writer attempted to dispel misconceptions about this territory. He pointed out

---

4. A good sourcebook for this era in Canadian history is Kenneth Osborne's *The Prairies: Selected Historical Sources* (Toronto: McClelland & Stewart, 1969).

that schoolchildren in eastern Nebraska and western Iowa would be astonished to read in geography books that they lived in a desert. He cites the irresponsible journalism of travelers like the influential Boston clergyman, Henry Ward Beecher, who wrote in 1878 that he was "riding night and day across the great desert plains." In a phrase that makes the contemporary reader shudder because of its racism, the *Lippincott* article assured readers that "not only have the savage tribes been conquered and exterminated, but nature herself has been subdued and overcome" (Shanks 736). The writer obviously felt that this representation of the situation would powerfully sway the attitudes of easterners. This essay is significant because it demonstrates that negative images persisted into the late nineteenth century.

The great expanse of grasslands presented a new terrain to immigrants, one which challenged the cultural stance shaped in the East or in the Old World. The Canadian artist Paul Kane, touring the West in 1846, wrote: "The country here is not very beautiful; a dead level plain with very little timber, . . . scarcely a stick or stump upon it" (49). The new topography demanded new attitudes, values, and techniques; Ray Billington summarizes these problems in *Western Expansion* when he analyzes the responses of immigrants arriving in Illinois after all the wooded areas of the state had been occupied:

> How could they make the transition from accustomed timber lands to the prairies of Illinois where cheap land alone remained? The task was formidable; to conquer the grasslands pioneers must discard their prejudices, shatter past traditions, and develop an entirely new frontier technique. They had, for generations, judged the richness of the land by the density of its forest growth, used wood for everything from homes to fences, and obtained fuel, game, and water from the wilderness. Now they must settle on a barren waste apparently incapable of supporting forests, unprotected from winter blasts or summer heat, without logs for their cabins, rails for their fences, or fuel for their fires. They must dig wells rather than depend on rippling forest streams, and provide drainage to carry spring rains from level lands. Worst of all, they must devise some means of breaking the tough prairie. [307]

These problems become personalized when we turn to an 1819 publication, *Letters from the West; or A Caution to Emigrants*. John S. Wright wrote to acquaintances about his travels in Ohio, Indiana, and Illinois during 1818–19 when he was considering emigrating. Prefacing his description of an Illinois prairie with the statement that his observations were rooted in *facts*, not in whim or fancy, he proceeded to describe the prairie and the people he encountered: "Every thing seemed to invite me to select a spot, begin my improvements, and enjoy my happy fate. But, ah! like the enjoyment of forbidden pleasure, there is a sting behind. Not only is an exorbitant price demanded, but the inhabitants, the people among whom I must spend my days . . . are sufficient to dispel the gay vision" (33–34).

He observes that the population is made up of a "motley assemblage" of southerners and Yankees and that through intermingling and intermarriage the Yankees have degenerated to the level of the southerners. Also, he insists that the climate contributes "a deteriorating principle" which "enfeebles" both mind and body (35). In weighing the advantages and disadvantages of the terrain, he notes that the land is easy to clear, but only small portions are truly fertile, and these are usually the "low" prairies which are "most certainly unhealthful." He doesn't like the "high" prairies either, because a good many of them "are merely oak barrens; of a clayey or sandy soil; the grass they produce, is a tall wild kind; . . . it affords a nourishing luxuriant pasturage while springing up, but soon becomes so hardened that cattle cannot eat it" (37). A disillusioned Wright returned East and wrote his book to warn others to read with suspicion the "thousands" of accounts which he believed were written by travel writers to "amuse" and to "astonish" uninformed readers.

A decade later, in the 1830s, another traveler to the Illinois prairies, William Cullen Bryant, described his reactions in "The Prairies." Bryant had grown up in western Massachusetts in a landscape quite similar to Wright's New York environment; his reactions, however, were quite different. He was so moved by his first glimpse of the prairies that he wrote a poem which emphasized the positive qualities of the landscape:

> These are the garden of the Desert, these
> The unshorn fields, boundless and beautiful,
> For which the speech of England has no name—
> The Prairies. I behold them for the first,
> And my heart swells.

It is the garden, not "the Desert," that finally emerges as the dominant image of the prairie in both Canada and the United States during the settlement eras.[5] The reason the garden image finally wins out is related,

5. In "The Garden Myth in 'The Prairies,'" Edwin R. Booher observes that Bryant's journal and letters revealed "diverse and conflicting impressions" of the prairie that are absent from the poem (15).

of course, to fundamental values. At the time Wright wrote his analysis of the prairies, there were still lands available in the east where he could live among his own kind of people; obviously his values required not only good land but a community representing backgrounds, interests, and values similar to his own.

While Wright chose to stay in New York, many moved West over the next decade and, through letters, magazines, newspapers, and books, encouraged others to follow. As early as 1831, according to J. M. Peck's *Guide for Emigrants,* the process of civilizing the American prairie lands was well under way. He argued that the area discussed in his guide (the states of Indiana, Illinois, and Missouri and the Wisconsin territory) "in all respects offers as many advantages and as few inconveniences to the emigrant" as any "tract of country in all America." Knowing that people had a very imprecise understanding of the prairies, he is painstakingly specific in his descriptions so that emigrants will choose the right kind of land: "To a careless observer, and especially one accustomed to a hilly surface, all our prairies will seem level; but a little attention will enable one to distinguish between a sloping surface, and one entirely level, or a little concave. It is a very common notion amongst the people of the Atlantic states, that a prairie is necessarily wet. Nothing is more inaccurate. *Prairie* is a French word signifying meadow, and means any description of surface, covered with grass, and entirely void of timber and brush" (106–07). Peck then describes each type of prairie, pointing out that "many suppose a prairie necessarily to be a swampy, wet soil, hardly fit for cultivation. Others imagine it to be a sandy and shrubby plain."

Peck's *Guide* carefully details the crops that do well in each area; he tells prospective immigrants how much money they need, what tools they should bring, what kinds of buildings they should plan to construct. He acknowledges, however, that many are worried about illnesses: "As the public mind abroad is extremely sensitive on this subject, and as certain sickness is the evil, which most of all others, haunts the imagination of those who desire to emigrate to the west, I shall devote a number of pages to this subject" (200). He proceeds to quote from an 1826 publication, *Family Physician,* which specifically addresses illnesses and ways of avoiding them or procedures for dealing with them on the prairie frontier.

Peck's goal, certainly, is to attract others to the Midwest, but he is not one of those whom John Wright accused of writing to "amuse" and "astonish." He wants to see the area settled by people who are well informed and sensible. He does not seem to share Wright's concern with the social or educational backgrounds of potential emigrants. The responses of Peck and Wright to the prairie provide significant examples of Yi-Fu Tuan's central thesis: people will see the landscape and the possibilities for settlement according to their deeply personal attitudes and values.

Another factor reflecting attitudes, at least in the United States, was the pervasive theme of Manifest Destiny. Politicians and businessmen, especially those supporting expansion of the railroad system, worked energetically to replace the image of the "Great American Desert" (and in this context *desert* did *not* mean "garden") with the image of the "Garden of the World." Slogans such as "the rain follows the plow" emerged during this period to encourage farmers to seek new homes in the West.[6]

Hard times frequently drive people to take chances and emigrate. Volcanic eruptions in Iceland, famine in Ireland, persecutions in Russia, and rigid class lines in the Scandinavian countries were a few of the reasons the second wave emigrants were predisposed to viewing the prairie in positive terms. Also, when it became apparent that all the best lands had been settled, immigrants and, of course, land settlement companies reevaluated the unsettled territories. For example, all of Illinois but the Grand Prairie had been settled by the 1840s; then the prairies filled and, subsequently, people moved into the rolling hills and prairies of Wisconsin. Most of Iowa filled during the 1850s, although the prairies (as in Illinois) were developed after wooded areas had been taken up.

The 1850s marked a turning point in Canadian attitudes toward the prairies. As Doug Owram indicates in *Promise of Eden: The Canadian Expansionist Movement and the Idea of the West, 1856–1900*, Canadians were beginning to realize that they needed more agricultural lands to accommodate a growing population. In addition, as Owram points out, "A combination of pride in achievements to date and concern for the future led a good many Canadians to conclude that failure to expand would result in stagnation. Canada was outgrowing its boundaries; if room for Canadian energies was not found, the colony would sink into

6. Henry Nash Smith's *Virgin Land: The American West as Symbol and Myth* is, of course, the classic American study of the Garden myth. Doug Owram's *Promise of Eden: The Canadian Expansionist Movement and the Idea of the West, 1856–1900* shows how the myth developed in Canada.

obscurity" (47). Ramsay Cook believes that while Americans wanted to "Americanize" the West, Canadians were "engaged in laying the basis for 'the Britain of the west.'" He quotes from an 1874 magazine which predicted that the western frontier would provide a place "to reproduce the British constitution with its marvellous heritage of balanced power and liberty; and to do this across the whole breadth of a continent— these are objects which are worth some labour, some sacrifice to obtain" (Cook 12).

In the 1860s and 1870s the Canadian government entered upon an ambitious propaganda program which is well exemplified by Thomas Spence's 1880 publication. The title page demonstrates the belief that the Garden of the World extended northward beyond the forty-ninth parallel:

The Prairie Lands of Canada;
Presented to the World as
A New and Inviting Field of Enterprise
for the Capitalist,
and
New Superior Attractions and Advantages
as a
Home for Immigrants
Compared with the Western Prairies of the United States

In the preface to this book, Spence remarks that "no longer will the Prairie Lands of the United States occupy the attention of the whole world. Canada can now cry aloud in every language to millions: Every one that wants a farm, come and take one, where you may enjoy health, happiness and freedom under the flag 'that's braved a thousand years,' and where the industrious will soon attain that end to which all men aspire, INDEPENDENCE" (5). Although the first agricultural settlement had been established in the Red River Valley in 1811, the mid-1880s marks the beginning of the major settlement era in the Canadian West.

Some of the conflicting responses to the prairies in both Canada and the United States can be attributed to whether the writer was a traveler or a settler—obviously a very important distinction. Visitors, Yi-Fu Tuan observes, will be more inclined to evaluate the landscape in aesthetic terms according to some formal criteria of beauty which may be superficial but nonetheless significant (64). We saw sharp contrasts between William Cullen Bryant and Paul Kane—the prairie suited

Bryant's aesthetic requirements but not Kane's. Nevertheless, Tuan cautions against automatically rejecting the traveler's judgment; his perceptions are often fresh. Also, the traveler frequently "perceives merits and defects in an environment that are no longer visible to the resident" (65). The settler, who is taking physical and economic risks, will be inclined to see the landscape in terms of survival; only those elements that are potentially destructive or sustaining are significant enough to enter this particular field of vision. Also, "once a people have settled down and adapted somewhat to the new setting, it is difficult to know their environmental attitude for, having become natives, they lose the urge to make comparisons and comment on their new home" (Tuan 68).

Thus far I have traced dominant attitudes toward the prairie during the nineteenth century, relying on Yi-Fu Tuan's insights to help explain the variety of attitudes held at different times and the reasons for changes in those attitudes. We can now return to the intriguing question, What did women write about the prairies? What were their expectations and, once they actually saw the prairies or lived on the prairies, what were their impressions? No women can be counted among the dominant image-makers—not even Margaret Fuller, whose *Summer on the Lakes* (1844) detailed her prairie travels. Nevertheless, Fuller's book and others like it, along with women's novels, letters, and contributions to newspapers and magazines, serve as indispensable sources for information about the attitudes of women toward the prairie and the frontier experience; in addition, they help us to make sense out of the fiction written by women who actually lived on the prairie for substantial portions of their lives.

One fascinating account is by the eighteen-year-old bride of George Simpson. Simpson had been appointed governor of the Northern Department of the Hudson's Bay Company after its coalition with the North West Company, and Simpson subsequently played a key role in the development of the West. When Simpson returned to England for a "leave" in 1829, he married his cousin Frances. The wedding took place on February 24, 1830. During this same period Simpson's friend and colleague, John George McTavish, a former Nor'Wester, also took leave and he, too, married.

In May 1830, the Simpsons and McTavishes left Montreal. Frances Simpson's diary for May 2 noted: "Left La Chine at 4 A.M. in two Canoes manned by 15 hands each, all strong, active, fine looking Canadians. The passengers consisting of Mr. & Mrs. McTavish, & Maid Servant in the one, and Mr. Simpson Myself & Servant in the other." The editor of the diary, Grace Lee Nute, points out that Simpson conducted the trip at an "incredible speed," yet Frances remains uncomplaining despite enormous hardship (50). One episode in Frances's diary provides a delightful contrast to all the stereotypical portraits of the reluctant female emigrant patiently enduring the hardships of the journey. She describes rising the morning of May 10 after an extremely cold night. While it was still dark, they began to wade "thro' a Morass knee deep." On the other side, the men built a fire "for the purpose of warming ourselves & drying our clothes." Then they reached a portage that was waist-deep in spots: "To cross this, baffled the skill both of Mrs. McTavish & Myself (good walkers as we flattered ourselves to be) and accordingly after mature deliberation, it was agreed that each should be carried by a man chosen for the purpose."

Simpson relates the fact that Nicholas Monique, an old Indian, volunteered to carry Mrs. McTavish; a man named Tomma Felix "took up" Mrs. Simpson:

> Tomma pushed on, despite of every difficulty making however many stumbles & false steps—but Nicholas' load being rather heavier, he absolutely came to a stand still, in the midst of a bog, and declared he could not take the Lady a step farther in his arms, but if she would get on his back, he thought he might accomplish the journey.
>
> Mr. Simpson who was coming on after us, persuaded Mrs. McTavish (with some difficulty) as a last resource to do as Nicholas recommended, which at length she agreed to, and on the back of Nicholas accordingly mounted: the scene however was so ludicrous that the bystanders could not resist a laugh, in which Mrs. McTavish joined so heartily, that poor Nicholas was thrown off his equilibrium, stumbled forwards, fell on his face, and gave his unfortunate rider a summerset over his head, into the mud: throwing her into a situation the most awkward, and ridiculous that ever poor Lady, was placed in.
>
> After extricating her with much difficulty, she was at length dragged to the end of the Portage, where we all washed & dried ourselves, and had Breakfast. (Nute, Dec. 1953, 54)

This episode gives us a good idea of the high spirits and good humor that characterized some female travelers. (See fig. 1 for Frances Ann Hopkins's painting of a woman traveling with voyageurs.)

Mrs. Simpson's journal also includes a description of her first sight of the Red River colony, details that help us to imagine life in a very early settlement.

Fig. 1   MRS. F. A. HOPKINS, *Canoe Manned by Voyageurs.* Courtesy of Public
Archives Canada C-2771.

6th   Mr. Simpson being anxious to get to Fort Garry (about 100 miles
distant) today, gave his usual "Lève Lève Lève" at 12 P.M. and although it
blew very hard, occasioning a heavy swell on Lake Winnipeg when we
embarked, we got to the mouth of Red River at 11 A.M. The beauty of this
Stream surpasses that of every other I have yet seen in the Interior. The
banks are richly clothed with Timber of large size, and greater variety than is
generally met with, and the soil when properly cultivated is fertile as that of a
manured garden.

This rich Country forms an immense sea of level plains which extends
upward of 500 miles back, on the West side to the foot of the Rocky
Mountains. . . .

On advancing in the Settlement, signs of civilization began to appear
in the form of houses built of Logs, and surrounded by patches of ground
which bore the marks of the Plough & the Spade. (Nute, June 1954, 14).

Although Frances Simpson stayed in the Northwest only four years,[7] her
diary gives insights into the mind of a curious and spirited female traveler.

7. Van Kirk says that Frances Simpson's health was not good, and the death of an infant
son in 1832 further contributed to her ill health and depression. George Simpson made this
observation of his wife: "She has no Society, no Friend, no Relative here but myself, she cannot

At Fort Garry, Mrs. Simpson would have met a woman whose strength and spirit sustained her through fifty years on the Red River— Marie-Anne Gaboury Lagimodière, the first white woman to settle in the Northwest. In 1806 Marie-Anne had insisted on traveling with her new husband and the voyageurs. She refused to stay in Quebec and wait, as all the other wives waited, for his return two or three years hence. In the West, she made frequent moves with her husband throughout the Northwest territory. For years she lived in tents and even, for a time, in a cave. She bore her children with the help of Indian women. In 1817 she and her children survived the Seven Oaks massacre because they were housed and protected by Chief Peguis (her husband was away, having been hired by Hudson's Bay Company to carry messages requesting military reinforcements). By 1830, the time of Frances Simpson's arrival, Marie-Anne's vision of a home in the West had been fulfilled: she had a house and a garden on the banks of the Red River, a land grant gift to her husband from Lord Selkirk.[8]

At the same time that Marie-Anne Lagimodière settled into a stable routine on the Canadian frontier, Rebecca Burlend, equally satisfied with life in Illinois, described her experiences in an emigrant's guidebook. Burlend, with her son, wrote a book entitled *A True Picture of Emigration: or Fourteen Years in the Interior of North America; Being a Full and Impartial Account of the Various Difficulties and Ultimate Success of an English Family Who Emigrated from Barwick-in-Elmet, Near Leeds, in the Year 1831*. Burlend wanted to dispel stereotypes and present the prairie as accurately as possible:

> Having referred to the prairies, it may perhaps be necessary to be a little more explicit. Many persons in England have a wrong idea of the uncultivated lands in America, imagining they are all wood. This is by no means the case. In Illinois there are thousands of acres with not a tree upon it, but covered with a sort of strong wild grass, growing sometimes three or four feet high. These lands are termed prairies, and require only to be broken up with a prairie plough, and they become at once fine arable land. As I

move about wt. me on my different Journeys and I cannot leave her in the hands of strangers . . . some of them very unfeeling" (quoted by Van Kirk 199).

8. For more information on the adventurer Marie-Anne Lagimodière, see Jean Johnston's *Wilderness Women* (Toronto: Peter Martin Associates, 1973), 121–52. Two historical novels have been published recently. *"My Name is Marie Anne Gaboury"* by Mary V. Jordan (Winnipeg: Prairie Publishing Co., 1983) was probably intended for young adults, but it suffers from sentimentality and poor writing. The second novel is by the historian Grant MacEwan, *Marie Anne: The Frontier Spirit of Marie Anne Lagimodière* (Saskatoon: Western Producer Prairie Books, 1984).

before intimated, this kind of land, though the soonest cultivated, is not the most productive being, as the farmers term it, of a stronger quality than the other. The soil of both prairies and woodland is quite black, probably owing to vegetable matter, which for ages had decayed thereon. At the season of the year now under notice, these prairies present to the eye a most charming appearance. Let the reader imagine himself by the side of a rich meadow, or fine grass plain several miles in diameter, decked with myriads of flowers of a most gorgeous and varied description, and he will have before his mind a pretty correct representation of one of these prairies. Nothing can surpass in richness of colour, or beauty of formation many of the flowers. [83–84]

True, Rebecca did not feel this way about the prairie when she got off the boat at Philip's Ferry early one November evening in 1817; in fact, she confesses that both she and her husband burst into tears at the sight of the empty landscape (43). This experience represents one common reaction. Even the stout-hearted need to learn how to look at a new landscape, as Margaret Fuller pointed out. As Burlend's subtitle indicates, her family overcame the difficulties and ultimately enjoyed success to such an extent that Burlend encouraged others to emigrate, as long as they understood the drawbacks and were willing to work hard and make sacrifices.

In 1843 a traveler by the name of Catherine Stewart published a book entitled *New Homes in the West* describing the land and people encountered on her trip from Chicago to Galena in 1836. Stewart writes: "The emigrant who goes to a new country with a heart braced for privation and hardship, will soon have cause to congratulate himself on his many unexpected comforts" (135). Her descriptions of the undulating land, luxurious grasses, and fragrant fields of blossoms perhaps served as models for descriptions of prairie settings in dime novels of the 1850s and 1860s. She also describes a later trip in 1842 in which she records the changes that had occurred in the landscape over a six-year period: "Fine farms, with substantial houses and barns, good fences, and all the indications of comfortable living, realize the most sanguine predictions" (127). She insisted that "it is not unusual to hear a lady from the eastern states assert, that though her domestic duties are more arduous, she would not exchange her situation for one of greater ease, that denied the prospects this country holds out to her rising family" (133–34).

The foreword to the 1966 reprint of *New Homes in the West* indicates that nothing is known about the author. Therefore we have no way of knowing Stewart's motives for describing the prairie landscape and the pioneer women in such positive ways. We should keep in mind that she was a visitor on the prairie and as such described the people and the environment as an outsider who had made no apparent commitment to or investment in a home in the West.

In contrast, we have a fairly clear idea of Margaret Fuller's motives in her descriptions of the prairies and the women she observed there: she wanted a different and better kind of education for young women, and she used her travel accounts to justify her demands for change. I respect and admire her purpose in using *Summer on the Lakes* as a public forum, and I grant that it may have lured some unsuspecting readers into listening to her views. Yet we have to recognize that she adjusted her descriptions to suit her purpose and that this resulted in some distortion through selection of materials. Fuller says that women were confined to their cabins, and even if they were free from their interminable chores, they would not have known how to ride and enjoy the luxurious prairie landscape (44–45).

Fuller tells about reading the letters of an Englishman named Morris Birkbeck. She applauds his attempt to establish a model prairie community in Illinois. Curiously, she does not mention the letters of the Birkbeck daughters, in which they describe the long and frequent rides they took across the prairie. These kinds of detail would not have supported Fuller's thesis. The Birkbeck women also describe enthusiastically, for friends and family in England, the activities and rewards of prairie life. Elizabeth tells her correspondents that the prairie is presently in a "wild state," but that she and Prue enjoy walking about, imagining "how pretty the homesites will look when cultivated" (Thomson 54). When the Birkbecks are joined by another family from England, the Woods, Elizabeth observes that the Woods daughters "are highly delighted with the Prairies" (60). They assure their English friends that despite the drawbacks of pioneer life they "contrive to go pretty cheerfully through the difficulties thrown in their way and amuse themselves with what would be called real misfortunes by the down hearted" (54).

In contrast to the Birkbeck daughters, the women Fuller describes on the prairie homesteads were confined by their chores to their cabins. Only one Englishwoman seemed to be "contented," and that was because conditions in England had been so distressing that "the hardships of this [country] seemed as nothing to her" (Fuller 58). Others, Fuller goes on to say, "found their labors disproportioned to their strength, if not to their patience; and, while their husbands and brothers enjoyed the country in hunting or fishing, they found themselves confined to a comfortless and laborious indoor life. But it need not be so long" (58).

This last phrase, certainly, is significant. Fuller believes that the next generation of women, especially if educated properly, should adapt successfully: "To a girl really skilled to make home beautiful and comfortable, with bodily strength to enjoy plenty of exercise, the woods, the streams, a few studies, music, and the sincere and familiar intercourse far more easily to be met with here than elsewhere, would afford happiness enough. Her eyes would not grow dim nor her cheeks sunken in the absense of parties, morning visits, and milliners' shops" (46). Fuller seems to be talking about middle-class emigrants. Certainly lower-class girls were neither educated nor confined to their cabins—they would have been responsible for numerous outdoor tasks as were lower-class girls in the East.

Fuller seems to be saying that "those who determined who was to live on what landscape and how they were to live there" were men, not women. At least this is Annette Kolodny's interpretation in her study of women and the frontier, *The Land before Her: Fantasy and Experience of the American Frontiers, 1630–1860* (1984). Kolodny points out that Margaret Fuller and her mother had once reluctantly followed Timothy Fuller on a disastrous "retreat" to the country, a retreat that brought enormous hardships to the women. In fact, Fuller wrote to one of her brothers that because of the move from Cambridge to the family homestead in Groton, her mother's health had been "injured" and her own health "destroyed" (quoted in Kolodny 119). It is not surprising, according to Kolodny, that Fuller interpreted the western migration in similar terms: Fuller and her mother "had followed an imperious male to a rural domestic nightmare. Whole generations of women going west were now following [men]"—and here Kolodny quotes Fuller—"'as women will, doing their best for affection's sake, but too often in heartsickness and weariness'" (128). Kolodny suggests that the "heartsickness and weariness" were "insupportable" because they were the dominant feelings to emerge from a situation that should, instead, have been characterized by a sense of satisfaction that comes with beginning a new home and garden in a new land (128). Clearly, in interpreting Fuller's impressions of women's lives on the prairie, we need to recognize and make allowances for her personal attitudes toward men in relation to the decision-making process. Then we can understand why she sees the situation in ways that contradict the descriptions of many other travelers and homesteaders.

Kolodny's interpretation, then, is that women followed men west as reluctantly as Fuller and her mother followed Timothy Fuller to the country. On the prairie frontier, immigrant women endured hardships that could have been avoided if they had stayed in the East, just as the two Fuller women could have been more comfortable in Cambridge. Rather than acknowledging the possibility that Fuller distorted materials, Kolodny insists that Fuller, because of her own suffering, was more capable of accurately describing women's lives than, for example, the domestic fictionists.

Kolodny argues that the voices of two women who should have been heard—Margaret Fuller's and Caroline Kirkland's—were drowned out by the voices of popular writers. The realistic assessments of prairie life, Kolodny says, were ignored. Rather, women chose to read "promotional tracts promising one form or another of the Edenic domestic fantasy. In works like Mary Austin Holley's *Texas: Observations, Historical, Geographical and Descriptive* (1833) and Eliza W. Farnham's *Life in Prairie Land* (1846), the flowered garden of the prairie beckoned, apparently offering easy prosperity, familial security, genial climate, and physical freedoms for women unheard of in the east." In these works, according to Kolodny,

> The American landscape became for women what it had always been for men—a realm for the projection of gratifying fantasies. But just as the realities of actual settlement had so often thwarted the fantasies of men, converting an inviting feminine terrain into the specter of violated maternity and ravaged virginity, so too now—as Margaret Fuller began to perceive—the demands of frontier life also thwarted the fantasies of women.
> The prairies might indeed be beautiful and welcoming in their appearance, with flowered meadows bespeaking "the very Eden which earth might still afford." But the landscape, as most women too late discovered, was not their domain of action. For them, the new home constituted not any flowering garden but only a rude cabin, sometimes without even windows from which to gaze out on the surrounding beauty. [129]

Kolodny concludes the chapter on Margaret Fuller's work with this observation: "Her *Summer on the Lakes* . . . finally did little to persuade an eagerly westering nation that, where women were concerned, their newfound frontier fantasies might, in fact, turn into domestic captivity" (130).

In the 1840s, whom could readers believe—Catherine Stewart's glowing account of beautiful prairies and contented women homesteaders, or Fuller's account of equally beautiful prairies but of women imprisoned in their cabins? This question also engages Kolodny in her study. In her search for answers, Kolodny turns from Fuller's account of the prairies to Caroline Kirkland's *A New Home—Who'll Follow? or, Glimpses of Western Life* (1839), which was published under a pseudonym: "By Mrs. Mary Clavers, an Actual Settler."

Caroline Kirkland had emigrated with her husband William to the Michigan frontier. On the basis of this experience, she was well qualified to describe and interpret western life. What distinguishes Kirkland from other writers, according to Kolodny, is her emphasis on realism: "That impulse to protect others from her own 'sentimental' expectations (as she called them) provided the impetus for what was to become the first realistic depiction of frontier life in American letters" (Kolodny 133). Certainly this appears to be an extravagant claim on Kirkland's behalf. Nevertheless, it can be justified because of Kirkland's careful reportage. Like Beck and Burlend, who also published in the 1830s, she acknowledges in her preface that she has written "a sort of Emigrant's Guide" for which she claims "the merit of general truth of outline" (31). On the opening page, Kirkland promises "a veracious history of actual occurrences, an unvarnished transcript of real characters" (33). I do not find fault with Kirkland's descriptions, but with Kolodny's use of one particular episode. Kolodny selects the story of Cora and Everard Hastings as the "fullest portrait of a model frontier couple" to appear in *A New Home;* it "pits book-learned fantasies against economic and geographic realities" (Kolodny 141).

The Hastings episode begins with a description of their "cottage" as first seen by Mary Clavers, who is out riding with her husband. (Note that here is another example of a woman who is *not* imprisoned in her cabin!) The Hastings' homestead is situated in a valley which was "beautifully diversified with wood and prairies" (*A New Home* 193). Mary Clavers is introduced to Cora Hastings, who "looked far lovelier in her woodland simplicity" than in the fancy ball dress she was wearing the last time Mary had seen her—for the two women had met back east. The next twenty pages trace the Hastings' story, beginning with Cora's obsessions with sentimental romances, her equally romantic elopement with Everard, followed by the near death of Cora and her baby. After these events, Cora and Everard become a serious, practical young couple. When the opportunity arises, they gladly accept a homestead in the Michigan wilderness where they can begin a new life. The silly Cora has become, according to Mary Clavers, "a new creature, a rational being, a mother, a matron, full of sorrow for the past and of sage plans for the future" (*A New Home* 211).

Kolodny cites this passage and suggests that "the chastened Cora, forerunner and pattern of the chastened and experienced New World Eves who would soon populate a rash of domestic fictions set in the west, is now ready to enter the garden" (143). Kolodny points out that Cora's Michigan home is "handsome and picturesque-looking," but it bears little resemblance to the fantasy homes of Cora's imaginings prior to the sobering experiences which forced her to live in the real world. "Most importantly, however, the economic realities ignored in the 'glenny' dell of Upstate New York are here given their due," Kolodny argues: in Michigan Cora and Everard possess "a fine fertile tract, managed by a practical farmer and his family" (144).

This phrase—"managed by a practical farmer and his family"— makes it difficult to accept Kolodny's endorsement of the Hastings as a model frontier couple; even a part-time hired man was a luxury few immigrants could afford. It is also difficult to accept Kolodny's view that the story's significance lies in the "economic realities" it portrays. The Hastings' farm is a fairyland when compared to the Burlend's. When placed in the context of a much larger collection of writings about prairie settlement, the Hastings would hardly qualify as "a model frontier couple." We need to look elsewhere in nineteenth-century writings for a model couple. In fact, we need to continually keep in mind that there were numerous models representing a variety of classes and ethnic backgrounds as well as rural and agricultural backgrounds.

Gro Svendsen represents one such model. She wrote letters to her family in Norway during the 1860s and 1870s. She conscientiously reported her impressions of the prairie. A second wave woman, Svendsen knew her letters would be given serious attention by the curious as well as by those with "American fever."[9] She heatedly denied that America was "paradise"—"My love for my native land is far too deep and too sacred. I could never prefer another country to my own" (29). Yet her faithfulness to the country of her birth does not hinder her from appreciating the new land. She is unrestrained in her praise for the prairie near Estherville, Iowa, where they had settled: "Our land is beautiful, though there are few trees. Trees, however, can be had and planted at the cost of from five to ten dollars per acre. We have good spring water near by. Best of all, the

9. Frank C. Nelson points out that Norwegians with "American fever" read as many American letters as they could. These letters passed from "family to family and community to community. Everywhere they spread information about America and stirred interest in the prospect of emigration" (6).

land is good meadowland and easily plowed and cultivated" (44). Svendsen, in recounting her husband's and her success, feared the readers of her letters might think she was bragging: "Now that we have our land and a wagon and oxen, we are self-sufficient and can even help others. It's wonderful to be able to do so. I am not telling you this to make us seem important, but I just chanced to think about it. We are by no means rich, but we cannot be called poor; that's just as certain" (53).

Gro Svendsen and Rebecca Burlend are representative of a group of women that is larger than previously suspected.[10] These women are candid about isolated conditions and deprivations; nevertheless, they leave their readers with a sense that the advantages of emigration far outweighed the disadvantages; cultural preferences for a particular kind of landscape and way of life could be put aside and alternatives accepted even when there was considerable stress. Some, as an Ella Hartt photograph demonstrates (see fig. 2), found time to play out-of-doors.

This flexibility on the part of women is demonstrated in Canadian women's writings during the pioneer era. Two sisters—English gentlewomen—married and emigrated to Canada in the 1830s. They pioneered in a variety of locations in both the bush country and the clearings of Ontario. Their works provided literary models for women describing the new prairie frontier. In 1854, Catherine Parr Traill published *The Female Emigrant's Guide*, which directly addressed the questions of English gentlewomen about Canadian life in unsettled areas. As early as 1836, however, her London publication entitled *The Backwoods of Canada* had become a handbook for emigrants (Klinck xii). Her sister, Susanna Moodie, was equally influential through her Ontario sketches published in the 1840s in the *Literary Garland*, a Montreal magazine. Her 1852 publication, *Roughing It in the Bush*, has become a Canadian classic. These two women provide fascinating contrasts as pioneer models: Susanna clings to her role as a gentlewoman and only gradually develops pride in her ability to dig up a garden and steer a canoe. Catherine immediately and enthusiastically takes control of the house and garden, and develops domestic skills as well as a strong sense of confidence and independence (see Fowler 128; 80–81).

Mary E. Inderwich assumes a tone much like Catherine Parr Traill's in her prairie frontier writings. Accompanied by her maid, Inder-

10. See Fairbanks and Sundberg, *Farm Women on the Prairie Frontier*; Elizabeth Hampsten, *Read This Only to Yourself*; Glenda Riley, *Frontierswomen: The Iowa Experience*; and Joanna Stratton, *Pioneer Women*.

Fig. 2   Miss Ella Hartt, *Mrs. Ed. Hartt wearing wooden shoes and riding in a wheel-barrow pushed by her husband.* Courtesy of Glenbow Archives, Calgary, Alberta.

wich left Perth, Ontario, with the intention of joining her brother. On the way she met an Alberta rancher, fell in love, and married a few months later. Her letters, written with the hope that they would be published, represented the views of a woman conscious of her role as image-maker when she described the land, the people, and the way of life. "Dear, This is the life!" she writes. "I have any number of troubles, in fact too numerous to mention, but I forget them all in this joyous air with the grand protecting mountains always standing round the western horizon. . . . They are the dearest and most constant friends" (1). While it is clear that the mountains are the most significant aspect of her environment, she wants her readers to understand there is a distinct difference between *plains* and *prairie;* she notes that there are "no plains here but the most glorious ranges of hills and rolling prairie" (1). In another letter, after describing encounters with a mountain lion and a grey wolf, she says: "Ah, I should not tell you these things, for I am sure they sound terrifying to you in the lap of luxury. They would have to me a year ago, but they are only incidents of interest and little excitement now" (3). These passages indicate that Inderwich wished to present herself as exhilarated by the pioneer experience.

A 1914 publication by another Canadian immigrant, Georgina Binnie-Clark, represents a woman's relationship to the land in "the last best West" in a more serious light. Binnie-Clark, with the financial backing of her father, homesteaded four miles from Fort Qu'Appelle and wrote about her experiences in *Wheat and Woman*. She argued that there were alternatives for single women who preferred not to marry but who would find work in business or industry monotonous and routine. (See fig. 3.) She recommended farming to those with money for a "fair start" and temperaments that would respond to "grateful animals and the varied labours on the land" (304–05). Throughout the book she comments on her love of the wild flowers and on the challenge presented by virgin land that must be broken and "cleaned"; she never glosses over the errors she had made, the deprivations to which she had to adjust, or the isolation that came with homesteading.

On the basis of the images provided by these writers, we might expect that many women packed their covered wagons or stepped aboard steamboats and trains with considerable assurance that, with good health and perseverance, a new life in a new land could be achieved. Then why is it that when we look at a prototypical painting by the popular nineteenth-century artist Emmanuel Leutze, we seek in vain for any expressions of optimism and excitement on the faces of women journeying to the promised land? In the center background of *Westward the Course of Empire Takes Its Way*, ca. 1861 (see fig. 4), a woman has been laid out for burial. To the left, a woman seated on a rock ledge with a child in her lap rests in the shadow of the larger-than-life male figure and refuses to look in the westward direction toward which the man is pointing so eagerly. Slightly to the right, another woman, who is attempting to drive the horses, puts hand to forehead in a gesture of despair as two men try to bring the excited horses under control. In the foreground, a fourth woman, walking, focuses all her attention on the child she is carrying, while a fifth woman—the only one facing westward—appears to be half rising

Fig. 3   *Two Lady Homesteaders*, circa 1912. Sabrine Jacobson and Johanne Solberg each had a homestead near Square Deal. Courtesy of Glenbow Archives, Calgary, Alberta.

from the wagon seat and gazing with mixed awe and fear toward the new territory.

    Feminist historians who have grappled with women's responses to the pioneer experience provide insights into the reasons why such images of women as presented by Leutze have dominated a significant portion of art, literature, and history during the nineteenth and twentieth centuries. Susan H. Armitage presents one perspective: "The frontier myth is a male myth, preoccupied with stereotypically male issues like courage, physical bravery, honor, and male friendship. While these are important themes, they by no means encompass the reality and complexity of the frontier experience" ("Women's Literature" 5). Yet for writers and

Fig. 4   EMMANUEL LEUTZE, *Westward the Course of Empire Takes Its Way*, circa 1861.
Courtesy of National Museum of American Art, Smithsonian Institution.

painters who wish to glorify this myth, there is no better way for showing
courage, bravery, and honor in males than by placing them beside helpless, fearful females.

What a painting like Leutze's does not show is that in some cases,
both men and women failed in their emigration ventures. For example, in
Went to Kansas (1862), Miriam Colt described how she and her husband
enthusiastically joined the Vegetarian Settlement Company; they in-

deed went to Kansas, but once there they discovered they had been swindled. Subsequently, Colt's husband and son died and she returned to the East, sad and defeated, with her daughter.

A great many women interested in emigration would have read articles and books such as Colt's in addition to a wide variety of travel books and emigrant guides. They were most likely, however, to read "dime novels," especially those published by Beadle, whose "total sales between 1860 and 1865 approached five million" (Smith 90–91). Three novels in particular are useful for this study because they provided nine-teenth-century readers with images and ideas about the prairie and fron-tier life. Some novels included descriptions of the picturesque prairies that are interchangeable with those found in Stewart's and Fuller's travel books. For example, in Frances Fuller Victor's *Alicia Newsome; or The Land Claim: A Tale of the Upper Missouri* (1862), four young squatters come upon the unexpected sight of Alicia Newsome picking the luscious strawberries that abound on the prairie (18). True, the pastoral scene is undercut by the presence of a snake, and the "young English beauty" has to be rescued by the four gallants.

Another dime novel writer, Mrs. Metta Victoria Victor,[11] de-scribes the prairie in equally picturesque terms, but without any threaten-ing element. In *Myrtle, the Child of the Prairie*, the hero discovers a child lying among tall grass and exquisite blossoms. The villain of the story had kidnapped the mother and left the baby behind.

> The infant, not more than a year of age apparently, was a little girl in a white frock, the sleeves of which were looped up with corals; she had round, rosy limbs, and a sweet face. A few flowers were grasped in one hand, the other was under her cheek; one shoe was on, the other lost, while her little mantle of blue silk was crumpled beneath her feet. As if in protection, a rose-bush leaned over her, from some of whose fullest blossoms the leaves had dropped into her gold hair. [5]

The hero takes the baby to his prairie home, adopts her, and raises her outside of society where, he hopes, she will be free from the false values, lies, and dishonest actions that characterize those living within society, even on the prairie.

The Edenic environment receives even fuller development in other dime novels. In Mrs. Metta Victoria Victor's *Uncle Ezekial and His*

---

11. Mrs. Metta Fuller Victor was the wife of one of the Beadle editors, Victor J. Orville; Frances Fuller Barritt Victor was her sister.

Exploits on Two Continents (1861?), the rich prairie soil gives way easily to Peter Potter's plow, enabling a poor man from the East to become a prosperous and independent farmer. Peter Potter's foster child, Edith (the daughter of an English aristocrat), romps on the prairie as a child; later, as a young woman reunited with her father in England, she yearns for the rose-scented prairie. Mrs. Henry Thomas, the author of *The Prairie Bride*, is more restrained in her descriptions of the prairie; she notes the lack of habitation, of shelter, and of trees for building fires. Nevertheless, she presents a self-reliant protagonist who delights in running away from a stifling home situation in the East and who demonstrates an ability to accept the prairie on its own terms.

Novels such as *The Prairie Bride* and *Uncle Ezekial and His Exploits on Two Continents* were printed in quantities of 60,000 and then reprinted as many times as necessary to meet readers' demands (Smith 90–91). Thus the sentimental versions of prairie experience provided by women writers would have influenced the views of numerous female readers—at least those who defied their mothers and ministers and read popular novels.

Two writers who directed their works toward more sophisticated readers than those who devoured dime novels were Caroline M. Kirkland and Caroline A. Soule. They also developed themes relating to the beauty of the prairies, the growth of midwestern settlements, the practical and kindly nature of common folk, the possibilities for adventure and heroism for genteel female characters. Prefaces in both Soule's *Pet of the Settlement: A Story of Prairie-Land* (1860) and Kirkland's *Western Border Life; or What Fanny Hunter Saw and Heard in Kanzas and Missouri* (1856) assure the reader that the materials upon which these works are based reflect the observations of writers who had actually lived in frontier communities and directly experienced situations similar to those described in the novels.

Soule describes the prairie as a place of "new life," "beautiful health," "tranquil joy"; it is, in fact, a new and improved Eden where the "trail of the serpent" could be forgotten for a time (79). The particular settlement Soule describes is near the Des Moines River in "Indian land"; her descriptions are frequent and extensive: the luxuriousness of flowers, shrubs, trees; the magnificence of the prairie at various times of day and at different seasons of the year. True, the black bear, the unscrupulous white adventurer, the winter blizzard, and the warring Sioux threaten to disrupt the tranquil existence, but eventually goodness wins out. The town prospers economically and morally; it welcomes immigrants who were homeless, debt-ridden, and hungry in the crowded cities of the East, and it offers them a new beginning in the West.

Kirkland, who focuses on social and political issues in *Western Border Life*, is not as ecstatic about the landscape as Soule or the dime novelists. The prairie still has appeal, however, as Kirkland shows when the New England schoolteacher arrives on the prairies and finds them delightful. As in *A New Home—Who'll Follow?*, Kirkland is committed to providing realistic details about the people and the situation. As the preface notes, she proposes to "sketch a picture of the social and moral life which the border counties of Missouri are endeavoring to force upon the new territory." She proceeds to describe what Fanny Hunter saw and heard in Kansas and Missouri: abuse of slaves by southern mistresses; rigid class structures barring poor whites from education and economic opportunities; permissive attitudes which allowed dancing and drinking on religious holidays; and blatant disregard for the law.

These novels by Soule and Kirkland trace the impact of a new territory on genteel, educated characters who have emigrated to the prairie in attempts to maintain their independence and/or to improve their economic situations. These situations are, of course, similar to those found in the dime novels. Even while idealizing New Englanders, Soule and Kirkland demonstrate that the simple, uneducated plains people have admirable characteristics as well. In *The Pet of the Settlement*, the huntsman Billy and the paragon Grandma Symmes initiate newcomers into the ways of the wilderness; in *Western Border Life*, an old black woman provides a religious and moral center in the midst of southern aristocratic decadence. Most importantly, the central characters of both novels demonstrate their ability to adapt to primitive conditions, to act daringly and intelligently; moreover, Fanny Hunter makes specific gains against superstition, immorality, class and racial prejudice, and religious slackness. Similarly, Margaret Belden in *The Pet of the Settlement* educates and converts two Indians to the Christian way of life; she also serves as a capable, refined, and educated role model for other women in the new settlement.

Yet according to Kolodny's study of women writers and their characters, genteel, educated women were unable to adapt to the frontier. She says that Caroline Kirkland, for example, "fled a blighted western Eden" (158). Kirkland's female hero in *Western Border Life* did not. Although Kirkland and her family had not been able to make the necessary adjustments to the Michigan wilderness, Kirkland as writer is able to construct a fictional situation in which a woman like herself could make a lifetime commitment to staying in the West. In fact, Kolodny omits this important novel in her study, yet this work is central to any discussion of the prairie frontier because it shows Kirkland imagining possibilities for financial prosperity as well as for improvements in the social, political, and spiritual fabric of the new prairie state. Kirkland and her husband left the frontier community they had helped to establish in Michigan because, according to one biographer, "both were disillusioned by the provincial attitudes of the frontier" (Kirkland, A New Home 8). But in Western Border Life Kirkland shows that people who are educated and committed to improving society—and, we should add, able to adapt to frontier conditions—can have an enormous effect on the social, political, and religious institutions of a new frontier community.

Although she herself returned to the East, Caroline Kirkland imagined the kind of woman who would stay in the West. I can think of no better example of a woman who made a lifetime commitment to staying in the Prairie West than Kate Simpson Hayes, who said: "In no country under God's sun is there the same chance and opportunity for woman's hand as in the new, western world" (quoted in Savage, Foremothers 19). Hayes's own story is more romantic than any to appear in a dime novel. She was born in New Brunswick and went to Prince Albert in 1879, where she worked as a governess for a brief time. Shortly thereafter she married and lived in western Ontario, where her two children were born. She left her husband and, with the two small children, went to Regina where she immediately became a part of the social and cultural life of the new town and began an astonishing affair with Nicholas Flood Davin, owner of the Regina Leader and soon-to-be elected representative to Parliament in Ottawa. Hayes provided Canadian readers with the first fiction about the prairies published in the West—Prairie Pot-Pourri (1895), a collection of poems, short stories, and a novella.[12]

An 1896 article on Canadian women writers made this pronouncement: "Far out on the prairie from the town of Regina, the capital of the Canadian North-west Territories, has recently come a voice fresh and strong. Kate Hayes knows well how to embody in a poem something of

12. For more information on Kate Simpson Hayes see Grant MacEwan's And Mighty Women Too: Stories of Notable Western Canadian Women (Saskatoon: Western Producer Prairie Books, 1975), 33–41. She appears as a character in a historical play by Ken Mitchell, Davin: The Politician (Edmonton: NeWest Press, 1979).

the rough life and atmosphere found in the prairie settlements of the West" (O'Hagan 791–92). As Dick Harrison notes in his study of prairie fiction, Hayes's stories are important because they "all share an evident desire to present the West through Western eyes. There is a preference for western ways and an assumption of western values, whether White or native" (*Unnamed Country* 65). This characteristic of Hayes's work takes on special significance because Hayes was not western by birth. That she wrote "through western eyes" demonstrates how quickly she made Regina her home ground.

In the short story "The La-de-dah from London," Hayes's first description of the prairie woman is a positive one. Two men traveling together from Ontario stop at settlers' houses. They note that "the wife—always an Ontario woman it seemed—with homely grace, bustled about" (*Prairie Pot-Pourri* 14). One of the travelers, an Englishman whom westerners nickname the La-de-dah, describes the two main female characters in the story, Mrs. O'Toole and her daughter, Mollie. The mother, he thinks, is an "extremely vulgah looking pehson"; she does not meet his criteria of gentility. The daughter, however, has been sent to St. Mary's Academy in Winnipeg for "educational advantages equal to eastern and much older cities" (25). He immediately approves of her and delights in finding a wide variety of labels to describe her—she's "a prairie nymph," "a pink apparition," "a pink divinity" (23). As the La-de-dah becomes better acquainted with Mrs. O'Toole, he is less perturbed by her deficiency in manners and diction; she makes up for these shortcomings by devotion and service to her husband, her daughter, and other prairie settlers. And he discovers that Molly is much more than "a pink apparition": she can ride a horse, make bannocks, play a melodeon, and tend the chickens efficiently and enthusiastically. Not until the La-de-dah has lost his fortune and professed the values of hard work and simple living does the prairie nymph agree to marry him.

Clearly, the pioneer experience and the prairie landscape brought a variety of responses from travelers, early settlers, and fiction writers. The complexities involved in analyzing the attitudes and lives of fictional characters within the frontier prairie setting are revealed when we consider one specific work. Gabrielle Roy, a French Canadian who grew up in the St. Boniface district of Winnipeg, on the edge of the prairie, writes in the 1970s about a Ukrainian woman who emigrated to Manitoba in the early 1900s. Why should we accept a French Canadian's interpretation of a Ukrainian woman's response to the prairie? I would argue that three reasons exist for trusting Roy's story. First, Roy is an insider who knows the prairie. Second, she knows the people because her father was a government official in charge of helping immigrants to resettle; he frequently told her about the people and their perceptions. He provided Roy with information and insights to which most people would not have access. Third, Roy was unsparing in presenting the grim reality of her characters' situations (Mitcham 163). Through observation, discussion, and reading, Roy had acquired the necessary insights for telling an immigrant woman's story. Therefore when she writes about Maria Marta Yaramko, we can believe in the reality, if not the fact, that such a woman passionately loved the prairie despite its loneliness and harsh climate. To use Geertz's terminology, we feel that Roy has gone through the important process of making guesses, assessing the guesses, and interpreting a woman's life according to the best guesses.

In "Garden in the Wind," Maria Marta Yaramko is isolated from her neighbors, separated from her children, and alienated from her husband. Yet she finds joy and companionship with the grasses, the trees, the wind, and—especially—the flowers in her garden. Why does Marta find fulfillment when others have not? Her children have grown up and moved to Moose Jaw, Prince Albert, and Rorketon. Her neighbors have given up: after the first few bountiful harvests were followed by several years of droughts, they too left. The town they had envisioned as early settlers never developed. Stepan, Marta's husband, had been reluctant to emigrate in the first place; now he focuses his anger on Marta for "loving life . . . despite the bitter blows" (Garden in the Wind 152).

If the cultural stance were the key factor affecting individual response to the landscape, Marta, Stepan, and the neighbors from the Ukraine would have responded in similar ways to the landscape—they all came from the steppes; they had all escaped from famine in the old country. Therefore it becomes apparent that what has made Marta an ally of the prairie has more to do with her personal perceptions and personal strength rather than with cultural attitudes. In this situation Roy draws on what she has learned about a particular group and about human nature in general; she concludes that the majority of people do not have ties to the land sufficient to sustain them during difficult times but that there are always some, like Marta, who find "inexhaustible consolation" in the "eternal play of wind and grass and sunlight" (141).

One reader of "Garden in the Wind" seems to distort the text because of her own attitudes toward Marta's situation. In "Roy's West,"

Allison Mitcham says that "despite the fact that Marta is dying of cancer in a lonely prairie *shack* bullied and ignored by turns by a harsh and brutal husband who takes out on her his own failure to cope with their alien environment, she retains to the end a faith in life. She is indeed lonely and deeply puzzled about life and her role in it, but the essential positiveness of her nature is symbolized by the way in which she toils unflaggingly to preserve the delicate flowers which she has nurtured year after year, despite the *hostile environment* and her husband's mockery" (my italics, 162). The wording *shack* and *hostile environment* reflects the critic's view, not Marta's. True, Marta once thought of her house as a shack, but that was when she had first arrived and before Stepan had brought her the snapdragon and poppy seeds with which she had begun the transformation of her particular corner of the prairie. So to refer to Marta's environment as hostile is to overlook the fact that Marta, despite the years of hardship, still has a vision that usually occurs only to young people just settling a homestead: "Once again the thought crossed her mind that the plain was deep in a great dream of things to come, and was singing of patience, with the promise that all things, in their time and place, would yet be accomplished" (146).

I use this example of a particular critical response to a work of prairie fiction to point out the layers of complexity that a critic must work through. A critic may be genuinely sympathetic to a work, strive for objectivity in description, summary, and interpretation, and still, in the middle of an interpretation, distort the text because of personal attitudes and/or cultural stance. Not one of us, as readers and critics, will be able to avoid these occasional lapses.

No subject related to the prairie is more difficult to approach objectively than the landscape itself—the preceding survey of images and attitudes has made this point. If we let the stories speak for themselves, however, they will entertain us with a surprising and challenging variety of perspectives.

In *The Land before Her*, Annette Kolodny says that women cultivated small gardens in order "to render Home a Paradise" (54). She finds ample support for this statement in the domestic fictions of the nineteenth century. But the subject of prairie females and their gardens is far more complex than Kolodny and the writers in her study allow. There are two reasons why this is so. The writers represented in Kolodny's analysis of frontier prairie women were educated, middle-class easterners. They may have known hard times and, as in the case of Margaret Fuller, they may have had rigorous household responsibilities at some time. Nevertheless, their identities are rooted in their work as writers, not as farmers or as the wives of farmers. As writers, of course, they fulfill an important function—they provide a female perspective on the prairies and the frontier during the early periods of settlement. It is a mistake, however, to generalize about prairie women on the basis of the experiences and writings of the domestic fictionists without taking into consideration the much broader corpus of writings by women—especially the works of women who lived on the prairie.

Moreover, neither Kolodny nor the authors of domestic fictions seem to have a very real sense of what is involved in gardening.[13] Kolodny insists that women created gardens in an effort to "render Home a Paradise." The women writers who provide the material for my study, however, would hesitate to make such an elaborate claim. Their characters, in most cases, are lower- and middle-class women who have grown up on farms or have tended small gardens in town. They certainly plant flowers whenever and wherever possible, but they also recognize that their gardens mean physical and economic survival of the family. Agricultural historians have frequently noted that men homesteading by themselves often failed because they did not have the time to break the sod for field crops and also plant a garden, harvest, preserve, and store the products. Most prairie women writers who have described the lives of women during the pioneer era show women devoted to making frontier homes secure and, if possible, comfortable. Almost without exception the characters are plain, practical women who would simply smile politely at the suggestion that what they were *really* doing was "making Home a Paradise," although some would have been aware that this was the message of women's books and magazines. This jargon simply does not appear in works by either serious or sentimental writers.[14] For the last

---

13. Caroline Kirkland is an exception. Describing a frontier garden in *A New Home— Who'll Follow?* she warns of the difficulties of preparing the ground; nevertheless, she assures her reader, "Even on the first turning up, it furnishes you with all the humbler luxuries in the vegetable way, from the earliest pea to the most delicate cauliflower" (117). On the subject of flowers she writes, "I scarcely dare trust my pen with a word, so sure am I that my enthusiastic love for them would, to most readers, seem absolutely silly or affected. But where the earth produces spontaneously such myriads of splendid specimens, it would seem really ungrateful to spare the little time and pains required for their cultivation" (115).

14. I use the term *sentimental* to describe works that "idealize the pretty and tender" in addition to "elevating feeling above all else"; this is only one of several definitions provided by Nina Baym in *Woman's Fiction: A Guide to Novels by and about Women in America, 1820–1870* (Ithaca: Cornell Univ. Press, 1978), 25.

hundred years, women writers have been providing, in fiction, innumerable realistic details that lead to a rethinking of prairie women's lives.

Two examples will illustrate the concrete details found in women's writings when they describe women and their prairie gardens. In "Garden in the Wind," Marta works among the cosmos, talking to them, "congratulating them on their good nature—flowers of the poor, making no demands, living in almost any soil, born again of seeds they had dropped in autumn. But no less than these she had loved certain of her plants that she had taken great pains to save" (129). She turns to the peonies and notices, with great disgust, that some worms have attacked a blossom: "Och, she thought in vexation, because of a greedy grub it's turned to worm now, and it could have been two or three great flowers, moist and proud. And what good did it do, for the worm itself will surely be eaten today!" She crushes the worm, and then looks around at her garden: "Each year the flowers appeared to her as a wonder she would never see clearly enough; but the care they demanded was equally inexhaustible" (129). Marta's love of her garden has nothing to do with "Home as Paradise"; the flowers nourish her very personal, wonderfully selfish greed for beauty. In addition, she repeatedly proves herself an equal adversary in the battle with nature's destructive forces.

In Lois Phillips Hudson's *Reapers of the Dust: A Prairie Chronicle,* a girl visits her aunt on a nearby farm. While helping to weed the garden, she discovers what to her is a wonderfully enormous green tomato worm. She keeps the surprise to herself, however, fearing that her aunt will not share her appreciation. Inevitably the aunt, who is following her down the row of tomato plants, discovers the worm and, of course, hacks through it with a hoe. The girl, though regretful, understands why her aunt had to kill the worm: she is a child of the prairie who recognizes the most fundamental of all relationships on the prairie—the one that exists between the gardener and nature in the daily struggle for survival.

Kolodny notes that some women were "enchanted with [the] new open and rolling prospects" of the prairies, the "ready-made park at the end of the trail" (97). She argues that while these responses to the prairies helped women to adjust to life on the new homestead, the most sustaining factor was related to their "fantasy of a landscape that might figuratively reconstitute some prior domestic community": by recreating the landscapes of their former homes, women could lessen "the sense of irrevocable loss" (97–98). Certainly any sensitive emigrant will recreate, in whatever way possible, the conditions and practices of her former home; those who are adaptable—even if not enthusiastic pioneers—will take pleasure in an appealing landscape.

The "park" at the end of the trail and the garden that "figuratively reconstitutes" the landscape of the former home, however, are only two of the many kinds of gardens that make up women's environments on the prairie. If we let dozens of characters speak for themselves, they will acquaint us with a variegated landscape that can be classified in four broad categories: Prairie as Garden, Prairie as Wilderness, Prairie as Real Estate, and Prairie as Wasteland.[15]

Prairie as Garden

This category has three subdivisions: prairie as garden plot, prairie as fertile farmland, and prairie as Garden of the World.

Prairie as Garden Plot. For Marta in "Garden in the Wind," the prairie is her plot of land where she grows the rose of India, the dahlia, and the gladiolus. True, she is intensely aware of the vast surrounding prairie and accepts it on its own terms, but her primary focus continues to be *her garden* because it enables her to find contentment and meaning; she also thrives on the challenges presented by her adversaries, wind, worms, and drought. A small plot can be watered except in times of severe drought; it can be filled with flowers that are reminders of the old country—as Kolodny suggests—or of special gifts from friends or even from a stranger. Marta's garden, for example, contains a rose of India grown from seeds that her friend Lubka in the Ukraine had taken from her own garden, dried, and mailed to Marta. The dahlia and gladioli bulbs had been the gift of an unexpected visitor who stopped to admire Marta's garden; subsequently he mailed her the bulbs, a gesture denoting the unexpected pleasure her garden had provided (151).

Sometimes the prairie at large is the garden (see fig. 5). In an 1880 story, Mary Hartwell Catherwood, probably conscious that her *Lippin-*

---

15. For additional insights into why people perceive a landscape in different ways, see Rees, "Nostalgic Reaction and the Canadian Prairie Landscape." He cites the psychoanalyst Michael Balint who "has identified two personality types based upon fundamental differences between people in their need for security. The two types are labeled *ochnophil* and *philobat*. According to Balint, the ochnophil is hesitant and fearful, and his world consists of objects (refuges) separated by 'horrid empty spaces.' . . . The philobat's world is the converse of the ochnophil's: the horrid empty spaces are, instead, friendly expanses interrupted by occasional hazards that have to be negotiated" (159).

Fig. 5   Harvey Dunn, *The Prairie Is My Garden*. Courtesy of South Dakota
Memorial Art Center Collection.

cott's *Magazine* readers might have an imprecise image of the prairie,
begins a story with an affectionate description: "The prairie was at that
time a rolling wilderness of sedgy 'slews,' grass, flowers, rosin-weed and
rich black loam; a sea, with two or three small arks of houses within its
horizon; a whistling, shrubless plain, with a wonderful sky shifting over
it. The sky comes very close to the prairie, as if it pitied the poor bald-
headed thing and wanted to cover it" ("Career" 706). Then we see
through the eyes of the farmer's wife and his sister:

> His young bride and his sister found the situation novel. They watched
> the spring prairie flush—there is no other word to express its sudden over-
> spreading with tender shades of green—curdle with white, and make solid
> banks of yellow, margins of purple all around the slews, and pink acres of wild
> rosebushes. Indian moccasins were there, growing mouth downward on the
> stem—a golden-colored shoe, now extinct or very rare—and miles of pale-

yellow sensitive plant with black stamens. . . . The newcomers drove at
hazard off the road through billows of rosin-weed and "nigger-head" which
reached the horse's shoulders. ["Career" 707]

These women delight in the expanse of prairie as others delight in their
small garden plots.

Even during the droughts of the 1930s, a character in a Manitoba
novel willingly substitutes the prairie for her own garden: "The prairie
had won," she cheerfully concedes: "The prairie was best. She had been a
long time coming to it. This year she had not even planted flowers,
which needed such a lot of watering and attention. No flowers. The
prairie bred the only flowers it needed, pale hardy blossoms in the sweet-
smelling grass." She describes this acceptance of the prairie flowers as a
kind of wedding: she had come to the prairie town as a foreigner from
Scotland; she had tried to recreate gardens from her homeland in the
prairies. Over the years, however, she has come to a sense of belonging.
This triumph, she feels, is symbolized by her "wedding" with the prairie
flowers. She gives herself to them without regret, no longer preferring the
familiar flowers of home. The prairie is self-sufficient: "It wants no plow,
no pansies or nasturtiums or anything else we give" (Blondal 94). Her
role is limited, simply, to loving it.

Prairie as Fertile Farmland. In the 1906 novel *The Plow-Woman*,
Eleanor Gates attempted to intervene in the mythmaking process and
radically alter stereotypical thinking about western women and their
relationship to the land. She describes a woman at work in her garden
plot: "To aid her in making better progress, as well as to cool her ankles,
[Dallas] brought the bottom of her skirt through the waistband, front and
back, and walked in her red flannel petticoat" (4). Rather than being
disconcerted by the sight of Dallas plowing, a townsman who has just met
her (who later falls in love with her) feels "that she must have sprung as
she was from the plains one day—grave, full-grown, gallant" (14). Thus
Dallas becomes a powerful symbol of a frontier hero: a woman farmer
plowing her fertile lands.

One critic for *The New York Times Book Review* failed to recognize
Dallas Lancaster's splendid courage as a farmer, dismissing the novel as
"very slim," concerned merely with "the wanderings of the Lancaster
family and the love affairs of two daughters" (674). The critic is unable to
interpret *The Plow-Woman* as the story of a woman who primarily loves
the land and *wants* to work with it on its own terms; the words *taming* and
conquering are not a part of Dallas's vocabulary when she talks about her

feelings for the land. In fact, she talks about the *blossoming* of the prairie (29) and derives enormous satisfaction from her role in turning the prairie into a productive garden. Perhaps the critic was bothered by the image of a woman with rough hands or by a woman planning a future without the advice of a man. Whatever the case, the structures of significance, especially the one relating to woman's response to the land, were completely overlooked. The critic expected a love story from a woman's novel; that is all she found.

Prairie as Garden of the World. Numerous writers in the tradition of prairie women's fiction consciously use the terminology associated with the Garden of the World myth: the prairie is an Eden, a New Jerusalem, a Utopia; it is virgin land, fertile and beautiful; it is associated with new beginnings and with progress. For example, in Laura Goodman Salverson's *Dark Weaver,* a woman who had been a reluctant emigrant undergoes a conversion:

> But now, as she crossed the lush meadow, a sudden whirring of wings brought her sharply back to the teeming present. How plentiful are the grouse, she mused, following the scattering birds with smiling eyes. And suddenly the cloudless sky, broad fields and stately trees seemed to give tongue proclaiming the inexhaustible riches, inimitable beauty and boundless generosity of this marvelous country. "Look at me," waved the forest, "my virgin breast and fertile loins waiting to fulfill the harvest." "And at me," sang Little River, "for mine is the power that maketh alive. I am the spirit of the wild land; I am the leaping, plunging, free running soul of the West."
>
> Never before had the new homeland so moved her; never before had her heart gone out to it. [66]

This passage demonstrates that even women who had no choice in the decision to emigrate came to accept the dream of the New World garden as their own.

Prairie as Wilderness

The tradition of women's prairie fiction does not present us with any female Natty Bumppos. An old Indian woman in Dana Faralla's *Circle of Trees,* however, initiates newcomers. Flying Cloud teaches Kersti Nielsen and her brother that nature should be accepted and respected on its own terms. The children's mother represents the opposite point of view. She refuses to stay on the Minnesota prairie unless some trees are planted. She orders linden trees from St. Paul; these are subsequently eaten by grasshoppers. Faralla recognizes that some newcomers to the prairies have "tree hunger": "In the planting of trees it seems that the prairie sojourners themselves acquire roots. They come home" (131). At the same time, Faralla believes that the most successful settlers are those who adapt, at least to some degree, Indian attitudes toward the land.[16]

When the children try to transplant trees from the river edge to the house, Flying Cloud tells them that "the trees and the river are one country. . . . The prairie and the buffalo grass is another country. When you want to see trees, you go to tree country" (174–75). In another passage she tries to teach them the wisdom of Indian ways: "The Indian is like the wind that passes through the grass" (201). Everything is allowed to grow in its natural habitat. Her views about nature are supported by Reilly-O, a man who stays with the Nielsens one winter. He tries to help the Nielsens adjust to the prairie: "It can't be the same for you as it is for a person who has been born here," he tells Kersti's father; "But once you take hold, once you get the rhythm and the spirit of the prairie you'll see things differently" (131). As a result of her apprenticeship to Flying Cloud and Reilly-O, Kersti gradually takes root in the prairie and values those portions that are still wilderness.

Prairie as Real Estate

In *O River, Remember!* Martha Ostenso presents a woman whose response to the land is diametrically opposed to Flying Cloud's. While innumerable novels have dealt with male acquisitiveness for the land, Ostenso provides an exceptional view of a woman who is interested in the land only as real estate (1). Magdali marries Ivar Vingar not in spite of the fact that he is going to America but *because* he is going. Magdali, in contrast to the women in the Leutze painting, is described as sitting "sharply alert to exclaim upon each new feature of the land as they neared their home" (50). Unfortunately, after they have established themselves on their own homestead, she begins casting a covetous eye on neighboring lands. "Magdali's eyes missed nothing of the features of the Endicott land where the trail crossed it. . . . She saw its firm, good level,

16. For an analysis of Indian attitudes toward the land, see Susan J. Scarberry, "Land into Flesh: Images of Intimacy" and Elaine Jahner, "A Laddered, Rain-bearing Rug: Paula Gunn Allen's Poetry."

rising from the river bed, and the rich covering of growth the summer had given it, yellowing now under the late season. Her lips straightened with contempt for a man who had not the enterprise to make the most of what was immediately under his nose. Such people had no right to be settlers in a new land" (75). Her husband sees the lands of Minnesota as an opportunity for experimenting with wheat grains, thus improving the quality of lives for farmers. Magdali sees the land as real estate to be purchased at minimal prices when people like the Endicotts fail, and then to be held until demand brings an enormous profit.

Prairie as Wasteland

Some women find the prairie, from first sight to last, an unmitigated wasteland; these are almost without exception minor characters in the stories. Their view is represented by a Dakota woman in Lorna Doone Beers's *Prairie Fires:*

> Mrs. Erickson put down the plate absently and gazed out of the window across the prairie, lighted by the last level rays of sun. But for her it was not there—only the yellow unbroken expanse of that former pale prairie grass, the blinding stretch of snow with no relieving color, not a bush, not a tree to save the nothingness; the drifted sod-banked shack was but a heap of snow in the midst of the snow. . . . Oh, those endless days and longer nights. [47]

In this passage we are taken into the thoughts of a woman who feels victimized by what to her is only a wasteland.

In some cases, major female characters may see the prairie as partially a wasteland; at the same time, however, they identify the prairie with some kind of promise. This is the case in Loula Grace Erdman's novel about nesters in Texas, *The Edge of Time.* A young woman, Bethany, proposes to a man, marries him, and leaves Missouri to emigrate with him to the Panhandle. Here is her first impression of the prairie:

> The first thing Bethany saw was nothing. Nothing at all. She pitched her mind in nothingness, found herself drowning in it as a swimmer drowns in water too deep for him.
> Here was more sky than she had ever seen before. That was all there was—sky. No houses, no trees, no roads. Nothing to break the landscape. She shrank back from it, as one draws from sudden bright light. [53]

The word *nothingness* appears here as it did in the response of Mrs. Erickson in *Prairie Fires.* The important difference is that Bethany feels something besides the nothingness: "She had a sense of exhilaration, as if somewhere ahead of her in all this nothingness she was going to find something pretty fine" (35). At the end of the novel, she and her husband are still struggling to make their farm prosper; she wonders if she can go on facing the land. Then she observes the clouds, "ever-changing, ever-lovely," and realizes that they have made the earth "more comfortably small, more a thing she could understand" (270). Finally, we are told,

> A strange thing happened to her. She found that she could look at the level and limitless land with no sense of pain at all. She thought, "Of course, this isn't like Missouri. All the time I've been trying to compare the two of them. They aren't supposed to be alike. This country is like nothing but itself."

A Canadian prairie critic and novelist, Henry Kriesel, has identified two polar images of man on the prairies: "man, the giant-conqueror, and man, the insignificant dwarf always threatened by defeat" ("Prairie" 256). When Kriesel says *man* he obviously means *males*. Women have not been trapped in this dichotomy. They have rarely identified themselves as giant-conquerors and thus have been able to accommodate themselves to a landscape that insists on being accepted on its own terms. In fact, nineteenth- and twentieth-century women were socialized to adjust to almost every situation and relationship they encountered. Thus women occupy a very different space from that which men occupy. Having very little compulsion to conquer space, they can establish themselves within space and, despite loneliness and isolation, establish a kind of compatibility with it. Women may feel exposed to the blizzards, the droughts, the grasshoppers, the fires. In most cases, however, they do not seem to associate the land with emptiness and meaninglessness. In fact, a woman may find in the land the same power to create and to give birth that she has: "The country seemed to reach out, to renew itself so that each mile added more miles; so that each new mile was, in turn, the seed for other uncounted miles as yet unborn. 'It's like creation,' [Bethany] thought. 'It's like my baby—'" (Erdman, *Edge of Time* 271). I would argue that a woman on the prairie, like the Hindu goddess emerging from the womb, is, simply, "garmented with space." The pioneer woman goes naked and vulnerable into a new world. But she can project onto this new space, this vast prairie, the potential to clothe and protect her. She does not have to control or conquer the land.

Again and again in prairie women's fiction, female characters establish an intimate relationship with the landscape in much the same way as they deal with the large, flat area that is to become a quilt. Their gardens, like their patchwork quilts, contained a wide range of associations which combined pieces from their own pasts as well as the pasts of friends and strangers. In addition, some portions were new: sometimes a woman enjoyed the luxury of buying a special piece of cloth for her quilt. In a similar manner she purchased seeds or plants for her garden, especially plants that she learned would survive and flourish in the prairie environment. These practical and yet visionary women focused, as quilt-makers must, on future possibilities.

CHAPTER THREE

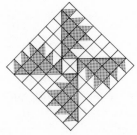

First Wave Women

Four statues provide a starting point for analyzing the iconography of pioneer prairie women. They represent the Prairie Angel, the Prairie Victim, and the Frontier Hero. *The Pioneer Woman,* a bronze statue by Bryant Baker (see fig. 6), was unveiled near Ponco City, Oklahoma, in 1930. She stands tall and erect; the folds of her long skirt suggest strength and vigor in the body beneath. Her chin is slightly lifted as she looks into the distance. A small bag hangs from the crook of her right elbow; her fingers firmly grip a Bible. Her left hand clasps the hand of a half-grown boy who stands slightly behind her as he gazes upward. She represents the Prairie Angel. Her role is threefold. The child at her left reminds us of the responsibilities of motherhood, and it is symbolic that the child is male: nineteenth-century women were charged with overseeing the moral and intellectual development of the sons who would become future leaders. Her second responsibility is represented by the bag, which would typically contain food and medicine for the needy. Her third responsibility as culture-bearer is represented by the book.

A statue from a Ukrainian village near Edmonton, Alberta, represents the Prairie Victim, although it exhibits the mildest possible form of victimization (see fig. 7). Leo Mol's statue of a Ukrainian couple shows a newly arrived emigrant woman who is not apparently suffering physically, but she is certainly suffering emotionally from the pain of leaving her family and her homeland, knowing how difficult it will be to recreate the old way of life in an alien land. The husband stands by her side, looking forward; his comforting hand rests on her shoulder. The wife looks downward, cradling an infant in her arms; beside her, a child, like the father, shows eager anticipation at the prospect of settling in a new land.[1] Although this woman lacks the assertive, forward-looking pose of the Bryant Baker statue, she nevertheless exudes a quiet strength which should carry her through the ordeal of relocation.

The Frontier Hero is represented by two additional statues. One stands on the state capitol grounds in Topeka, Kansas. Created by Robert Merrill Gage, it is dedicated to the "Pioneer Women of Kansas" (see fig. 8). She is seated, but looking directly ahead despite the infant cradled and asleep in her left arm and the boy kneeling beside her, reading a book. A dog rests at her feet. The madonna-like pose insists on her traditional qualities as mother and nurturer; however, a gun rests across her lap, forcing our attention to the different role that she plays compared to that of the Baker figure. The gun represents fierce independence and self-sufficiency, the ability of a woman to feed and protect herself and her children and to survive in the wilderness. Gage posits, through his work, that the Frontier Hero can, certainly, be a woman.[2]

Another version of the Frontier Hero, John Weaver's *Madonna of the Wheat*, stands before the City Hall in Edmonton (see fig. 9). The title of this work encourages a cluster of symbolic interpretations. *Madonna*, of course, suggests sacred motherhood. But by placing a sheath of wheat in her arms rather than a child, the sculptor gives greater emphasis to her qualities as earth mother or even as earth goddess. The wheat, too, serves as a reminder that the rich farmlands of the prairies have the potential to feed the world.[3]

The iconography of frontier women is, of course, more complex than indicated by these examples of the Prairie Angel, the Prairie Victim, and the Frontier Hero.[4] Nevertheless they provide a starting point

1. A writer for *Alberta Magazine* describes the woman as sitting "patiently, a dream on her face." The sculpture of this Ukrainian immigrant family was commissioned for Alberta's Ukrainian Cultural Heritage Center, a few miles from Edmonton. Leo Mol was born in the Ukraine in 1915 (Lang 8).

2. Another work by Gage was commissioned by the Council Grove Daughters of the American Revolution and called *Madonna of the Trail*. This figure carried a baby in one arm, a rifle in the other; a little boy clings to her skirts.

3. The plaque on the statue includes a quotation from John B. Weaver: "The young woman cradles the wheat in her arms as though it were a child. She feels the good earth beneath her feet and turns her face to the warm sun. Without words she is giving thanks for the miracle of the wheat." The statue was dedicated "to all the pioneer women of Alberta" by the Alberta Branches of the Ukrainian Women's Association of Canada.

4. In "Cowboy Knights and Prairie Madonnas" Kirsten H. Powell says that "of the various myths of the West, the myth of the frontier hero and heroine has traditionally been one of the most appealing to the American imagination. While in the nineteenth century the western hero was

Fig. 6 BRYANT BAKER, *The Pioneer Woman.* Courtesy of The Glass Negative, Ponca City, Oklahoma.

for a discussion of first wave women. The structures of signification are equally complex, but a short scene from the first act of Susan Glaspell's play, *The Inheritors,* is equally helpful in establishing the fundamental motifs of the pioneer experience—the journey, the work, the ordeal, and the satisfactions. The setting is an Iowa farmhouse in 1879, "on the

frequently a specific person whose deeds had granted him hero status, by the early twentieth century, heroes were more often generalized types rather than historical persons" (50). In a chapter entitled "The Madonna of the Prairies and Calamity Jane: Images of Westering Women," Sandra L. Myres summarizes the dominant images: the "weary and forlorn frontier wife, a sort of helpless heroine"; "the sturdy helpmate and civilizer of the frontier" who is also known as "the Madonna of the Prairies, the Brave Pioneer Mother, the Gentle Tamer" (2–3). The third image, the Bad Woman, is associated with the far west rather than with the prairies.

Fig. 7   LEO MOL, *Ukrainian Immigrants*, located at Alberta's Ukrainian Cultural
Heritage Village. Courtesy of Alberta Photograph Library.

rolling prairies just back from the Mississippi." Grandmother Morton
enjoys educating a young visitor, named Smith, about some historical
events in which she actively participated in the 1820s. She tells him she
came to Iowa in a wagon; when he suggests that the trip must have been
dangerous, she abruptly reminds him that "them set on safety staid back
in Ohio" (5). Clearly, Grandmother Morton was not a fainthearted
emigrant. When Mr. Smith tries to extend his sympathy for the isolation
she had to endure in the wilderness, she scoffs: "No, we weren't alone.
We had the Owens ten miles down the river" (5). When he asks about
problems with the Indians, he expects her to respond with typical anti-
Indian sentiments. He says, "I should think the Indians would have
wiped you out." Again, Grandmother Morton refutes the stereotype: "I

Fig. 8   ROBERT MERRILL GAGE, model of the statue *Pioneer Woman*, which is
located on the statehouse grounds, Topeka, Kansas. The base of the statue
carries the inscription "Dedicated to the Pioneer Women of Kansas."
Courtesy of the Kansas State Historical Society.

threw an Indian in the cellar and stood on the door. I was heavier then."
She goes on to say that Black Hawk and his people had reasons for their
anger: "We roiled them up considerable. They was mostly friendly when
let be. Didn't want to give up their land—but I've noticed something of
the same nature in white folks" (3). Grandmother Morton boasts about
the homesteading years: "We worked. A country doesn't make itself.
When the sun was up we were up, and when the sun went down we
didn't" (8–9). She goes on to say that men may run the town in the
1870s, but that *she* was one of the founders of the town and she intends to
get credit for it: "This town began to grow the day I got here, " she says.

Fig. 9 JOHN WEAVER, *Madonna of the Wheat*, located at Edmonton City Hall.
Courtesy of Alberta Photograph Library.

Smith is incredulous: "You—you began it?" "My husband and I began
it—and our baby Silas," Grandmother replies complacently (4).

In this one short scene Glaspell discredits the traditional images of
women pioneers as reluctant emigrants terrified of Indians and devastated by the loneliness of an isolated homestead. Instead, Grandmother
Morton shows that some women worked as equals with men in the
difficult years of establishing farms and, indeed, even shared responsibilities in building new prairie towns. As we examine the structures of
signification in prairie women's fiction—the journey, the work, the
ordeals with nature and isolation, the satisfactions of watching farms and
community grow—we learn that Grandmother Morton's experiences are

not one of a kind. She is an archetypal Frontier Hero in fiction as well as in fact.[5]

Twenty-one women writers (fourteen American and six Canadian) describe the experiences of first wave women throughout the American and Canadian prairies. Although the agricultural frontiers of Texas, Oklahoma, and the Dakotas were settled in the latter part of the nineteenth century, as were the Canadian prairies, works set in these areas have been included as first wave fiction; pioneer conditions were alleviated only slightly by transportation and communication networks.

To discuss the *waves* of settlement on the prairie is appropriate, one critic observes, because the settlers (like the travelers, fur traders, and explorers before them) described the landscape according to familiar images associated with the sea (O'Connor 161). In the United States, the first wave was dominated by settlers from the states bordering the grasslands, from the East, and from the British Isles. Illinois, Iowa, southern Wisconsin, southeastern Minnesota, and the far eastern portions of Kansas and Nebraska were widely settled by the 1860s, although the true prairies were the last lands to be acquired. As noted in chapter two, immigrants bought up wooded areas and settled along water routes before moving onto the prairies. Some families were still homesteading in the early part of the twentieth century, as a 1915 photograph of the Lyons family reminds us (see fig. 10). Fiction by Catherwood, Aldrich, Wilson, Donovan, and Heacock describe this era, but only Catherwood grew up during the period she describes.

The Dakota boom years between 1868 and 1878 are described by Gates, Lane, Wilder, and Breneman/Thurston. In *The Edge of Time* Erdman describes an early farm venture on the scarcely populated prairies of northeastern Texas; a farm family settling in Oklahoma after the land rush is described by Aydelotte in *Trumpets Calling*. In this group only Wilder drew on personal experiences.[6]

---

5. In a critical biography of Susan Glaspell, Arthur E. Waterman summarizes Glaspell's private vision in such a way as to emphasize the archetypal midwestern qualities of a Grandmother Morton. "At first glance," Waterman says, "we feel [Glaspell's] heroines are out of touch: they appear to be eccentrics who don't belong to the world they live in. But we sense their isolation because they are old-fashioned pioneers living in a time when the independence, stubbornness and discipline associated with pioneering are out of date. They seek what the new urban Midwest has lost: individualism, integrity, a love of nature, and a faith in man. In recovering these ideals for themselves, the heroines lead the community back to the forgotten vision" (118).

6. William T. Anderson discusses Wilder's commitment to accuracy in "The Literary Apprenticeship of Laura Ingalls Wilder." Her daughter, Rose Wilder Lane, in defending a "discrepancy in dates" in *Little House on the Prairie* says, "A fiction writer myself, I agree that my mother could

Fig. 10   *The Lyon Family in Nebraska, 1915.* Courtesy of Mrs. Minnie Avery.

While most American works focus on the period from 1850–80, Canadian works represent several different phases of settlement over a hundred-year period. Knox's *Red River Shadows* centers on the Red River settlement of the early 1800s and Rolyat's *Lily of Fort Garry* depicts the same settlement a few decades later, when frontier conditions still per-

have added to artistic effects by altering facts, but she did not write fiction. She did not want to" (Anderson 288). Although Catherwood and Wilder are the only two writers referred to in this chapter to describe scenes and situations as they might have observed them, numerous others have been intimately knowledgeable about the people and places described in their works. Aldrich grew up hearing family stories about homesteading in Iowa—her mother had driven "one of the teams all the way out from Illinois" ("The Story behind *A Lantern in Her Hand*" 239); Donovan, according to Suzanne L. Bunkers, "modeled the central chracters in *Black Soil*, Nell and Tim Connor, on her parents . . . [who] came to Iowa from the East by wagon and ox team" (4). Heacock and Sapergia also drew on family history; Erdman and Aydelotte thoroughly researched the frontier history of the places they wrote about. Lane, of course, grew up in DeSmet, South Dakota, and, after publishing her two prairie novels, urged her mother to write autobiographical stories for children.

sisted. The major settlements of the grasslands in the prairie provinces began in 1880, and by 1914 all the good land was gone.[7] Hayes, McClung, and Parsons, immigrants during this time, describe the early settlements. Hayes and McClung came from Ontario in the 1880s; Parsons came from Iowa.

Many of the first wave works include minor characters who have emigrated from both western and eastern Europe, thus demonstrating the overlapping waves of immigration. Non-Protestant, non-English-speaking settlers arrived during the first phase of settlement. Works by Aldrich (*Spring Came on Forever*) and Ostenso (*O River, Remember!*) could be included in first wave fiction, but because the structures of signification emerging from these stories are different in some ways from those of English-speaking immigrants, they have been included with second wave works in chapter five.

The major female characters in first wave works have certain common characteristics. Some of the women had no role in the decision to emigrate to the prairie; they represent what the historian Glenda Riley has called "an appendage of the male migrant" (*Frontierswomen* 5).[8] However, several women appear to have shared in making the decision, although some were more enthusiastic than others. Many were brides, young women in love with adventurous males; they shared the men's optimism about life in the new territories. Several female characters emphatically contradict the popular myth that women were reluctant emigrants. In Eleanor Gates's *Plow-Woman*, Dallas Lancaster has had a great deal of responsibility thrust upon her, first by her mother's death and then by the subsequent care of a younger sister. When her father is injured and unable to continue work for the railroad, Dallas encourages emigration to the farmlands of the Dakotas. Two other women propose to men they know are emigrating West—one because she has loved the man since childhood (Bethany in Erdman's *Edge of Time*) and the other because she is tired of seven years of seclusion in her Pittsburgh bedroom after having been jilted (Castle in Heacock's *Crinoline to Calico*). An exceptional example of a woman emigrant is found in Margaret Lynn's *Free Soil.* In this novel, Ellen Truman is described as a Lady Galahad with

---

7. See Roy's essay "Mon héritage Manitoba." Roy relived the frontier era of the late 1800s through the tales of her grandmother and mother who came from Quebec. She recorded versions of their experiences in *The Road Past Altamont.*

8. For further discussion of the reluctant frontierswoman, see Riley, *Frontierswomen* 177 and Faragher 167, 171.

a clear vision of her mission into the wilderness. When her husband warns her about the chances she's taking by going with him to Kansas, she says: "It's the chance I want. . . . Just think that it might be my duty as well as yours. You are not the only abolitionist in this pair" (9). During the last part of the boat trip to Kansas City, another woman asks Ellen if she is "goin' out on the perraira." Ellen replies that she is indeed going to the prairies; in fact, she feels as though she is "on a cloud" or "moving into the sunset"—this venture is "something of that golden kind" (24). A male passenger questions the wisdom of joining her husband in Kansas. He says that the political issues related to whether Kansas will be a free or slave state will inevitably lead to violence. He tells her there are not many women or children on the prairie. Ellen firmly replies that if Kansas is "to grow into a country . . . there will have to be women and children" (25). Later in the story Phoebe, a young friend from New England, joins Ellen. She shares Ellen's conviction that men alone cannot settle the country nor the political issue of slavery. At one point Phoebe stands aside, observing Ellen: "Ellen . . . seemed to her to have the greatest chance that could ever come to womankind" (65). When given the opportunity, Phoebe, too, chooses to stay in Kansas and fight for abolition.

Women's letters, diaries, and reminiscences remind us that many women did not want to emigrate. Novels by prairie women writers help us to empathize with these women. The discussion that takes place between Ma and Pa Wilder is representative:

> One day in the very last of the winter Pa said to Ma, "Seeing you don't object, I've decided to go see the West. I've had an offer for this place and we can sell it now for as much as we're ever likely to get, enough to give us a start in a new country."
>
> "Oh, Charles, must we go now?" Ma said. The weather was so cold and the snug house was so comfortable.
>
> "If we are going this year, we must go now," said Pa. "We can't get across the Mississippi after the ice breaks."
>
> So Pa sold the little house. [*Little House* 2–3]

A Canadian equivalent to Ma Wilder is found in Gabrielle Roy's semiautobiographical story, "My Almighty Grandmother." The little girl Christine listens to her grandmother's complaint:

> "I have twice built a home," she told me, "having followed your trotting horse of a grandfather from one part of this vast country to another. I began all over here in Manitoba what I'd already made back in Quebec, made once for all, I thought—a home. . . .

"Your grandfather Elisée . . . such a trick to play on me, the gay
adventurer . . . to [die first], without waiting for me, leaving me all alone on
this western prairie, in exile."
"Manitoba isn't exile," I said. "It's home."
"All the rest of you too," she went on. "You'll be just like the others.
You're all like him—independent, selfish, travelers every one of you. You all
have to be off somewhere." [*Road* 15–16]

In another story, Christine's mother comments on the grandmother's
isolation: "I was thinking how lonely she must have been among us, her
husband and her children, who were all, you might say, of a different
breed" (*Road* 128). The French-Canadian grandmother, like Ma Wilder,
was never able to share her husband's and children's enthusiasm for
traveling and pioneering.

Although there has been a large quantity of information about the
journey by river, by canal, by lake, and on the overland trail,[9] most
women writers have not been imaginatively inspried by this aspect of
pioneer experience. Most writers emphasize the last lap of the journey—
the first sight of the prairie or the last few miles across the prairie to the
homestead site. Therefore no prototypical journey emerges from the
fiction. Certainly the journeys overland were under the direction of men;
in two novels that discuss the journey in great detail—Laut's *Lords of the
North* and Knox's *Red River Shadows*—the main characters are men.

Fortunately one writer shows what the trip might have been like.
When Mary Hartwell Catherwood published *Old Caravan Days* (1880)
for children, the publishers' advertisement proclaimed that it was "a
veritable record that reads like a romance, of the Westward journeyings
of a merry household in a 'mover's wagon'" (2). Grandma Padgett had
been born in Virginia, had emigrated to Ohio when it was still "un-
broken wilderness" and, at the opening of the story—1857—is emigrating once again, this time to Illinois. She has loaded her belongings into a
covered wagon which is driven by Zene, her hired man; Grandma drives
the carriage (see fig. 11). She is accompanied by two children, her
grandson Robert Day—nicknamed Bobaday by his fellow traveler, Aunt
Corinne, who is two years younger than her nephew. The dogs, Boswell
and Johnson, trot along beside them.

On the morning of their departure, a neighbor predicts that
Grandma Padgett will be back soon: "'The Wild Western prairie country

9. The journey is analyzed in Jeffrey 38–50 and even more thoroughly in Faragher's
Women and Men on the Overland Trail, which is based on 169 trail diaries.

"HASN'T THE CREEK ANY BOTTOM?" CRIED GRANDMA PADGETT.

Fig. 11   Illustration from Mary Hartwell Catherwood's *Old Caravan Days*, 1884.

won't suit you at all,'" he says. Grandma admits that she would prefer to
stay in Ohio, but her son Tip, she says, "'can do very little here, and he
can do well out there'" (12).

The trip from Reynoldsburg, Ohio, to the Illinois state line takes
about three weeks. At one point they stop with a group of twenty or
thirty families who are traveling to California.[10] When Grandma says
she's too old to go that far, they boast that they have "a granny over
ninety" with them (122). One of the women tells Grandma that "they
were going to California because her husband had the mining fever. He
had wanted to go years before, but she had held out against it until she
saw he would do no good unless he went. So they sold their land, and
started out with a colony of neighbors" (127).

10. Although the image of the lone covered wagon persists, many families traveled in groups,
as Faragher's study demonstrates (25–34).

When they go through prairie country, the narrator defends the landscape: "Whoever calls it monotonous has never watched its varying complexions" (200). The small towns, however, are pretty much all the same. They "did not differ greatly from the Ohio villages located on the Turnpike: There was always the church with a bonny little belfry, and the schoolhouse more or less mutilated as to its weather boarding. The 'pike was the public street, and such houses as sat at right angles to it, looked lonesome, and the dirt roads weedy or dusty" (204). When they pass through Indianapolis, which is still a small city, Bobaday feels "exalted" by the sight (261). Catherwood certainly uses Bobaday to express her own remembered feelings about those sights.

> She had grown to girlhood there [in Ohio] with the steady stream of Westward migration flowing past her door. Her family had joined the moving column when she was nine or ten, just old enough for her to feel the full tide of hope which enthusiastic young parents had seen in an undeveloped neighborhood on the Illinois prairies. The migration and the feelings attending it probably colored the rest of her life, for even in the severest of adversities—and she suffered from many—Mrs. Catherwood never lost the peculiar optimism of outlook which the West still symbolized in American thought during her formative years. [Price, "Critical Biography" 13]

Old Caravan Days is a charming story that takes on significance when we learn that Catherwood is describing a journey similar to the one she took in 1857. Her father, a doctor, felt that he (like Tip in the story), could "do well out there." Within two years, however, both of Catherwood's parents died and Catherwood made the trip back to Hebron, Ohio, probably in 1858.[11]

Only Margaret Wilson discusses the impact of the ocean voyage on a woman. In *The Able McLaughlins*, Jeannie McNair loses three children when a smallpox epidemic breaks out on the ship. Jeannie never forgets the image of the bodies being buried at sea or the sharks following the

---

11. Robert Price discusses the circumstances associated with Catherwood's journey to Illinois in "A Critical Biography" (31–34). Price notes that Catherwood grew up with "the Old National" passing her doorstep, so to speak: it was "the major route to the whole American West, and in the minds of a main portion of the general populace in that decade [the 1840s] the road to the American future. Its west-moving line of migration, that marked many of the days when Mary Hartwell was growing into awareness of her world as the oldest child in the home of a young country doctor in Luray, must have seemed the biggest and most vital thing in life. Not only was she to grow into early girlhood with this road a normal part of the daily nature of things, but afterward she was to make the most momentous trip of her life as part of its Westerly current" (18–19).

ship, waiting for their prey. She never recovers her former energy or
enthusiasm; she never shares the optimistic vision of her traveling companions of a good life in America (26–27).

None of the writers chose to "re-vision" the long, boring hours,
the discomforts, indeed, the agonies, of the sea journey. North's *Morning
in the Land* opens with the arrival of a family in Milwaukee. Mrs. Moore
in Rolyat's *Lily of Fort Garry* may talk about hard times and famine in
Ireland, but not about the sea voyage. The author of *The Curlew Cried*
ignores Victoria Sewall's voyage from Liverpool to Winnipeg and begins
the story with the last jouncing miles that the newlyweds take across the
prairie, south of Regina, Saskatchewan, to the new homestead (Parsons
10–18).

In a fictionalized account of her grandmother's trip from Pennsylvania to Iowa, *Crinoline to Calico,* Nan Heacock describes the journey of
Castle Gayle. Castle tries to picture her future home and community,
hoping they are better than the settlements they see on the way. "Surely," she thinks, "where they were going there would be respectable
people . . . not just riffraff" (14). When they near their homestead site,
she asks her husband where the town is. She's horrified when he tells her
there are no towns, only small settlements. She says: " 'Well, we can't
live right out in the middle of this . . . wilderness!' " Her husband replies
with an irritated " 'Why not?' " and reminds her that if she wanted to live
where there were people, she shouldn't have proposed to him and asked
him to bring her to Iowa (ellipsis in original; 4).

Castle represents the dreamer, the kind of person who has refused
to pay attention to what people have said about living conditions in
newly settled portions of the prairie. A woman in North's *Morning in the
Land* represents the other extreme. The Wentworths pause in Milwaukee
before buying land. When Ann Wentworth realizes her husband is too
proud to ask for information about places to settle, she goes to the nearest
trading post once a week to get supplies and to eavesdrop. She justifies
her actions this way: "Well, he was stubborn, was Tommy. He would
have nothing to do with the foreigners, and to him every man was a
foreigner who was not English and a Wesleyan Methodist. Ann knew it
would be no use to argue, so she set herself the task of finding out
everything she could about the western settlement from the conversation
of others" (22). By the time they decide on a location in the Rock River
Valley, she knows better than her husband what to expect. She is still
taken by surprise: "This was the Paradise for which they had set forth,

about which they had heard so much in Derbyshire. The rich Wisconsin prairie, land of flowers. Who would believe such a place existed beyond all those miles of swamp and forest?" (47).[12] In *Black Soil* a German immigrant woman makes the decisions. When they reach the north-western Iowa prairie, Mr. Schwartz suggest a site. His wife, Katto, responds with a firm no, and points to a rise in the land: "My house shall be there," she announces (Donovan 30–31).

Laura Ingalls Wilder's description of the journey probably represents a typical situation: Charles and Caroline Ingalls, emigrants from the Wisconsin "border" had grown up in comparatively new agricultural settlements. The Ingalls females might have been astonished by the flatness of the prairie land, but not by the sparsity of the population and potential difficulties with Indians. Thus the first fifty pages of *Little House on the Prairie*, based on Wilder's own experiences as a girl in Kansas, establish a journey motif upon which future writers within the tradition of prairie fiction can perform variations.

Once the journey is completed and the homestead site selected, the first home absorbs a good share of the attention of the woman settler. Frequently the shanty, cabin, dugout or soddie is cruder than anticipated, but the women "make do," optimistically planning ahead to the time when a frame house will be built with such conveniences as a wooden floor, a cooking shed, a pantry, a kitchen pump, and even such luxuries as a sitting room and a separate bedroom for the children. In Wilder's story about Plum Creek, the cow climbs up on the dugout, but Caroline Ingalls copes with the problem: she admits it "had given her a turn to see it [the cow's leg] coming down through the ceiling," but, she adds, "there's no great damage done" (*Plum Creek* 50).

The house frequently serves as a symbol for the relationship of a wife and husband. If there are problems in the relationship, these problems enter into decisions regarding the house. In some instances the husband purchases more land while the house remains primitive, thus ignoring the wife's needs and even adding to her burdens. In Margaret Wilson's *Able McLaughlins*, McNair brings a second wife back from Scotland after the death of the first. The bride, Barbara, is subjected to prolonged introductions to her new family. When finally left alone with her husband, she tells him that she is not pleased with her new home:

"Ye never telt me you lived in a sty!"

---

12. North is describing a section between Madison and Milwaukee in the 1840s.

"Huts, woman! 'Tis no sty!"

"And I thinking you like a laird, with so many fine acres!"

"It's a new country!"

"It's an old sty!" Had she not from the train seen many a snug place among comforting hills, livable little places! But that had been, to be sure, far from this, in the east. The further west they came, the more they traveled into desolation. Lonely enough places she had seen, but none so uncompromising as this sty. [99–100]

Many prairie women—the real ones and the fictional ones—would have accommodated themselves to a bad situation, thinking there really were no other options but to "make do." Using Barbara McNair as a model, Wilson argues that not all women tolerated their husbands' indifference and stinginess. Barbara McNair, as her son-in-law observes with a hint of admiration, "refused to adjust herself to the new country. She just sat tight, and let the great significant country adjust itself to her as best it might" (147). Barbara begins a low-keyed but persistent campaign for a new house. McNair refuses to "adjust." One day he discovers that she has not only learned to harness the team but has packed and driven the team to town, where she intends to take a train. Fearing the ridicule of his neighbors, he goes after her:

He found her the next afternoon, in the hall of one of those long, shanty-hotels which comprised the town. . . . They faced each other in her room, he, tall, gaunt, black-eyed, ragged, she small, dainty, red-haired, bedecked. Her placidness, as usual, disarmed him. He began:

"You can't go back to Scotland! Are you daft?"

"I canna' live in a sty."

They were off, then. He urged decency, morality, economy, honesty, pride, race, the waning reputation of Glasgow. After each argument she simply said, like one born foolish;

"I canna' live in a sty." (155)

Barbara wins, and places her order: "three good big rooms downstairs, and two upstairs, a wee porch, all painted white, except the green shutters with closets and windows . . . and besides a wee white house for the fowls" (156).

Bethany Cameron, the traditional bride portrayed in Erdman's *Edge of Time*, is also stunned at the first sight of the dugout her husband has built: " 'It's like a cellar,' Bethany thought, 'Or maybe like a cave.' " However, when she realizes her husband is waiting for her response she replies, simply, "It looks fine" (56, 58). In this novel the couple is working toward a goal that the wife has fully accepted; thus she adjusts to the primitive conditions.

Although Barbara McNair and Bethany Cameron represent different responses to the new home and different relationships with their husbands, their values are the same: they plant flowers in a symbolic effort to make the new place a home. Bethany's father, the morning of her departure from Missouri, dug up a rosebush for Bethany to transplant in Texas. Barbara McNair, having acquired a suitable house, returns to town to arrange for the final stage of settlement, a flower garden. She walks down a muddy lane, pushes open a gate, and approaches a large woman bending over a washtub:

> "I have come to see your flowers!"
> The woman wiped her well-soaked hands on a limp apron, and replied in perfect Pennsylvania Dutch:
> "I don't understand you." But she smiled a smile of extraordinary width.
> They faced each other, Scotland and Germany, curiously for one moment. Then Barbara pointed dramatically at the pansies. There was that look on her face that was understood by frontierswomen of many tongues. The German began babbling sympathetically about her display, pointing out one beauty after another, breaking off little sprays to hold near her visitor's longing nose. [Wilson 160]

In both *The Able McLaughlins* and *The Edge of Time*, the women recreate—to some extent—through the flowers the civilized environment they left behind. At the same time, they make a commitment to staying. Like Marta, the Ukrainian woman in Roy's "Garden in the Wind," they make the landscape their own.

Women's work is the most thoroughly described and analyzed aspect of pioneer prairie women's experiences. The first wave women, as described by women writers, are a remarkably traditional lot. Among the main characters, most women work within the nineteenth-century norms for female behavior; only a few deviate from the division of labor which distinguished between inside work and appropriate outside work for women within a sphere that was carefully separated from the male's. Yet even the traditional women's roles are more complex than a statue or painting of the Prairie Angel with her bag and book suggests. Nicholas Karolides emphasizes this point in his chapter on pioneer women in *The Pioneer in the American Novel, 1900–1950*, pointing out that the "heroine is a worker. And she does not engage merely in semi-laboring tasks that meet a minimal requirement of usefulness. She is a housewife, child-rearer, doctor, nurse, weaver, seamstress, butcher, food preserver." He goes on to note that Bess Streeter Aldrich belittles, in her novels, the female character who stoops to working in the fields. But Aldrich's characters, Karolides insists, are exceptions: "The heroine who assists her husband in the fields as well as managing the household work is more common in the literature, and this routine is common to the non-heroine woman as well" (91).[13]

In one of the earliest prairie stories, a frontier couple turn their home into an inn. In "The Apples on the Crane (At the Red Pump Tavern)" (Catherwood, 1886) the boy narrator explains that his father hadn't intended "to set up a stand for travellers, but so many came by and it was on the country road, and the mail hack always stopped with us; so, finally, he took money for it just to keep from being eat up" (13). This means that his mother had to cook and look after an enormous pantry of "hams and flour and kegs of corned beef and molasses and sugar and dried fruit. . . . The preserves and honey and cider and apple-barrels were there, too" (Catherwood 14). Fortunately a girl named Ellen helps— she's "our girl that we took to raise," the boy adds; "mother put dependence on her" (15).

In *Free Land*, Rose Wilder Lane describes a prairie woman who rebels against the perimeters of a role set by her husband and society. Mary grew up in new territory in Minnesota; with her marriage to David she left the comfortable home that her parents had established and moved to the Dakota Territory. During the first couple of years she becomes depressed because David's work is demanding and meaningful, and her work is so slight by comparison—there is no garden to plant and weed, no attic or parlor or cellar to clean, no chickens to tend or butter to churn and sell (87). When David has an unexpected opportunity to sell a field of turnips, Mary insists on helping: "They worked with bare hands because bare hands are quicker and the sap of the turnip tops would soon soak mittens. The strong-smelling sap corroded their hands. In the cold, the shriveled flesh cracked, and one day when he emptied a full basket David noticed smears of blood on the turnips. Mary's hands were bleeding" (226). David tells her to quit work and take care of her hands. When she refuses he becomes adamant. Finally she shouts at him: " 'I've got a right to be some use!' " (227). He relents. They take beeswax from Mary's sewing basket, melt it, and fill the cracks in their hands. They harvest the turnips, together.

13. Of the works Karolides draws on for his descriptions of women's role, eighteen are by men and only five are by women.

Curiously, Lane creates a male character who wants his wife to perform traditional, socially acceptable roles—to be the Prairie Angel. Yet he is attracted to a young neighbor girl, Nettie, who represents the Frontier Hero. Nettie is the daughter of a man who has moved from Illinois to Kansas and then to the Dakotas. David first sees Nettie on his trip to Yankton, before his marriage, when he takes out a claim: "A girl had come out of the slough grass. She was perhaps sixteen years old, and carried a rifle. Her hair, redder than a buckeye, hung in braids beside her cheeks, like an Indian woman's hair, and her thin face was as brown as an Indian's. Her eyes were bright blue" (23). When David asks her about the Indian country her family had tried to settle in Iowa, Nettie says it was "beautiful and rich and wild"; they could hunt and fish. They built a log house and a barn there and broke sod. She loves the prairie frontier—whether it is Iowa or the Dakotas.

When David returns with his new bride, Mary, he is severely frostbitten during a blizzard. He is nursed by Mary and Nettie. At this time David ponders the responses of women to hardship and comes up with two types of reactions among women. Nettie's mother and Mary are the type who would "slap at trouble," talk about it, and eventually conclude that "what can't be cured must be endured." Nettie, from David's perspective, represents another, more heroic, type: "This girl," David thinks, "would say nothing; endurance was in the marrow of her bones" (68). Obviously he admires the stoicism usually attributed to male heroes. Nettie nurses the sick; she also swings a scythe and fills in for her father behind the plow. Then when there's finally enough money for shoes, she goes to school; eventually, she becomes certified for teaching so that she can bring fifteen dollars a month home to her parents. She's the woman with the gun, the bag, *and* the book. She's perhaps by necessity a minor figure in the story; as a primary character she would be too heroic to be credible.

A similar pairing of types—the Prairie Angel and the Frontier Hero—appears in Loula Grace Erdman's *Edge of Time.* Bethany Cameron is a young bride from a middle-class Missouri family. She has married the first man to take a sod plow into the Texas Panhandle and to fence off his land with the new barbed wire. In fact, her husband was what the cattlemen disdainfully called a "nester"—a farmer trying to grow crops in ranch country. Bethany, a loyal and hardworking wife, adjusts admirably to primitive conditions and isolation. It is her neighbor

Lizzie Dillon, however, "a tall woman in a soiled mother hubbard," who represents what Erdman calls the "true" pioneer type:

> There was no age about her; she was like the hills in her look of strength and endurance. Her face was the sort that was meant to be forever framed by the bow of a covered wagon; her body was one that carried children easily and bore them, if not without pain, at least without great fuss. Birth and death— and what was most mysterious of all, life itself—gave her no great concern. She took everything as it came, bearing within herself an animal's power of self-healing. She was the true pioneer type—the one who is destined never to eat the fruits of the vineyards she has planted. [92]

Erdman nevertheless undercuts this image when she describes Lizzie's submission to her husband's and children's insistent demands to move on to new country in New Mexico: "And she had given up to them. Other stronger (or maybe weaker) women would plant a vine and refuse to leave it. Because of them, the men would stay, too. But not Lizzie Dillon. She would go on with Tobe Dillon, her very endurance a kind of weakness, a submission. She would endure all the hardships of a new country save the hardest one of all—staying there. Never the vine for her, or the hearth-stone" (168–69). Thus Lizzie Dillon represents some ambivalence and uncertainty about this version of the female Frontier Hero. Is she weaker, or stronger, than the women who "stick it out"? Is it easier to go on and try to make a success of things further on than to stay and survive the first difficult years?

When depicting women's work roles on the frontier, prairie liter-ature offers one recurring refrain: when a certain job needs to be done, whether it is considered women's work or men's work, the woman will do it. In *Black Soil* Nell Connor, a New England doctor's daughter educated at one of the first schools for young women, does the outside work after immigrating to the Iowa prairie: "They had had a good crop and a fine garden. She had helped with both. She had taken a man's place in haying and shocking. Work to her had become negligible—what was heavy work if obstacles were on hand to be overcome?" (Donovan 52). One day when Nell pays a visit to the Steindler's farm, the section adjoining the Connor's land, she finds two girls herding the cattle, another snaring gophers, and the two oldest in the fields helping their father break the sod:

> She heard the wrenching of stubborn roots of grass like ligaments tearing a human body, followed by smoother passages where the girls' share cut into

the soil with a murmur like that of gurgling blood. The full skirts and long-curtained bonnets of the girls blew in the spring breeze; their shoulders and arms curved, contorted and grew rigid as they clung each to a plow handle. . . .

Nearer the house, Nell encountered another daughter who was also assisting with the breaking. She walked beside a yoke of oxen, directing them with a goad while a young hired man held the plow handles. [35–36]

Nell moves beyond the field to the house, where she and Mrs. Steindler talk about the girls' work. Mrs. Steindler hopes the girls will get married. "My gels," she says, "they got it so hard here. That is why I want they should marry quick" (37).

In another story, Caroline Ingalls frowns when Laura suggests helping Pa with the haying. "'Why, I guess you can,' Ma said doubtfully. She did not like to see women working in the fields. Only foreigners did that. Ma and her girls were Americans, above doing men's work. But Laura's helping with the hay would solve the problem" (*The Long Winter* 4). The best-known example of a woman plowing is, undoubtedly, Cather's Ántonia. Jim is indignant when he hears that "Ambrosch hired his sister [Ántonia] out like a man, and she went from farm to farm, binding sheaves or working with the threshers" (*My Ántonia* 147).

One other example of a first wave woman as Prairie Angel deserves note because she might be a precursor to a realistic revisioning of prairie women by contemporary writers: Nan Heacock provides a dramatically different version of the Prairie Angel. To others in the novel, Castle is the Prairie Angel who shares recipes and quilt patterns, who delivers babies according to the instructions her husband reads from the medical encyclopedia—Castle had never learned how to read. However, Heacock's delineation of Castle reveals a proud, stubborn, self-centered, prejudiced, and occasionally cruel and devious woman. While creating a character whom readers gradually respect for her dogged perseverance and dignity, Heacock at the same time challenges those versions of prairie women which are idealized or sentimentalized.

Although some men took responsibility for teaching their children "the basics," the task was frequently shared by both parents or assumed by the woman during the first period of settlement when the population was too small to support a school. Teaching certainly represents another kind of work for prairie women. In *Women Teachers on the Frontier*, Polly Kaufman points out that many women became teachers to avoid being dependent on relatives when their parents or husbands died (14).

Catherwood's perception of a frontier community in "The Career of a Prairie Farmer" includes a protrait of a young woman from Indiana who had come to Illinois to teach. Her father had died, leaving her mother to support several children. "I have to teach," she tells the farmer's sister. She needs to be self-supporting because the man she had expected to marry, she discovered, already had a wife in another town (710–11).

Ostenso's O River, Remember! provides one of the fullest descriptions of a prairie schoolteacher. Kate Shaleen takes a position in a Red River community in northern Minnesota; she was "untrained and fortuitously hired, but resolved to implant within the hearts and minds of her young charges an idea of beauty, of gentleness and courage and a right way of living" (174–75). Her first job does not last very long because a blizzard leaves her stranded in the schoolhouse with her students, and the parents decide a man could handle such situations more competently. Kate Shaleen moves to another school where, throughout a long career, she influences many students. A less glowing account of a teacher is reported in A Circle of Trees. The children behave well when a school board member visits; they have discovered they will be rewarded with a long recess and a new song: "It was as though they [the children] shared a conspiracy, that lessons were not really to be taken seriously." Miss Morris was "gay, vivacious, pretty," but a poor disciplinarian who spoke only English and lost patience quickly with her students who knew little English (Faralla 136).

Several girls who grow up on the prairie during the first generation of homesteading teach school not so much as a mission or a profession, but to make money to help their families or to establish their own independence. Both Black Soil and Little Town on the Prairie describe young women going through the examination process to become teachers. In Red River Shadows the priest urges Hélène, an unhappy young wife, to become useful by teaching in his school. In Country People, the daughter of a German immigrant couple teaches school, but this responsibility is temporary. When one of the young farmers is looking for a wife, her competence as a teacher is irrelevant: "He liked her. He wondered if she was pretty strong. She seemed to be able to get through with a lot of work. . . . She taught country school in the Benning Township schoolhouse, but she knew how to wait on threshers" (Suckow 36). In Crinoline to Calico, a widow is asked to teach school when there is a scarcity of teachers in the area. The narrator notes that her grammar was "faulty," but children learned because of their teacher's curiosity" (Heacock 188).

Many of the prairie writers had themselves been schoolteachers, but Mary Hartwell Catherwood undoubtedly had the most dramatic history as a teacher: at the age of thirteen she passed her teaching examination, but because she was so young she waited a year before taking a position.[14]

The first wave women discussed thus far represent women in situations where men ultimately determined the success or failure of the homestead. Three additional works point out that women, in some instances, determined whether or not the homesteading venture would succeed: Jane Rolyat's *Lily of Fort Garry*, Dora Aydelotte's *Trumpets Calling*, and Josephine Donovan's *Black Soil* describe women's work roles when men are absent.

The Lily of Fort Garry is notable for its portrayal of women's roles and work during the early 1860s in southern Manitoba. Margaret, the "lily," is trained to be a lady. The mother, on the other hand, is described as "a woman with a body like iron, preferring work in the open to work in the house, up by sunrising, building fires in the great clay oven outside, milking, planting, weeding; roughening, deforming her hands, chafing her skin, torturing her clothes" (36). Perhaps Elizabeth Moore does prefer outside work; yet she has very little choice in some matters because her husband is away months at a time on hunting expeditions or searching in the wilderness for his lost brother. Until the oldest son takes over responsibility for the farm, Elizabeth must make the decisions so that there is money for her daughter's schooling and land for her sons to farm. A similar situation is described in Aydelotte's *Trumpets Calling*. When Martha Prawl realizes her husband will never take responsibility for the farm, she urges him to get a job in town. She tells her husband that she and their sons can manage the farm (95).

Nell Connor, the main character in *Black Soil*, has already been described working with her husband, Tim, but more and more of the responsibility for the farm falls to her as Tim becomes involved in community affairs. He organizes the Mill Creek township, peddles cutlery, secures signatures for the Central Railway, campaigns for political candidates, and conducts the affairs of the school board. Nell raises the children, runs the farm, rides horseback at midnight to nurse neighbors, and teaches English to the immigrant woman on the adjoining farm.

The women in these novels, though the mainstays of their fami-

14. The most fully developed portrait of an early twentieth-century prairie schoolteacher is Gabrielle Roy's *Children of My Heart*, which undoubtedly records impressions and observations from her teaching experience in southern Manitoba.

lies, have at least some help from men. Eleanor Gates, in *The Plow-Woman*, explores the situation of a woman who is even more independent. This young woman, Dallas Lancaster, is the "Madonna of the Wheat," the sod-breaker, the planter, and the harvester. Her father, crippled from a railroad accident, can help only in limited ways; in addition, he is hot-headed in his decisions and unreliable in his actions. True, a concerned and much-interested townsman keeps a protective eye on Dallas as she works to establish the homestead, as does Squaw Charley, an Indian who has become good friends with her. Dallas's father objects to her position of authority: "It was all very well for her to do the outside duties as if she were a man; that did not privilege her to ride roughshod over his opinions, or to rule affairs in general with a heavy hand" (88). Gates resolves the conflict with the father's death during a blizzard.

Dallas is content with her choice of roles, although she occasionally wonders what fashions women wear in Bismarck and what it would be like to be a lady at the fort. But when her lover expresses a desire to make life easier for her by hiring outside help for the plowing, planting, and cutting, she laughs: "Outside work is fine. . . . Better than cooking over a hot stove or breaking your back over a tub. Men have the best half of things—the air and the sky and the horses. I don't complain. I like my work. Let it make me like a man" (300). It is the captain of the fort who voices, perhaps, Gates's attitude about women like Dallas: "And let me say that I heartily commend them. They are made of the stuff of our forefathers, who pushed their way into the wilderness. Their spirit is the spirit of the frontier" (256).

Whether Prairie Angle or Frontier Hero, the ordeals are the same. Droughts test the settlers' determination and provide situations for comparing those who stay with those who get discouraged and leave. Rains, floods, and high winds strike unexpectedly; hail and tornadoes wipe out the crops on one farm while an adjoining farm remains unscathed. Blizzards severely threaten individual life; they are typical and anticipated. Nevertheless, they bring suffering in fiction as in real life. A tombstone from a pioneer cemetery in Saskatoon reads: "Erected in Memory of / My brother / Edward William / Meeres / Who lost his life on the Prairie / during a blizzard on / Jan. 14, 1888 / Aged 27 years / Not forgotten."

Droughts and grasshoppers, though typical of the prairie region, are not as inevitable as winter blizzards and, when they do occur, they wipe out an entire year's work. The settlers have greater difficulty adjusting to these losses and react variously with rage, depression, or submission to the ways of God. In "The Wind Our Enemy," the Canadian poet Anne Marriott describes the effects of several years' drought on the land and on the people. In part III of the poem she places side by side the promise of an abundant wheat crop and the reality of the drought:

> A man's heart could love his land,
> Smoothly self-yielding,
> Its broad spread promising all his granaries might hold.
> A woman's eyes could kiss the soil
> From her kitchen window,
> Turning its black depths to unchipped cups—a silk crepe dress—
> (Two ninety-eight, Sale Catalogue)
> Pray sun's touch be gentleness,
> Not a hot hand scorching flesh it would caress.
> But sky like a new tin pan
> Hot from the oven
> Seemed soldered to the earth by horizons of glare.[15]

These ordeals are faced by both men and women. Some abandon their dreams and their homesteads, but—in women's prairie fiction— these are always the minor characters. Moreover, some women have the ability to keep the catastrophes and the blessings in proper perspective. The contemporary poet Martha Mihalyi, after reading women's descriptions of the locust invasions, put herself in the place of a nineteenth-century woman:

> The Locusts Return
>
> blotting the sun and in darkness
> we set fire everyone at the same
> time sets fire to the prairie,
> our faces flickering at the edge
> of the blaze, smoke rising
> further than god.
>
> we do not speak of crops
> burned, crops burning.
> at night we pray: there are

---

15. In Angus, *The Prairie Experience*, 9. The editor, Terry Angus, observes that Marriott "has encompassed within a poet's lines the frustration and heartbreak experienced by men and women battered by the searing winds of the dust-bowl years when the lamp at noon was the symbol of a wind-and-drought-tormented wasteland." He goes on to point out that the dust-bowl years in Saskatchewan marked its inhabitants in a way others of the prairies were not marked (4–5).

the children there are still
the children who must live
to leave our arms.

we will tuck them into
sleeping, we will make
for them a blanket of stars
as the earth wheels
slowly beneath us

as the smoke lifts away.

The land may be devastated, but the stars, at least, are still there to give
to the children. And the children symbolize future possibilities for fulfillment, or at least for new beginnings: "the earth wheels slowly beneath."
Cycles bring death; they also bring birth and renewal.

Isolation and loneliness, the most pervasive ordeals endured by
women, are represented in a variety of ways, even within a single work.
For example, in *The Land They Possessed,* a South Dakota woman listens
obsessively to a seashell when she can no longer endure the sound of the
wind in the grass (Breneman/Thurston 68). Eventually she is taken to an
institution in Yankton. Another woman, Mavis, enjoys a certain degree
of economic stability and the companionship of a woman helper living in
the house; she still complains because the "land is so empty" and most of
the people around are foreign immigrants (Breneman/Thurston 31). The
authors are critical of her inability to accept Germans or to adapt to the
prairie. The hero of the novel is Mavis's daughter, Michal, who loves the
prairie. In one scene she watches a beautiful sunset which "transform[s]
the faded stubble to a sea of tawny gold. For an instant she felt keenly the
beauty and immensity of the fields and the labor that had produced them,
and thought, as she had so often, the prairie is a lovely place." Then she
thinks of her friend's young husband who has just committed suicide. She
realizes "for the first time in her life, there on the sweep of prairie . . . its
supreme indifference to those who walk upon it" (235). This recognition
does not affect her own attitude toward the prairie, but it helps her to
understand why others react negatively to what they perceive as emptiness and indifference.[16]

16. Sandra L. Myres comments on the fact that loneliness and isolation need to be viewed
from different perspectives than those provided by "hundreds of books of both fact and fiction"—
"The physical isolation imposed by distance or weather soon came to an end; new settlers arrived;
the comforting sight of smoke from a neighboring cabin could be seen on the horizon; the long

The subject of loneliness has engaged both historians and literary critics because people react so differently to isolated conditions. Susan Armitage's insights, therefore, help us to evaluate specific examples: "A common theme in the accounts of pioneer women . . . is loneliness. Loneliness has many forms—psychological, physical, social—and can foster strength as well as weakness. . . . Now that we know this, we can move beyond the pitying and limiting stereotype of women as reluctant pioneers" ("Reluctant Pioneers" 48).

Even those committed to homesteading on the prairie endure agonizing periods of doubt. For example, Rose Wilder Lane describes a young wife left with her baby in a South Dakota dugout. The nearest neighbors, an immigrant couple, have left because of the drought. Caroline's husband has gone back to Minnesota to make enough money to plant the spring crop. After a three-day blizzard, Caroline forces open the door:

> Then she saw the immensity of whiteness and dazzling blue. She confronted space.
>
> Under the immeasurably vast sky, a limitless expanse of snow refracted the cold glitter of the sun. Nothing stirred, nothing breathed; there was no other movement than the ceaseless interplay of innumerable and unthinkably tiny rays of light. Air and sun and snow were the whole visible world—a world neither alive nor dead, and terrible because it was alien to life and death, and ignorant of them.
>
> In that instant she knew the infinite smallness, weakness, of life in the lifeless universe. [*Free Land* 128]

Caroline is the Frontier Hero, however, who refuses to be intimidated by the elements. She emerges from the dugout: "It was a moment of inexpressible terror, courage and pride. She was aware of human dignity. She felt that she was alive, and that God was with life. She thought: 'The gates of hell shall not prevail against me'" (129).

Canadian settlers, according to some historians, were not as isolated as some of their American counterparts. Lewis G. Thomas, for example, notes that by the 1880s Indians and Métis provided very little resistance to white expansion in the prairies; the Canadian transcontinental railroad cut across the prairie provinces; government institutions

---

winters ended; spring came again. But isolation and loneliness were not the same thing. Frontier women were rarely isolated from people; they were surrounded by husband, children, hired hands, often Indians or other native peoples; but they were still lonely. They missed their old companions and family members" (167–68).

were well established; moreover, the Royal Canadian Mounted Police "performed services to the emerging community far beyond the normal demands of police duties" (62). Thus Nellie McClung has sound basis for her cheerful portrayals of pioneer life in her 1912 collection of stories, *The Black Creek Stopping-House,* which she dedicated to "the Pioneer Women of the West." In the title story, "The Black Creek Stopping-House," McClung explores the responses to the prairie of two types of women. Maggie, who runs the stopping-house with her husband, sees herself as "a finger-post on the way to right living," perched as she is "on the very edge of civilization" (16). She is guardian of morals, enforcer of etiquette, and, moreover, the Prairie Angel who looks out for the new-comers. She assumes responsibility for a young, upper-class Ontario bride who shows all the signs of becoming a victim of the prairie unless some-one helps her to adjust. Maggie wonders what the young woman will do when the dismal fall weather sets in and how she will react to a crisis with the crops, "when the wheat's spoilin' in the shock, and the house is dark, and her man's away" (35). This section of Manitoba is still an un-developed territory; the first settler had arrived only three years before. Therefore Maggie is determined that the bride is going to be around to watch the miracle that happens every spring when "it seemed as if every grain sowed had fallen upon good soil and gave promise of the hundred-fold" (37). Because of efficient mail and train service, Maggie is able to arrange a reconciliation between the bride and her estranged father, thus demonstrating that Canadian pioneers, at least on the Manitoba prairies between the Assiniboine and the Souris, were not as isolated as some prairie settlers.

Whether women were isolated from other women by long dis-tances or by weather conditions that made travel impossible, they found comfort in needlework. Of course many sewing tasks were essential to survival and required long hours of dull labor—patching, darning, knit-ting socks and mittens for the cold seasons, spinning and weaving to provide fabric for the family's clothes when dry goods were unavailable. On the other hand, many women found time or made time for "fancy work," although these items too were usually practical and necessary. In one story a farmer gives his housekeeper "a dress length of light blue muslin, imprinted with blue cornflowers, red poppies, and white daisies" to express his appreciation for the care she has provided for his children and his house (Faralla 111). No other gift could have given Zelia more hours of pleasure as she chose a pattern, cut, and sewed the dress. In another story, a woman "in spare moments . . . knitted and crocheted afghans of intricate design and made beautiful silk blocks for a patchwork quilt which she featherstitched together" (Ford, *No Hour* 162). In *Children of My Heart* a Russian immigrant woman who lives "on the edge of the city dump" grew flowers in her little garden through the summer and, in the winter, made exquisite cloth flowers: "From this ill-heated cabin came jonquils so delicately made that you wanted to sniff them like real flowers" (Roy 23).

In *Crinoline to Calico*, Castle Gayle, who usually concentrates on her own needs, spends a contented week ripping seams out of old dresses and petticoats to make them into dresses for the young neighbor girls (Heacock 65). Although Castle feels superior to all the neighbor women, when they ask if she has quilt patterns, she takes enormous satisfaction in bringing several patterns up from the depths of her trunk and watching Abigail choose her favorites, the *Bridal Wreath* and the *Sunburst*. These novels emphasize that rituals related to sewing bring women together; in fact, a sewing circle or a quilting bee provide an acceptable occasion for socializing. (Fortunately such rituals persist today; see fig. 12, "Lone Star" quilt from a midwestern quilt show in 1985.) Aydelotte's *Across the Prairie* provides an amusing anecdote that reveals the quilting bee's possibilities for social interaction. Tenny, a widow, thinks about how she had outsmarted the gossips the day before. She had gone early to the quilting and stayed late so that the women couldn't talk about her being "courted" by the minister—the older women had to content themselves with "looking daggers" and the younger women with "nudges and sly winks" (98).

Aydelotte also uses quilt imagery to describe Tenny's confusion. Tenny thought she had settled down permanently in a little prairie town on the Kansas-Oklahoma border. Then her daughters start clamoring to join the "Boomers" and move to Oklahoma: "The way things were happening, Tenny Travis could no longer see life as a planned and orderly pattern. It seemed more like a crazy quilt with some pieces the wrong color and others that wouldn't fit in anywhere, no matter how she tried. Since it was beyond her to make the scraps and pieces one harmonious whole, she left that to the Master Designer and quit worrying" (195).

Women put gardens in their quilts and quilts in their gardens. They carried quilt patterns west with them just as they carried seeds. *Ship's Wheel* was renamed in the midwest and became *Harvest Sun;*

Fig. 12   T. A. Browne, *Mrs. Jones's "Lone Star" Quilt.* Many white women wrote
about learning crafts from Indian women; the star pattern, such as the one
pictured here, became a favorite of many quilters. Courtesy of the
photographer.

likewise, the *North Carolina Lily* became the *Prairie Lily* in both Canada
and the United States. They carried patterns for *Grandmother's Garden,*
Log Cabin, and *Indian Trails.* They created new patterns to reflect their
new homes—for example, *Kansas Dugout;* in the *Kansas Troubles* quilt,
women kept alive the memory of the political troubles attached to the
making of a free state. With the *Prairie Queen* patterns and "prairie
points" for making borders on the quilts, they made their own contributions to the art of quilting.

When planting gardens, some women arranged them according to
quilt compositions. Marta, "lacking the strength to make rows or com-
pose her intricate designs with groups of plants—diamonds, points or

squares—that she had taken such pleasure in improvising every spring, she had let them grow this time according to chance and providence, and the effect was perhaps the more striking because of it" (Roy, *Garden* 137). Indeed, her garden has become a crazy quilt which delights her as much as the formal gardens she had made when she was young and strong.

The importance of needlework in women's lives—whether done in groups or in isolation—cannot be too strongly emphasized.[17] The simple, powerful statement of one Wisconsin woman shows that quilt-making can be the most sustaining factor in a woman's life over a long period of time:

> It took me more than twenty-five years, I reckon, in the evenings after supper when the children were all put to bed. My whole life is in that quilt. It soares me sometimes when I look at it. All my joys and all my sorrows are stitched into those little pieces. When I was proud of the boys and when I was downright provoked and angry with them. When the girls annoyed me or when they gave me a warm feeling around my heart. And John, too. He was stitched into that quilt and all the thirty years we were married. Sometimes I loved him and sometimes I sat there hating him as I pieced the patches together. So they are all in that quilt, my hopes and fears, my joys and sorrows, my loves and hates. I tremble sometimes when I remember what that quilt knows about me. [quoted in Smith-Steffen 8]

The quilt has become a significant presence in the woman's life, a companion that is not only a witness to her joys and griefs but also a concrete symbol of her creative energy sustained over a quarter of a century.[18]

17. Michael W. Berry (curator, Museum Services, National Trust for Historic Preservation) argues that along with the recognition of quilting as an art form has come a "tendency to romanticize both the quilt and the quiltmaker. All too frequently enthusiasts read into the making of an antique quilt a 1980s attitude. Often the modern quilter writes of the joy and enthusiasm that a quilter of the 1850s must have felt in arranging the colored patches, and suggests that the quilt reflects an otherwise suppressed artistic personality." To prove otherwise, Berry quotes from an 1822 letter wherein a woman complains of the tediousness of putting "a bed quilt in frame." Anyone who has any familiarity with needlework knows that this is a small part of the process and a necessary nuisance. In addition, a quilt created because someone in the family needs another blanket in no way diminishes the satisfaction of having made something. Berry insists that "quiltmaking was a household duty along with cooking, sewing and raising a family"; hence, the experience of putting together a quilt as quickly as possible cannot be interpreted as being artistically rewarding (23). Yet both in factual records and fiction women have provided sufficient evidence to discredit Berry's view; both the simple, practical quilt and the elegantly worked bedcover provide satisfactions for the creator.

18. As numerous authors on the subject of quilting have pointed out, quilting bees provided women with a reason for getting together. Smith-Steffen, in her study of several Wisconsin

As this passage indicates, small things can make a woman's spirit rise: "It soares me," she says of her quilt. The passage also serves as a reminder that sorrows and annoyances and grief and hate were part of these women's lives. Even the contented survivors on the prairie, who lived to see their farms become profitable and their children healthy and successful, still acknowledge certain losses. Bess Streeter Aldrich's novel about her mother, A Lantern in Her Hand, is cheerful and optimistic; nevertheless, Abbie Deal never paints the pictures she yearned to paint, and she never writes the stories she had to tell. She must be content with her children and grandchildren doing the things she might have done if she had not become a homesteader. Similarly, Willa Cather's "Wagner Matinee" describes the agony of another Nebraska woman who returns to Boston and, after a concert, expresses intense grief and despair because she has had to forgo music, the most important thing in her life. Instead, she dedicated her life to helping her husband and raising their children on a Nebraska homestead.

Mary Hartwell Catherwood was one of the few women writers who focused an entire story on a Prairie Victim. In "The Monument to the First Mrs. Smith" (published in 1878 in the Kokomo Weekly Dispatch), Catherwood provided a subtitle, "A True Story of Today"; twice within the story the author emphasizes that it describes "an every-day affair," "a common case." Many women, Catherwood insists, encounter the fate of Susan Smith, one of the pioneer women. Male readers of the Kokomo Weekly Dispatch who noted this story on the front page and took the time to read it must have been somewhat disconcerted by the bitter tone with which the author describes a fresh, girlish bride shriveling, year by year, in her husband's service:

> She worked for him and waited on him and the two or three big "hands" who assisted him; and never in all the years of her servitude did he think it necessary to give her a servant to help bear her loads which were twice as heavy as those his laborers shared with him. He could not afford conveniences in those days. The farm had to be paid for before cistern or well could be dug; so Susan cheerfully carried water from neighboring wells or distant streams. She never minded wearing her wedding bonnet seven years, while

---

quilters, says that "the genteel, upper class parlor quilting bees of the East gave way to a new type in the mid-West. It became an event which was a natural and necessary outgrowth of pioneer loneliness and seclusion" (12). She describes several different circumstances for quilting bees—an "album quilt" would be presented to someone moving westward or to an honored citizen, commemorating local events; "freedom quilts" were made for young men going off on their own; "bridal quilts" were made for young women (13–19).

they were paying for the farm. . . . They never took the county paper; after the farm was paid for Smith said he would subscribe for a paper if the crops were good. Susan had no time to read, however. She had all the babies to nurse, and all the domestic machinery to keep in order. The tired ceature used to wonder how it would seem to have everything in plenty, and no mortgage on the farm. But when she remembered what an abundance of children she had, she felt ashamed of murmuring even in her own mind. [1]

On the basis of this passage we can identity some recurring charac- teristics of pioneer prairie women. The great majority were committed to helping husbands to achieve their goals, no matter how selfish or mate- rialistic the goals were. There is a kind of innocence and trust about these women who, despite evidence to the contrary, believe that their hus- band's ultimate goal is to achieve comfort and security for the entire family. Therefore the Mrs. Smiths sacrifice themselves physically and psychically, forgoing all present conveniences and pleasures for the sake of future comforts and security. They are so imbued with a sense of responsibility and obedience to husbands and so intensely concerned with the welfare of their children that they feel guilt when they even silently complain or criticize. With a child on one hip and a laundry tub on the other, they cheerfully go about their work.

Like Susan Smith, however, some die before the handsome brick house is built. It is Mr. Smith's young, thoughtless second wife who enjoys the advantages of a pump in the house, closets with shelves, bedrooms to spare, and a front hall. Catherwood ends her diatribe against selfish, materialistic prairie farmers by admonishing young girls: "MORAL —Girls, if you must marry Mr. Smith, don't take him on the first bal- lot—i.e.: wait till the monument is built, and then enter as the second Mrs. Smith" (1).

If there seems to be a disproportionately small number of prairie women victims in this analysis of first wave women's lives, the responsi- bility is not entirely that of the writers. Editors, finally, determine the content of the stories published in newspapers, magazines, and books. A rejection letter received by Zona Gale provides an example: "We regret exceedingly," the editor writes in a September, 1935, letter,

> that we can not accept your short story, "Flying Acres," because we have set a policy for the present of keeping out of our fiction columns the stories of tragedies that farm readers would like to forget.
>
> This policy is based upon the wish of our readers themselves. As they express themselves upon the matter, they show a desire to put behind them

the unpleasant years they have had and to avoid fiction that brings them
back to memory in a vivid way. [19]

"Flying Acres," the story rejected by *The Farmer's Wife*, focused on
farmers in Kansas who, as one farmer says, "tried to turn a grazing
country into a farming country, uprooting the stocky grass that would
have bound the soil to the earth" (10). After several years of drought,
there was nothing to hold down the topsoil. One particular winter there
had been very little snow; although it was April, there had been no spring
rains. The farmers could see that another desperate year lay ahead.
Nevertheless, there was no question but that they would "stick it out":
after the worst dust storm they had ever seen, "the air cleared and the
land lay smiling. They all agreed that they'd 'stick around.' Thwarted,
defeated, in all the loss from that early mistake of cultivating, they yet
wanted to see it through" (19–20). The heroism of the farmers of a Kansas community, however, was not sufficient reason to publish a story. [20]

In the hundred years since the publication of Catherwood's story,
therefore, the delineations of the first Mrs. Smiths, the Prairie Victims,
have continued, but usually the victims are minor characters in women's
fiction and major characters only in novels written by men. In other
instances, such as in Gale's "Flying Acres," the family or the entire
community are the victims, not a specific female. There are no equivalents to the Garland women or to Beret Hansa in the first part of
Rölvaag's *Giants in the Earth*. Clearly, women writers are rebelling against
pervasive images of the frontier woman as victims. To say that their
optimistic stories are unrealistic is to sidestep the issue. They are committed to recreating the heroic women they saw around them or heard about
through family, acquaintances, interviews, and historical documents.

While supporting the goals of these women writers, we must not
overlook or minimize the victimization that was a very real part of the
experience of some females on the prairie. [21] Leona Gom's poem "Farm
Women" summarizes one form of victimization:

19. Zona Gale Papers, Wisconsin State Historical Society.
20. In 1934 Gale sold a prairie story about a winter blizzard, "The Night of the Storm." In
this story a lost child is found by a neighbor who is an enemy of her father. This man saves the
little girl's life and the story ends happily with reconciliation between the two farmers. While
depicting a struggling farming community, it nevertheless had a positive theme and did not dwell
on the desperate farming conditions created by the drought; thus it was publishable material.
21. As Jeannie McKnight notes, "to view women *only* as victims is as hazardous as it is
misleading. Some specific women responded to life on the western frontier in different ways.

you labor for years
in the cold fields of this country,
in the hot kitchens of your houses,
in the birthing of unwanted children
    (you do what you must
    there is
    no other choice you
    survive)
to this final appraisal
in a man's court of law;
your easeless years
rewarded with a feudal wage,
  your room and board;
your work betrayed as
    just a normal contribution for a wife
and you sit with your large-knuckled hands
crumpled on your laps
beyond even anger
as you see the empty harvests of your lives,
your plantings doomed from the start
by the dry injustice
of these judgments:
your work worthless,
the farm theirs. [56]

These lines demonstrate the bitterness a farm woman feels who has sacrificed everything, it seems, and knows how difficult it is to win against both nature and men: sometimes she cannot even claim part ownership for the farm in court.[22]

Even when couples work together, it is a hard life, as Mrs. Feather testifies in *Morning in the Land*: "It's a hard life here, when you can't sell your pork, but got to trade it for flour. Why did we come so far west, I ask

---

Depending upon health, level of education, cultural or religious background, proximity to family, relationships, the immediate circumstances of her life, a woman might be more or less resilient to the hardships that inevitably arose" ("American Dream" 26).

   22. According to the editors of *A Harvest Yet to Reap*, wives and single women could establish homestead claims in the United States, but in Canada women had to be head-of-household; thus families with daughters could not expand their holdings as could families with sons. In Alberta, the Married Women's Relief Act of 1910 provided that a judge could "overrule a man's will if he left his wife an inadequate inheritance"; finally in 1920 the Interstate Succession Act "set aside a third of one spouse's holdings for the other if they had children, and the entire estate if they were childless." Of course there were loopholes with both acts (Rasmussen et al. 148–49).

Josh, when our children are all buried in Ohio except George who aint dead yet, and we never thought to raise him he was that puny? Four graves and nobody to tend 'em. It's a hard life" (North 45).

Ordeals associated with illness and childbirth are prominent structures in first wave prairie novels. The birth of a son or daughter occasionally shatters a male character's sense of authority, control, and self-sufficiency, forcing him to recognize the precarious conditions of child-bearing as well as his dependence upon woman and child for his emotional well-being. Parturition can be used also as a powerful symbol. The birth of a child symbolizes the cyclical nature of all life on the prairies; an equally powerful symbol is the death of a woman in childbirth, which represents the sorrow and failure of one generation in addition to the renewed hope in the life of the newborn infant.

In *Foreigners,* Luba is working in the garden when her mother calls her to come to the house. She helps her mother give birth to three baby girls. Luba is frantic, not knowing what to do. Then a fourth baby, a boy, is born. Luba wraps each baby in a diaper, telling herself that no one has four babies! When her father comes to the house, they wash each baby, but only the boy lives. The father tries to comfort Luba, telling her she did everything she could possibly do (Sapergia 101–04, 112). As this story indicates, a childbirth adds tension to the plot because the reader knows women and babies frequently died in the childbed; a birth brings women, even strangers, together in a bonding situation; and childbirth serves as an initiation of young females into the mysteries of woman-hood.[23]

While the novelists are quite frank about childbirth, other structures relating to female conditions are missing. No one discusses "female problems" such as *prolapsus uteri,* menstruation, and "uterine madness"—all subjects that William A. Alcott undertook in his 1855 publication, *The Young Woman's Book of Health.* A later publication, *Perfect Womanhood* (1901), promises on its title page to provide "full information on all the mysterious and complex matters pertaining to women." Exactly three paragraphs, however, are devoted to "Regulating Number of Offspring." Curiously, novelists are equally reticent on such subjects, as though they had entered into a conspiracy with their foremothers to discuss nothing that those women themselves had not been willing to

23. See childbirth ordeals in the opening scene of Gates, *The Biography of a Prairie Girl;* in Aldrich, *A Lantern in Her Hand,* 105; in Donovan, *Black Soil,* 113; in Lane, *Let the Hurricane Roar,* 12, 18–19; in Knox, *Red River Shadows,* 256.

reveal. Catherine Beecher, as early as 1855, pointed out that women were reluctant to discuss health problems; either pride or prudery kept them from talking to close friends or family members about health problems (264).

An excellent example of the situation described by Beecher is found in *The Edge of Time*. After a pregnant Lizzie Dillon has driven two horses and a wagon with her children and another woman through a devastating prairie fire, she insists that she is all right—she simply needs to lie down for awhile. When Bethany notes how sick she looks, Lizzie firmly tells her there's nothing she can do: "If I lay right still, like this, until morning," Lizzie replies, "I'll be all right. I ain't never lost one yet with a mishap, and I ain't a-goin' to lose this one" (Erdman 161–62). Frontier Heroes don't complain.

Works rarely particularize "intimate" problems. *The Land They Possessed* is an exception: the daughter expresses anger that her mother had been too discomfitted by discussions of female functions to prepare her for menstruation (Breneman/Thurston 190). Later her mother refuses to tell her what to expect in the marriage relationship, although she did, in an after-the-fact way, leave behind a book on midwifery before emigrating further west (329).

Several novels with male protagonists include stories of abused women as a way of enhancing the male's heroism. In *The Able McLaughlins*, a girl is raped by her cousin, but the hero marries her anyway, publicly claiming the child as his own. A minor character in *Trumpets Calling* sacrifices personal happiness by marrying a girl he doesn't love to save her reputation. In both situations, the sacrifices of these heroes are eventually acknowledged and rewarded. In *Morning in the Land* the male protagonist realizes his father has been unfaithful to his mother; he says to his brother, " 'Look at mother. Never a day's rest nor a penny of 'er own. Father can hire ten men at harvest and such, but no help for mother, and she has to feed them and make their beds and wash their clothes. Then on top of it all, this business with Molly Beeson' " (124). In all of these works the reader is kept at a distance from the female character who is being subjected to the humiliation. There are no in-depth analyses of the female's situation nor of her psychological reactions except through another character.

Other kinds of personal problems are avoided. The impossibility of maintaining any kind of privacy in a one-room dwelling never becomes an issue; the fiction writers, like the pioneer men, women, and children, avert their eyes or turn their backs. They look away, too, from both physical abuse and sexual desire among respectable people. One of the few exceptions is Heacock's *Crinoline to Calico*. While Heacock, too, avoids many issues, she is frank in her description of Castle and Jonathan's sexual relationship—the only time they are compatible is when they are in bed. Heacock also describes the beatings Jonathan gives Castle when she refuses to do anything. We understand his frustration—after all, he can't do both the inside and the outside work; she had wanted to come west and once there had no business playing the lady. This situation was not unusual. In his study *Women and Men on the Overland Trail*, John Mack Faragher points out that "husbands were recognized by law as the heads of their families; to them was delegated the obligation to control and discipline their wives. Hence husbands were permitted to physically punish their spouses within 'reasonable limits'" (162). Even Heacock, however, avoids discussing the method Castle uses to induce an abortion because she has decided she is not going to do all the work and care for "a bunch of brats" (35).

Fleeting references to prostitutes do exist, but the women themselves are kept at a distance from the respectable characters observing them.[24] David, the protagonist in *Free Land*, hears "the screaming laughter of girls and drunken shouts, a maudlin uproar" (Lane 28). Only *The Land They Possessed* involves a prostitute in the action of the story. During a prairie fire, the women of the "Bad House" work with the other townspeople to save the buildings on the edge of town. In another passage in the novel, the girl Michal contemplates the future and what it means in sexual terms: life seems like a threatening fire on the horizon—"Marriage and birth lay coiled darkly in the future . . . of men going drunkenly to That House and of dogs tying openly in the streets" (Breneman/Thurston 208–09). In a novel about the Oklahoma Boomers, the relationship of David Payne and his mistress, both historical figures, is treated sympathetically:

> Vic Sullins was only a name to most people and Tenny had seen her but once—a small, timid-acting woman all in black and wearing a heavy veil, hurrying along the street in Border City. There was a mystery about her;

24. See Carol Leonard and Isidor Wallimann's "Prostitution and Changing Morality in the Frontier Cattle Towns of Kansas," *Kansas History* 2 (1979): 34–53. As more analyses like Leonard and Wallimann's become available, fiction writers will be able to recreate the ways women thought about and dealt with issues such as prostitution. This study illustrates the kinds of documents (such as newspapers and court records) that reveal information about prostitution.

some said she and Payne just took up together, while others insisted that she
had to run away from a husband who beat her savagely and who, after she fell
in love with the Boomer Captain, wouldn't give her a divorce so they could
get married. She and Dave had a son who went by his mother's name, and
she lived quietly in Border City, keeping to herself and giving the gossips
little chance to talk. [Aydelotte, *Across the Prairie* 85]

When we turn to another significant structure in prairie women's
fiction—female relationships—we discover that women come to terms
with the capriciousness of nature; grueling chores, and troublesome husbands when they have women friends. A simple, uneducated male narrator, Rough Ben, makes exactly this point in one of Kate Simpson
Hayes's ballads. He tells the story of a neighbor, a young, educated
Englishwoman, whose "fool of a brother" has just died. He finds her
sitting near the brother's grave, crying, and says:

> All at once I see'd her trouble,
> 'Twas want o' wimmin to cuddle her in,
> An the nearest petticoat, too, by thunder!
> Thirty miles off—an' *she lived by sin!*

Ben goes on to explain that she could have endured the problems related
to the homestead and the Rebellion if there had been the support of
women. But she marries him because, he says, she was "jest frightened"
into "a-bein" his wife. This kindly, adoring man recognizes that she had
no alternative; at that particular time, a female friend would have met
her needs better than a husband ("Rough Ben" 138).

Describing a rural farm tragedy in a much later era, Susan Glaspell's "Jury of Her Peers" shows two women coming to the realization
that their friendship could have saved a woman from murdering her
husband. Isolated on her Iowa farm with a husband who is too penurious
to allow her trips to town or the pleasure of a telephone, Minnie Wright
finds comfort in her little yellow canary. The husband, apparently, gra-
tuitously kills the bird, binding a string around its neck. This act moves
Minnie to the extremities of despair: that night when her husband has
fallen asleep she slips a noose around his neck and chokes him to death.
The next day, as neighbor women pack some of Minnie's things to take
to her at the jail, they find her sewing basket which contains quilt pieces
and the strangled canary. They notice the erratic stitches and recognize
how distressed she must have been. Both women realize they should have
taken time to talk to her. Clearly, this was another case of "want o'
wimmin to cuddle her in."

A Canadian story that describes strained relations between husband and wife illustrates the redemptive potential of friendship between women. During her seven years on a homestead, Helen Harwood has become bitter. A productive farm does not compensate for the loss of a baby or for a work-driven husband, "blunted and dulled" by pioneer life: "Mated to this silent being, living miles from any woman, Helen Harwood had lived years as dry and lifeless as the dust of the pyramids" (Elston, "A Mess of Things" 438). Helen decides to return to England and goes to her baby's grave one last time. Here she discovers a very young woman who envies her because she, at least, has a grave to visit and to "hold" her to the place. The girl announces that she is going to the city, adding, " 'I guess it isn't Jim's fault. . . . Men don't know what it means to be lonely' " (440).

That night Helen tells her husband, John, that she has come to hate the place and is leaving. Filled with despair, John keeps repeating, " 'I guess I've made a dreadful mess of things' " (441). Startled by the depth of his feelings, Helen asks him if he has ever loved her. He replies: " 'Loved you, lass? I've worshipped the ground you walked on. But I'm afraid the dreadful years before you came have changed me. They've made me this quiet clod, I'm no fit mate for you.' "

By revealing their deepest feelings, John and Helen are reconciled. Helen realizes that the young woman she met at the baby's grave might also be reconciled with her husband. After John hears the story, he saddles the broncos and they ride together to the train station where the girl will be waiting for the train. "By the moving lights from the train the woman descried a desolate little figure waiting on the platform. Helen was beside her as the conductor stepped from the train. The girl put out both hands and Helen Harwood gathered them in hers" (443). The girl had never been truly sure that leaving her husband was the best solution, so she accepts Helen's advice: "Side by side with my path of duty lies my path to happiness" (443). But this sentiment only partially explains how a woman can find happiness. There is another way, although it is never articulated in the story: the discovery of an unexpected and compatible neighbor woman diminishes the sense of isolation.

In Mary Hartwell Catherwood's story "The Career of a Prairie Farmer" (1880), several types of female relationships are represented. The dominant one exists between the wife and the sister of the farmer. They are first seen riding across the prairie, both delighted by the landscape. Together, through their "human kindness," they win the good

will and respect of less fortunate neighbors who initially resent their
"airs" and silk dresses. The two women gradually blend with the countryside: when the silk wears out they put on calico like everyone else.
While Catherwood doesn't press the point, it is obvious that the relationship sustains them as the years pass by. In fact, the friendship between two women can be more important than the wife-husband relationship.[25]

Abbie Deal, in A Lantern in Her Hand, is dragged through a blizzard
by her German neighbor, who refuses to abandon her; until that event
Abbie had felt superior to Germans. This dramatic scene is one of many
recurring in women's fiction, showing that barriers between classes and
cultures are broken down when women reach out to help each other. In
Black Soil Nell Connors teaches her neighbor to read English so that the
woman doesn't have to depend on her husband, whom she mistrusts, to
translate her letters. In return, the woman nurses Nell during childbirth.
Another neighbor, Katto Schwartz, plows a fireguard around Nell's
buildings when she realizes both Nell and Tim are away from home. In a
semiautobiographical novel, Upon a Sagebrush Harp, Nell Parsons describes her feelings about an aunt's thoughtful Christmas present that had
been planned months in advance—a box of chocolates in a "blue box
with white lilies on the cover." Parsons recalls that she cherished the box
for years (88). The quiet, self-sufficient mother in The Lily of Fort Garry
finds enormous satisfaction in being able to release years of pent-up
frustrations in a discussion with her only daughter, who is finally old
enough to understand the problems her mother has faced, married as she
is to an adventurer. These relationships help women to endure the stress
that accompanies the pioneer experience.

Even men most sympathetic to pioneer women have difficulty
seeing them as adventurers. In The Passing of the Frontier (1918), Emerson Hough described the emigrants who headed for Oregon. He insisted
that his readers reconsider their image of the pioneer hero as a male:

> The chief figure of the American West, the figure of the ages, is not the long-
> haired, fringed-legging man riding a raw-boned pony, but the gaunt and sad-

25. Many historians and literary critics have relied on Carroll Smith-Rosenberg's article
"The Female World of Love and Ritual: Relations between Women in Nineteenth-Century
America," to guide analyses of female relationships in real life and in fiction. John Mack Faragher,
however, convincingly argues that Smith-Rosenberg "really shows . . . that in their writings
women allowed men to appear in only shadowy ways. In itself this says nothing about women's
actual behavior" (205).

faced woman sitting on the front seat of the wagon, following her lord where he might lead, her face hidden in the same ragged sunbonnet which had crossed the Appalachians and the Missouri long before. That was America, my brethren! There was the seed of America's wealth. There was the great romance of all America—the woman in the sunbonnet; and not, after all, the hero with the rifle across his saddle horn. Who has written her story? Who has painted her picture? [93–94]

Certainly by now part of the story of the woman in the sunbonnet has been told—that of the female Frontier Heroes on the prairie who populate women's fiction. Obviously Hough would have difficulty finding his stereotype among the many robust, enthusiastic, independent female homesteaders in these works. Not Hough's "sad-faced" woman but Aydelotte's "resolute" Martha Prawl is prototypical:

> It was stepping wide of the truth to say that their place was at the edge of town. To Martha, gazing across the sweep of prairie, it seemed more like the edge of nowhere. She had wanted to live close in and have near neighbors, but out here they were going, and here they would have to stay. But there would be room for garden and chickens, and plenty of pasture for the stock, and by the time she got some flowers to growing and set out trees, they would have a real home.
>
> So she said, trying to make the best of it, "One thing sure: we'll have plenty of elbow-room, living out this far. And another thing; we can always see a long way off."
>
> No question about the view. Straight to the sky-line swept great waves of prairie land, lifting in one grassy swell after another. In every direction it was the same—miles of bare, rolling country. . . .
>
> The pioneering instinct quickened in Martha's blood. Her features firmly cut and resolute, were a heritage from ancestors whose courage in the face of danger helped to conquer new frontiers. Her figure, tall and angular, had strength and endurance graven in every line. Her hands, lean and capable, could ply a needle or guide a plow down the long furrows—or, if need be, grip firmly the barrel of a gun.
>
> Men were needed to tame the wilderness, but it took women like Martha Prawl to make its waste places blossom like the rose. [*Trumpets Calling* 58–59]

CHAPTER FOUR

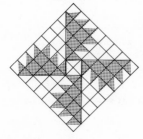

White Women and Indians

A buckskin-clad youth sits beside an old Indian woman and learns to bind an arrowhead to the shaft. Nearby, some old braves gamble with cherry stones while plump, happy children tumble among the puppies. In the background, a Frenchman, dressed for the wilderness, leans against the lodge. From where he stands he can see the Rock of St. Louis a mile upstream, the Indian women and children in the cornfield frightening away the crows, and the burial platforms of the Illinois tribe standing just beyond the fields. The year is 1680; the place is Fort St. Louis on the Illinois River.

This scene was created by Mary Hartwell Catherwood in "The Little Renault: An Episode of Tonty's Life in Illinois Country." It provides the first glimpse of a white female in Indian territory to be found in prairie women's fiction—what appears to be a boy making arrows is actually a girl, the daughter of a Frenchman. This story and Catherwood's novel *The Story of Tonty* describe an early period in midwestern history, thus enabling readers to imagine the life and landscape before the arrival of the first white settlers on the prairies. In addition, the characterization of "the little Renault" and of Barbe Cavelier in *The Story of Tonty* is consistent with dozens of other female heroes who dominate the pages of prairie women's fiction: they, like the male heroes of the American and Canadian prairies, are undaunted by the dangers of the wilderness or by the potential hostility of Indians.

When writers choose the frontier years for their subject, they have a wide range of options in plotting their stories and developing their characters. From an abundance of images of the Indians, they have to decide which ones their characters will carry with them into the prairie wilderness. They have to show how these images are reinforced or broken down as women encounter Indians on the trail and in the early settlements. The ethnocentrism of the characters can prevent them from learning about and understanding the different Indian tribes. On the other hand, when confronting human beings rather than abstractions, women can be shown to undergo significant changes in attitude. They might not accept and like certain traditions or practices, but they can at least learn something about the Indian culture and society and, perhaps, come to respect Indian religions, marriage customs, gender roles, attitudes toward nature, social rituals, childbirth, and childrearing practices. Thus prairie women's fiction serves as a useful supplement to historical documents by showing how numerous women writers have molded their materials according to their readings, interviews, memories, and imagination. As readers, we become more aware of the varieties of experiences and relationships between white women and Indians on the American and Canadian prairies.

Five works describe whites, Indians, and mixed-bloods[1] living together in a community: Catherwood explores the late seventeenth-century encampment of La Salle's men among the Illinois at Fort St. Louis; four Canadian novelists—Agnes C. Laut, Kate Simpson Hayes, Olive Knox, and Jane Rolyat—describe life in the Red River settlement. White settlers' reactions to Indians on the Iowa, Kansas, and Nebraska frontiers are explored in works by Bess Streeter Aldrich, Laura Ingalls Wilder, Nan Heacock, and Elisabeth Ford. Three other novelists, Dana Faralla, Eleanor Gates, and Josephine Donovan, give examples of the ways whites and Indians helped each other. Insights into intermarriage between whites and Indians as well as the victimization of Indian women by white males are provided in works by Donovan, Martha Ostenso, Gabrielle Roy, and Laura Goodman Salverson. These issues, presented from the perspective of white women writers, are also discussed in an autobiographical novel by Maria Campbell, *Halfbreed.*

In the opening scene of Catherwood's "Little Renault" (described above), the situation appears serene. The French explorers and the Illinois Indians, however, are joined in an uneasy alliance. La Salle and his lieutenant, Henri de Tonty, are waiting for reinforcements and sup-

---

1. In her study of women and fur-trade society, Sylvia Van Kirk uses the term *mixed-blood* "to describe people of Indian-European origin. Like the French word "Métis", it accommodates all gradations of racial mixtures and does not carry the pejorative connotations of the word 'half-breed'" (255).

plies that will enable them to move westward.[2] In the meantime, La Salle is "holding ground" in the midst of what is described as "a suspicious savage tribe" (558). If he had built a camp apart from the Indian village he would have increased their mistrust. He needs their protection, and the Illinois need his help because the Iroquois are a continuous threat. La Salle's vision of his role in Illinois country is patriarchal and expansionist: "They would soon fortify the Rock and make it a feudal castle to these timid savages. Neighboring tribes would gather close and help to form a strong principality. It would be easy from this vantage-point to penetrate that unexplored river called the Mississippi" (561). This passage reveals La Salle's blind feudalism. Although the white man can build his fort in the wilderness, he cannot command a position of authority and patronage typical of a seigneur. He underestimates the Indians' courage and their commitment to retaining their lands on their own terms. He will indeed penetrate those new territories beyond the Mississippi, but he is tragically naive in his assumption that whites and Indians can form "a strong principality." The ways of the two groups are too different; in addition, the prejudices and ethnocentrism of whites erect additional barriers to establishing a harmonious community.

This short romance by Catherwood, published in *Century Magazine,* provided readers with an interpretive description of white-Indian relations in prairie country. It also presented a cameo of the spirited, adventurous French girl who enjoys learning Indian ways while under the guardianship of Henri de Tonty at Fort St. Louis. Her sojourn in the wilderness, however, is short-lived. Almost immediately after making her first arrow shaft, the Iroquois attack by surprise and she is wounded. She refuses, however, to consider herself a victim of the wilderness. While delirious, she describes her joy at having had this adventure with Tonty:

> She thought she was dancing in a whirl along peaks, or fishing in the river with L'Espérance, or shooting arrows at a mark with young Indians, or moving across the prairie with Tonty on his errand to the Iroquois. Through every act ran gladness. She exulted upward through the fire-gilt branches.
>
> "O Mother of God, what joy thou hast given me! If there had been no Monsieur de Tonty—think of that! [565]

A young female reader in the nineteenth century would have been

---

2. Catherwood's interest in the French explorers of the Mississippi led to *Heroes of the Middle West* (Boston, 1898), in which she describes La Salle's vision and Tonty's role in history.

distressed by the death of the charming little heroine; nevertheless she might conclude that even a short life has its distinct rewards: the excitement of an adventure with the early explorers among the Indians. The story's real significance, however, lies in its picture of the whites and Indians living together and providing mutual support despite different goals and values.

Readers of Catherwood's fiction found another adventurer in *The Story of Tonty*, which begins in Canada. In the first scene, eleven-year-old Barbe Cavelier has temporarily escaped from the nuns to walk with La Salle, her uncle, through the streets of Montreal during a beaver fair. Like the "little Renault," she too is placed under the protection of Tonty: he guides her through the melee of Indians and merchants and voyageurs to the security of the convent. During their walk, Tonty tells her that "a woman should learn to pray, even as a man should learn to fight. . . . He stands between her and danger, and she should stand linking him to heaven." Barbe, however, refuses to accept such a mundane role: "I can fight for myself," she tells him, "and everybody ought to say his own prayers" (30).

Later in Book I, Barbe asks her uncle if the only way out of the convent is through marriage. When he says yes, she announces that she would like to marry Tonty, and La Salle agrees that he would make a good husband for her. Once married, Barbe says, she would run for the wilderness and Tonty would not be able to catch her. In a more serious vein, she tells La Salle of her longing to go west, and La Salle, equally serious, tells her: "If the wilderness thus draws you, you will some time embrace it. Cavelier blood is wild juice" (62, 63). The charm of this passage lies in La Salle's respect for the adventurous spirit—even in a young girl. He sees no reason to lecture her about Indians, blizzards, arduous journeys, crude accommodations, or isolated dwellings.

Book II opens five years later, in 1683, at Fort Frontenac on Lake Ontario. Father Hennepin has just returned from the West after "great peril and captivity" (74).[3] La Salle's return is imminent, but he has lost the financial and political support of the king of France and the governor

---

3. Catherwood gently pokes fun at Father Hennepin. When he is accused of being an overzealous colonizer, he "swell[s] his stomach and inflat[es] his throat" as he defends his motives: "'Why should I enter the mendicant order of Saint Francis, and live according to the rules of a pure and severe virtue, if I felt no zeal for saving souls?'" He then proceeds down the street, talking to himself "until some derisive savage pointed out this solo" (37–38). Catherwood implies that his motives had more to do with power and fame than with saving souls.

of New France for having sided with the Illinois tribe against the Iroquois. Barbe Cavelier, "freed unaccountably from her convent, and brought on a perilous, delightful journey to so strange a part of her world" (99–100), is ready for further explorations, and after Tonty arrives she tells him of her lifelong affinity with the West:

> "Monsieur," said Barbe, "there is something on my mind which I will tell you. I was thinking of the new world my uncle La Salle discovered, even before you came to Montreal. Now I think constantly of Fort St. Louis of the Illinois. Monsieur, I dream of it: I go on long journeys and never arrive; I see it through clouds, and wide rivers flow between it and me; and I am homesick. Yes, monsieur, that is the strangest thing—I have cried of homesickness for Fort St. Louis of the Illinois!" [119]

She refuses to be intimidated when Tonty tells her what a difficult time he has had mediating between the Iroquois and the Illinois: "'How would mademoiselle like to . . . carry the wampum belt of peace on the open field between two armies, and for your pains get your scalp-lock around the fingers of a Seneca chief and his dagger into your side?'" (118).

Barbe remains undaunted and her dream of seeing Fort St. Louis is fulfilled in Book III. Now in the care of another uncle, Abbé Jean Cavelier, she arrives at Fort St. Louis. While the Abbé regrets that Barbe and her brother Colin were not sent back to France, Barbe expresses satisfaction with the arrangements La Salle has made for her. La Salle, having spent Barbe's inheritance on his explorations, is determined to repay her by providing the opportunity for her to see the fort and, in addition, to be given a land grant. As the travelers approach the fort, Barbe sits in one of a long string of canoes under Tonty's command. She is absorbed in the landscape:

> To Barbe this was an enchanted land. She sat by the Demoiselle Bellefontaine and watched its populous beauty unfold. Blue lodge-smoke arose everywhere. Tonty pointed out the Shawnee settlement eastward, and the great town of the Illinois northwest of the Rock—a city of high lodges shaped like the top of a modern emigrant wagon. He told where Piankishawa and Weas might be distinguished, how many Shawanoes were settled beyond the ravine back on the Rock, and how many thousand people, altogether, were collected in this principality of Monsieur de la Salle. [190–91]

Barbe's brother, whom she has not seen in four years, is at the fort; he has little tolerance for adventure, she discovers, and yearns to return to France. "For myself," Barbe replies, "I love this wild world" (199).

Fortunately, Barbe is allowed to stay because the Abbé knows she will be unmarriageable in France without a fortune of her own; he therefore decides that a marriage between Barbe and Henri de Tonty would be appropriate.

Immediately following the wedding and the departure of the Abbé, the group at the fort receives news that La Salle has been killed. Tonty grieves over his friend's death and at the same time recognizes the precarious existence of the Indians, who will now be vulnerable to attack from the Iroquois: "Tonty heard tribe after tribe take up the lament for the dead. Not only was it a lament for La Salle, but it was also for their own homes. [La Salle] and Tonty had brought them back from exile, had banded them for strength, and helped them ward off the Iroquois. His unstinted success meant their greatest prosperity. The undespairing Norman's death foreshadowed theirs with all that silence and desolation which must fall on the Rock of St. Louis before another civilization possessed it" (221). That subsequent civilization is described in the last chapter of the book, entitled "To-Day." The Rock of St. Louis was renamed Starved Rock, according to Catherwood, because the Iroquois, in the late eighteenth century, had surrounded the Illinois on that spot and starved them. Then the Iroquois were forced westward and Indian lodges were replaced by homesteads and towns.

A few years after the publication of Catherwood's romances about La Salle and Tonty, a Canadian novelist, Agnes C. Laut, published *Lords of the North*. Like Catherwood's works, this too is an adventure story that has been carefully researched and written to appeal to readers who want a combination of historical fact, excitement, and suspense. A marked difference between the two writers emerges when we focus on the attitudes of whites toward Indians. While the main characters in Catherwood's stories respect Indian ways, the opposite is true of Laut's novel; white racism pervades the story. The first of several novels by women about the Red River settlement, *Lords of the North* brings together three sets of people: Indians and mixed-bloods; traders, voyageurs, and bourgeois associated with the fur-trading companies; and white settlers.

Laut's central character is Rufus Gillespie, an educated young man from Montreal. The adventure begins in Montreal when a villainous Iroquois kidnaps the wife and child of Rufus Gillespie's friend Hamilton. Outraged, Rufus signs up as a clerk with the North West Company and leaves for the West, assuming that the fur traders will follow a route similar to the one taken by the kidnappers.

In the introduction to his adventure, Rufus establishes his position in regard to the Indians: "On the charges and counter-charges of cruelty bandied between white men and red, I have nothing to say. Remembering how white soldiers from eastern cities took the skin of a native chief for a trophy of victory, and recalling the fiendish glee of Mandanes over a victim, I can only conclude that neither race may blamelessly point the finger of reproach at the other" (3–4). However, Rufus as narrator is unrelenting in his prejudice against the Indians, even when he records the impressions of others. For example, he asks an old trader about the tribe camping near his friend's house and is told that they are "mongrel curs, neither one thing nor the other, Iroquois canoemen, French half-breeds intermarried with Sioux squaws!" (31). Although Laut's story is set in a period when those attached to the fur-trading companies were relatively free of racism, she imposes on the character Rufus an attitude which is more characteristic of the second half of the nineteenth century. The derogatory word *squaw* was not used with any frequency until after the mid-1850s in Canada.[4]

As Rufus begins the search for Miriam Hamilton and her son, he seeks information at an Indian camp. Here he meets a college friend from Laval who, according to Rufus, already shows the corrupting effects of a wild life among Indians and voyageurs. The Indian and mixed-blood women tending the fire are described as a "motley throng of fat, coarse-faced squaws." One in particular has a "hideous, angry face": "She might have been a great, bronze statue, a type of some ancient goddess, a symbol of fury, or cruelty" (46). She is the daughter of a Sioux chief, a condition that usually elicits praise and respect from a male adventurer; Rufus Gillespie, however, never discerns "the noble savage" in the Indians he encounters.[5]

4. Van Kirk points out that while the "parent society" held prejudices against Indians, many individual males in the fur trade did not. She notes "a sharp rise in the expression of racist sentiments . . . when European women appear upon the scene" (6). It was during this period, not earlier, that the derogatory word *squaw* began to replace other expressions such as "my woman," "the mother of my children," "the guid wife" (201). Van Kirk clarifies the differences in sexual mores between the two cultures: "Most officers subscribed to a European ideal of womanhood, which emphasized the necessity of female modesty and chastity. . . . Thus, the amount of sexual freedom allowed to women in Indian society seemed scandalous to the traders" (23).

5. One of the most interesting aspects of Van Kirk's discussion of Indian and mixed-blood women in fur-trade society relates to their relationships with white men. Clearly, many strong relationships survived the stress of different cultural values and disapproval, especially from the Europeans. In 1821, according to Van Kirk, the newly organized fur-trading company "took steps

Nor does Rufus appreciate the colorful character and life-styles of the voyageurs. When they reach the Great Lakes, he describes another Indian camp:

> Indians, half-breeds and shaggy-haired whites—degenerate traders, who had lost all taste for civilization and retired with their native wives after the fashion of the north country—came from the Nipissangue encampments and joined our motley throng. Presently the natives drew off to a fire by themselves, where there would be no white-man's restraint. They had either begged or stolen traders' rum, and after the hard trip from Ste. Anne, were eager for one of their mad *boissons*—a drinking-bout interspersed with jigs and fights.
>
> Stretched before our camp, I watched the grotesque figures leaping and dancing between the firelight and the dusky woods like forest demons. [79–80]

Gillespie watches with interest one figure in particular seated before the fire—a man who is oblivious to the activities going on around him. When a trader tells Gillespie that this man is homesick for his wife, Gillespie finds the situation comical: "The idea of an Indian sentimental and love-sick for some fat lump of a squaw!" (80). Clearly Gillespie thinks only white men like his friend Hamilton can grieve for a missing wife.

If Laut is critical of whites' lack of respect and compassion for Indians and their culture, she never reveals it. Gillespie disapproves of the traders who have "retired with their native wives after the fashion of the north country"; there is no other voice to remind readers that some white men loved their Indian families and stayed with them.

In another passage Gillespie records a conversation between two traders. One describes the hardships of a winter without enough food. The other man tells him he should have avoided difficulties by marrying an Indian woman as he has done. The tone of the conversation discredits Indian women and the important role they played in the lives of the fur traders. Although the novel has been complimented for having given "a fairly accurate historical picture of the Métis"[6] the biases of the author

---

to standardize the social customs which had evolved in the Indian Country. In order to regularize marriage *à la façon du pays,* a marriage contract was introduced which emphasized the husband's economic responsibilities" (117).

6. Wolfgang Klooss argues that Agnes Laut's novel, unlike other popular novels about the Canadian West, approaches the Métis with historical accuracy. "Laut integrates documentary material such as authentic Métis songs into the general flux of the plot. Although the tone of her

prevented her from recognizing the essential role of Indian women in the fur-trade society. They ground corn, chopped firewood, washed clothes, preserved foods, and made snowshoes, moccasins, and other articles of clothing. They skinned buffalo, sliced and dried the meat (pemmican), harvested rice, caught small game and fish, and waterproofed canoes. They even paddled canoes and served as guides and interpreters on expeditions.[7] Many men respected the Indian women for these talents, but this perspective is missing from Rufus's interpretations of the fur traders and their relationships with Indian women.

Rufus himself is adopted by an Indian chief in one unconvincing episode which conforms to the conventions of the western adventure story. Even while receiving the protection of his adopted tribe he continues to be critical and disapproving. Only thoughts of the woman he loves prevent him from becoming a barbarian: "Hers was the influence that aroused loathing for the drunken debauches, the cheating, the depraved living of the Indian lodges" (232).

As soon as possible, with the coming of spring, he leaves the Indian camp and travels to the Red River settlement. Here he sees the beginning of the Seven Oaks massacre: he observed that "the empty threats of half-breeds to butcher every settler in Red River had evidently reached the ears of the women. Some trembled so they could scarcely walk" (356).[8]

But what about the attitudes of the female protagonist of the story, Frances Sutherland? This young woman had emigrated with her father when Lord Selkirk brought Scots settlers to the Red River. Rufus describes Frances's courage and strength, but he remains strangely silent about her opinion of the Indians. Rufus first meets Frances when, having overheard his plans to find a boat with which to rescue Miriam, she reveals herself, scrambles over a wall, and leads him to a place where canoes have been concealed. Rufus praises Frances because she is willing to risk "life and reputation, which is dearer than life, to save another

---

novel is primarily romantic, she turns realistic whenever the Métis are mentioned." Klooss quotes from The Oxford Companion to Canadian History and Literature: "Lords of the North . . . despite the fantastic plot and her inability to handle conversation, conveyed in terms acceptable to her age and the drama and unscrupulousness of the struggle between the North West Company and the Hudson's Bay Company for control of the Fur Trade" (154). Neither critic seems disturbed by the distortions which result from racist attitudes toward the Métis.

7. For a detailed analysis of women's work, see Van Kirk 53–63, 110–11.

8. For a brief overview of the Red River settlement era, including the Seven Oaks massacre, see The Beaver, special issue 1983, 45–48.

woman!" (130). Frances is an intriguing character. Wherever she appears in the plot, she is knowledgeable about the wilderness and quick to make good decisions. If she contemplates the conditions of Miriam's captivity, she apparently never reveals her thoughts to Rufus. Instead, we are given Rufus's anxieties: "Forebodings of terrible suffering for Miriam haunted me. I could not close my eyes without seeing her subjected to Indian torture" (216). His fears, apparently, are unfounded. The few glimpses we have of Miriam in captivity show her sitting quietly with her child or sleeping. She is frail, tired, and despairing—as well she might be—but she is not being abused or tormented. When her escape is effected, she joins her husband with great joy and expresses gratitude for her release. If the trials of her captivity included physical and sexual abuse, Laut does not recount the wounds. This suggests that Rufus's imagined tortures were worse than any Miriam actually experienced.[9]

The following passage is the closest Agnes Laut comes to sympathizing with the plight of the people whose lives were uprooted by the fur traders and, in the mid-1800s, by the growing numbers of farmers: "So it was," Laut writes, "with the great fur-trading companies at the beginning of this century. Each held the Indian in subjection and thought to use him with daring impunity against its rival" (327). As recent research shows, however, the early years of the fur trade were often characterized by mutual cooperation and respect.[10]

The popularity of *Lords of the North*—in spite of its racism—shows the tolerance of readers for works that made heroes out of white males who despised Indians, Métis, and other mixed-bloods. Once a man is able to apply the term *savage* to others, he can begin the process of conquering their lands and obliterating their cultures. In fact, Laut dedicated the novel to "the Pioneers and their Descendants, whose heroism won the land." She is clearly on the side of the white aggressors. While Laut's novel does not illuminate the subject of the emigrant white woman's relationship with Indians, it does provide insight into the attitudes of

9. For an analysis of white women and Indians, including a discussion of women in captivity, see Riley, "Rumors and Alarms on the Trail and in Early Settlements," in *Women and Indians on the Frontier*, 83–119.

10. "In the fur trade, white and Indian met on the most equitable footing that has ever characterized the meeting of 'civilized' and 'primitive' people. The fur trader did not seek to conquer the Indian, to take his land or to change his basic way of life or beliefs. The Indian in Western Canada was neither subject nor slave. Even as late as the mid-nineteenth century, the Hudson's Bay Company did not exercise direct authority over the tribes in Rupert's Land" (Van Kirk 9).

those who made up the dominant culture of the late nineteenth century. These readers, both female and male, would have concurred that the land had to be won and that the inhabitants had to be "civilized."[11]

A certain element of surprise is in store for readers who turn from Laut's *Lords of the North* to the introduction she wrote for a book by Kate Simpson Hayes, *The Legend of the West*. Here is Laut's introduction:

> The Indians are the Arabs of America, with all the picturesque poetry and romance of the desert runner; only we have no Bayard Taylor to make vocal that poetry; and I have often wondered why no one has embodied in art of some sort—picture or allegory—the legends of our North-West Crees, as Longfellow's "Hiawatha" eternally preserves the legend of the Ojibway, and the epic of "Kalevala" the legend of the Finnish people. We must be quick about it and the work must be done now, or the race will have gone down the trail where all tracks point one way!

In this passage Laut has established a suitable tone for Hayes's subject matter in this "Legend." In an author's note, Hayes says that "there is inexpressible pathos in the passing of the Red man. This is now taking place in what was once known as 'The Great Lone Land.'" A narrator tells about the coming of Yotin (the Winds) who speaks in tones that make the earth tremble. Yotin recalls the days when great people met in council; now the peace pipe is broken and brother fights brother. Yotin expresses his sorrow: "The chase is abandoned—the camp-fire but a circle of ashes. A once great Race is now as a broken reed, and for the children there shall be no tomorrow."

The narrator asks for Yotin's pity, reminding him that "the land is parched—the Hunting-grounds bare—nature sterile—and emptiness has come upon the land. . . . Children who made music now only sigh." After listening to Yotin's speech, the narrator falls into a deep sleep. When he awakens, he describes the sight before him:

> . . . a new Moon upon whose pale horn the Tomahawk should never again hang. Flower and fern smiled—leaf and branch danced; by laughing waters pale-faced children played—and on the sweetened air came the Song of Toil!
>
> In the morning light shone a new Trail and upon it rose a city greater than any.

---

11. In her journal Frances Simpson commended the Red River chaplain for having entered "very zealously into the humane and laudable objects of reforming the loose & savage lives of the Indians, and of training their Off spring in the paths of Virtue, by instilling into their minds at an early age, the doctrines and precepts of the Christian Religion" (Nute, June 1954, 15).

But the lodges of my people—the children of my race? They were no
more: the War-Cry died out when Moos-toos [buffalo] sent a last call to his
mate by lost rivers.

Where my people sat in Council is a great Silence. My people! . . .
They have become as a wraith and as a shadow!

I tell these things that the Moons to come shall keep memory of my people.

This apologia by Hayes is free, at least, of the racism that pervades *Lords
of the North*. Her friendship with the mixed-blood poet E. Pauline Johnson perhaps influenced her attitude toward Indian history and made her
more sensitive than many white writers were to the lost cultural heritage
of the Indians. Hayes's legend suggests issues dealt with more directly in
Johnson's poem "A Cry from an Indian Wife":

> They but forget we Indians owned the land
> From ocean unto ocean; that they stand
> Upon a soil that centuries agone
> Was out sole kingdom and our right alone.
> They never think how they would feel to-day
> If some great nation from far away,
> Wresting their country from their hapless braves,
> Giving what they gave us— [*White Wampum* 17]

Fortunately two additional works show other, and more complex,
images of whites and Indians in the Red River settlement. Olive Knox's
Red River Shadows covers the period 1818–50; Jane Rolyat's *Lily of Fort
Garry* takes place in the 1860s. Knox's novel falls into the genre of
sentimental adventure stories, and Rolyat's has been called a potboiler.
Yet they are useful because they present positive images of Indians,
mixed-bloods, and Métis; in addition, they acknowledge the existence of
prejudice against Indians but at the same time show characters who
respect Indians and their traditions. These works come close to recreating the white-Indian relationships which characterized the early years of
the Red River settlement.[12]

In the opening pages of *Red River Shadows* Knox demonstrates that
prejudice against Indians existed. A small group of emigrants is about to
set out from Quebec with some voyageurs and two priests. Among them
is the central female character, Hélène LeStrange: "She had not wanted
to leave Montreal and go to a savage country. But she was an orphan; and
now at sixteen with her schooling finished at the Convent, she had no

---

12. I am, of course, relying heavily on Van Kirk's research on Indian-white relationships in
the fur-trade society of the Canadian Northwest.

home but with her childless Aunt Pauline and Uncle Victor. . . . 'I'll hate living among the savages,' she had stormed" (4). Her fate, however, is to marry a white "savage"—an Englishman who, as secretary to the chief factor, wears a civilized countenance which initially conceals an arrogant and corrupt disposition. The plot centers on this question: Will Hélène eventually be reunited with the dashing, kind, honest, brave voyageur who accompanied the expedition from Quebec? The answer is yes, but this plot, in itself, is obviously not very interesting. The historical figures who appear in the story line and the analysis of white-Indian relationships are the elements that sustain the interest of contemporary readers.

When the voyageurs and emigrant party land at Fort Douglas, the settlers rush out to meet the priests. One woman "throws" herself at Father Provencher's feet. She is introduced as "the wife of Lagimodière" (15), the first white woman to settle permanently in Indian territory. Knox makes no attempt to develop the comparison between the fictional Hélène, a reluctant emigrant, and the real-life Marie-Anne Lagimodière; nevertheless, Marie-Anne's presence is a reminder that the pioneer spirit usually attributed to men can be found in women as well. She was willing to adjust to wilderness conditions and, because she had known Indians in Quebec, she was not as intimidated by rumors as some women would have been. In fact, when the Métis attacked the Red River settlement in 1816 (the Seven Oaks massacre), an Indian chief, Peguis, took Marie-Anne and her children to his camp so she would be safe.

Three other historical figures provide insights into intermarriage between whites and Indians. When the new settlers arrive, Andrew McDermot is also on hand to meet them. He had come out with the first group of Selkirk settlers and become a trader. At that time, his marriage to an Indian woman assured profitable and fair dealings with members of her tribe.[13] At the end of the novel McDermot and another man, Chief Factor Ballenden, are influential in breaking the hold of the fur-trading companies so that hunters do not have to channel all their furs through Hudson's Bay Company or the North West Company. Although the novel doesn't reveal the fact, Ballenden also had a Métis wife.[14]

Knox keeps the dominant romantic interest focused on the

13. Van Kirk says that some Indian women would have preferred marriages to fur traders because of the likelihood of an easier way of life: more permanent homes, less strenuous physical work, lighter domestic duties, more comforts (80–82).

14. Mrs. Ballenden's story is told in part in Van Kirk (223–25).

Quebec couple, Hélène and her voyageur, Jean Ritchot. At all times, however, the reader is aware of the complex relationships of the people around them. Jean's friend Michael, a hunter, has an Irish father and an Indian mother. When Michael marries "a Red River girl," the daughter of one of the new settlers, the fur-trading society demonstrates its approval by holding "three days of dancing, and then a 'bee' to build them a cabin" (63–64). Other situations demonstrate the social equality of mixed-bloods. When grand parties were given at the forts, "all the elite were invited." It is apparent from the description of the women that "the elite" included mixed-bloods as well as whites: "Candles flickered in bracket sconces and candelabras, throwing a golden glow over young women whose blond, brown, or black hair was parted in the centre to fall in curls over the ears. White, creamy, and golden-bronze shoulders gleamed above low-cut gowns of every colour" (227).

These examples represent the positive side of intercultural relationships in the settlement. Petty—and sometimes vicious—prejudices existed as well, and Hélène's husband, Stanley Bowman, represents an extreme case. Despite the attractions of Jean Ritchot, Hélène married Bowman because he had a good position with the North West Company and fine manners. First Hélène discovers his "selfish passion" in bed. Then she discovers that he seduces the Métis girls while at the same time despising them. Other men who have administrative posts with the fur-trading companies or with the government are also exploitative in their relationships with Indian or mixed-blood women. The narration points out that George Simpson, the governor-in-chief, had "turned off" his Indian wife, "who had a daughter and two sons by him," after bringing an eighteen-year-old bride from England.[15]

In addition to these insights into relationships, Knox helps us to imagine life in the settlement where whites and Indians mix together. During a grasshopper plague, Marie-Anne Lagimodière is in tears as she looks at the fields crawling with grasshoppers. Her plight is especially poignant because she spent years living in tents until Jean-Baptiste finally agreed to build a cabin on the banks of the Red River. In contrast, the

---

15. "Turning off" involves making arrangements for separation from one's wife. Van Kirk says that "'turning off' resulted in part from the Indian view that marriage did not constitute a permanent bond, but there were undoubtedly some traders who unfeelingly exploited this attitude to suit their own purposes" (51). For information relating to George Simpson's "country wives" see Van Kirk, who comments that Simpson "regarded mixed-blood women primarily as objects for sexual gratification" (161).

Indians and Métis are described as "taking the disaster stolidly, even gathering buckets of grasshoppers, pulling off their legs and wings, and frying them in grease, or making them into soup" (25). On a happier occasion, New Year's Day, 1836, the settlers call out greetings: "Happy New Year"; "Bonne et Heureuse Année"; "Bliadhna Mhath Ur!" "Gluckliches Neues Jahr"; "Ke Ku we meyo ooske-uskewinisse!" (123–24).

The author recognizes many of the problems that forced settlers from Scotland, Ireland, Switzerland, and eastern Canada to seek homes in the West; at the same time, she is aware of the consequences for the Indians and presents their perspective through the words of Chief Peguis:

> "Many years I am friend of my white brothers," Peguis began. "But the white man has taken many things from the red man. Before he came our rivers were full of fish and our buffalo many on the plains. Now the buffalo herds grow smaller . . . our fish are harder to catch. Sometimes our women and children go hungry. Now the white man take our land, too. [81–82]

In *The Lily of Fort Garry*, which is set in the 1860s, the Indians' situation is described in bleaker terms: "Once on this land they had been sole owners and lords. Here and out on the plains they now moved in obedience to the commands of the great Company. Once they had been in the foreground of the picture, but now silent, sometimes sullen, always passive, they occupied the background" (64–65). When we compare this passage with Chief Peguis's speech, we see that conditions have indeed worsened by the 1860s. Indians who had once participated in the fur trade and intermarried with the Scots, the English, and the French no longer have control over their lands and their way of life. *The Lily of Fort Garry* shows that some Indians had remained beyond the control of the fur-trading companies. They are described as "impressive and commanding." Their lives have not been disrupted by whites: "Far away where they roamed they were not in the background, but still the reigning force one felt. Certainly there was an importance about them, not shared by other groups of Indians" (65). At the end of the novel the protagonist chooses to marry the leader of this tribe rather than a wealthy Irishman who would introduce her to the luxuries of civilization.

Rolyat, author of this novel, goes a step further than Knox does in *Red River Shadows*. Knox showed that intermarriage between whites and Indians was accepted, but the white hero and heroine marry within their race. Rolyat dared to wed her "lily" with an Indian leader. Roger Mac-

Fig. 13   *Le petit Fort Garry,* from *L'Opinion publique,* Montreal, 31 August 1871, p.
423. Courtesy of Public Archives Canada C-7622. Today Lower Fort Garry
is a National Historic Park; its buildings have been restored to appear as
they did between 1835 and 1875.

Lachlin is a mixed blood but he has been educated in Europe; in addition
he elicited the respect of both government and fur-trade officials.[16]

Certainly the novel is a romantic adventure story, but like *Red
River Shadows* it provides descriptions of life at Upper Fort Garry. Moreover, the novel enables us to see settlement life during the 1860s from a
woman's perspective: it is essentially Margaret Moore's story—she is the
lily of Fort Garry. Margaret lives on the fringe of the white community,
close to the Métis settlements along the Red River. "Society" includes
those who live at the fort: the chief factor, the bourgeois, and the traders.
(See figs. 13 and 14.) Margaret Moore's family is respectable, but her
father is a nonconformist whose relish for the winter hunting trips with

16. By plotting her novel in this way, Rolyat was vulnerable to attack for indulging in
fantasy; indeed, a contemporary critic has dismissed *The Lily of Fort Garry* as a "potboiler"
(Thompson 152).

AN INDIAN LODGE IN THE NORTH-WEST.

Fig. 14   *An Indian Lodge in the North-West,* from *Canadian Pictures* by the Marquis of Lorne.

the Indians and Métis makes him insensitive to the needs of his family. His wife and eldest son are forced to assume full responsibility for the farm, which provides more security than the income earned by Moore through fur trading.

Margaret is educated at the Red River Academy along with the children of the fort people.[17] At the opening of the novel, her education has been completed and she is back on the farm with her mother and brothers. Although her mother does outside work, Margaret is limited to traditional female chores inside the house: "If she should tan or sprout even the tiniest freckle, or if her hands should be other than very white and very soft, it would be a tragedy" (17). Margaret finds these limitations frustrating; she wants to be more useful to her family. Her mother, however, is training her to be a lady so that she can marry into the elite of

17. The Red River Academy was founded in 1832 (Van Kirk 148).

Fort Garry. Margaret suspects that the man has already been identified—
Colin Currie, whose father is described as "an important personage" in
the settlement: "Besides being a skilful farmer he was a merchant and a
'free-trader.' That is, he dealt with the Indians on his own account and
himself operated a line of boats to York Factory, connecting with the
ships overseas. He was on both sides of Scottish parentage but he had a
wife 'of the country.' 'Wild Rose' as Mrs. Currie was still called, in all
fondness, now almost helplessly fat, was reputed to have been in girlhood, one of the most beautiful of Cree princesses" (60). This portrait of
a mixed marriage is both unexpected and rare. As Van Kirk points out in
her study of the early fur-trade society, Red River settlement women who
published their reminiscences had heard the real-life stories of their
families in the Red River settlement; nevertheless, they did not admit
that these were mixed-blood families in the 1923 publication, *Women of
Red River*. Therefore Rolyat's description of the Currie family is interesting and unique. In fact, the Currie family is probably modeled after the
Andrew McDermot family referred to in *Red River Shadows* and discussed
in Van Kirk's *Many Tender Ties*.

Colin Currie and his sisters have been educated in the East; they
live at the center of the social life of the settlement. Margaret, isolated
on the Moore farm a long walking distance from the fort, envies the
secure social life and interesting activities of the Currie family. She even
wonders if part of her isolation isn't the result of having "pure transatlan-
tic blood" (152)—of being the "lily" rather than being mixed-blood.
Given this context, it becomes understandable why Margaret eventually
chooses to marry an Indian: what better way to "belong" than to marry a
man who will be at the center of tribal affairs?[18] One of the first times she
sees Roger MacLachlin, the mixed-blood whom she marries, he is talking
with the elders of his tribe. They tell him that they want him to return
and, if he wishes, he may bring a white wife as well as the white man's

18. Glenda Riley's comments on intermarriage are useful in interpreting Margaret's actions:
"It might be hypothesized . . . that the female value system permitted relatively easy adjustment
to the concept of intermarriage. Female values made it possible for women to enter into warm and
comfortable situations with Indians in which intimate relationships could develop. In addition,
because female ideals focused on home and family, women were not usually as dedicated as men to
the eradication of native Americans and the seizure of their property. Thus, it can be argued that it
was at least possible that white women were more accepting of the idea of marriage between
themselves and native men than were their white menfolk" (*Women and Indians* 182).

religion: " 'You belong in part to us, my brother, yet we do not wish you to live again the religion of Tapatamee, your mother, unless you so desire. We believe that the Great Spirit of all has made our religion good and sufficient for us, but it may not be sufficient for you. And if you have, my brother, while here, chosen a pale princess as your bride, we will be pleased to carry her thither with you, to our happy land where the plains look up to the great high hills' " (72). At this point Margaret does not even know MacLachlin's name, but she finds him attractive in a way that Colin Currie, also mixed-blood, is not.

Another passage provides further preparation for Margaret's attraction to Roger MacLachlin. "What was the difference, she began to wonder, between those of Indian blood and themselves, in essence?" The Currie girls are handsome; Colin is not. Roger MacLachlin is handsome. She recalls her sight of him earlier that day, standing with her father who had just returned from the winter hunt: "Did one imagine that when he removed his hat, the sun shining on his raven hair lent it rainbow tints?" (126). At this point her attraction to MacLachlin is primarily physical.

Other scenes, described from Margaret's perspective, show the reasons why Indian customs appeal to her. The mixed-blood families who live nearby are described as "their nearest and best neighbors" (15) and as "their laughter-loving, philharmonic neighbours" (16). When the hunters return, Margaret contemplates their celebrations: "What laughter, rippling, sunny as the water, the laughter of a people who lived in a golden age in a gold land, a land of plenty, who had gone forth on an adventure, had met the buffalo" (120). The rest of this description, however, takes a serious and sardonic turn: the hunters have returned with enough furs to trade for "fine velvet, even enough to buy sparkling liquors to quench a long prairie drought" (120). The Indians' golden age has been tarnished by the white man's customs.

Margaret's father also prejudices her in favor of the Indian way of life. When he returns from the winter hunt, he gives one of his favorite lectures:

> "By gad, the Indians, thinks I, have the way that shoots the country. It's thim that has the best way. The Indian to my way of thinkin'—called a savage, whatever—is a highly developed human bain', highly developed in the wilderness and by the wilderness. Sure ages ago he took the world as he found it and everything was ready for him, wasn't it?—and he didn't try to alter the Divine Creation at all, at all, but tried to grow to mate it and in time he fits himself to it, the world as he finds it. . . .
>
> "The white man makes a great mistake. He sets out to change the

airth, brings in his quare machines and all, loses his muscles and his interest
and destroys the very manes of sustenance intinded for him." [145]

This passage foreshadows the eventual disappearance of the father, who
fails to return after the next winter's hunt. During the summer months at
home he refuses the offer of an important job at the fort; this refusal
frustrates his wife, who realizes that he is incorribibly attracted to the
wilderness. After sporadic attempts at helping his oldest son with the
farm, Robert Moore signs up for another expedition. He is never heard
from again.

In a "colophon" which concludes the novel, some picnickers read
a gravestone at an old Indian mission:

> Sacred to the Memory of Samuel Moore
> 1785–1855
> Beloved Husband of Sally, Daughter of
> Chief Wessagun

This is Margaret Moore's uncle—the uncle her father presumably
searched for every time he went on the winter hunts. One of the picnickers had known the Moore family and she says that there was gossip
about the possibility that Robert Moore, too, had a country wife.

Margaret, like her father and uncle, chose the Indian way, as did
Roger MacLachlin, who had his choice between living in the Indian
community or in the fur-trading community. He was respected by the
white community and could have played an important role in colony
affairs. His commitment, however, was to "The People." The picnicker
comments on these events in a way that suggests how the Fort Garry
community reacted to Margaret's decision. The picnicker says that the
family had made great sacrifices for Margaret, but she " 'chose her own
husband—something of a victory in her day—every age has its victo-
ries—who was so meek—but who inherited the earth while on it—after
upsetting it. . . . At any rate she broke countless hearts when she took
that long journey with her dusky husband, that long, hard journey across
the plains—so long undiscovered as to prove, surely, undiscoverable—
to some point of devastating crudity—it was thought—after Fort Garry' " (287). Margaret is, finally, her father's daughter, searching for the
golden age of the Indians.

One American novel describes an early community similar to the
Red River colony—Maud Lovelace's *Early Candlelight,* which is set at
Fort Snelling in the early 1800s (see fig. 15). This novel, too, inter-
weaves the lives of several groups of people: the easterners attached to the

Fig. 15   *View of Fort Snelling,* attributed to Edward K. Thomas. Courtesy of The Minneapolis Institute of Arts, The Julia B. Bigelow Fund.

fort, including the military men and their families;[19] the "squatters" who "ran their sheep and dug in their gardens and gave thanks to the good God that they had a bit of this pleasant land for their own" (15); the voyageurs, traders, and guides; and finally, the Sioux and Chippewas who came and went, depending on the time of year. The Indian villages of Black Dog, Penichon, and Shakopay are a short distance away. On the one hand, ladies at the fort sipped wine in front of the fireplace or danced quadrilles with the soldiers and officers; in contrast, Indians "huddled" in

19. Van Kirk's study of male-female relationships in the fur-trade society of the Canadian Northwest is useful in helping readers to imagine the society that surrounded Fort Snelling in its early years. Van Kirk points out, however, that "the fur-trade society of Western Canada appears to have been exceptional. In most other areas of the world, sexual contact between European men and native women has usually been illicit in nature and essentially peripheral to the white man's trading or colonizing ventures" (4). Because many of those who lived near Fort Snelling had come from Canada, some attitudes and situations parallel those found in the early Red River settlement.

tepees, traders waited for spring in their stockades, voyageurs existed on corn and tallow, "singing their wild songs to pass the long nights" (63–64).[20]

The main character is a young girl, Deedee DuGay, whose mother is an Irish immigrant and whose father is a French Canadian. Her father's first wife had been an Indian woman who died; therefore Deedee has mixed-blood brothers. She grows up moving freely among the settlers, the Indians, and the traders. She feels somewhat less comfortable among the people at the fort because their manners, speech, and living habits seem so elegant. She speaks some Sioux, the French of her father and the voyageurs, and the English of her mother. The DuGay family has adopted some Indian ways and respects those ways that are different. The author explains, for example, that "the DuGays never refused food to the Indians. They understood better than did the later settlers the red man's primitive conviction that while anyone had food, no one should go hungry. They accepted with tactful enthusiasm the beaded moccasins and shot bags, the well made bows and arrows, which the Sioux never failed to bring them in return" (175). The author's tone in this passage is somewhat patronizing, but the description of settlers living in harmony with Indians is a refreshing one.

Midway through the novel, when the Sioux and Chippewas sign the treaty which brings them money (but robs them of their land), they celebrate at the DuGay cabin: Deedee's mother knows a party has been arranged when three Indians arrive, make the announcement, and then curl up on the floor to sleep. Deedee's mother is at ease with the Indians. When one of her stepsons, Narcisse, falls in love with a Sioux girl, she approves of the choice. When forced to choose between Indian custom and white ways, however, she sometimes sets limits. Deedee asks for an Indian cradle for carrying the babies around; her mother objects and Deedee has to settle for a less convenient but more "civilized" cart.

The novel traces the inevitable erosion of Indian rights as the Sioux and Chippewas are manipulated, deceived, and finally forced from their lands. At the same time, Lovelace weaves into the plot a stereotypic but nevertheless appropriate form of exploitation—the abuse of an Indian girl by a captain from the fort. Narcisse DuGay, one of Deedee's stepbrothers, has negotiated with an old Indian woman to marry her

20. For an account of life at Fort Snelling, see Charlotte Ouisconsin Van Cleve's reminiscences, "Three Score Years and Ten": Life-Long Memories of Fort Snelling, Minnesota, and Other Parts of the West.

granddaughter, Light Between Clouds. The woman reminds Narcisse that her granddaughter is very beautiful: "Her father could get blankets and ponies and kettles and much red cloth if he were to marry her to a chief of his own people or to a great white trader." Why, she asks Narcisse, is he not marrying Light Between Clouds immediately? Narcisse replies that he wants it to be "a real marriage in a church, such as white women have" (80). Narcisse, by choosing to do things the white way rather than the Indian way—remember, he is part Indian himself—loses Light Between Clouds. He goes away on an expedition, planning to return with a priest. While he is gone, Captain Mowrie arranges to take possession of Light Between Clouds. The grandmother, however, should not be blamed for making this possible: from her perspective the captain is not only an important person but also wealthy. She assumes that he will treat her granddaughter with the same respect and dignity that an Indian would show toward a second wife.[21] When Narcisse returns and discovers his loss, he shoots and wounds the captain. While the two men are fighting, Light Between Clouds hangs herself.

This novel, like *The Lily of Fort Garry*, develops the story of a white girl growing up among whites, Indians, and mixed-bloods who accept each other as friends and equals. Deedee, however, marries the wealthy, educated New Englander, Jasper Page, who watches over the settlement with the benign eye of a seigneur. In both novels the most prejudiced and the least tolerant of cultural differences are the upper class, with the exception, of course, of Jasper Page.

Several novels present images of Indians and Indian-white relationships in the Midwest. In three of Bess Streeter Aldrich's novels, people react to Indians in typical ways. In *Song of Years*, set in the 1850s, rumors of Indians are rampant in the Red Cedar Valley, eastern Iowa. Jeremiah Martin, the hero, observes that he has heard rumors for two years, but there has been no real trouble. Reference is made, however, to the deaths of fifty settlers resulting from an Indian attack at Lake Okoboji in March 1857. In *Spring Came on Forever*, the new settlers take great satisfaction in the fact that Nebraska, just admitted as a state, is "no longer a place to pass through but a place to stay" (80). Nevertheless, a young German immigrant, Amalie, finds it difficult to adjust. She feels the strain of hard work and trying to please her husband; moreover, she is

---

21. Attitudes toward polygamy are discussed in Van Kirk (37–38, 82–83) and in Riley, *Women and Indians* (230–39).

haunted by the fear of rattlesnakes and "marauding Indians" (93). In *A Lantern in Her Hand*, Aldrich describes an "Indian scare." When a rider sends out word that Indians are on their way, each family loads food and other essential supplies into a wagon and, as quickly as possible, drives to the biggest, sturdiest house in the community: "Already the men were stationing guns near windows and barring and barricading doors. Several women were running bullets in the little salamander stove. . . . One woman was hysterical; another a little out of her mind from fear, kept wanting to go back outdoors where there was air" (19–20). They wait all night, but nothing happens. The next day word arrives that the Indians had turned north: "The Indian scare, then, had come to nothing. The wagons went lumbering back across the prairie and through the damp, dark river" (20).

As Glenda Riley has pointed out in her study of white settlers and Indians, women headed west expecting the worst from Indians. Riley summarizes some of the attitudes of white emigrants:

> Most westering women struck out for the trans-Mississippi West with their minds conjuring apparitions of inferior native people, who were hostile, vicious, and evil, interspersed with enigmatic visions of superior native beings, who were friendly, kind, and courageous. Because the likeness of the "bad" Indian was usually dominant, however, most female migrants' expectations tended to be negative rather than positive. When they finally reached the trail, their nerves were taut with fearful anticipation; they were ready for the worst of fates in the hands of American Indians. [*Women and Indians on the Frontier* 83]

Once on the prairie, women's fears persisted because of rumors of attacks; Aldrich's novel effectively describes this situation. In addition, Riley points out that historical documents such as diaries and letters "were punctuated by impending crises and predictions of doom, only to end on a rather anticlimactic and peaceful note" (91).

Another motif recurs in the fiction: women not only feared Indians but also hated them. Hélène, the young woman in *Red River Shadows*, insists that she'll "hate living among the savages" (4). In *Little House on the Prairie* the Wilder family leaves Wisconsin and heads for Kansas, which is still "Indian country." Laura repeatedly expresses her desire to see one of the papooses Pa has spoken about. She is curious about the Indians in spite of the fact that Ma and even the dog Jack have expressed their dislike for Indians:

> "Why don't you like Indians, Ma?" Laura asked, and she caught a drip of molasses with her tongue.

"I just don't like them; and don't lick your fingers, Laura," said Ma.

"This is Indian country, isn't it?" Laura said. "What did we come to their country for, if you don't like them?"

Ma said she didn't know whether this was Indian country or not. She didn't know where the Kansas line was. But whether or no, they would not be here long. Pa had word from a man in Washington that the Indian Territory would be open to settlement soon. [46–47]

Pa Wilder balances Ma's negative attitude toward Indians: "Indians would be as peaceable as anybody else," he believes, "if they were let alone. . . . They had been moved west so many times that naturally they hated white folks" (284).

Several other writers who record the experiences of settlers in a variety of locations provide examples of women who dislike Indians. Nell, the hero of the Iowa settlement novel *Black Soil*, has "a horror of Indians" (Donovan 169), but her German neighbor has neither fear nor respect: she chases Indians off her land with a pitchfork (168). Nell, who is reasonable and likeable in almost every situation, is irrational about Indians, proclaiming that an Indian is bad enough in his right senses, but given distressing circumstances will invariably act in the worst possible way.

Another settler enters Iowa with some of these stereotypical preju-dices against Indians. In Heacock's *Crinoline to Calico*, Castle begins fussing about Indians and her husband, who has had some experience with Indians, simultaneously discredits and compliments them. He tells Castle that if Indians think white people are afraid of them, they'll take everything they can get: "Cowardice is the most contemptible of sins in the eyes of an Indian," Jonathan tells Castle (36). Indeed, Castle is manipulated by an Indian who is so intimidating that she loads him down with corn from the corncrib when he asks for it. Later in the story an Indian takes some precious supplies and then, passing by the clothesline, plucks off Castle's red petticoat. Castle is outraged and runs after him, screaming abuses. The Indian laughingly returns her garment (37).

In Elisabeth Ford's novel *No Hour of History*, Elizabeth Ash is asked to support her husband David's new business venture in Iowa. Her first reaction is typical: " 'But the Indians—' It was Elizabeth who spoke fearfully" (44). She is assured that the Indians had been moved further west to Kansas a few years earlier, in 1846. Part one of the novel ends with the two men contemplating the profits to be made from eight hundred acres of rich farmland in Iowa. Part two opens with this passage, which represents the author's view of expansion into the West: "By the time David crossed the mighty Mississippi the white man had nearly finished his dark and dastardly business with the Bronze People. By conquest and chicanery he had slowly driven them westward for two and a half centuries. The brave and simple savage faced only the farther ocean and the setting sun. Civilized man's uncivilized theft of an inheritance was almost complete" (47).

These examples show that women novelists were well aware that many women carried with them, as they traveled west, vivid images of threats and harassment by Indians. After settling into their new homes, they continued to hear rumors and, in some cases, went through the ordeal of conflicts with Indians.

Many stories about the early years of settlement provide examples of women who adapted to "the Indian situation." Two patterns emerge: some women have fleeting encounters with Indians, like Castle who reclaimed her red petticoat; others depend on Indians for survival and develop friendships.

Usually Indians surprise the unsuspecting mistress of the household, but in No Hour of History five Indians find only a small boy at home. These are Sac and Fox Indians returned to their old Iowa home from Kansas in the 1850s. The narrator says that "the red men were for the most part peaceful and harmless . . . although there persisted vague rumors of their attempted kidnappings of white children" (Ford 70). One day when Elizabeth Ash is at a neighbor's, her eight-year-old son, Jimmy, sees Indians coming and shoves his little sister under the sofa. The Indians enter, look around, and pluck a feather from the parrot. Although Jimmy has heard stories about the Spirit Lake massacres, he nevertheless dares to block the doorway when he sees the Indians are about to enter the sacred Sunday parlor. The Indians turn and leave as quietly as they had come (69–71).

An example of an Indian visit in Little House on the Prairie is typical. Laura and her sister Mary are playing out on the prairie when they see "two naked wild men" walking along the Indian trail; they enter the cabin and Laura is terrified that they'll do something to Ma and the baby. When Laura reaches the cabin, she finds the two Indians standing by the fireplace. Ma is cooking cornbread for them, which they eat with great enthusiasm, even picking crumbs from the floor (Wilder 134–140). Again, fears of the settlers are shown to be unfounded.

Wilder described another episode with Indians in The First Four

Years, the novel about her first years of marriage to Manly Wilder. Although Laura has grown accustomed to Indian ways over the years, she knows that "Indians nearly went on the warpath a little way west, and even now they often threatened the railroad camps" (31). On one occasion Indians come to the house while Manly is away. When Laura won't let them in, they go to the barn. Her horse, Trixy, is in the barn and, thinking that they might steal Trixy, she runs to the barn and orders them out. One of the Indians touches her arm and she slaps his face. This makes the Indian angry, but the others laugh. The one who appears to be the leader apparently likes her spunkiness: "Then with signs pointing to himself, his pony, and then with a sweep of his arm toward the west, he said, 'You go—me—be my squaw.'" When Laura stamps her foot, he smilingly accepts her rejection.

Wilder's stories also demonstrate that Indians are frequently helpers. In *Little House on the Prairie* the Ingalls family has trespassed in Indian territory and, Pa realizes, the only reason the Indians do not harm them is that an Osage leader, Soldat du Chêne, has given orders to the tribe that insure the protection of the Ingalls family. In *The Long Winter* an old Indian enters Harthorn's store where Pa is talking to some men. "'Heap big snow come. . . . Heap big snow, big wind. . . . Many moons,'" the Indian tells them, using his fingers to show how many. "The Indian meant that every seventh winter was a hard winter and that at the end of three times seven years came the hardest winter of all. He had come to tell the white men that this coming winter was the twenty-first winter, that there would be seven months of blizzards" (61–62). Pa trusts the Indian's experience and immediately moves his family to town for the winter.[22]

Other novels examine in greater detail the ways Indians helped settlers. *A Circle of Trees* opens with two children, Danish immigrants, playing in the foundation of an elegant house that had been razed during the New Ulm massacre. Most Indians have moved further west, but some who are friends of the whites remained behind. One of these is Flying

22. Research focusing on Indian-white conflicts has drawn attention from the ways Indians helped whites to adapt to the frontier. Riley discusses the exchange of goods and services and the interest of some women in attending Indian celebrations and ceremonies as well as in visiting Indian homes. According to Riley, men were much less apt to form friendships with Indians (*Women and Indians* 168–75). Wilder's prairie books are apparently typical in describing the formal relationships between a white man and the Indians he meets. Ma Wilder, however, is unreceptive to any kind of contact with Indians.

Cloud, who tells the children that "she stays here because she always lived here, and she'll stay until her husband [who is dead] tells her in a dream to go" (Faralla 33). When she gathers herbs and roots for medicines, she takes the children with her so they can learn to identify the plants. She teaches them Indian folklore and, in the process, tries to teach them reverence for nature. The children remember that when they first came to Minnesota, before their mother died, they had eaten unripened berries and vomited. Flying Cloud came on her horse, carrying a leather bag which was decorated with quill embroidery. She fixed a tea that made the children feel better. On other occasions Flying Cloud and the mother sit and talk together.

The children are fortunate because two of the adults living in their home respect Indians. The housekeeper, also an immigrant, tells the children to learn everything they can from Flying Cloud. Reilly-O, who has accepted an invitation to stay with the family through the winter, used to live among the Indians; he shares with the children the Indian wisdom he has acquired. Reilly-O has adopted Indian clothing, Indian tobacco, and Indian views of nature. He tells the children "there's no use shaking your fist in the face of the elements. . . . Be humble, ask for mercy and the grace of pity. That's what the Indian does, because he knows he's helpless in the hands of Nature. And acknowledging this he also has confidence in the supernatural. He seeks wisdom from it and guidance and security" (87).

When Bestemor, the children's grandmother, becomes ill, Flying Cloud brings her a tonic made of herbs, roots, and juniper berries. These two old women find comfort in each other, both being close to death. Flying Cloud says she is being summoned by the ghost of her husband beating the medicine drum. Bestemore has heard "the Death Horse so often now that she was certain he would show himself at the window one day before long." Flying Cloud contradicts her: surely she has been hearing drum beats, not horses' hoofs. " 'One and the same thing,' " Bestemor said. 'Drum beats, hoof beats,' " thus acknowledging that the images may be different but the experiences are the same (36).

A humorous view of an Indian helping white settlers is provided by Josephine Donovan. An Indian named Wild Goose has been lying in the long grass watching some young people. He is especially interested in the girl named Sheila. He had seen her once before and affectionately named her Sun-in-the-Hair. When he sees a boy named Herman teasing Sheila, Wild Goose runs to her and takes her by the arm. Sheila screams: the rumors have led her to expect the worst from an Indian. One of the boys hits Wild Goose on the head with a candlestick and Wild Goose falls, unconscious, to the ground. Sheila's stepmother, Nell, has him placed on a cot. She washes his wound and watches him through the night. Katto, her German neighbor who was going to stand guard with her, has fallen asleep. Nell, frightened and fatigued, feels disoriented. The night seems long and Katto's pitchfork has fallen to her side. Nell feels alone and "cut off from life." She realizes how ridiculous it is—"she guarding the Indian, Katto guarding her." She feels so far away from the New England home where she had grown up and worn clean, neat aprons to school and had heard Jenny Lind sing at the opera house. She wonders: "'Did those things ever happen really?'" She listens to the sounds of the train in the distance, wolves, the hounds on the next homestead, Katto's snores. Reality returns. She feels bound to the Indian; in fact, she feels bound to the "strange prairie: she was part of it, influencing other lives, becoming affected by others. This was the West" (194–96). She unties Wild Goose, having concluded that he is harmless and that the children had misinterpreted his actions.

She does not, however, approve of his fondness for Sheila. Therefore, a few days later when she agrees to take a neighbor girl to town to meet her lover and the preacher—the father won't consent to the marriage—Nell realizes she has to take Wild Goose with her to keep him away from Sheila. It isn't until after the marriage when she is ready to return to the homestead that she realizes that she and Baby Alice will be alone with an Indian. All her old fears of Indians return to haunt her and she comforts herself with the words of a friend: "'I trust an Indian further than lots of white men.'" Her husband, she recalls, had said "'Treat 'em decent and they'll let you alone'" (217). Near home, when they realize a prairie fire is surrounding them, Wild Goose drives the oxen into a slough where Nell and Baby Alice wait in safety while Wild Goose flails the grass with his wet shirt until the fire dies down. Nell has been rescued by Wild Goose; she trusts him, but she still fears the attraction that he feels for Sheila, to which Sheila seems to respond.

The Donovan novel provides one answer to questions raised by Glenda Riley in her study of white women and Indians: "How then would women react when they were actually exposed to individual natives on a personal basis? Would they see only the Indians whom they had been prepared to encounter, or would they prove to be flexible and open enough to revise their views once they had confronted real people?"

(*Women and Indians* 119). Initially Nell was, if not hysterical, at least deeply distressed by the presence of Wild Goose. But common sense, combined with Wild Goose's kindness, helped Nell to judge the young man on the basis of his actions alone, apart from whatever stereotypes she might have retained about Indians as a group.

Riley also points out that many women found the first Indians they met were not nearly as troublesome as they had anticipated (*Women and Indians* 124). An example is found in *The Plow-Woman*, in which Eleanor Gates explores the possibilities of a mutually supportive relationship between an Indian and a young white woman named Dallas.[23] At the beginning of the novel, Dallas nurses an injured Indian, nicknamed Squaw Charley. Out of gratitude, Squaw Charley provides Dallas with sticks for fuel. From this point their friendship is firm, demonstrating that individual whites and Indians could trust and help each other even when the two groups were in conflict. The irreconcilable differences between white ways and Indian ways is symbolized by the confinement of Ojibwas at the fort, and the novel ends with Indians attacking the fort to free the captives.

In describing relationships between white women and Indians, some writers choose to analyze two additional possibilities—intermarriage and the condition that has been popularly referred to as "gone Indian." In the novel by Rolyat, Margaret, the "lily of Fort Garry" did both: she married an Indian and went with him into the wilderness where the only whites were traders or voyageurs. In Donovan's *Black Soil*, Nell discovers that Wild Goose had a white grandmother who "went Indian":

> His grandmother had been a white woman. She was loved by a chief and lived in happiness with his people. When old, she became ill. His grandfather carried her back to her people to see "good medicine man." She recovered and asked to go back to the Indians, but her people said never would they let her go back. In the spring she began to fail again and spoke often of her husband and children. . . . One morning when the trees were shooting forth green leaves and spring scents filled the air, she could remain no longer; she disappeared, traveling east instead of west, to elude her people. She picked up with movers headed west who were afraid of Indians. She promised them a safe trip, and they carried her as far as Big Muddy. [164]

At the end of the novel Sheila Connor, too, chooses the Indian way of life, a choice that baffles one critic and leads him to discredit the novel as

23. Another work by Gates, *The Biography of a Prairie Girl*, is quite negative in its portrayal of Indians.

a whole: "It is difficult to take seriously a novel in which a girl named Sheila Connor is discovered to be part Indian and in the last chapter rides off into the sunset with her Indian lover" (quoted in Andrews 34).

A frequent motif in adventure stories of the westward movement has been the male who has chosen Indian society rather than white culture. When the same choice is made by a woman, however, the effect is quite different. White women who were attracted to the wilderness and identified themselves with the Indian way of life threatened many American males.[24]

Prairie women writers are willing to explore the positive aspects of white-Indian relationships. At the same time they examine mixed marriages that don't work and relationships in which Indian women are victimized by white men. Examples from the Red River settlement novels have already been discussed, but other significant illustrations deserve comment.

In the early years of the fur trade Indians recognized that both the individual and the tribe could beenfit when a native woman married a white man. However, not all white men had the appropriate qualifications from the Indian's point of view, as a white man points out in Ostenso's O River, Remember! Julian Fordyce, sent to Canada by a fur-trading company, met "a girl with eyes blue-black as grapes on a vine, and hair like the mane of a wild horse. Slim and beautiful—half Scotch, half Cree." Fordyce explains that she died in childbirth: her Cree mother had put a curse on her for marrying "an outcast Englishman" (63).

Another man expresses bitterness because his Indian wife would not stay with him: "Between all the things I could lay at her feet, this house—and it cost a pretty penny—and the expensive furniture, and dresses made in Winnipeg, . . . even servants to look after my Indian,

24. This attitude persists because, as Susan Armitage says, "the frontier myth is a male myth, preoccupied with stereotypically male issues like courage, physical bravery, honor and male friendship. While these are important themes, they by no means encompass the reality and complexity of the frontier experience" ("Women's Literature" 5). Glenda Riley asks the question: "Why haven't the stories of white women [who have formed alliances with Indian males] received attention from novelists and screenwriters? Where is the media saga of the female settler who sent west to become the happy wife of an Indian and the fulfilled mother of 'half-breed' children? When nineteenth-century media did broach this theme, it usually described female captives who wanted to return to their Indian husbands and children. The standard explanation for such 'odd' behavior was that these women had been permanently dehumanized through their association with American Indians or that they were ashamed to face white society because of their debasement" (Women and Indians 183).

well, between that and the tribe, it was the wigwam, the reservation, she chose" (Roy, *Children of My Heart* 144). The angry husband does not try to understand his wife's dissatisfaction with white ways and values, nor does he acknowledge the pain she felt when he would not permit her to take the child with her. Another variation occurs in North's *Morning in the Land.* A few years before the story begins, a white woman had been scalped by Indians; her daugher, Maria, was then raised by the Indians. When Maria grew up she married a Winnebago who, from the point of view of the male hero, had a "strange hold" on her. Thinking her husband has been killed, Maria marries the hero. The Indian husband returns, however, and Maria goes away with him, taking her Indian child but leaving her white child with the father. She leaves a note behind, telling her white husband that she didn't want to leave. This implies, of course, that marriage to the white man was better than the marriage to the Indian. The situation in the novel is dissatisfying to the reader because there are too many innuendos about Maria's life with the Winnebagoes. It is never clear if the hero's prejudices against the Indians interfere with his ability to understand Maria's situation or if the author herself has negative attitudes toward Indians.

Sometimes white religious practices interfered in relationships. Many missionaries, Protestant ministers, and Roman Catholic priests disapproved of marriage *à la façon du pays* and failed to recognize the integrity of long-term commitments in mixed marriages.[25] In *Red River Shadows* an Indian woman was converted to the Roman Catholic religion. When she realized that her "country marriage" was not recognized by the Church, she left her husband, a captain at the fort, and took her child back to her tribe (Knox 77). She rejected white culture because it adhered to a religion that had failed to acknowledge the sanctity of a couple's relationship.

A story by Kate Simpson Hayes centers on the victimization of a Métis woman. Hayes exhibits a curious combination of respect mixed with condescension. The narrator of the story "Aweena" describes him-

25. According to Van Kirk, missionaries condemned marriage á la façon du pays as immoral. "While they eventually succeeded in gaining wide-spread recognition for the necessity of church marriage, this attack on fur-trade custom ironically had a detrimental effect on the position of native women. The double standard arrived with a vengeance. Incoming traders, feeling free to ignore the marital obligations implied by the 'custom of the country', increasingly looked upon native women as objects for temporary sexual gratification, not as wives" (145–46).

self as a "beggarly red-coat." He is a low-ranking policeman in love with Aweena, the daughter of Chief Factor McDonald and his Indian wife.[26] Aweena has returned from four years at a finishing school in Scotland, and invitations have been distributed for her coming out party. Almost simultaneously, the narrator is issued orders by his rival in love, who is also his superior officer. The narrator must ride ninety miles to arrest an old Indian chief by the name of Wap-et-ah-wok.

The narrator finds Wap-et-ah-wok weeping over a grave and is, of course, moved by the man's grief. He listens as the old man tells about losing his wife many years before. This wife, also named Aweena, became ill; he carried her many miles to the white medicine man. The medicine man fell in love with her, drugged Wap-et-ah-wok, and secreted the woman away. When Wap-et-ah-wok recovered he was told that his wife was dead and the medicine man showed him a fresh grave. Later Wap-et-ah-wok discovered his wife was not dead, stabbed the medicine man in the back, and then fled.

As he listens to this story, the narrator realizes that the "medicine man" is Chief Factor MacDonald; the Aweena of the story is his own Aweena's mother. When the narrator returns to the fort with the old chief, MacDonald witnesses the painful reunion between Wap-et-ah-wok and his wife, confesses his guilt, and allows his daughter to marry the man of her choice.

The victimization of Métis women by white men is recounted in numerous other prairie novels over the next hundred years. The Métis character seems to have considerable appeal, first, I expect, because of the renowned beauty of the Métis women. Also, the Métis women were more vulnerable than Indian women because they frequently straddled two worlds—the Indian's and the whiteman's—and some were forced to sever bonds with their tribes and live entirely in the white community. At the opposite end of the continuum from Hayes's stories is Byrna Barclay's *Summer of the Hungry Pup*. A ninety-six-year-old Cree woman tells how a woman was victimized by both an Indian and a white man. The Indian man, Scratches, had never earned a "Real Name," according to the Old Woman; he failed to do anything to earn status within the

26. Earlier in the century a chief factor by the name of Archibald McDonald had been committed to a marriage á la façon du pays for ten years; then he and his mixed-blood wife were married in a church ceremony which, McDonald makes clear, had less meaning for him than the first marriage. Van Kirk notes that McDonald was anxious about supporting and educating a large family of thirteen children, but he loved them and was proud of them (137–38; 157–58).

tribe. Because he is an outcast, he doesn't hesitate to make himself useful to the white men at the fort: "'He is one of those we call Government-blanket people or Old-Blue-coat-people,'" Old Woman says, "'and he lives by trading women instead of beavers'" (163). As a result of these dealings between Scratches and the soldiers, an Indian girl is raped. Old Woman recalls how she pitied the girl. In fact, she arranged for her own husband to take the girl as a second wife in order to protect her and to give her status within the tribe.

Salverson's *Dark Weaver* includes an important subplot involving a Métis woman and one of the emigrant leaders. Captain Marcusson, permitted by the mores of his class to have whatever women he wants, attends a Métis betrothal party. He dances with a lovely Métis woman, Marie Batoche, and subsequently arranges for her to be taken as a servant into the household of another family to insure that she will be kept nearby. When all the families move to the area designated for their new town, Marie moves with the settlers. She is pregnant with Marcusson's child when he becomes infatuated with another woman from Marie's tribe. Black Crow, the chief, reprimands Marie, telling her she should not "Meekly see [Marcusson] take another woman before our faces, as his kind takes our lands and lakes and furs and buffaloes!" (77). The white man's exploitation of Indian women symbolizes his usurpation of everything that had once belonged to the Indians.

The other woman, having dishonored the tribe by stealing Marie's lover, disappears after being beaten by members of her tribe. The Indian woman, not the white man, pays the consequences of an ill-advised affair. Marie, too, feels as though she is being punished when she becomes terribly ill after childbirth. When Marie dies, Oline, the woman for whom she has worked, adopts the child and raises her as her own to compensate for the disruptions in Indian lives caused by the white settlers.

At the time when Marcusson's exploits disrupt the tribal community, Black Crow confronts him and tries to make him understand the effects of his behavior. He tells Marcusson that "centuries before the coming of thieving traders, Black Crow's people had been a power in the land. A tribe strong and fearless and quick to avenge insult to its women long before the loose-moralled white man came out of the northern mists to steal their country and debauch their women. Even yet they held their women high. Marie Batoche was only an off-shoot—a frail creature tainted with white blood—but, none the less, they meant to see justice done her, justice to satisfy the Great Spirit!" (95). Black Crow goes on to remind Captain Marcusson that the tribe is dying out and is unable to protect its own people. He therefore charges Marcusson with raising Marie's child.

Another white man, Oscar Brear, listens to Black Crow's speech. His response to the situation is a chilling reminder of white racism. Although Oscar acknowledges Marcusson's "villainy," he nevertheless sympathizes with him: "Those sanguinary faces staring out from the rim of firelight were as savage as a circle of wolves waiting to pounce on their prey. Those horrible brutes, on whose faces cruelty and cunning marked the limits of intelligence, represented the sort of progeny Ephraim was asked to accept into his ancient line. Mein Gott!" (95). In the next paragraph the author continues where Oscar's thoughts leave off: "In face and form, disposition and temperament Marie might be French, but that could not alter the disagreeable facts of dual ancestry. Endearing or not she was likewise the innocent and helpless repository of savage traits and instincts" (96). This passage clearly reveals Salverson's prejudice; its wording echoes a 1930 autobiographical essay in which she writes about living on a farm near Selkirk, Manitoba, and watching Métis who were camped in a nearby field: "Another of my outstanding memories is of the marshy field in front of our house dotted with small fires round which grotesque and drunken figures rotated idiotically. These were Breeds, I learned; and very ably did they demonstrate the worst of a dual inheritance" (71). She is an outsider who incorrectly interprets the dance and, moreover, a racist who refuses to try to understand the rituals of another group.

Prejudice like Salverson's enabled white settlers to move into Indian territory and settle homesteads while feeling minimal guilt or, in some cases, none at all. One of Laura Ingalls Wilder's stories provides an excellent example. In *Little House on the Prairie* Wilder presents the Indians as the rightful owners of the land; nevertheless, Pa, though honest and respectful with the Indians, has the white man's irrational attitude that permits him to take land that rightfully belongs to the Indians. In the following passage, Laura represents the minority voice in society when she objects to violations of the Indian-government treaties.

> "Will the government make these Indians go West?"
> "Yes," Pa said. "When white settlers come into a territory, the Indians have to move on. The government is going to move these Indians farther west, any time now. That's why we're here, Laura. White people are going to

settle all this country, and we get the best land because we get here first and take our pick. Now do you understand?"

"Yes, Pa," Laura said. "But, Pa, I thought this was Indian Territory. Won't it make the Indians mad to have to—"

"No more questions, Laura," Pa said, firmly. "Go to sleep." [237]

Old Woman, in *Summer of the Hungry Pup*, teaches whites the difference between the Indian's and the white's feelings about the land. Four things, she says, cannot be given away: land, grass, trees, and animals. " 'They belong to Father-to-all.' " The prairie, she maintains, should have been "home" for all people. The white man, in possessing the land in a legal sense, has sinned (343). Old Woman's story dramatically illustrates the effects of white aggression on a Cree woman's life. As a young woman she calls herself First Woman; she is the first wife of Horse Dance Giver. She gives birth to her first child while her tribe is moving from Saskatchewan to Montana after their leaders have been killed, imprisoned, or forced into hiding. In Montana they are haunted by starvation, the "hungry pup," and yearn to return to their home ground.

This era in Saskatchewan history is also recounted by Maria Campbell in *Halfbreed*. In the introduction, Campbell says: "I write this for all of you, to tell you what it is like to be a Halfbreed woman in our country. I want to tell you about the joys and sorrows, the oppressing poverty, the frustrations and the dreams" (2). In order to tell her own story, Campbell begins by describing Saskatchewan in the 1860s before there were farms, fences, and towns. She then traces the key political events affecting the lives of the Indians and mixed-bloods. After the 1885 defeat of Louis Riel, Gabriel Dumont, Poundmaker, and Big Bear, Campbell's people settled northwest of Prince Albert which, at that time, was free of settlers. They could hunt, fish, and trap. Then the land was opened for homesteading, and Indians had to choose among accepting treaty lands from the government, building cabins in the narrow strips of "Crown land" along highways, or seeking new homes further away in the bush country.

Campbell's narration provides additional insights into the issues discussed in this chapter: attitudes of Indians toward white settlers and the relationships between the two groups. As Thomas Flanagan points out, "there is quite a large imaginative literature about the Métis, most of it dealing with Riel, but this, of course is not the same thing as literature produced by one's own people." Flanagan comments that Maria Campbell's *Halfbreed* is unique in its portrayal of the Métis people who have "a continuous historical experience of about 250 years" ("Métis Literature" 137). *Halfbreed* is also unique in prairie fiction about the frontier era; it is the only novel not written by a white woman.

Campbell's great-grandmother, Cheechum, married a Scotsman named Campbell. He beat her. He kept her with him at all times because he was afraid she would be attracted to other men. In fact, he took her to political meetings related to the Riel Rebellion. Cheechum listened carefully, then "passed on all the information she heard at these meetings to the rebels and also stole ammunitions and supplies for them" (from the Hudson's Bay store that her husband ran (10). When the new settlers came, Cheechum found an effective way of dealing with them: she simply "ignored them and refused to acknowledge them even when passing on the road." Later, when asked why she hadn't become a Christian, Cheechum said that "she had married a Christian and if there was such a thing as hell she had lived there; nothing after death could be worse" (11).

After her husband's death, Cheechum went to live with her mother's people. There she built her own cabin, hunted, trapped, and raised her son. When the Royal Canadian Mounted Police tried to remove her from the land, she shot over their heads. After that they left her alone. Through Cheechum, Maria learns what life used to be like before the settlers came: old women and little girls did all the work—cleaning, cooking, tending the babies, mending the fishnets. The older women, Cheechum recalls, were also good trappers and hunters; some were better than the men (42).

Maria Campbell's Grandmother Campbell had nine children; the eldest (Maria's father) was eleven when his father died. Campbell's description of this grandmother provides another portrait for the gallery of heroic plow-women:

> After Grandpa died, Grandma Campbell went to a white community and hired herself and Dad out to cut brush for seventy-five cents an acre. She wrapped their feet with rabbit skins and old paper, and over this they wore moccasins. . . .
>
> In the spring after the farmers had broken the brushed land, they would return and pick the stones and roots and burn the brush, as the farmers wouldn't pay the seventy-five cents an acre until all this was completed.
>
> In the fall they went to work harvesting. They did this until they had enough money to buy a homestead. She and Dad [Campbell's father] built a cabin and for three years tried to break the land. Because they only had one

team of horses and Dad used these to work for other people, Grannie on many occasions pulled the plough herself. [12]

Campbell goes on to say that although her grandmother cleared the settlers' land, delivered their babies, and took care of their sick, they never visited her even though her home was open to anyone. Clearly, whites were not willing to accept her as a friend. On the other hand, three old Swedes came to her funeral, demonstrating that race was not always a barrier.

This detail from Campbell's story coincides with a situation in Barclay's *Summer of the Hungry Pup,* which describes the long, deep friendship between a Swedish immigrant woman and a Cree woman. The fact that no white women visited Campbell's grandmother raises the question, How frequent *were* friendships between white women and Indian women? Several white women writers included details of these friendships in their novels. The recounting of such incidents is not inaccurate—many friendships indeed existed, as Riley's study demonstrates.[27] Some Indian women, like Cheechum, did not want friendships with white women; others, like Grandmother Campbell, would have appreciated a closer relationship with white women but found them unable to set aside their racial prejudices and class biases.

Campbell's Grandmother Dubuque had married a French Canadian whose father had been a coureur de bois. When faced with making a choice, the Dubuque family chose to become "treaty Indians" and receive land for farming. Ironically, as Cheechum points out to Maria, "treaty Indians" were frequently "more half-breed" than those who identified themselves as half-breeds. Maria says that treaty Indian women were quiet; the half-breeds were not. Significantly, Maria chooses the

27. Riley provides examples of several friendships between white and Indian women in *Women and Indians* (173–76). The importance of continuing to develop such friendships is the focus of Paula Gunn Allen's "Who Is Your Mother? Red Roots of White Feminism." Allen agrees with the "traditionalists" who say "we must remember our origins, our cultures, our histories and our mothers and grandmothers, for without that memory, which implies continuance rather than nostalgia, we are doomed to extinction" (40). Allen reminds readers that "the earliest white women on this continent were well acquainted with tribal women. They were neighbors to a number of tribes, and often shared food, information, child-care and health care." Allen concludes with this statement: "It should be evident that one of the major enterprises of Indian women in America has been the transfer of Indian values and culture to as large and influential a segment of American immigrant populations as possible. Their success in this endeavor is amply demonstrated in the Indianized lifestyles that characterize American life" (41).

label *half-breed* for herself; this is the matriarchal line with which she identifies most strongly.

The most important point Maria makes about her family is this: "My people have always been political. They get involved in political campaigns for local white politicians. As a child I remember listening to them talk and argue far into the night about why this party or that was the best. They talked about better education, a better way of life, but mostly about land for our people" (72). Although the Indians and mixed-bloods have been unable to control a great many things in their lives, the sense of political efficacy persists in some. Maria Campbell's book is a political act, aimed at educating people, changing attitudes, and altering stereotypes. She writes in the introduction that there is no home to which she can return: "Like me the land had changed, my people were gone, and if I was to know peace I would have to search within myself. That is when I decided to write about my life. I am not very old, so perhaps some day, when I too am a grannie, I will write more" (2). As more women like Maria Campbell recognize that there are still many stories to be told and write them down, we will have a better sense of what relations have been between the two groups of women on the American and Canadian prairies. Gradually the voices of all prairie women will fill in a history that is perilously close to being lost: the voices of Indian women and mixed-blood women will, let us hope, join with the voices of black women and white women. Only then will prairie women begin to understand their regional histories and identities.

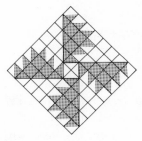

CHAPTER FIVE

Second Wave Women

Mary Hartwell Catherwood's story "The Bride of Arne Sandstrom" begins with a young Swedish woman getting off a train in a midwestern prairie town, "dazed by long riding and partial fasting, and dumb terror of finding no one to receive her at the end of her great journey" (254). Then she notes the not disagreeable surroundings—the prairie stretching westward and the "perky architecture" of the town. Two young American males watch her, deciding that she has come from the old country for the wedding that is being held by a prosperous Swedish family, the Lunds. They envy the lucky Swede bridegroom and speculate about their chances of winning one of the younger Lund daughters. The tired traveler receives directions from these young men, one of whom understands some Swedish. She then makes her way to the Lund house and peers through the windows of the house, which teems with laughter and prosperity. She sees "Svensky wooden spoons and beautifully painted and polished Russian bowls" as well as "unheard-of Amerikanski things"—symbols of prosperity yearned for but unattainable in Sweden (263). From snatches of conversation she concludes that her betrothed has chosen another bride.

Nevertheless, she asserts herself. Stepping across the threshold, she calls to Otto Jutberg, a young man who came to America with her lover Arne. Expecting his derision, she is greeted instead with warmth and happy astonishment. It is finally explained to her that there are two Arne Sandstroms, and it is the other one who is marrying the Lund girl. The story ends happily with a double wedding.

On the continuum of prairie women's fiction, Catherwood's "Bride of Arne Sandstrom," written about 1885, is the first story about a second wave immigrant woman on the prairie. Typically, the story is told by a representative of the first wave of immigrants. It was not until the late 1920s that a second wave descendant published a novel. In a study of immigrant fiction on the midwestern frontier, David Lynn Dyrud notes: "The first generation of foreign-born immigrants was too involved in establishing itself on the inhospitable prairie to have the leisure to record its experiences. Someone must step forward to speak for the dead who can no longer speak for themselves." Dyrud then goes on to say, "The record succeeding generations leaves, however, may suffer from not being firsthand and may, worse, be clouded by a patina of nostalgia" (23). But when we turn to women's prairie fiction, we realize and accept the fact that writers like Catherwood stepped forward and filled the gap, although they too could not speak "firsthand" and were, on occasion, nostalgic and sentimental. Mary Hartwell Catherwood, Willa Cather, Nellie McClung, and Gabrielle Roy filled the gap until the descendants could tell their own stories.

Catherwood's story of the Swedish bride portrays a close-knit and prosperous immigrant group well on its way to realizing the promises of America that they first heard about through American letters, railroad and government propaganda, or enthusiastic travelers. Indeed, the situation offered the new Mrs. Sandstrom is considerably more agreeable than that of the first Mrs. Smith, the victim in one of Catherwood's earlier stories. Even though the story is tinged with nostalgia, the underlying structures reveal a consistent and usually convincing view of second wave women's experiences.

As noted in chapter three, foreign-born, non-English-speaking women were present on the North American prairies from the beginning of settlement. A few isolated examples give insight into the settlement population during the early frontier periods. In 1850, Iowa's total population of 192,214 included 9,734 immigrants from Great Britain and Ireland; 1,756 from British North America; and 7,152 from Germany. By 1870 there was a total population of 1,194,020 with 66,162 from Germany and only 65,442 from Great Britain and Ireland, along with 17,907 from Norway and 10,796 from Sweden; the number from British North America leaped to 17,554. However, the largest wave of non-English-speaking foreign-born came between 1890 and 1912 (Bogue 14).

In Canada, Swedes and Swiss were included in Lord Selkirk's 1812 settlement; 6,000 Mennonites came to Manitoba between 1874 and 1889. Large numbers of Icelanders came in the 1870s, Jews in the 1880s,

Fig. 16   O. S. LONGMAN, *Polish Settlers at Sundance, Alberta*, September 1930.
Courtesy of Glenbow Archives, Calgary, Alberta. This photograph was
taken four months after the family arrived from Poland with $1425.
Within a few months they broke forty acres and put in a crop; cleared ten
more acres; bought four horses, two cows, thirty chickens, a wagon,
seeder, gang plow, disc, and harrows; and planted a one-acre garden.

and Norwegians and Finns in the 1890s. In 1893 Sir Clifford Sifton,
minister of the interior, recruited Poles, Czechs, Hungarians, and Doukhobors. In addition to these groups, 75,000 Ukrainians had made their
homes on the prairies by 1910 (Woodcook 82–84, 88, 90).[1] As one of
Barbara Sapergia's characters says, "We are all foreigners here" (28).
(See fig. 16.)

1. According to the 1981 census 3.9 million Canadians were born outside Canada (*Canada
Today/D'aujourd'hui* 15.2 [1984]: 9). For stories about the Doukhobors and Ukrainians see Roy's
Garden in the Wind. Roy's *Fragile Lights of Earth* includes several essays on Canadian immigrants.
See also Aldrich's *Spring Came On Forever* and Fernald's *Plow the Dew Under*.

The last two decades of the nineteenth century and the second decade of the twentieth have received the most attention by prairie women writers. Second wave immigrants, like the first wave immigrants, came for land—they hoped for land that was cheap and fertile. A few like the men in Salverson's *Dark Weaver* and McDonald's *Amalie's Story* intended to establish businesses in booming prairie towns. Some came for religious reasons: the immigrants in Sapergia's *Foreigners* were escaping the power of the priests in a small Romanian village; other eastern Europeans were escaping from religious persecution or national laws that clashed with their religious beliefs. A typical situation is described by Gabrielle Roy in "The Well of Dunrea": "In their own country they had possessed nothing—or so very little: a skimpy acre or two on the arid slopes of the Carpathians to feed an entire family; and they had left that behind them without too great pain. But now they had all sorts of things—hay, sugar beets, wonderful wheat, full barns, really every thing" (*Street of Riches* 81). Natural catastrophes such as the volcanic eruptions in Iceland spurred others to seek alternatives in the New World.

Many realized that they would not be bound to poverty in the lower social classes if they were able to establish successful homesteads or businesses. Most of the characters, it seems, whether American or Canadian immigrants, at one time or another had heard the voice of "the great parent" referred to by de Crèvecoeur:

> "Welcome to my shores, distressed Europeans; bless the hour in which you didst see my verdant fields, my fair navigable rivers, and my green mountains!—If thou wilt work, I have bread for thee; if thou wilt be honest, sober, and industrious, I have greater rewards to confer on thee—ease and independence. I will give thee fields to feed and clothe thee; a comfortable fireside to sit by, and tell thy children by what means thou hast prospered; and a decent bed to repose on. I shall endow thee beside with the immunities of a freeman. . . . I will also provide for thy progeny; and to every good man this ought to be the most holy, the most powerful, the most earnest wish he can possibly form, as well as the most consolatory prospect when he does. Go thou and work and till; thou shalt prosper, provided thou be just, grateful, and industrious." [63–64]

The immigrant's choice between Canada and the United States usually depended on the presence of friends or relatives in one of the countries, or on the propagandist with the most convincing arguments.

In second wave fiction, women's roles in the decision to emigrate are significantly different from those of women in first wave fiction. One explanation for this change is the fact that there were many brides in the first wave group who were willing to let their new husbands make the choices. Only one bride is included in the second wave group—Catherwood's Swedish bride—as compared to almost a dozen in the first wave works. Thus the emphasis shifts instead to women who have been married for several years; they are apt to be more practical than their younger counterparts.

Frequently goups rather than individual couples or families made the decision to emigrate. While the authority of the group usually rested with the men, Helen Clark Fernald demonstrates the full participation of one woman character. As a German Mennonite family makes its way to a new Kansas settlement, the husband's spirits sink while the wife's spirits rise. They see that a recent grasshopper invasion has stripped the land of all plant life, but Sophie Palevsky assures her husband, Nicholas, that the "bare, bitten prairie" is only temporary." "'This is a good place,'" she tells him (*Plow the Dew Under* 37). At one point, when the horses need to be disciplined, Sophie symbolically takes the whip from her husband and forces the horses to behave.

Nicholas observes that "she was not at all frightened. He was a bit puzzled at the thought which crossed his mind: *What's this? The woman looks as if she actually enjoyed it!*" (36). And she does—the new land, bare and bitten as it is, is unimportant when compared to the prospect of establishing a new home. Still later, after her family and the other settlers are asleep, "Sophie slipped out through the open end of the house and stood alone in the night. Sharp bright stars burned above the prairie, spangling the deep blue bowl of the sky. A cool wind swept across the plain from the southwest, freshening Sophie's whole body as if she had been dipped in water. . . . As she looked at the prairie, it seemed as if she could see fields out there, bright green." (38). Even women who have not had a major role in the decision to emigrate can, Fernald suggests, experience a kind of rebirth in a new land.

Several of the main characters in second wave fiction are girls. In Cather's *O Pioneers!* and *My Ántonia*, Faralla's *Circle of Trees*, Aldrich's *Spring Came on Forever*, Salverson's *Viking Heart*, and Sapergia's *Foreigners*, daughters accompany their families. The decision is made, obviously, by adults, but the girls show no reluctance.

As in first wave works, some second wave women regretted leaving the homeland. Cornelia James Cannon describes how Brigitta Swenson's husband arranged to emigrate after listening to a steamship agent:

The slow and cautious Nils was fired, and, when argument failed to rouse Brigitta, he sold the accumulations of a laborious life without her knowledge, bought tickets to Minnesota for them and their only surviving child, a five-year-old boy, and returned to his impoverished home to tell her that a new and better life was beginning for them all. Brigitta shed tears of anguish, but she hid them from Nils. In dull acquiescence she packed her household goods, said goodbye forever to the little mounds on the hillside [their dead children], and followed her husband on the long journey into the unknown. [*Red Rust* 5]

In fact, Cannon later reinforces the myth of the reluctant pioneer woman: "'The true woman pioneer is a rare creature,'" one character says. "'Most of the women who pioneer do not go into the wilds of their own choice, but follow the men they love, and, victims of a fate stronger than their will, bear what must be borne. Lena Jensen loved her children, and like a frantic mother bird followed them from one temporary shelter to another'" (37). Cannon does not contradict this statement through the narrative voice or another character.

In a similar vein, the mother in Cather's *O Pioneers!* is represented as a woman who never quite forgave her husband for "bringing her to the end of the earth." Once in Nebraska she asked for nothing more than "to be let alone to reconstruct her old life in so far as that was possible" (30). In *My Ántonia*, however, Cather presents the reverse situation: Ántonia tells Jim Burden that her mother forced her father to come: "All the time she say: 'America big country; much money, much land for my boys, much husband for my girls'" (90).

Stefan Dominescu in Sapergia's *Foreigners* had emigrated to Manitoba so that his family would be educated. He reminds a fellow Romanian that in their old village only the priest could read, write, and do arithmetic. Stefan rebeled against having to pay the priest for his help, so when he heard that all the children in Canada were sent to school he made up his mind to emigrate. A short time after arriving in Canada, the younger Dominescu boy dies. Stefan's wife, Sophie, grieving, exclaims "'I am sorry we came to this country!'" Stefan reminds Sophie that she had wanted to come too, but she denies this: "'You talked about it day and night till I agreed. I could see you would give me no peace'" (29). After giving birth to quadruplets, Sophie falls into a disordered state of mind and tells Stefan they should never have come. She feels they are being punished for having left home and that it is wrong to learn new ways; in fact, she refuses to learn the language. She also is convinced that their land is bad; they will never succeed (104).

Sophie recalls the horror of the sea voyage: the storms, the wind, the lack of air: "people sick everywhere, they could not help it i would not be sick, i would not let it happen, and yet the smell alone would turn your stomach i would close my eyes and scream and scream in my mind, but on the outside i kept quiet so the children would not be afraid . . . i never thought we would get here alive" (105).

The journey remains a minor structure in second wave works. Only Julie McDonald recreates the feelings of a woman anticipating the sea voyage. In *Amalie's Story*, Amalie hears a song at a fair:

> Proudly o'er the ocean waves
> Sped the steamer *Austria*
> Passengers it had in numbers
> Going to Amerika
>
> To the captain who commanded
> Never dream came of the blow
> Which fate for him upon this voyage
> Unluckily prepared had. [138]

The narrator of the novel, Amalie, describes how she turned away from the singer, not wishing to hear the rest of the song: "But somehow I could not go. I stayed to listen to the horrors of fire on shipboard: women throwing their children over the side, then being swallowed up by red and yellow flames. The listeners gasped in sympathy, and when the last note faded, the troubadour passed his hat. I dropped a few øre into it and stumbled away, shaken" (138). After her husband decides to go to America to investigate business opportunities, Amalie's perspective changes: "Across that frightening infinity of water lay the America I now longed for. Peter's descriptions of the shoulder-high prairie grass, the groves of trees beside small streams, and the fertile land glowed in my mind, and his face was in the foreground" (145–46). Fascinated by such descriptions, Amalie, like others before her and after her, embarked on the sea voyage.

Laura Goodman Salverson is the only writer to detail the land journey of a second wave emigrant. Her own mother had lost two children en route from Iceland to Winnipeg in 1887 (Clara Thomas, "Women Writers" 47).[2] As a result, Salverson felt very deeply the ordeals of

2. Salverson's indebtedness to her mother's stories is acknowledged in "An Autobiographical Sketch": "Always, despite her arduous life and many babies, she found the time to sit with young things around her telling of the marvelous and the true. Nothing dour. Romance filled the room so completely with its compelling sweetness that somehow I never remember what sort of chairs we sat on or what happened to be about in the way of furnishings" (72).

travel as women experienced them. Also, Salverson herself traveled extensively. In an autobiographical essay written for the *Ontario Library Review*, Salverson noted that she had moved thirty times in fifteen years of marriage and, she writes, "I cannot remember how many times before" (73), referring to the frequent moves back and forth between Manitoba and several plains states during her childhood. Both her father and her husband continually searched for better places to live and work.

Salverson drew on her experiences and those of her mother to recreate the immigrant woman's journey to a new home. In *The Viking Heart*, Salverson traces two days of the boat trip taken by a group of Icelanders to the immigrant sheds of Winnipeg. Although laughter and song rang out, no one could overlook the "pinched faces" and "little thin hands" of the babies, the "young women with the bloom faded from their round cheeks," the older women hunched over in "pathetic silence" (24). In *The Dark Weaver*, the journey is briefly summed up by one of the Danish women, Oline Vedel Boyen:

> Oh, but she was weary! As weary as though she had lived a dozen lives in the weeks that separated her from home and civilization. From the first the trip had been a horrible nightmare—storms at sea, the protracted delay in Ontario where John [her husband] had arranged to meet this body of homeseekers, the comfortless trains to St. Paul, and finally these bone-shaking prairie vehicles the like of which she had never conceived. She could understand how one might weep and feel the better for it. [33]

When the leaders of the immigrant group finally choose land south of Winnipeg, the last lap of the journey is planned without regard for Oline's advanced stage of pregnancy. One of the older women in the group comments that it would never occur to Oline's husband—one of the leaders—that "even his wife is subject to the same mortal risks that killed poor little Gerty Holmquist [who had died in childbirth earlier in the journey] and annoyed him so much by halting the caravan three days!" (39). As it turns out, thirty miles from Winnipeg, Oline's pains begin. Fortunately a clear-headed young Métis woman traveling with them makes life-saving decisions which lead to a safe delivery for the mother and infant.

We see that childbirth and travel are not always as traumatic when we compare this account by Salverson, which demonstrates women's perspectives on the journey, with a thirdhand account told by Cather's male narrator in *My Ántonia*. In a very charming story, Jim recalls the winter nights when their hired hand, Otto Fuchs, could be persuaded "to talk about the outlaws and desperate characters he had known" (68). The example Jim proceeds to recount, however, is about Otto's ocean voyage to America when he accompanied the wife of an acquaintance:

> In mid-ocean she proceeded to have not one baby, but three! This even made Fuchs the object of undeserved notoriety, since he was travelling with her. The steerage stewardess was indignant with him, the doctor regarded him with suspicion. The first-cabin passengers, who made up a purse for the woman, took an embarrassing interest in Otto. . . . The trip to Chicago was even worse than the ocean voyage. On the train it was very difficult to get milk for the babies and to keep their bottles clean. The mother did her best, but no woman, out of her natural resources, could feed three babies. . . . When [the husband] met his family at the station he was rather crushed by the size of it. He, too, seemed to consider Fuchs in some fashion to blame. [69].

Jim recalls that his grandmother, "who was working her bread on the bread-board, laugh[ed] until she wiped her eyes with her bare arm, her hands being floury" (68). Certainly the story is comic and ends happily. Nevertheless, Jim's grandmother, who had herself traveled from Virginia to Nebraska, must have realized that the situation easily could have taken a sharp twist toward the tragic at any number of points.

A major difference in structures emerges when second wave men are compared with first wave men as portrayed by women writers. First, male characters are less important, playing major roles only in *Plow the Dew Under* and sharing the story line with a female character in several other works. In *A Circle of Trees*, Faralla's interest in children's adaptation to a new landscape remains evenly balanced between the boy and the girl. In *Red Rust, Spring Came on Forever, My Ántonia*, and *O River, Remember!*, both male and female roles receive close attention, but in every instance the women gradually dominate because of strong personalities or because, simply, the woman lives longer than her male partner and therefore continues to demonstrate strength: they do whatever it is that has to be done.

Secondly, while many first wave men conform to the popular image of the Canadian or American Adam, the second wave men are more apt to be flawed as pioneers and failures in their work or in their health. They contrast sharply with the strong, tall, handsome men of energy, vision, integrity, intelligence, and responsibility that are found in first wave works by McClung, Heacock, Lane, Aldrich, Wilson, and Parsons. The two fathers in Cather's novels are admirable men but not survivors on the prairie frontier. Mr. Shimerda in *My Ántonia* had made his living in the old country as a musician, not as a farmer; when he couldn't take care of his family, he committed suicide. *O Pioneers!* opens with the serious illness of John Bergson, and he charges his daughter Alexandra with the care of his farm.

Some of the male characters are kind, hardworking, and moderately successful farmers—Bjorn Lindal in *The Viking Heart*, Var Vinge in *O River, Remember!*, and Matts Swenson in *Red Rust*. They are not, however, the dynamic personalities and community leaders that their first wave equivalents were made out to be. In *Amalie's Story*, Amalie's husband is successful and loving; he promises her that if she will go to America he will make it rain lemonade. As a businessman, he comes close to doing that; still we sense that he is too quickly Americanized to completely satisfy Amalie's needs and values. Two other businessmen in Salverson's *Dark Weaver* are prosperous and "founding fathers" in their community; on the dark side their motives and/or morals are suspect.

In the first wave fiction only one man is portrayed as hard, uncaring, land-grabbing, and life-robbing—Mr. Smith in Catherwood's "Monument to the First Mrs. Smith." In three other works men are flawed: Tom Wentworth in North's *Morning in the Land*, physically handsome and popular as a community leader but hypocritical and materialistic; the shadowy figure of the husband in Cather's "A Wagner Matinee"; and the adventure-seeker in Rolyat's *Lily of Fort Garry*. These men all fail to meet the deepest needs of their wives and families. Nevertheless, they are portrayed in less harsh terms than the patriarchs in several second wave works. For example, the German immigrant in Aldrich's *Spring Came on Forever* expects to prosper because he has "160 acres, a good team and a woman" (67). The prospect for his wife Amalie is dismal: "as always the hard work and the attempt to please Herman in every way so there would be no loud fault-finding" (93).

Even harsher portraits are presented in Ukrainian novels by Vera Lysenko and Mary Ann Seitz. In Lysenko's *Yellow Boots*, the father builds the largest log house in the district and dreams of accumulating more and more land. To assure success, he harnesses his children to the plow, hires out a fragile daughter to work on a relative's farm, and, when she comes of age, tries to arrange a marriage for her that will bring him more land. Seitz's *Shelterbelt*, a story about east European immigrants at the very end of the frontier period in Saskatchewan, describes a father who is unnecessarily harsh in his discipline; even though times are easier, he expects his children to sacrifice all personal desires for the sake of the farm.

Women writers delineating the first wave experience usually created larger-than-life males; those writing about the second wave immigrants refused to idealize their male characters. This cannot be attributed to the fact that American- or Canadian-born writers are prejudiced against foreign-born males, because descendants of second wave immigrants are frequently even more critical of the males in their groups. Nor are attitudes affected by the era in which the stories were written: in both groups of fiction, the largest number of stories are told forty to sixty years after the end of the frontier era.

One explanation might be that second wave works were, on the average, written two decades later than the first wave novels and thus reflected the increase of feminism in society as well as the increase of realism in literature. Also, the first wave works, emphasizing as they do the experiences of young brides and heroic males, appealed to and perhaps were intended for popular reading audiences. Many of the second wave works—especially fiction by Cather, Cannon, Faralla, McDonald, Roy, Barclay, and Sapergia—are aimed at an audience that demands a better quality of literature.

In addition, many writers of second wave works took advantage of the opportunity to read and evaluate earlier works of prairie fiction and to learn from those works. As Dorothy Livesay, a Winnipeg-born poet, has noted, "I don't think a mature novel can arise in a country unless there's been a lot of popular writing at a base" (137).

The next question is, then, Are second wave women less heroic? In the fiction about first wave women, three major women characters come close to being ideal Frontier Heroes—self-sufficient women, nurturers, and survivors on the prairie with or without the help of men. All of these characters—Elizabeth Moore in *The Lily of Fort Garry*, Nell Connor in *Black Soil*, and Dallas Lancaster in *The Plow-Woman*—are in relationships with males who, to varying degrees, provide support. The four women I would identify as Frontier Heroes in second wave fiction exist in parallel situations, but they are shown as more independent and better able to draw on their own resources. This situation is best described by the fantasy of one character. In Cather's *O Pioneers!* Alexandra has a recurring "illusion": she imagines "being lifted up bodily and carried lightly by some one very strong. It was a man, certainly, who carried her, but he was like no man she knew; he was much larger and stronger and swifter, and he carried her as easily as if she were a sheaf of wheat. . . . As she grew older, this fancy more often came to her when she was tired than when she was fresh and strong" (206–07). Two of Alexandra's brothers, who are part owners in the farm, are strong, hard-working men, but unfortunately conservative and narrow-minded in their approach to farming. Her youngest brother, Emil, is sent to the state university because Alexandra believes the reason her father came to America was "to have sons like Emil, and to give them a chance" (117)—a chance, it is implied, to do something besides farming. Alexandra's childhood friend Carl eventually returns to stay with her, but he has failed as an artist and attained only moderate success as a lithographer and a gold-seeker in Alaska. Not one of these men could lift or even share Alexandra's burdens.

The same situation, with some variations, is repeated in Cather's next prairie novel, My Ántonia. At the age of fifteen, Ántonia put on her father's boots and assumed a man's responsibilities in life. At a later stage, she leaves town where she has worked as a domestic and returns to her brother's farm. Here she gives birth to her illegitimate child. Then she takes up the plow, eventually marries, and develops her own farm while raising her family. When Jim Burden returns to Nebraska after a twenty-year absence, he sees Ántonia as

> a battered woman now, not a lovely girl: but she still had that something which fires the imagination, could still stop one's breath for a moment by a look or gesture that somehow revealed the meaning in common things. She had only to stand in the orchard, to put her hand on a little crab tree and look up at the apples, to make you feel the goodness of planting and tending and harvesting at last. All the strong things of her heart came out in her body, that had been so tireless in serving generous emotions. [353]

In this passage we see Ántonia through Jim's eyes as the archetypal prairie woman rooted and flourishing spiritually in a land which has been harsh and deadly to innumerable other men and women. In fact, her vitality is so powerful that she has been able to bind her husband, a city man, to a way of life which, without her and on his own, he would have rejected.

Lena, another Frontier Hero, caused critics considerable trouble in their 1928 reviews of Red Rust. Reviewers for both Outlook and The Saturday Review of Literature express uncertainty about which character is the main protagonist—Lena or her younger, second husband who develops a rust-free wheat grain. Obviously Cannon has succeeded in creating a powerful female character if critics are unsure whether Matts, who resembles in some ways a Norse agricultural god, is indeed the hero. The novel itself gives us some confusing signals. Matts, in analyzing his younger sister's situation, asks: "Was it possible that women did not feel the joy in life, the thrill of experience, that stirred in him from morning to night? Were they, instead, so crushed by hard work that they had no energy left for happiness?" (115). At the point when this question is asked, the reader cannot determine if it is the author speaking through Matts or the author presenting a male's perception of female experience.

As the novel progresses, however, and Lena's characterization becomes more fully developed, the reader recognizes that the answer to Matts's question is a definite no. While Lena is presented, appropriately, with many traditional female qualities, she is not immune to life's possibilities and the thrill that comes from living and working. Lena sits up at night with Matts, helping him to record data, even though she does not understand his experiments with soil types, origins of the seeds, dates for planting, cross-fertilizing, and self-fertilizing. She is an ideal nineteenth-century wife in her "yearning to protect the man who could plan such miracles and dream such dreams" (213).

It is understandable that critics have erred in their interpretation of the novel; Lena, in some ways, seems more like a helper than a hero. Allan Nevins's reading was distorted by stereotypes of gender roles:

> Mrs. Cannon's central figure is Hans Mattson [sic] . . . pursuing his cross-fertilizations, wondering over the diversity of grains and trying to define the laws of inheritance; and it is hard to give such an embodiment of scientific zeal sufficient life to make him more than a lay-figure. A love story runs through the book, and at times quite dominates the interest. It is the heroine of this love-story, the poor abused widow whom Hans marries and who then blooms into a second youth, who in retrospect seems the author's most vivid creation. She is far more vital and appealing than Hans. We see her first as the wife of a brutal immigrant, who is mercifully killed in an accident before he kills her. . . . Somehow, Hans is not so important to us as Lena, and the wheat arouses our emotions less than the throbbing chronicle of family happiness and unhappiness. [63]

What Nevins has failed to recognize is that Cannon has carefully built up role reversals for Matts and Lena most of the time. Matts has a highly developed feminine side, as evidenced by his creativity in his grain experiments and tenderness with his family; unfortunately, he has absolutely no sense of the marketplace—he is not profit-oriented or competitive or aggressive as his father and neighbors are. Because he lacks

expertise in these matters, Lena assumes the male responsibility of making ends meet; she assigns the chores, plows, digs potatoes, husks corn,
manages the threshing and winnowing, and—when she realizes there
will not be enough food to get them through the winter—teaches the
children how to dig up ginseng roots to sell so that they can feed the cows
and themselves.

While Nevins concludes that "the necessities of the novel demand
that Lena be kept a subordinate personage" (63), a feminist reading
enables Lena to emerge as the hero. One further detail contributes to the
latter interpretation. Nevins notes that "the heroine of this love-story,
the poor abused widow" marries Matts and "then blooms into a second
youth." This is a serious misreading of the novel and it demonstrates how
easily literary clichés and social stereotypes can get in the way of what is
really going on in a story. Actually, the story says that Lena, once freed
from the tyrant husband,

> could not think tragically of the future. The years of struggle ahead, whose
> difficulties she knew only too well from the years of struggle behind, looked
> to her like years of joy. She would move no more. Here, in this new country,
> she and her children could build up a home in which there would be no more
> harsh words and no more shrinking from the horror of blows. . . . The
> beautiful world would speak to her with a new voice, the voice of her own
> revived life. [148–49]

At this point, Matts sees her and notes that "far from being crushed and
aged by the heavy responsibilities that had fallen upon her, she had about
her a look of youth and sweet freshness" (151). And soon afterwards they
are married. The blossoming takes place *before* her courtship and marriage to Matts.

Nevins was not the only critic to find the book flawed because of
uncertainty about whether Lena or Matts is the hero. Frances Lamont
Robbins in an *Outlook* review noted that "Lena lacks the heroic quality of
those who defy nature and fall under her revenge" (475). This is another
traditional (and usually male) assumption: the land must be subdued; in
subduing the land a person becomes heroic. True, Per Hansa in *Giants in
the Earth* and Abe Spaulding in *Fruits of the Earth* represent man-the-
conqueror. Even those who "fall under nature's revenge" are heroic in
their efforts. The relationship between women and the land is different.
Women writing in the tradition of prairie women's fiction generally insist
on women's heroism arising out of their ability to work *with* the land.
Cather expresses this relationship in *O Pioneers!* when Alexandra is

described by her friend Carl: "Her face was so radiant that he felt shy about asking her. For the first time, perhaps, since the land emerged from the waters of geologic ages, a human face was set toward it with love and yearning. It seemed beautiful to her, rich and strong and glorious" (65). The conflict in O Pioneers! and in Red Rust is not between women and the land; it does not involve "nature's revenge" and human failure or success. Rather, the conflict evolves around the situation of a woman assuming a male role, the criticism she must face when she does so, and the degree to which she can succeed under trying circumstances.

One ordeal—isolation—has diminished in second wave works. Only Faralla's Circle of Trees shows a family isolated from a group. Even this family, however, has relatives nearby. Although relations are strained, they gather for holidays and times of illness. All other major characters in second wave works belong to well-defined, protecting ethnic groups. In several works (Cather's My Ántonia and O Pioneers!, Cannon's Red Rust, Ostenso's O River, Remember!, Sapergia's Foreigners, and Riley's "Pies") there are mixtures of immigrant groups and first wave settlers, and while there may be problems between individuals of different groups and within a group, no character is without recourse to help of some kind. The conflict between the isolated farmer and nature, in some instances, has been replaced by a variety of personal or cultural conflicts.

Group support emerges in various forms. The church provides one kind of support in Amalie's Story. Amalie chooses to conform to the occasionally restrictive regulations of the Lutheran church and thus preserve her identity as a Danish-American as well as maintain the protection of the group. For example, when her husband insists on attending Christian Church where an infant's baptism is postponed until "the age of discretion," Amalie secretly arranges for her new daughter's baptism by a Lutheran minister (168, 170). On another occasion Amalie innocently enjoys an American dance; when she realizes her fellow church members disapprove, she gives up dancing (172).

The unity and strength of a religious settlement is detailed in the story "Hoodoo Valley" in which Gabrielle Roy describes a group of Doukhobors "gathered like an immense family" in tents and converted railroad cars near Verigin, Saskatchewan. They refuse to be separated; they consider the other settlers immoral and refuse to mix with them: "And the people here, the ones who'd been living in this solitude awhile, what strange ones they were! Eaters of meat and other forbidden foods, they squabbled among themselves as if life wasn't hard enough already;

or, carried away by a different madness, they'd dance till the tavern tables jumped. They couldn't be Christians, these folks who used alcohol and tobacco and never seemed to tire of spatting viciously among themselves" (*Garden* 107–08). In another passage, an old, valiant woman scolds some discouraged women, reminding them of the "dark years" when they roamed Russia and fell before the soldiers because they refused to fight in the czar's wars. Roy reminds us that they were a group with painful memories trying to find a home in the new land, but their common past—and shared present and future—sustained them, giving them enormous emotional and spiritual advantages not available, for example, to the first wave individualist.

Gabrielle Roy, a French Canadian from the St. Boniface district of Winnipeg, drew on her experiences as a young teacher in Manitoba for *Children of My Heart*. Standing at her classroom window, the narrator watches the children coming across the prairie. Some live in the section called Little Russia that includes mostly Polish and Ukrainian families; others come from French-Canadian homes, like the teacher's; still others belong to Italian families. When she is preparing to leave the school to take another position, she worries about what they will do without her: "I felt I was abandoning them," she says, "and that those silent, overwhelming, dismal spaces in all their vastness were closing around them, cutting me off from my poor deserted children" (168). She knows that the children are outsiders and will remain so until education or financial success brings them into the mainstream. She recounts, in each chapter, the particular problems of an immigrant child.

A Jewish immigrant novel by Adele Wiseman, *Crackpot*, describes a family who are outcasts from their own group. Rahel, hunchbacked, with a blind husband and small daughter, must find housework to house and feed her family:

> Work was not easy to find, for she did not look very strong, and besides people did not like the idea of a Jewish woman hiring herself out to do what they considered to be demeaning tasks. . . .
>
> In effect, Uncle Nate had thrown them out, though he hadn't actually had to go that far, for Rahel, gentle always in her actions, though not necessarily in her judgments, had not waited for him to behave as badly as he gave indication that he was capable of doing. Gaging very quickly the temper of the uncle's household she had gone out, found and rented the shack, and moved her family into it. Then, since she had no other skill, she went among the neighbours and offered herself as a charwoman. [12]

This example shows that immigrants who expected and deserved support from a group were sometimes disappointed in their expectations.

Cultural as much as religious bonds sustain many characters. Mary Ann Seitz, in *Shelterbelt*, describes Christmas when the Polanskis and Chorneys got together:

> The grownups didn't dance on the Holy Night. They drank and told stories and laughed. Sometimes Dad told a joke; then all of them roared and slapped their thighs. They laughed in English, Francie thought. Even though she could not understand what they said, she knew it was funny by their laughter. . . .
>
> Silence fell on the group around the table. Dad filled everyone's glass, then his own. They lifted the glasses, a longing upon their faces that Francie could not understand. [38–39]

Francie, Canadian-born, knows neither the language nor the longing for the old country. The adults toast one another on festive occasions—*Die Boza zdrowla,* God grant us good health; group bonds are reestablished which sustain them in the months that follow.

Keeping old world traditions alive also diminishes the inevitable sense of loneliness and alienation for those living among "the English." A Ukrainian mother's life is enriched by teaching her son songs from the homeland. At Christmas, when the teacher asks the boy to sing for the old people at the nursing home, the mother writes: "We lend Nil to the old people." Her signature, the teacher notices, "looked like embroidery"—Paraskovia Galaida (Roy, *Children* 46). In fact, embroidery and other arts, like music, carry the values and skills of the Old World into the New. Second wave women, like first wave women, take pride in their needlework. Sofie, in *Foreigners,* loves "the wool soft against her fingers, the best and silkiest fleece, spun as fine as she could with her hand spindle. She used the thinnest needles, straining her eyes over stitches that looked like a band of lace. Sofie liked to make pretty things, and she was proud of her work" (Sapergia 12). In the past she had disliked carding fleece; then one summer she started spinning sitting in the garden, rather than saving the task for the winter months: "She would sit for one hour, two, as much as she could save after her other chores, and the carded wool slipped and sifted through her fingers, the spun wool winding round and round the spindle. . . . Then she took the dried washed wool from the day before and wound it into a big light ball. Ah, the feel of the soft clean yarn" (212–13). As the years pass, Sofie gradually joins her family in community activities and mixes with the Anglo-Canadians. She enters the competition at the fair and wins two dollars and a blue ribbon for her tablecloth embroidered in red and yellow (248–49).

Numerous stories illustrate the way positive female relationships balance the ordeals and help women to survive. In Breneman/Thurston's *Land They Possessed,* a German woman of peasant stock, Mrs. Haar, brings the New England woman a burial gift when her baby dies: a pillow lovingly made "of softest down and covered with a linen case in the exact center of which, against a light blue silk background, a square of beautiful old linen lace was knitted in a pattern of the Christ Child with Mary in the manger, while Joseph, leaning on his staff, watched with shepherds kneeling in adoration, above hung a great star." There are tears in Mrs. Haar's eyes as she hands the bereaved mother the memorial gift. Mavis moves into the circle of the woman's arms and cries on her shoulder, soothed by the woman's foreign, incomprehensible words (71–72).

Occasionally second wave women are portrayed in isolation— Lena in *Red Rust,* Marta in "Garden in the Wind," Ántonia at the time she gives birth to the illegitimate child. In *O River, Remember!* Magdali is alienated from other women and her daughters because she invests all her energy in making money, but she is an exception. Most women share childbirths, deaths, illnesses, church, and community activities with other women. Their relationships bridge gaps inherent in different national origins, ages, and classes.

The aristocratic Isabella Marcusson establishes a friendship with Leona Schulz, her husband's business partner and former mistress. After the two women have met, liked each other, and realized that they have great deal in common, Leona says: " 'This is the sort of happiness I used to hope and long for. . . . The compassionate satisfaction I was once fool enough to expect from men. I know better now! There is no such thing as true companionship between men and women. Self-gratification, or to put it bluntly, the irrepressible tyrannies of sex interfere and utterly prevent any such happy condition. But ah, how I have longed to be accepted as an individual—not a biological factor!' " Isabella agrees and then points out her admiration for Leona: " 'Women like you, Leona, may eventually emancipate the rest of us. You have at least demonstrated a female can execute other offices than that of wife and mother.' " The scene ends with them entering Isabella's house together, "laughing like schoolgirls" (Salverson, *Dark Weaver* 154).

Another woman in *The Dark Weaver,* Illiana Petrovna, is a "mad" pro-worker, anti-aristocracy socialist. She nurses the babies of upper-class women, chats with the mothers, organizes a school, and, generally, becomes indispensable to the women of the community. In *The Viking Heart* women's relationships take on other variations: a "despised Magdalene" helps a stranger recover from her grief over a drowned child; a Miss Thompson from Winnipeg goes to the Icelandic community at Gimli where she restores order to the household and provides much-needed friendship for an insane Scandinavian woman.

Fear of intermarriage deters many potential friendships. In *Foreigners,* when the Dominescu daughter, Luba, is courted by a Métis youth, her father, Stefan, visits another Romanian family and hints that the time has come for their son, Paia, to start visiting Luba with the intention of proposing marriage. Although Luba feels that Lachance is more attractive and "new"—"so full of energy and passion," she chooses Paia who "had a stronger claim": "He had cared for her such a long time. . . . And he was one of her people, spoke the same language, played the same music. . . . Finally she thought of one thing that was decisive. Paia wanted to marry her and raise sheep, the same work tata did. If she married him, they would both live here in this same house with mama and tata, probably for many years. She wouldn't have to leave her family" (Sapergia 155, 158–59).

An English couple fear their daughter Margaret will marry the son of their tenant, Nicu Dominescu, Luba's brother. They don't realize the Romanian family is equally opposed to intermarriage. In fact, Sofie Dominescu tried to keep the children from attending school because she feared that they would "mix" with the English and inevitably leave her. Margaret's family, when they suspect Margaret's growing attachment to Nicu, send her to a school in town. The young people continue seeing each other, and Margaret becomes pregnant. One night Margaret comes to the Dominescu house and Stefan accepts her as his daughter-in-law. Sofie is forced to give way: "Sofie was in the kitchen, she had the fire going and she was making coffee. She looked confused, all of her fears were coming to pass. Nicu would marry the pale girl, the English girl, the Chisholm girl. His children would be pale and bloodless—like skim milk or white" (291).

Margaret's relatives also have to resign themselves to the marriage. The wedding dance takes place at the Sweet Grass schoolhouse in the final chapter of the book. The participants in the wedding festivities symbolize the multicultural nature of the prairie community. Although the mother of the groom and the mother of the bride are sitting apart, their presence demonstrates support for the young couple. "A tall dark-haired woman sits by herself, because her husband has gone home without her, taking his two flinty sons." This is Margaret's mother. "Near by, on a wooden bench, the other mother sits. She thinks for a moment of the children she has lost and the boy who died at sea. Then she watches her oldest son dancing, and wraps herself more tightly in a wonderful shawl embroidered with birds and flowers." This is Sofie. She is wearing a shawl made especially for her by an Englishwoman—and Sofie had thought the English incapable of creating any kind of needlework as beautiful as that of the eastern Europeans! Young Canadian men from the brick yard where Nicu works swing the bride. A Chinese couple and their son drink tea as they watch the dancers. Another woman, "with hair the colour of wheat stubble"—formerly a dressmaker from Regina—hands her baby to the Chinese woman and goes to dance with her husband, a Romanian friend of the groom. The scene suggests that cultural barriers still exist, but some—the Chinese woman and the Canadian woman from Regina, for example—have established ties that surmount ethnic, religious, and class differences.

A recently published story by Wilma L. Riley provides a humorous and perceptive view of the way female friendship can transcend cultural differences. In the story "Pies," a German woman named Elena Meuser clashes with a Polish woman named Mary Cherwak. The conflict develops because Elena, in taking a shortcut through the field to the village, steps in a "cow pie." Usually Elena stepped carefully through the "clean dry prairie grass," but one day, her arms full of groceries, she is frightened by Mary Cherwak's cow and she steps in one of the cow droppings (100). Elena insists that Mary Cherwak has no right to keep a cow in their village. When Elena goes to Mary's to tell her that she has to keep the cow penned, we witness a scene that illuminates the difficulties of immigrant women from different cultures, with different languages and lifestyles, trying to live together in the new land: "Elena didn't understand Polish and Mary didn't understand German, so they spoke in the new language neither had as yet mastered, due to their relative isolation in their homes" (102). The scene ends with Mary pushing Elena into more cow droppings.

In the days that follow, Elena realizes that her husband and daughters are unsympathetic to her cause and perhaps even amused. She becomes more and more depressed, neglecting both her house and her family. She felt "there was a part of her which would not heal . . . until she had vengeance for her defilement and utter loss of face" (104–05). She finally discovers a solution to her problem. With her former energy she resumes domestic responsibilities and announces to her family that she is going to invite Mary Cherwak for coffee and offer her friendship. What she doesn't say is that, while assuming a position the village will interpret as noblesse oblige, she plans to substitute some of Bossie's dung for the applesauce in the dessert.

Mary arrives, spotless from kerchief to shoes and carrying a dish covered with a snowy-white cloth. Mary obviously regrets that they have fought and appreciates what she interprets as Elena's kindness. They talk about Elena's doilies, Mary's knitting, and, of course, the wonderful pie Elena has served her:

> "Ho, la, la. Is very much spice, much sugar. Is nice, very nice."
>
> "Tank you," replies Elena. But this moment, which should have been so rich, so full, was somehow flat. It was like feeding poison to a trusting child. . . .
>
> "You like new statue of Holy Mother in church?" Mary asked suddenly.
>
> "Yah. Is very . . . fine," Elena replied, trying not to follow the downward movement of Mary's fork with her eyes.
>
> "I alvays pray to Holy Mother," Mary continued with a sly smile at the corners of her mouth. "I alvays say Holy Mother is little bit like me. She is poor voman, vork hard, and she know vat it is to have troubling child." Elena stared at her in surprise. The sly smile had reached the corners of Mary's eyes and Elena saw that she was having a little joke. Suddenly, Elena found herself giggling hysterically. Mary laughed heartily. "Is true, yah? Everybody got trouble with their kids now, yah?" [108]

Mary expresses her hope that they will now be friends, a wish she has had "for much time"; then, we are told, "Elena knew what she had to do. There was only one way, really, to redeem herself for this shameful act. She put another piece of pie on Mary's plate and then cut a generous slice for herself." And she ate it (108–09).

Riley's story takes on another level of meaning when considered within the context of the tradition of prairie women's fiction that has explored again and again relationships between first wave women and second wave women, and relationships between women within a group. "Pies" illustrates the need for a neighbor's friendship and a willingness on the part of women to reconsider values and eliminate stereotypes in order to assure that the friendship survives. This does not mean that these women are to be melted down, their unique identities lost in the proverbial melting pot. Rather, the bonds of femaleness are occasionally strong enough to overcome individual or group customs and prejudices.

Women writers—at least the better ones—choose to describe positive female relationships rather than focusing on the ordeals of marginality which would logically make up a dominant structure in immigrant fiction. Only in the most sentimental work in this group of second wave novels do we find an emphasis on British and American hegemony and its effect on new immigrants.[3] One example can be found in *Plow the Dew Under*, a novel about German Mennonites in Kansas. Immigrants are ridiculed and insulted by a number of citizens in the Kansas town. When one of the men shows signs of success, his cracker factory is destroyed by Americans who resent competition from a foreigner. One critic analyzes marginality in *Plow the Dew Under*:

> Assimilation is inevitable for Fernald although she indicates clearly in her novel the isolation experienced by the immigrants in the face of Yankee harassment. The trauma of the immigrant experience for Fernald is not the uprooting from the European homeland or in the struggle to adjust to a new natural environment, but rather exists in the harsh treatment of immigrants by Yankees or other immigrant groups with slightly more experience in America. [Dyrud 103]

This critic is correct as far as he goes, but because he focuses on the dilemmas of the main male character, he fails to note that issues relating to marginality and assimilation are different for female characters.

A very minor character in *Plow the Dew Under*, a young woman named Aganetha, sells three "old country" kerchiefs to purchase a train ticket and escape from the immigrant village to the town of Parsons; there she hires out as a maid and enthusiastically begins the process of assimilation. The male protagonist, Ilya, envies her escape into the mainstream, realizing that she "had probably been smarter than he, and had known where she was going and what she was going to do" (Fernald 104–05). Actually, this analysis was not the case; Americans, simply, were more willing to hire a young girl for domestic work and accommodate her interest in improving her language and getting an education. Foreign-born women were not a threat—they were expected to marry and raise fine American sons. Ilya's attempts to establish a cracker factory, however, were more public and more threatening.

3. Dorothy Skårdal outlines the four stages of assimilation: 1) new immigrants are exposed to a mixture of amusement and contempt; 2) Americans fear the growing numbers of immigrants and envy their success; 3) Americans fear the political solidarity of the immigrants; and 4) Americans finally accept immigrants as worthwhile citizens (96–97).

Two other dimensions of women's marginality are explored in *Plow the Dew Under*. When Ilya's mother comes to visit him in Kansas City, she is accompanied by the neighbor girl, Iliana. Iliana is enthusiastically entertained by a young American newspaper man, but then ignored when he meets a fascinating American girl. In this minor plot, Fernald explores the expectations and disappointments of a young woman who is attracted to American people and American ways but has not acquired the education and sophistication that must eventually replace her foreign charm if she is to become the wife of an American. The situation is much easier for Ilya's mother, Sophie. We have seen that Sophie was an eager immigrant who intuitively responded to the new landscape and faced the homesteading experience optimistically. She mediates not only between her conservative husband and adventurous son; but also between two cultures. A minor incident taking place in Kansas City symbolizes Sophie as the "ideal"—from Fernald's point of view—immigrant. Sophie wants a dress like the ones American women wear, but when it is completed she feels that it is too worldly for a Mennonite woman. She keeps it, but she also makes a few appropriate alterations (206). The dress is an excellent symbol of a very delicate process: Sophie accepts and respects American ways, but modifies those aspects which conflict with her old country values and customs. She simultaneously stands for progress and for traditional Mennonite values.

Several works provide glimpses of new immigrants suffering from the slights of the first settlers. In "The Hired Girls" section of *My Ántonia*, Jim notes that "the country girls were considered a menace to the social order. Their beauty shone out too boldly against a conventional background. But anxious mothers need have felt no alarm. They mistook the mettle of their sons. The respect for respectability was stronger than any desire in Black Hawk youth" (201–02). Jim also comments on the envy of first wave settlers for the success of the newcomers. American farmers, according to Jim, refused to let their daughters become domestics. Among the Bohemians and Scandinavians, however, there was no such reservation. As a result, daughters worked at neighboring farms or in town and sent home much-needed money. "One result of this family solidarity," Jim notes, "was that the foreign farmers in our country were the first to become prosperous. After the fathers were out of debt, the daughters married the sons of neighbours—usually of like nationality—and the girls who once worked in Black Hawk kitchens are to-day managing big farms and fine families of their own; their children are better off than the children of the town women they used to serve" (200).

Open hostility and prejudice against newcomers is expressed in Salverson's *Viking Heart*. The Icelanders who settled near Gimli, Manitoba, were at the mercy of the immigration officials and even the English doctor. When smallpox broke out, Dr. Thomas refused to help: "On being told of the illness and the skin eruption, he put it off with the gentle admonition that if they were less dirty this sort of thing would not happen. 'It's just a kind of itch contracted from filth,' he told them" (43). A more widespread effect of prejudice is analyzed by one of the Icelanders:

> "When I remember the wild plans I had in youth of gaining recognition and position after a few years in this country, it seems a huge joke. You know the attitude that the people had towards us. Suspicion, distrust and contempt. A little of that faded when we proved our worth in the rebellion—it has never been said or ever will, I hope, that a Norseman can't defend his home. But we Icelanders are still a curiosity to many. They think us creatures of doubtful habit and uncertain intelligence. They tolerate us because we are useful— because we are doing what they refuse to do, being of such superior clay." [187–88]

In Salverson's view, however, the second generation dispels this kind of suspicion and gains the respect of their countrymen.

Ostenso's *O River, Remember!* and McDonald's *Amalie's Story* detail kinds of problems that emerge within both the group and the individual family because of different attitudes toward Americanization. Some embrace the process; some take the line of least resistance some acknowledge with regret the inevitability of assimilation, while others actively struggle against it.[4] Magdali Vingar represents the first type— she embraces the process because she is expedient in achieving her goals to make money and to establish the kind of town she wants her children to grow up in. To her husband's dismay, she changes their name from *Vingar* to *Wing*, the first of many changes that eventually lead her son, many years later, to make this comparison between his parents: "It came to him sharply then that his mother had gradually discarded every vestige of her immigrant past, while his father was still—well, what *was* his father? Surely an American now, but with the best, the most vigorous

---

4. The hegemony of "the American way of life" is perceived differently at each stage of assimilation and, of course, individuals react in a variety of ways. See Skårdal 87–88.

and honest and spiritually simple qualities of the old land giving something to the new" (Ostenso 308).

In McDonald's novel the tension rising from the clash between
American and Old World values is more intense because both husband
and wife are firm in their commitments. When a fellow Dane accuses
Amalie of "going Yankee," Amalie feels defensive because she knows
that she has drifted away from her countrymen. Although Amalie pro-
tests, she feels guilty about her "American church, rare roast beef, and a
houseful of Yankee furniture" (189–90). Amalie, by her own choice,
would not have gone Yankee. She is married to a businessman, Peter,
who has an American partner; Americanization is essential for maintaining his business relations. Also, her husband is by nature the kind of
immigrant who embraces Americanization because it is easier to fit into
the new culture than to maintain old customs that seem ridiculous to
uninformed Americans. Peter says, "We have taken a new country, and
our children must spend their whole energy learning its ways" (191).
Amalie resists. Her statement about learning and speaking English gets at
the crux of the problem: "I quailed at the thought of learning English. It
would mean the re-making of my soul, for one does not know a language
until the emotions can move in it. From the English I had heard, I
considered the language of America an inhospitable womb for the feelings" (159–60). Peter and Amalie quarrel also over their daughter's
education—Amalie wants her to go to the Danish folk high school and
Peter wants her tutored by an American college graduate (191). Like
most second wave novels, however, *Amalie's Story* concludes on a concil-
iatory note. The foreign-born immigrants affirm the New World experience.

Conflicts may arise because of marginal status, but the novels
delineating the experiences of second wave women are in the comic
tradition: the gains are greater than the losses. One character, Oline,
observes that the New World falls short of the immigrant vision:

> Had they not expected miracles of liberty in America, in return for almost
> miracles of effort? Yet what was the result? Cities, rife with the worst greed
> and vices of Europe, sprang up overnight. The combined forces of science
> had waved a wand over the new world a thousand times more effective than
> all the miracles of the scriptures. Waste lands grew fertile, the wilderness was
> inhabited with strange people all bent on sudden wealth; magnificent build-
> ings lined former ox trails and the simple, home-hungry pioneer had given
> way to speculators, promoters, and outright exploiters of God-given re-
> sources. [Salverson, *Dark Weaver* 196–97]

In fact, she feels her own daughter, self-centered and materialistic, embodies the worst qualities of the New World. An older woman finds Oline's tirade amusing. "But, my dear Oline, were you not just raving at the futilities of the centuries-long sacrifice of individual liberty and happiness? Perhaps our madcap rainbow chasers [their daughters and other young people] will fare less ignobly than we?" (197). In other words, "America"—both Canada and the United States—is flawed. Nevertheless, the younger women have options that their mothers and grandmothers never dreamed of. Laura Goodman Salverson, speaking through a minor character, affirms the immigrant life: "It is a great task and a noble one, this blazing a road to prosperity—this making a wide path for other feet to follow" (*Viking Heart* 115).

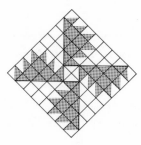

CHAPTER SIX

The Prairie Town

> She had come to a wilderness sick and resentful, where none there was
> to meet her, and the impenetrable forests terrified her every hour, with a
> man whose every act she disliked. . . . Yet this was the splendid recom-
> pense. A town of happy homes. . . . A habitation of men, made pleasant by
> the benefits of civilization, and safe by the gifts of science, had flowered in
> the bitter wilderness through the persistent husbandry of a plain man.
> [Salverson, *Dark Weaver* 346]

This passage reveals a great deal about the emigrant experience in the
pioneer prairie town: a reluctant emigrant, a woman without family
other than the husband she despises, forced to settle in a landscape she
abhors, gradually accepts her new home on the frontier and even respects
"the plain man"—her husband—who has helped to create it. Oline has
participated in the town's growth over a two-decade period and the result
brings enormous satisfaction. To what degree do other female characters
praise or condemn prairie towns? The fiction of prairie women writers
provides a wide range of responses as characters watch their towns grow
from a few canvas-and-board shacks to respectable public buildings and
comfortable homes.

Laura Ingalls Wilder, in her story about De Smet, South Dakota,
describes the spontaneity with which a prairie town appears: "Suddenly,
there on the brown prairie where nothing had been seen before, was the
town. In two weeks, all along Main Street the unpainted new buildings
pushed up their thin false fronts, two stories high and square on top.
Behind the false fronts the buildings squatted under their partly shingled,
sloping roofs. Strangers were already living there" (*By the Shores* 242).
While Laura is fascinated by many aspects of the growing town, she is

happy to leave the town when Pa announces that they can move to the new homestead site (259). Later, however, she looks forward to returning to town for the winter so that she can enjoy the prestige of being a town girl rather than a country girl (*Little Town* 131). Laura's vacillation is understandable: there are advantages and disadvantages to both town and country life. As an adult, Laura hesitates to marry Manly Wilder because he is a farmer, and a farmer's wife always has to work too hard: "I don't want to be poor and work hard while the people in town take it easy and make money off us," she tells Manly (*First Four Years* 4). On the other hand, she loves the horses and the "spaciousness of the wide prairie land." She concludes that it is "more fun living on the land than on the town street with neighbors close on each side" (6–7). She agrees to marry Manly with the understanding that if the farm doesn't pay off in four years, he will try another line of work.[1]

Laura's ambivalence about town and country is a familiar theme in American literature. Yi-Fu Tuan outlines the mythic opposition of urban and rural life:

> The theme of city corruption and rural virtue is popular enough to be classified as folklore. It is told repeatedly: first, decadent Europe and prelapsarian America provided the pleasing antithesis; later, as America took up manufacturing and was itself acquiring large cities, the opposition was perceived to lie between an industrialized and Mammon-seeking Eastern seaboard and the virtuous, agrarian interior. . . . During the nineteenth century the image of a contented and virtuous rural people became a dominant emblem of national aspirations. The ideal did not stop, or even much hinder, the amassing of wealth and devotion to technological progress that combined to make America into a great manufacturing nation. Yet it was far from being an empty rhetoric. [*Topophilia* 108–09]

Thus prairie women writing about the New World landscape north and south of the 49th parallel had to deal with both the powerful agrarian ideal and the equally strong belief in progress, which is intricately connected to the city's role in society. They had to decide upon the extent to

1. William Holtz discusses the "failure of the myth" in the cycle of Wilder's works: "the autobiographical detail of *The First Four Years* challenges the simple optimism of the earlier books. Ambiguities that had remained latent emerge as explicit alternatives to life on the homestead. Town life has permitted Laura's adolescent social growth and fulfillment, and the town itself, although ugly, now offers economic opportunities denied the farmer. The farm, on the other hand, furnishes a beautiful landscape but forecloses further horizons" (87). The new Eden, where a farm couple through hard work and commitment can flourish and prosper, never becomes a reality for Laura and her husband.

which they could support the image of "a contented and virtuous rural people" and—if their stories were to move beyond the initial homestead-ing experience—to establish the effects of growing prairie towns on the lives of their characters.

Clara Thomas, in her study of four Canadian women writing about the "new land," notes a tendency on the part of authors and their characters to take sides either for the country or for the town. Thomas draws an example of an idealized country landscape from Nellie Mc-Clung's autobiography:

> White-washed, Red-river frame houses, set in wide farm yards, well back from the road, stacks of hay and fields of ripe grain with men cutting it down with reapers, and in some fields with sickle and cradles—then long stretches of meadows, growing brown with autumn and then more houses. Over all the odor of wild sage, and goldenrod, that grew beside the road, and in the air flights of crows and blackbirds visiting the scattered grain fields, and sitting on wire fences, like strings of jet beads.

Without making an explicit comparison, McClung implies that the country is so pleasing that no one could possibly want to live elsewhere. As Thomas points out, this scene serves "as a central image for all McClung's work and all her lifetime's effort" ("Women Writers" 46). Country, for McClung, is better than town.

Thomas then presents a sharply different perspective found in Laura Goodman Salverson's *Viking Heart,* noting that Salverson "made quite explicit her ultimate faith in the city, not the country, as the agent of civilization and progress" ("Women Writers" 51). Thomas quotes the following passage from *The Viking Heart,* which describes Winnipeg as a young city: "Each pedestrian seemed to have caught some happy vision and so the very air vibrated with an abundance of good will. . . . For the soul of a city is the most wonderful thing in the world. It is fed by knowledge and ambition; it is tempered by adversity and grief; it is beautified by love and honor and it is made eternal through sacrifice and death" ("Women Writers" 51; ellipsis in Thomas). While Thomas finds clear-cut preferences in the works of McClung and Salverson, other critics examining other works find ambivalence. (See figs. 17, 18, and 19, which show a picturesque Winnipeg at several stages of growth.)

In "The Ambivalence of Rural Life in Prairie Literature," Diane Dufva Quantic describes conflicting feelings not only toward the farm but also toward the town. She infers from several novels that most writers felt that whatever culture was available was inferior. Townspeople were

WINNIPEG AS IT WAS.

Fig. 17   *Winnipeg As It Was*, from *Canadian Pictures* by the Marquis of Lorne.

WINNIPEG IN 1875.

Fig. 18   *Winnipeg in 1875*, from *Canadian Pictures* by the Marquis of Lorne.

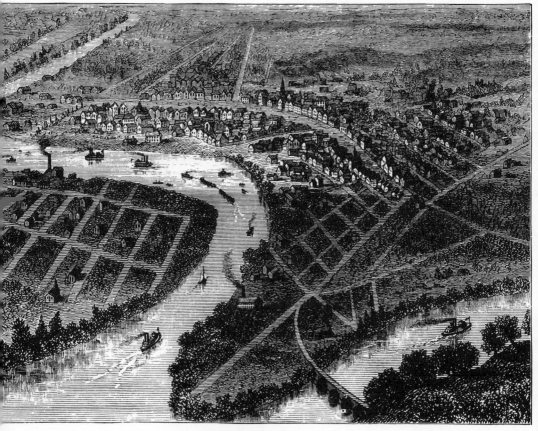

WINNIPEG IN 1882.

Fig. 19   *Winnipeg in 1882*, from *Canadian Pictures* by the Marquis of Lorne.

trapped in a pervasive cultural isolation, but the farm family, she argues, felt even more alienated because they depended on the town for supplies and school and church, but had no real place in town business or social structures. In Quantic's analysis, negative feelings about the town are replaced by ambivalent feelings for those "sensitive souls" who make up a small portion of any town. The town offers so little by way of imaginative and intellectual stimulation that the appearance of individuals with "a sensitivity to the land, to their place in the scheme of life on the prairie gives rise to surprise at first, and then ambivalence" (118).[2]

2. Quantic bases these generalizations on tall-grass works by Cather, Rölvaag, Wilder, Aldrich, Woiwode, and Morris, and on short-grass fiction by Mari Sandoz.

While Quantic acknowledges the ambivalence of characters and authors toward the town, she, like many other critics and historians, draws a negative picture of the prairie town.[3] I believe that if we isolate the three "true" prairie women writers (Cather, Wilder, and Aldrich) and examine their characters in relation to their towns, a degree of ambivalence may remain, but the prairie town appears as a generally favorable environment in which to live.

A Lantern in Her Hand describes a pioneer woman's feelings about the town. In this novel, Aldrich describes the frontier situation for the women of her mother's generation. In 1872 Abbie Deal's town consisted of her house, the Lutz's combination store and house, and the black-smith-preacher's house and shop. Abbie and Sarah Lutz didn't like people referring to the "Stove Creek store" or talking about picking up their mail "over at Stove Creek." They decided to name the town "Cedar-town" and began to correct any references to "Stove Creek" (66). Women like Abbie Deal—who named a town, initiated the Grange auxiliary, established the Literary Reading Circle, and participated in the dedication of the new frame church—certainly had a minimal amount of hostility toward their towns. The ambivalence, I suspect, comes with the second generation.[4]

In Cather's O Pioneers! the town of Hanover, Nebraska, is described as a "cluster of low drab buildings huddled on the gray prairie, under a gray sky" (3). But in My Ántonia, the town of Black Hawk is described as "a clean, well-planted little prairie town, with white fences and good green yards about the dwellings, wide, dusty streets, and shapely little trees growing along the wooden sidewalks" (145). Each description is appropriate for a particular character at a particular time in the action. To Alexandra in O Pioneers! the town would appear drab and gray on a late fall evening as she makes family purchases; we must remember that her thoughts are focused on her dying father. Jim Burden, whose position is considerably more secure than Alexandra's, sees the town as clean and green and neatly ordered when he moves there to begin a new and interesting phase of life.

---

3. See, for example, Dick Harrison's discussion in Unnamed Country 127–30 and the following novels: E. W. Howe's Story of a Country Town; Meridel Le Sueur's I Hear Men Talking; Sinclair Ross's As for Me and My House. In an essay in Heart of a Stranger, Margaret Laurence presents both the positive and negative sides of the prairie town ("A Place to Stand On" 13–18).

4. Aldrich's Rim of the Prairie describes the frustrations of the second and third generation growing up in a prairie town.

Even Ántonia, despite her periods of loneliness in town, the thwarted rape by Wick Cutter, and abandonment by her railroad lover, looks back on the time she lived in town as a good one: " 'Oh, I'm glad I went! I'd never have known anything about cooking or housekeeping if I hadn't. I learned nice ways at the Harlings', and I've been able to bring up my children so much better' " (343). The town provided Ántonia and several other immigrant farm girls with experiences and options that would not have been available on the homestead.[5] Certainly, as Michael Peterman points out, "the town speaks . . . to those elements of social and daily life which inhibit human behavior of a natural or spontaneous kind: conformity, prejudice, artificiality, habitual materialism, and what Cather calls 'respect for respectability' " (101). Certainly the small towns have some negative characteristics; they nevertheless offered some women important advantages.

In *Pioneer Women: Voices from the Kansas Frontier*, Joanna L. Stratton concludes her analysis of first and second generation frontier women and the town experience on a positive note. Her summary adds the voices of "real" women to those of fiction and provides a foundation for analyzing prairie towns in women's fiction:

> The prairie town was the mainstay of frontier society—a marketplace, a meeting place, a crossroads for interstate commerce and communication. Though women sometimes found it a rough and lawless place, they also loved the town for its hubbub and vitality. Those who labored on the family homestead went to town not only to shop but to join in church activities, sewing circles and literary societies where news was shared and confidences exchanged in a warm community of women. Those who lived in town often ran general stores, managed hotels, worked as dressmakers or served as postmistresses. Women united to organize the town library and support its expansion. In time, a number of women stepped forward to express their views at political rallies, . . . on temperance crusades and . . . the campaign for woman suffrage. Those women who lived more obscurely still had the pleasure of watching a raw town of dirt paths and shanties grow into a real metropolis. As Josephine Middlekauf wrote: "After sixty years of pioneering in Hays, I could write volumes telling of its growth and progress, more often under adverse conditions than favorable ones. . . . Suffice to say I have found it all interesting and worth while and feel I have been singularly privileged to have seen it develop from the raw materials into the almost finished product in comfortable homes, churches, schools, paved streets, trees, fruits and flowers." [204]

5. For an analysis of the hired girls in works by Cather and others, see Sallquist, "The Image of the Hired Girl in Literature: The Great Plains, 1860 to World War I."

Josephine Middlekauf's views—and those of other Kansas women in Stratton's study—prevent us from dismissing the fiction writers' positive responses to the town as mere nostalgia.

Why do some women accept the town or express ambivalence toward it while others reject it? Prairie fiction gives us some astonishingly different perspectives. Some works show characters defending the town; other characters criticize the town. Several works contain plots that develop not the characters of individuals but the character of the mid-western town. At the same time, prairie novels provide materials for analyzing the iconography of town women to determine the differences in roles and options between town women and homestead women.[6]

Laura Ingalls Wilder, as an adult, chose the farm a few miles outside of De Smet as a better place than town to live with her husband and to raise children. This preference for country is reflected in her daughter's work as well. Rose Wilder Lane, in a novel about her parents' generation of immigrants, *Let the Hurricane Roar*, describes a situation which leads a young wife to decide to live in town for the winter. Her husband has written from Iowa telling her he has been injured and can't get back to their homestead before the blizzards begin. On entering the town at sunset, Caroline feels intimidated: she is an outsider who is asking for shelter and work among strangers. The next morning, however, she finds the town less threatening: "The tall fronts of the buildings were thin boards; they had behind them only shanties, boarded up and down. The buildings tried to assert their importance, erecting painful vertical lines where all lines were low and level. But the great sky and the prairie ignored them. Barns, haystacks and a few little shanties straggled out and dwindled against the prairie, like a confession of futility" (103).

---

6. In "The Civilizers: Women's Organizations and Western American Literature," June O. Underwood raises some important questions about the ways women have been portrayed in relation to town organizations and the kinds of bonding that result from women organizing and working together for a specific reason. She points out that in literature women's participation in civic organizations has been "used to trivialize or reveal the malevolence of the women involved" or to show their indifference, their lack of enthusiasm or commitment. She argues that these images, although contrary to historical facts, have been perpetuated because of the idealization of the "loner, the individual who acts in isolation, and who, when his space gets too crowded, 'lights out for the territory'" (8, 9). Underwood concludes: "While fiction has tended to deny the validity of dignity of women bonding together in a separate sphere, autobiography has recorded it vividly. The women who civilized the West brought more than teacups and lace doilies with them. They brought the moral imperatives of humane nurturing and valuing, valuing not property—horses and lands and cattle—but other human beings. Out of their organized concern, the West became a different place" (13).

Every detail of this passage conveys the frailty of the new town and its questionable ability to fulfill human needs. As Caroline seeks room, board, and work, she is treated with suspicion by some; others ask her pointed questions while trying to estimate the money they could gain by helping her. She returns to the homestead, alone, where her existence and that of the baby's may be threatened by nature, but her dignity will be intact. The earliest stages of "city corruption," as noted by Yi-Fu Tuan, are represented in Lane's South Dakota frontier town.

Other works focusing on the homestead experience present similar preferences for the country. In Nellie McClung's story about late nine-teenth-century pioneers, "The Runaway Grandmother" (1912), Grand-ma answers an advertisement for a housekeeper and escapes to the farm of a bachelor near Souris River in southern Manitoba. When the young man expresses concern about harboring a runaway, Grandma tries to ease his conscience by explaining her reasons for refusing to live with her sons. Her lawyer son in Regina won't go to bed before 10:30 or dismiss the hired girl so that the grandmother can do the housework by herself. Her doctor son in Winnipeg dabbles in politics and, in her opinion, spends too much time away from his family (*Black Creek* 121). Grandma's complaints demonstrate that key values—the work ethic and the inde-pendent, family-centered home—are threatened in the progressive ur-ban centers. She manages a return to traditional values by introducing her granddaughter to the bachelor. The young people fall in love; Grand-ma is assured of a happy old age on a farm where everyone works hard and goes to bed early.

In McClung's "Black Creek Stopping-House," Winnipeg in the 1870s and 1880s is described as a cold, muddy city where men develop bad habits, such as drinking and gambling. However, one young man, John Corbett, falls in love with an Irish girl and promises to reform if she will marry him. They save money while running a boardinghouse and eventually purchase oxen and a covered wagon and, responding to "the cry of free land for the asking" (14) establish themselves among settlers of southern Manitoba. Human nature being what it is, there are villains and gossips and ne'er-do-wells among the settlers, too; fortunately, honesty and goodness predominate and John Corbett, influenced by the new land and a firm wife, never relapses into his gambling city ways.

The evils of town and the goodness of farm life become the domi-nant theme in McClung's *Painted Fires* (1925). A Finnish girl, Helmi, embarks on a quest for the garden she saw as a little girl on a postcard from her Aunt Lily in Minnesota. The ordeals Helmi undergoes in pursuit of the garden equal those of mythic male heroes. In St. Paul she finds Aunt Lilly tubercular and abused by her American husband. However, through a network that links domestics in St. Paul and Winnipeg, Helmi obtains a position at a respectable place in Winnipeg. As her new employer says, "Any girl that will wash dishes and scrub can always find a place, and if she's civil and clean and honest she'll get on" (11–12). Helmi learns not only the domestic service, but the language and customs of Canadians too. At one point she is even adopted by a socially minded single woman who lives in an "unimpeachable neighborhood"; for a brief time, Helmi enjoys life as a carefully supervised young girl participating in such activities as Canadian Girls in Training. Then Helmi is caught purchasing heroin tablets at the Chinaman's for a neighbor who uses them. Helmi, though innocent—she doesn't know that the errand she has been sent on involves illegal drugs—is sentenced by a jury prejudiced against Finns. She is sent to a girl's reformatory, and the inhumanity of Winnipeg's penal system is described in great detail.

When Helmi leaves reform school she escapes to Alberta. Prejudices against foreigners persist; moreover, everyone, it seems to Helmi, seeks wealth and freedom from responsibility. Early one spring Helmi marries a respectable young man; unfortunately he is gold-hungry and gullible. He leaves Helmi—temporarily, of course—and goes to work in a mine in which he has invested. By Christmas Eve, Helmi is alone in Edmonton, where she is taken in by a Mrs. Corbett at the North Star Boarding House and assisted in delivering her baby. Eventually Helmi returns to a prairie homestead in Alberta, property which she inherits from an Englishman she once nursed. It is here—not in St. Paul or Winnipeg or Edmonton—that she is able to create the garden she has yearned for since leaving Finland. And because she has endured disappointment and anguish, McClung rewards her not only with the homestead but with a coal mine that insures her future prosperity. However, near the end of the novel we are told that "unlike most mine owners, The Dorans [Helmi and her husband Jack] have not moved to the city, but have a large gray stucco house, with a red roof and many windows, on the banks of English River" (315).

Although *Painted Fires* is a maddeningly melodramatic story, it nevertheless documents what McClung perceived to be the economic and social climate of prairie province towns in the early twentieth century. No matter how outrageous McClung's plots may be, they are rooted in a reality she had examined firsthand as a pioneer in Manitoba and in her adult years in Alberta and Saskatchewan. As a social and political activist she embarrassed public officials in three provinces by document-ing deplorable conditions in housing, hospitals, jails, and factories.[7] Ultimately McClung's optimistic view of human nature leads her to acknowledge certain kindnesses—individual and institutional—in town as well as country.

Several writers present multiple reactions to country and town through pairs of characters: one prefers the town and one prefers the country. In novels by Rolyat, Breneman/Thurston, and Wilder, mothers and daughters represent those opposites. In *The Land They Possessed,* Mavis, the mother, laughs about the debate over the town's name: "'I don't care what they call it so long as we're here. Hetty, I feel like a new woman. My husband satisfied. The babies thriving. There'll be church again. And people'" (Breneman/Thurston 121).

The daughter in this novel, Michal, and Margaret, the daughter in *The Lily of Fort Garry,* understand and respect their mothers' feelings about the town and the kinds of security that even a newly formed town represents to some women; both daughters, however, reject proposals of marriage from townsmen. Margaret marries and disappears into the wil-derness with her mixed-blood husband, rejecting the affluent merchant's son in Fort Garry as well as the Irish aristocrat who tempted her with continental journeys and an estate in Ireland. Michal too has had an alternative; she jilts the lawyer's son who is accumulating degrees at a New England university. She chooses to elope with a German immi-grant, thus linking her life with those who, the authors make clear, truly possess the land.

In Wilder's fiction the new town of De Smet is described as "a sore on the beautiful, wild prairie" (*Little Town* 49). But Laura finds the town interesting and delights in the different people: they are unpredictable— sometimes funny and sometimes sad. In town there are horse races, dime sociables, a new church, and the "Literary" that holds spelling bees, musical programs, and charades. Of course, there is an unhealthy side of town life. Laura laughs until her sides ache when she sees two drunk men. One extraordinarily tall, thin man and one short paunchy man walk

7. See Candace Savage, *Our Nell: A Scrapbook Biography of Nellie McClung* for an overview of McClung's political activities; see also Veronica Strong-Boag, "Canadian Feminism in the 1920's: The Case of Nellie McClung," *Journal of Canadian Studies* 12 (1977): 58–68.

down the yellow-boarded sidewalk, arms linked. They are singing "My name is Tay Pay Pryor . . . and I'm drunk!" They pause at each door for the tall man to emphasize the lyrics by kicking in the mosquito netting in Brown's saloon, Beardsley's hotel, Barker's grocery, and Wilder's feed store. Ma, however, finds nothing humorous about the situation and concludes that the women are going to have to organize and do something about the two saloons (*Little Town* 54–55). From Ma's point of view, the town, with a railroad and strangers coming and going, represents a center for unethical business practices, widespread instability, and disregard for traditional customs and values.

On the basis of the town fiction reviewed thus far, we can conclude that female attitudes toward the town vary considerably. Thus women's prairie fiction supports Tuan's thesis that individual variations affect attitudes toward environment. "We need to know something of human physiology and temperament in all their diversity," Tuan insists; then we can understand how some individuals remain unaffected by dominant family or cultural attitudes toward place while others are swept completely away (*Topophilia* 45).

Fiction becomes a forum for the country-town debate. Nellie McClung, for example, used fiction as propaganda for the tolerant, democratic nature of the Canadian town. In "The Way of the West," a story first published in the prairie provinces in the Toronto *Globe*, a newcomer to the prairies is forced through a social ritual which results in his democratization. Thomas Shouldice, a loyal Orangeman, is outraged by the spectacle taking place across the road from his house: American settlers who have poured into the Souris Valley are having a Fourth of July celebration. Shouldice shudders at the sight of "Canadian-bred and born driving over to the enemy's camp" (*Black Creek* 210). Furthermore, his rage against the Yankees increases when he sees Father O'Flynn walking across the slough to join the others. He is sure the Americans and Catholics are "in league" against the British. In response to these activities Shouldice attempts to reinforce sharp boundaries between groups by organizing a Twelfth of July celebration to commemorate the Protestant victory over Irish Catholics at the Battle of the Boyne.

By the morning of the twelfth, Shouldice has been able to assemble only a faithful few. He heads the parade as William of Orange, riding an old mare and followed by a soloist and some members of the Carleton Place Loyal Lodge No. 23. However, the numbers grow: the seven Breeze children join in, followed by two American youngsters. Gradually more

Americans "fall in . . . two by two, men, women and children" (*Black Creek* 220). The priest, listening to the paraders sing—"We are not divided / All one body we"—observes that "the spirit of the West was upon them, unifying, mellowing, harmonizing all conflicting emotions" (*Black Creek* 222). Shouldice, as organizer, is lauded for his goodwill by the priest, who knows perfectly well that Shouldice's motives were to separate, rather than to unite, the townspeople. Thus Shouldice is drawn reluctantly into the life of a community that respects national and religious differences. McClung concludes the story by saying:

> Where could such a scene as this be enacted—a Twelfth of July celebration where a Roman Catholic priest was principal speaker, where the company dispersed with the singing of "God Save the King," led by an American band?
> Nowhere, but in The Northwest of Canada, that illimitable land with its great sunlit spaces, where the West wind, bearing on its bosom the spices of a million flowers, woos the heart of man with a magic spell and makes him kind and neighborly and brotherly! [*Black Creek* 224]

Like McClung, other writers use character and situation to establish the identity of the prairie town as democratic and culturally promising. Both Alice French and Mary Hartwell Catherwood tried to alter easterners' stereotypes of midwesterners and their towns through fiction. In "Mrs. Finlay's Elizabethan Chair" (1887), Alice French demonstrates that democracy flourishes on the prairie; she believes that midwesterners are superior to their New England counterparts who have become elitest, lost touch with their ancestors' mission, and reverted to Old World values which, in French's opinion, are inferior because of their emphasis on class. In a similar vein, Catherwood demonstrates in "The Spirit of an Illinois Town" (1896) that the jaded easterner can be rejuvenated and regain hope while living in a raw, energetic western town that nourishes both individualism and creativity.

In French's story, Emily Finlay, a New Englander, marries a man who "could not quite brush away the flavor of the prairies," although he had been educated at Harvard and Heidelberg. Tom Finlay's roots are so firmly established in his prairie town that no amount of exposure to the East and to Europe can alter his midwestern ways and values, which the narrator clearly admires (*Knitters* 101). Tom tries to mediate between the town and his wife, but Emily does everything possible to maintain her New England distinctiveness in a town she considers "stupid, censorious, [and] provincial" (*Knitters* 100). French, a New England descendant herself,[8] does admire certain qualities in Emily. She presents Emily as a good wife to Tom in every way—except in not sharing his affection for the town and its people.

The true hero of the story, the foil for Emily Finlay, is Violet Durham, described as making "one think of prairie flowers when the breeze shakes the dew from them" (*Knitters* 108). The plot of the story evolves around Violet's role in the planning and opening of the Wrenham Art Museum—the town has reached that stage in development which requires visible evidence of its historical and cultural roots. Mrs. Finlay, after considerable pressure from her husband and the museum committee, agrees to exhibit the Elizabethan chair that had been brought by a Finlay ancestor from Scotland two hundred years before. Its counterpart in the exhibit is the Jackson chair belonging to Mrs. Cody, the head of the museum committee. This chair is a hundred years old, "given to Mr. Cody by the General himself" (*Knitters* 110). In a subtle way, the two chairs represent the character of the midwesterner and the easterner. The lines of the Cody chair are "chastely plain," in contrast to the "florid carving" of the Elizabethan chair. We are told, however, "there was a general resemblance of form, if not of color, between the two chairs": both have arms and both have "imposing proportions" (*Knitters* 117). The reader then makes the appropriate comparison—the prairie townspeople and the New Englanders are attractive and, moreover, very much alike; the westerners, however, are simpler.

When the exhibit closes, everything is removed from the building but the two chairs, which are too large to be protected from the continuous rain that has hindered the removal of the artifacts. One night the building catches fire and, as the result of a series of errors, Violet Durham thinks she has rescued the white-sheeted Finlay chair but discovers too late that only the Jackson chair has survived the fire. While it is indeed regrettable that the Elizabethan chair was destroyed, the point of the story is, of course, that the Jackson chair must survive because it represents true American values. The Elizabethan chair, a product of a decadent European culture, must give way to the American chair. So too must Emily Finlay give way and acknowledge the fineness inherent in Violet Durham and, indirectly, in the prairie town. In coming to terms

8. Alice French has received relatively little critical attention. For more background on her characterization, themes, and values, see Susan McQuin, "Alice French's View of Women" and a very early essay by Mary J. Reid, "The Theories of Octave Thanet and Other Western Realists."

with the loss of her chair and Violet Durham's heroic attempt to rescue the chair, Emily is brought into harmony with the town's values, with its life and its spirit.

Alice French has been quoted as saying that a short story is "an incident . . . a single glimpse into life [which has to be] typical and significant" (Reid 100). In the case of "Mrs. Finlay's Elizabethan Chair," French effectively establishes the identity of a prairie town through a single incident. She accomplishes a similar task in the story "Tommy and Thomas" in which she returns to the theme of democracy and the mid-westerners' pride in their democratic and classless society. In this story, however, French demonstrates that the supposed equality among prairie people is a myth; nevertheless, intelligent and sensitive individuals can secure a place in "high society" through good education and manners. Tommy's grandmother had come from Ireland during the famine; his father is a saloon-owner who recognizes that money alone will not bring power and prestige. While most working-class fathers would have pulled their sons from school at an early age and put them to work, Mr. Fitz-maurice insists that Tommy graduate from high school. Tommy is in the process of memorizing his valedictory address when his friend Harry introduces him to Mrs. Carriswood, an elegant, widely traveled eastern-er. She is attracted to Tommy's Irish charm, although his speech, manner, and clothes need considerable polishing. She spends several eve-nings helping him improve his oratorical style, and is rewarded by the cheers and foot-stomping that follow his address on graduation night.

When Mrs. Carriswood meets him ten years later, he has gradu-ated from the state university and become a respected, even wealthy, lawyer. But, Tommy tells her, "'I'm on the outside of such a lot of things. . . . When I first began to suspect that I was on the outside was when I went to the High School. . . . You can't learn manners from books, ma'am. I learned them at Harry's. That is,'—he colored and laughed,—'I learned *some*. There's plenty left, I know'" (*Stories* 111).

More years pass, and when Mrs. Carriswood meets Tommy a third time he is an Iowa representative to Congress. During the course of a few weeks she watches him move with infallible manners and poise among the most sophisticated society. She is delighted to see that he is now on the "inside" until she realizes that her niece Margaret, who has turned down several continental nobles, has permitted him to become an inti-mate friend. Rather than sending off a telegram warning Margaret's mother, she decides to wait another day, assuming that Tommy will commit some faux pas that will make Margaret see what an inappropriate husband he would be.

Mrs. Carriswood and Margaret attend a congressional session and hear Tommy give what was later referred to as "the speech that made him" (*Stories* 126). Mrs. Carriswood spots his parents in the gallery and realizes they are keeping their presence from Tommy because they don't want to embarrass him in front of his elegant colleagues. When Tommy sees them, he calls to them and takes obvious delight in introducing them to his friends. At the conclusion of the story, Mrs. Carriswood calls him "Thomas" instead of "Tommy": this is her tribute to a man who has risen to a position of power and respectability but has not become a snob.

In Catherwood's "Spirit of an Illinois Town," the flaws of a newcomer are corrected by the positive influences of the prairie town. Seth Adams, a disillusioned young writer, has gone west after ruining his personal and professional relationships in the East. Like Shouldice in McClung's "Way of the West" and Emily Finlay in French's "Elizabethan Chair," Adams moves from outside to inside the community through the intervention of a local resident. In Catherwood's story, the helper is a young woman named Kate Keene whose alcoholic father (the former newspaper editor) has bequeathed her a love of books and paintings and theatre. With an eye to the practical, he also urged her to develop the domestic arts, so she dutifully learns housekeeping from an aunt, according to her father's instructions—so she'll have something to fall back on while preparing to "read in public." Without anyone's knowledge, Kate has devoted hundreds of hours to elocution. Perhaps there had been in her father's collection a book such as *Iliff's Select Readings for Public and Private Entertainment,* which, the subtitle promises, "contains choice selections of the most pathetic, gay, humorous, heroic, sublime and patriotic speeches and poems . . . together with appropriate elocutionary instructions."

As the result of one of Kate's performances in the small town's theatre, Seth Adams becomes a new man. In the following passage he describes his transformation during Kate's presentation to the Wilderness Club:

> It was a spell. None of the hollow tricks of the elocutionist broke it. She made people pass before our minds, magnifying our human experience. She was Perdita as white as a lily. She was Cleopatra with a Greek-Egyptian face. With sudden angularity she was Betsey Trotwood chasing donkeys. She was

a score of droll American forms which we recognized with shouts of laughter. She was age, youth, childhood, tears.

    She left us; and four times, five times, six times, seven times, we dragged her back to give us the joy of living a moment longer in the mimic world. And then the town of Trail, with its guests, stood upon its feet, and shouted and laughed and cried, until I felt something break away within me. [346]

Gradually, through Kate, Adams comes to love the town: "I myself was landed," he concluded (346). He is no longer an outsider; he acknowledges that Trail City provides the setting for a second chance, for renewal as a new "Adams" in the prairie town.

    Following Kate's performance, during what Adams calls the "resurrecting spring," he resumes his writing career. Kate provides intelligent criticism of his work; in addition, she is "like primeval air blowing across the prairies" (485). If Seth is the prairie Adam, Kate certainly is the prairie Eve. That resurrecting spring brought life, but it also brought death, including Kate Keene's. A tornado struck town. Later Seth recalled that "ragged lights of bird's-egg green zigzagged in [a] wall, and the faces of all around . . . were dim and ghastly. We smothered in an icy river of exhausted air and the wall came on with a million locomotive roars, crashes and screams rising in its course" (488).

    Seth Adams's partner, Sam Peevy, another easterner, provides Kate's eulogy:

    "I said to myself again and again, as I looked at her, 'The Spirit of this Illinois town!' Sprung out of hardship, buoyant and full of resources, big-hearted, patient, great,—how mightily she did express the soul of the West! . . .

    "The Spirit of this town,—that's what she was; just as a beautiful ideal woman expresses the Goddess of Liberty. Pluck and genius and humility, boundless energy and vision, and personal power that carried everything before it,—all of these covered with the soft flesh of a child just turning woman,—that was Kate." [490]

Contrary to traditional images of the West, it is the frontier woman, then, not the frontier male, who epitomizes the spirit of the new land. Kate is not the stereotypical culture bearer, conservative in thought and action; she is buoyant, resourceful, big-hearted, energetic, and visionary. And, as the story and title make clear, these are the characteristics of the prairie town as well.[9]

    9. Although Catherwood disliked a great deal about prairie towns, one critic noted that no other writer had "ever shown more convincingly the squalor, the rush, the intensity, the intoxication of life in a growing western town" (Price, "Critical Biography" 314).

Sam Peevy's impassioned description of the prairie town is balanced by a less highly colored description at the opening of the story in which Catherwood notes the different elements contributing to the town's personality:

> But the virgin town was still untainted with deep poverty or vice. It had kept itself entirely free . . . from that American institution called the saloon, so different from foreign wineshops. We were literally walking through a square mile of Ohio cheer, New England thrift and conscientiousness, Kentucky hospitality, New York far-sightedness with capital to back it, and native Illinois grit. The very air, resinous and sweet, had a peculiar tingle that a man, having once felt, cannot forget. Everybody was going to succeed, and on the way could put up with a few inconveniences. . . . Everybody wore a satisfied grin, because the days of rattlesnake-fighting were over and a long-looked-for millennium had come. . . .
>
> There were a great many passers, for people were continually walking about to gloat over the promised land, and brag. [169]

Price, in his critical biography of Catherwood, says that "her sentiment for the West as a land of hope never vanished" (104). Nevertheless, she disliked the midwestern towns, where she was forced to spend most of her years "close to ugliness of living and narrowness of thinking and feeling" (14). The fact that Catherwood has "the spirit" of the town killed in a tornado symbolically represents the erosion of the good things that Kate Keene stands for. At the same time, Seth Adams is rehabilitated, so the midwestern town has some redeeming qualities.

In Elisabeth Ford's *No Hour of History*, Victoria throws down her copy of *Main Street* and announces she would like to write a book called *The Other Side of Main Street*:

> "I'm sick and tired of a lot of fool notions people have about the Middle West generally. . . . You'd think the whole place had been settled by ignoramuses. I'd have them know that the pioneers brought with them their leather-bound classics as well as almanacs, and that they read them, too. We may say tomaytoes instead of tomohtoes but our fathers and mothers didn't all sit around in homemade rockers with patchwork cushions and stir straw ticks and act folksy." [307–08]

Catherwood's characters, at the beginning of the era, had confidently predicted a prosperous and culturally rich future for the prairie town. At the end of the era, Ford's Victoria Ash insists that good music and literature and intellectual pursuits were not only ideals but realities.

Interest in delineating the pioneer prairie town and its people continues in the work of the contemporary writer Margaret Laurence.

She draws on her personal family background, which includes two pioneer grandparents in the Manitoba town of Neepawa.[10] Laurence also had the advantage of evaluating the perspectives of other writers in the tradition of prairie fiction as she constructed her own imaginary town. Her 1964 novel, *The Stone Angel,* provides yet another interpretation of a pioneer town.

In this novel, Hagar Currie Shipley, a ninety-year-old woman, describes her father's attempts to found a prairie dynasty. He produced two sons who develop into "unspirited" boys and then a rebellious daughter, Hagar, whose birth takes the life of the mother. The father, Jason Currie, can mold the landscape to his liking by building a brick house (the second one in town) and by carrying birch trees from Galloping Mountain. He can also try to mold the values of his family and the town according to his Scot-Presbyterian beliefs in self-made men, economy of words and feelings, hard work accompanied appropriately by material success, good manners and education. However, he can't make his daughter love the town. Hagar says: "How bitterly I regretted that he'd left [Scotland] and had sired us here, the bald-headed prairie stretching out west of us with nothing to speak of except couchgrass or clans of chittering gophers or the gray-green poplar bluffs, and the town where no more than half a dozen decent brick houses stood, the rest being shacks and shanties, shaky frame and tarpaper, short-lived in the sweltering summers and the winters that froze the wells and the blood" (12). Hagar refuses to be his showpiece after receiving an eastern education. She marries the uneducated, coarse but virile Bram Shipley and, carrying with her all of her father's class prejudices and sexual and emotional restraints, chooses (at least for a while) the prairie farm with its voluptuos lilacs and terrifying horses. When her younger son is still a boy, she leaves Bram and moves to Vancouver, becoming a housekeeper for a retired seaman. She returns, briefly, to Manawaka when her husband is dying. Shortly thereafter her son is killed in a car accident. The town, without her "lost men," has nothing to hold her.

The iconography of prairie women also reveals the attitudes of women writers toward the quality of life for women in prairie towns. The Prairie Angel persists as a dominant image but with some new variations: she is a wife but also an unmarried domestic and, in one case, a school-

10. For insight into the role of Laurence's family in Manawaka, see the Neepawa Centennial publication (Neepawa Chamber of Commerce 1983), which describes the activities of her grandfathers on the Wemyss side and on the Simpson side of her family.

teacher. The town counterpart to the plow-woman is the businesswoman who cultivates new ground in the marketplace; considering the barriers she must cross to achieve her goals, she might very well be called a Frontier Hero. The Prairie Victim, the woman who is unable to adapt to the frontier environment, is a recurring type but with different problems; the physical isolation of the homestead is replaced by psychological isolation resulting from class or cultural alienation.

The angel of the house in prairie town novels has similar responsibilities and works as hard, in many instances, as the woman on the homestead.[11] Aldrich, Aydelotte, and Salverson provide examples of town wives and, at the same time, describe town settlement at four stages: the new, isolated prairie town in the 1870s; the Oklahoma boom town after the "dangerous days" are over; a small frontier town in Manitoba; and finally, the city of Winnipeg at the turn of the century.

In *A Lantern in Her Hand*, Abbie and Will Deal endure the drought years of the 1870s in Nebraska. Being part of the town, as noted before, alleviates the stress and reduces some of the deprivations. As a girl back in Iowa, Abbie had dreamed of a career in music or art, but the prairie town does not develop fast enough for her to pursue those aspirations. She is the archetypal nineteenth-century woman who sets aside her personal needs and arranges finances so that her daughters realize their dreams. While readers might see in the Abbie Deal types the Prairie Victim rather than the admirable Prairie Angel, we need only recall the rebuke Bess Streeter Aldrich received from her mother to put things in a proper perspective. Aldrich wrote: "I remarked that we daughters were sorry her life had been hard in her pioneering days, that it seemed unfair that we now should live in an easier era with all its modern conveniences. She looked at me with an odd little expression and said: Oh, save your pity. We had the best time in the world" (Aldrich, "Story behind *A Lantern in Her Hand*" 240).

Aydelotte's *Trumpets Calling* and Salverson's *Dark Weaver* describe women's situations in new towns after roads and railroads have been established. As Aydelotte puts it, "those dangerous days were over"—

11. The "angel of the house" was a dynamic image for young women imagining their roles, as editors and writers well knew. For example, a 1901 publication, *The Perfect Woman*, includes discussion under topics such as "Man Erects the Building, Women Enshrines It," "Home the Kingdom of Woman," "Love and Marriage Divinely Appointed"—all images complementary to angelic passivity but promising, at the same time, power. This book aimed to give practical, serious advice on the physical, emotional, and spiritual well-being of females.

those days when men worked new fields with rifles nearby and wom-
en"faced hardships valiantly, giving the look of home to a one-room log
cabin" (17). Martha, the daughter of a man who continually sought new
adventures in new lands, married a similar type. Unlike her mother,
however, Martha makes the decisions and when she agrees in 1893 to go
with her husband, Dave, to the Cherokee Strip in Oklahoma, she refuses
to live on an isolated homestead, but instead perches near town where
she can run her homestead and keep track of events in town at the same
time. When Dave gets restless during the dry years, she tells him he can
move on, but he'll have to go alone. Hence Dave stays with her and
diverts his frontier energies into fights with the railroad for a line through
their town, Cloud Chief, and when that battle is won, he schemes with
fellow citizens to steal "abstracts and things" so the courthouse will be
located in Cloud Chief (363). Meanwhile, Martha runs the farm, moves
easily between town and country activities, and achieves fame throughout the countryside as the doctor's assistant. In this novel, town represents a unifying force—people working together with common interests—and a stablizing force for men like Dave Prawl who are quickly
bored with homesteading.

In *The Dark Weaver*, Salverson provides portraits of the middle-
class Prairie Angel, the wives of businessmen who came to Manitoba
with money and business acuity. From the beginning the wives have
servants drawn from the lower-class immigrants in their settlement company and the Métis girls in the area. One of the women, Oline Boyen,
had married in order to save her parents' farm in Denmark and had
emigrated with great reluctance to Canada, as we saw in the quotation at
the beginning of this chapter. Nevertheless, she eventually accepts the
prairie town. This acceptance, I believe, results from the rewarding role
she plays in the community. As Prairie Angel she "rode pillion behind
Dr. Hartman, sometimes waded, booted and trousered, through mire and
sloughs. More often in addition to serving the sick there was stock to be
fed, wood and water to fetch. . . . Difficult, ugly, depressing chores, yet
Oline found herself coming alive to the manifold beauties of existence"
(75).

In another novel, *The Viking Heart*, Salverson provides two views
of Winnipeg and of Prairie Angels at work in the town of Winnipeg. In
the 1890s, Main Street has been improved so that a team of horses might
"travel its entire length through the town and not be in danger of
wallowing up to its haunches in adhesive mud. New industries and stores

were steadily springing up and the town was spreading north and west-ward" (126).[12] The young town is typically unkind to its poor. One of these, Mrs. Hafstein, is a widow whose husband had worked himself to death in a harness shop. Yet her poverty has not made her oblivious to others' trials. On a cold night she sees an old Indian huddled against the wall of a shanty, goes to him, and pointing to her little two-room house, makes gestures of warming her hands over a fire. She feeds him bannock and coffee, makes a bed for him, and is rewarded the next night by a huge cut of meat he has cunningly appropriated and deposited on her steps (128–29). The destitute of Winnipeg occasionally overcome cultural barriers to help each other survive.

At a later time in another part of town, Finna Johnson has what she considers a fine modern house on Maryland Street—"six rooms and a bath, a white bath as pretty as a dish, and a walk all around the house!" (156). Her husband, having given up the seemingly hopeless task of farming in Gimli, has become a carpenter in the growing town where there is a high demand for good craftsmen. This situation provides Finna with an opportunity to open her home to the young people from her former farming community as they come to Winnipeg to go to school or to work. When Finna's friend and former neighbor Borga Lindal comes to town, Borga is astonished at the changes that have taken place since she arrived at the immigrant sheds in 1876:

> Where was the snake-like muddy road? Where were the tumbledown houses? What was all this hustle and bustle and noise? This rattling of swift-moving traffic on hard smooth streets? Winnipeg was not a village—not a town. It was a city! Its streets were reaching out hungrily over incredibly large areas. Its business houses, its banks, its hotels, were everywhere. She was as one in an Arabian Night's dream when she fell upon Finna's welcoming bosom."
> [159]

The "city section" of *The Viking Heart* shows that the functions of the Prairie Angel have shifted only slightly: the women who assisted each other in childbirth, childraising, and illness on the homestead now look after the young people and help them to make their way in a modern world where, from Salverson's perspective, wonderful opportunities are available to the intelligent, serious, and highly motivated children of the Icelandic immigrants.

12. The humorous affection citizens felt for young prairie towns is represented by Alan Artibise in this comment on Winnipeg, a city famous for its mud in the early years: "Newcomers were told that if they ever saw a hat floating in the mud they were to throw it a line—there would be a man under it" (56).

A new type of Prairie Angel emerges in the literature of prairie towns—the domestic. Women without skills or husbands to support them could do laundry, cooking, cleaning, and childcare. From social histories of nineteenth-century women, we know that domestic work was generally exploitative—long hours, low pay, and hard work, accompanied by inferior social status. While prairie fiction implies some of these problems, the stories of several females demonstrate the satisfactions—the Prairie Angel–type of reward—accompanying domestic work.

We have already seen in Mary Hartwell Catherwood's "Spirit of an Illinois Town" the acceptance and respect Kate Keene receives as she keeps house for her aunt's boarders and studies elocution on the side. In McClung's *Painted Fires*, Helmi's competent domestic skills are her "in" to Canadian life despite the trials she endures as a foreign-born and vulnerable female.

In "The Hired Girls," Book Two of *My Ántonia*, Cather thoughtfully analyzes the positive and negative aspects of the roles of domestic girls in town. Many of the girls Jim Burden knows and describes are fortunate to be in the homes of women who feel responsible for the physical and moral health of their hired girls. Regardless of the concerns of the employers, the girls have easier work in town than on the farm where many, like Ántonia, hire out and do men's work, going from farm to farm with the threshers. If the hired girls suffer from the narrow-mindedness of townspeople, the country has its own restraints. Lena Lingard, herding cattle in open country near Squaw Creek, becomes a victim of a jealous wife's rumors because she talks to the neighboring farmer. Lena defends herself: "I never made anything to him with my eyes. I can't help it if he hangs around, and I can't order him off. It ain't my prairie" (169).

There are social and economic advantages for domestics in town. On winter evenings when the winds whip through town almost as savagely as in the country, there is companionship. On Saturday nights, Ántonia finishes her work in the kitchen and joins the Harlings and neighbors in the parlor; she sews as they listen to Mrs. Harling play the piano or joins in when Frances Harling teaches the young people to dance. Jim recognizes Ántonia's pleasure on these occasions: "After the long winter evenings in the prairie, with her brother Ambrosch's sullen silences and her mother's complaints, the Harling's house seemed, as she said, 'like Heaven to her'" (175).

Then when summer came and the Vannis set up their dance pavil-ion, Ántonia had another outlet: Saturday night dances. According to Jim, "Ántonia talked and thought of nothing but the tent. She hummed dance tunes all day. When supper was late, she hurried with her dishes, dropped and smashed them in her excitement." Because Ántonia was so popular at the pavillion, Jim notes, "a crisis was inevitable." One night a young man walks Ántonia home and tries to kiss her. As a result, Mr. Harling tells her she must quit dancing or quit her job. Ántonia an-nounces that she has to "take her good times when she can" and quits the job (200).

Town life presents certain hazards for young girls like Ántonia. Nevertheless, farm girls and lower-class town girls (whether foreign or native-born) receive training as domestics, which enables them to better enact their roles as Prairie Angels. Among town women they find models for speech, dress, and manners; some gain a little culture through books, music, theatre, or oratory. Some acquire a better sense of political, social, and economic issues. Some benefit from active involvement in church or school. Most are indoctrinated into the cult of womanhood: they become pious and pure, submissive and domestic.

Among the most interesting of the domestics are older women who have rebelled against the "true woman" role and who function as deviant Prairie Angels, contrasting sharply with traditional wives. Catherwood, Breneman/Thurston, and Salverson, in portraying domestics of the pre-vious generation, create lively nonconformists.

In "The Spirit of an Illinois Town," Catherwood looks back to the mid-1800s and, among a variety of female types in the new town, places some emphasis on the character Esther, who cleans the newspaper office for Seth Adams and Sam Peevy. On the surface, Esther appears to function in a traditional manner. In fact, she is described as a "big coarse Madonna" who cheerfully supports her widowed sister-in-law, several nieces and nephews, and the family pet, a sand-hill crane named Jimmy. One day in the newspaper office Jimmy swallows a considerable length of twine and Seth watches Esther patiently "unwind" him. Esther philo-sophically observes that people aren't "so easy to manage in their in-nards" as Jimmy. She should know: she has devoted her life to tending both the insides and outsides of a variety of people. But the narrator provides one piece of information that sets Esther apart from the usual Prairie Angels: she has been married "two or three times" to "no-account" men (339–400). Esther's ability to separate from these men suggests independence and lack of concern for what others think. While committed to serving others, Esther has no intention of being "God's doormat"; there are limitations to sacrifice.[13]

Another nonconformist appears in Breneman/Thurston's *Land They Possessed.* After the Ward family moves to town, Michal meets Achsah, the woman who lives across the street. Bringing the family a pot of beans, Achsah greets Michal: "'Oh, you'll love this town, child. It smells good, sort of clean and new, and it looks good. It even sounds good. Listen tomorrow for the sound of the blacksmith. . . . Like music it is.'" Achsah reflects an enthusiasm and zest for life absent in Mavis, Michal's traditional mother. Michal overhears another neighbor tell Mavis that Achsah does washing for the railroad men as well as providing other "services" (120, 123). Thus, in the portrait of Achsah, we have the Prairie Angel as prostitute with a heart of gold.

In *The Dark Weaver* Salverson creates another version of the domestic, one who is a political nonconformist. Illiana Petrovna, a widowed refugee from Russia via Denmark, cleans the houses of affluent townswomen, serves as their midwife, and rocks their babies. Back in Denmark she was condescendingly labeled "mad" for her radical anti-aristocracy, pro-worker views. In fact, her socialism led to the dismissal of her son from a teaching post; hence they emigrated to Canada. In the newly formed Manitoba town, Illiana "had come into her own" (109) with ample opportunity to do more than look after people's insides and outsides, like Esther in Catherwood's story. She could also oversee the development of their minds by becoming the chief agitator in creating a school for the isolated settlers. She "struggled over the roads tirelessly, inveigling, scolding this one and that one, representing now the glory of the work of building a new school, now its social opportunities" (112). The result? A new school, built by the commitment and energy and vision of a "domestic."

These three portraits of domestics are significant, first, because the writers obviously want their readers to like, admire, and respect the women despite their refusal to conform to traditional roles. The writers

13. See Susan Wood, "God's Doormats: Women in Canadian Prairie Fiction" Wood analyzes the images of women in popular fiction, noting that McClung's female heroes "do everything," but that secondary female characters conform to the prairie angel archetype.

were certainly aware that they were going against the grain: popular literature in the era of each writer (Catherwood in the 1890s, Salverson in the 1930s, and Breneman/Thurston in the 1950s) emphasized the blessings and rewards of conformity. Second, these writers remind readers that at any time and place there have been women who refused to conform. Their main characters may be fine models of traditional womanhood, but their secondary female portraits insist that some other kinds of women have taken risks, survived, and even earned respect.

Certainly domestics, whether young girls or older women, faced victimization in many situations, although most prairie writers chose not to analyze this aspect of females' lives in the new prairie towns. The women they did choose to portray as victims elicit little sympathy from the reader. Unlike the female victims in the homestead situation, the town victim frequently seems to deserve unhappiness and disappointment. She is usually the wife of a professional or a businessman without meaningful work or purpose in life. Secondary characters in three novels provide representative examples. In Breneman/Thurston's *Land They Possessed*, one doctor's wife drinks and smokes; her successor, a young woman from New York City, is incapable of adapting to a place where she can't continue voice lessons. At first she cries about "the awful prairie winds and [the] terrible town" (225); then she leaves her husband and goes back to New York. In Nellie McClung's *Painted Fires* the doctor's wife enjoys teaching English to Helmi, the Finnish girl; she is attracted by the novelty of Canadianizing an attractive young foreigner. However, this woman has no scruples about sending Helmi on an errand to the Chinaman's shop when her regular narcotics supplier is unable to fill her order. When Helmi is arrested and sentenced to the reformatory, the doctor's wife experiences moments of guilt but never feels compelled to confess.

In *My Ántonia*, Cather presents a more complex view of a victim of leisure in her portrait of Mrs. Wick Cutter, the wife of a Black Hawk moneylender. Although her relationship with her husband is humiliating, she never seriously considers separation. Her only outlet appears to be china painting, but even her art is abused: when Mr. Cutter attempts to show a visitor one of her dishes, he drops it and then ignores Mrs. Cutter's protestation: "Mr. Cutter, you have broken all the Commandments—spare the finger-bowls!" (212). Despite her middle-class comforts, she and her husband fight over his underwear, the front yard landscaping, their inability to have children, and his seduction of the hired girls. She is at odds not only with her husband but with other women, thus neglecting what could have been a source of comfort.[14]

By providing these examples of victimhood, the writers acknowledge that there will always be individuals temperamentally incapable of adapting to new situations or of finding and accepting challenges. The women, not the town and its inadequacies, are clearly at fault. These negative portraits of women, though irritating or pathetic, provide a realistic cross section of pioneer women.

While the writers portray these women as the self-made victims of their situations, others are victimized by situations which win them sympathy. In Salverson's *Viking Heart*, Mrs. Hafstein, as we saw earlier in this chapter, was a victim because she was dependent on her husband who, as a harness maker, received low pay and died from heavy work and exhausting hours. Yet it must be admitted that discrimination and the lack of social welfare institutions and legislation were typical of the times, not of the prairie town alone.

The businesswoman as Frontier Hero is not the unique province of the prairie town, either. Yet she is an important figure because traditional historians have ignored her presence unless they chose to introduce her as an oddity or as a peculiar contrast to the woman in the sunbonnet. A character in Alice French's story "The Face of Failure" (1893) serves as an example of the office worker. Alma Brown had to leave school at the age of twelve when her father died. First she was a "nurse-girl" and was fortunate in having a kindly employer who made sure she ate hearty suppers. Then she became a cook; "'I was a good cook, too, if I say it myself. . . . I am not a bit ashamed of being a hired girl, for I was as good a one as I knew how'" (69). Then she managed to go to a business college and learned bookkeeping, typing, and shorthand; these enabled her to enter the business world and earn enough money to educate her younger sisters.

Magdali Wing, one of the main characters in Ostenso's *O River, Remember!*, has been discussed in another context as an exploiter of the land and of unfortunate landowners. In some ways, Magdali is the female counterpart of the patriarch found in Grove's *Fruits of the Earth* and Rölvaag's *Giants in the Earth*. While we admire the vision and energy of this type of pioneer, we criticize the way they put their personal aspirations before the needs of the people closest to them. Magdali, for exam-

---

14. According to Mildred Bennett, a Red Cloud businessman, M. R. Bentley, was "the notorious 'Wick Cutter' of My Ántonia" (*World of Willa Cather* 82).

ple, robs her children of the dignity of making their own choices and contributes to their alienation from their home.

In Salverson's *Dark Weaver* Leona Shultz has had to put family needs first, like Alma Brown in French's story. Leona repeatedly gave up money she had been saving to improve her personal situation. When she meets the influential businessman Captain Marcusson, she is willing to ignore gossip and norms for female behavior in Manitoba of the late 1800s. The townspeople never really figure out the relationship between the captain and Leona; they see only the puzzling results of what is revealed to readers as blackmail: Marcusson, to avoid a scandal involving Leona's half-sister, agrees to train Leona in his business. She "learns figures" from an immigrant German professor and eventually manages Marcusson's new store. The town's bewilderment increases when Leona and Marcusson's wife become friends. Salverson's feminism, reflected in other female characters in both *The Viking Heart* and *The Dark Weaver*, surfaces in Leona's incensed words to Captain Marcusson: " 'I want to learn about business. Oh, you can laugh! I know women haven't been thought capable of it unless their useless husbands died! Just the same I mean it! I'm willing to pay any price for the experience, Captain Marcusson' " (124). Here is the assessment of the townspeople:

> For three years Leona Shultz had operated Captain Marcusson's store in Maple Bluffs. Her success was the talk of the district. Whatever her moral imperfection, she ways endowed with an indefinable quality that inspired confidence. In a hard-headed sense she was honest, and shrewd and un-alterably true to her given word. She drove a hard bargain, but stuck to her promise. . . . She was completely indifferent to the opinions of her own sex, and knowing well the foibles of men dismissed their wavering judgments with a shrug. [146]

A few years later Leona drives into town with an automobile; she is the first person in town to own a car, and it is "a splendid black monster" (280). Eventually she marries an elderly writer—further evidence of her eccentricity, according to the town gossips.

Leona Shultz is a significant example of role-reversal, especially within the Canadian context, as she fights for what she believes is hers. Both the Canadian pioneer male and the American midwestern farmer have been characterized as industrious, independent, and committed to domestic affairs and a growing national economy. The frontiersman of the American West, however, is characterized not only by independence but also by his heroism, his freedom, his adventurousness, and his assertion of self above man-made laws.[15] Leona Shultz conforms to the second type rather than to the first.

Cather provides other portraits of frontierswomen who fall into the same classification as Leona Shultz: two are traditional—at least in their conformity to acceptable modes of behavior; the other two refuse to conform. In My Ántonia, Mrs. Gardner runs the hotel and brings the latest fashions to Black Hawk. The banker's daughter, Frances, demonstrates that females can function intelligently and efficiently in the business world; also, she brings to business relationships a sensitivity to customers' problems and needs.

After an apprenticeship with a Black Hawk dressmaker, Lena Lingard (one of the "hired girls") becomes a successful dress designer in Lincoln, thus escaping from the farm where, she says, "'There ain't any end to the work. . . and always so much trouble happens.'" In Lincoln she picks up city manners and a reputation for style (161). She remains single because men, though "all right for friends," turn into cranky husbands and fathers after marriage. As Jim says, "Lena gave her heart away when she felt like it, but she kept her head for her business and got on in the world" (298). Another hired girl, Tiny Soderball, goes from Mrs. Gardner's hotel dining room to make a fortune running a hotel in the Klondike. Tiny and Lena eventually settle together in San Francisco where each can truly be "her own woman." One critic points to the emptiness of their lives—and Jim's—without children.[16] Lena has a response to that view of her life. Referring to the brothers and sisters thrust upon her at an early age, she says: "You can't tell me anything about family life. I've had plenty to last me" (272).

These examples demonstrate that the town could provide some females with a setting for developing their business talents or could serve as a "jumping-off place." The town also served as a cultural center, even in its simplest form, for the pioneer settlement. Considering the pervasiveness of the image of woman as culture-bearer on the frontier, it is puzzling to find this particular aspect of the Prairie Angel's mission minimized in women's fiction. Only Kate Keene in Catherwood's "Spirit

---

15. See definitions of the frontiersman in Barbara Howard Meldrum's "Agrarian versus Frontiersman in Midwestern Fiction" (Faulkner and Luebke, Vision and Refuge 45).

16. "If life on the land is incomplete, the life that Jim finds in the great world is even more so. He is childless. Like Lena Lingard and Tiny Soderball he has spent his creative energy in making a self and has none left over for sons and daughters. Jim returns home, but he can never fully be at home" (Klug 296).

of an Illinois Town" comes close to acquiring symbolic stature as a culture-bearer, but she is killed in the tornado; her potential influence on the culture of the new town is terminated, and the narrator emphasizes that there are no young women with the ability or interest to affect the culture of the town. Seven decades after Catherwood's creation of Kate Keene, Julie McDonald developed a character in *Amalie's Story* with the ability to put a spell on a prairie audience. Standing in the glow of the footlights, Lily Hertert symbolizes—to her friend Amalie, at least—"a woman who had climbed to the rooftops and stayed there, while [she] had scuttled down" (207). Lily's influence is undercut, however, by her idiosyncratic behavior: she is a Unitarian in a Lutheran town; she insists on her "predinner sherry as a mark of civilization" among people who are "temperance"; she influences her banker-husband's business decisions, thus interfering in the male domain.

Ida Meier, in Bess Streeter Aldrich's *Spring Came on Forever,* seems to be the only woman who excels in both the public and private domains without disrupting the norms for feminine behavior. Ida leaves teaching when she marries Matthias, a prominent young businessman in Lincoln. "She worked side by side with him in the store, never missing a day nor a chance to help her husband earn a penny" (168). The times were hard—the 1870s in Nebraska saw both grasshoppers and droughts, so the Carters lived in a boardinghouse for seven years before they could build a house. By the 1890s prosperity had returned; Matthias is vice-president of the bank and Ida takes a key role in organizing the Women's Club.

Only one female character attains heroic proportions as a culture-bearer—Kate Shaleen in *O River, Remember!*, who serves as a foil to Magdali Wing: she represents "intuitive religion of beauty" as compared with Magdali's "stinking materialism," to use the expressions of Magdali's grandson (13). Kate is the town's first schoolteacher; she brings the first organ to the community; she composes a song about the land—"O River, Remember!"; she gives her niece the *Rubaiyat of Omar Khayyam;* she takes the Wing boy to the theatre. She eventually moves to St. Paul and founds a girl's school.

We know from the research of historians and biographers that there were cultural giants in real life. One of the most dramatic examples is probably that of Kate Simpson Hayes, the first western woman to write about the Prairie West and to have a book published in the West. One historian, Earl G. Drake, notes that in Regina, in the 1890s, Hayes was "the best exemplification of the more independent and prominent role women were beginning to play" in the cultural life of a community:

> She did newspaper writing. . . . She wrote, produced, and acted in the first local comedy in 1892. In 1894 Mrs. Simpson Hayes wrote a more pretentious three-act serious drama which was produced under the Lieutenant-Governor's patronage. She was prominent in all stage activity for years, producing among other things in 1895, an engaging operetta-bouffe performed entirely by small children, which starred her own talented little daughter, Bonnie. All this was in Mrs. Simpson Hayes' spare time, for her working hours were spent as the Territorial Legislative Librarian. [60–61]

Many of Hayes's cultural activities were shared by an impressive gentleman, Nicholas Flood Davin, a lawyer who had come west with a vision for making Regina the cultural capital of the West. He began by establishing a newspaper, *The Regina Leader,* in 1883 when Regina was still a tent city. When a Winnipeg writer made fun of "the pile of bones"—the original name for Regina—and predicted that the new town would shortly return to its original state, Davin responded with verses of his own, playfully defending Regina as "a pleasant city on a boundless plain, / Around rich land where peace and plenty reign" (McCourt 86). In a more serious vein, he wrote an ambitious poem called *Eos: An Epic of Dawn.* Conceived originally as "A Prairie Dream," the poem describes the failures of ancient civilizations and the flaws of Europe and Great Britain, and it predicts a new beginning for man in the Prairie West.

The example of Hayes and Davin supports the hypotheses of several recent historians who conclude that both women and men made considerable commitments to the cultural growth of the newly established towns. Elizabeth Jameson rejects a sexual stereotyping of women as civilizers:

> Rather than assuming that all settlers arriving in the West internalized the idealized gender roles, we need to document what previous understandings of manhood and womanhood each group brought with them. If they were not white, Anglo-Saxon Protestants, if they were working class or had farmed previously, genteel expectations were more likely to be qualified by more realistic understandings of daily life and family options. . . .
>
> Second, we need to explore men's and women's experiences together to understand what values they shared. John Faragher found, for instance, that midwestern farm women and men shared a concern with practical economic considerations that may have played a major role in the decision to move west. . . . Rather than assuming that western men were mythic rugged individuals whom women were to civilize, we need to discover whether

women and men shared desires for stable communities and households, and how they understood their roles in achieving them. [6–7]

Fiction seems to support these conclusions. Women writers minimized or even contradicted the myth of woman as culture-bearer. In one novel the mother reads the Bible, the father reads the encyclopedia, and the daughter reads *Little Women* (Breneman/Thurston 93). In another novel, a daughter is reprimanded for filling her head with silly romance novels and the mother decides against joining the Shakespeare Study Group: "It's all too deep for me. . . . I'm just a plain prairie woman with sandburs in my skirts" (Aydelotte, *Trumpets Calling* 386). In *A Lantern in Her Hand,* Abbie Deal recalls that her father carried copies of Shakespeare to Dubuque, Iowa, in the 1850s, but her mother didn't read them: "She didn't read anything but the Bible" (Aldrich 13). Certainly women brought songs, popular stories, holiday rituals, embroidery and weaving techniques, quilt patterns, religious and national myths; these they passed on to their children and shared with other women. It is "high" culture that seems to be missing from the fiction.

In women's fiction we find images of men who loved the arts. Mr. Shimerda needs music to survive (Cather, *My Ántonia*); Pa Wilder organizes "the Literary" (Wilder, *Little Town*); Jason Currie sends to Italy for a Bernini-like statue to place on his wife's grave (Laurence, *Stone Angel*). Ivan Wing as an old man feels an enormous loss when talking about the move from the old land to the new. He says of his wife: "'She was building up a little empire, you see, here in the valley, beside this river, and Norway meant nothing to her any more. . . .' He hesitated, a little shyly, searching for the right words. 'There was—there was poetry—and music—in the light on those fjords and mountains in the midsummer night sun'" (Ostenso, *O River* 221). For Ivan, as for Shimerda, the landscape of memory was associated with the arts. When Ivan and Magdali's son wants to take piano lessons he tells his mother, "We've got all the new-fangled binders and mowers and hay feeders and sweep rakes and feed grinders and manure spreaders—and the whole shebang! Why shouldn't we have a piano?" (280).

Eventually the boy recognizes "that his mother had gradually discarded every vestige of her immigrant past, while his father was still— well, what *was* his father? Surely an American now, but with the best, the most vigorous and honest and spiritually simple qualities of the old land giving something to the new" (308). His mother, on the other hand, had abandoned the cultural values of the old land and absorbed the materialism of the new land. These examples of pioneer males require that we look again at the images of men not only in the historical context but in fiction.

When examining the iconography of women on the homestead, we do not look for nor bemoan the absence of social and political activists—in most women's fiction females are absorbed by the task of establishing homesteads. We do find women who helped to organize schools and churches. Yet none of the writers chronicling the homestead experience devoted significant portions of their stories to women's effect on the political structures of their settlements.

Ma Wilder in *Little Town on the Prairie* and Abbie Deal in *A Lantern in Her Hand* belonged to the Women's Christian Temperance Union. In *The Land They Possessed*, the W.C.T.U. was active, but the saloons were winning out over the churches, twelve to six. Magdali Wing in *O River, Remember!* informed a congressman that if a woman is fit to teach children, then "she is fit to have a voice in deciding who will run [the] government" (331); women's suffrage, however, is not an issue dealt with in the novel. In many novels, of course, there are references to local, state, and national elections and, depending on the era, to the Civil War in the United States, to the Riel Rebellion in Canada, or to World War I or II. Generally political events involve minor portions of the plot and minor characters.

In prairie fiction there is no Frances Willard, "a daughter of the Middle Border" who became part of the temperance movement because she saw the W.C.T.U. as a means of influencing women's attitudes toward increased rights for women. There is no Irene Parlby who, after an outstanding education in England, married an Alberta homesteader and became the first president of the United Farm Women of Alberta and worked for women's suffrage before being elected to the Alberta Legislature (Rasmussen et al. 224). There is no Kate Simpson Hayes who organized Regina's cultural life, worked for women's suffrage, and served as one of the founders of the Canadian Women's Press Club (MacEwan 33–41). The only woman in prairie fiction who goes west with a political mission is in *Free Soil*, Lynn's novel about the Kansas movement to keep the state free from slavery.

However, there *is* a Nellie L. McClung. In 1914 McClung participated in a play called "How the Vote Was Won" performed before an audience of one thousand in Winnipeg. The play was a protest against the Manitoba Legislature's decision to turn down the Political Equality

League's request for women's suffrage—an organization with which Mc-Clung had worked enthusiastically. A January 1914 newspaper article reported that McClung appeared before the curtain and explained to the audience that "they would have to use their imagination as political conditions [in the play] were reversed and women were in power. She couldn't see why women shouldn't sit in Parliament. It didn't seem to be such a hard job. She didn't want to—but you couldn't tell what your granddaughters might want to do" (Savage, *Our Nell* 88). In the play men asking for the vote were turned down. The premier, played by McClung, informed petitioners that *they* were worthy individuals; however, many were not: seven-eights of the crimes were committed by men; only one-third of the male population belonged to a church. McClung, according to the newspaper article, became eloquent:

> "You ask me to enfranchise all these. . . .
>
> "O no, man is made for something much higher and better than voting. Men were made to support families. What is home without a bank account? The man who pays the grocer rules the world. In this agricultural province, the man's place is the farm. Shall I call man away from the useful plow and harrow to talk loud on street corners about things which do not concern him! Politics unsettle men, and unsettled men means unsettled bills—broken furniture, and broken vows—and divorce. . . . When you ask for the vote you are asking me to break up peaceful, happy homes—to wreck innocent lives. [Savage, *Our Nell* 89]

This real-life situation is reenacted in McClung's novel *Purple Springs* (1921). Pearlie Watson, whom Canadian readers had already met and loved in two earlier novels, *Sowing Seeds in Danny* (1908) and *The Second Chance* (1910), plays Nellie McClung's role. In the chapter entitled "The Play," Pearlie gives the preliminary speech:

> The Woman Premier had risen. So intent was the audience in their study of her face, they forgot to applaud. What they saw was a tall, slight girl whose naturally brilliant coloring needed no make-up; brilliant dark eyes, set in a face whose coloring was vivid as a rose, a straight mouth with a whimsical smile. . . .
>
> She put her hands in front of her, locking her fingers with the thumbs straight up, gently moving them up and down before she spoke.
>
> The gesture was familiar. It was the Premier's own, and a howl of recognition came from the audience, beginning in the Cabinet Minister's box.
>
> She tenderly teetered on her heels, waiting for them to quiet down, but that was the occasion for another outburst. [281]

During the course of the "hearing," guardianship rights of fathers are debated. However, the legislators pay little attention—they read newspapers, eat chocolates, and powder their noses. One concentrates on her tatting. Next, the opposition pleads for dower rights to men, complaining that they devote their lives to the family but wives can sell their property "over their heads." Finally, a delegation of men urges that they be given the right to vote. Pearlie then gives—making a few appropriate adjustments—the speech the Manitoba premier had given a few months before to a delegation of women. " 'You do not know what you ask,' " she tells them gently:

> "You have not thought of it, of course, with the natural thoughtlessness of your sex. You ask for something which may disrupt the whole course of civilization. Man's place is to provide for his family, a hard enough task in these strenuous days. . . .
>
> "Man has a higher destiny than politics," she cried, with the ring in her voice that they had heard so often, "what is home without a bank account? The man who pays the grocer rules the world. . . .
>
> "Do you not know of the disgraceful happenings in countries cursed by manhood suffrage? Do you not know the fearful odium into which the polls have fallen? . . . No, history is full of unhappy examples of men in public life; Nero, Herod, King John." [283–85]

Although women's suffrage was won five years before the publication of *Purple Springs*, McClung kept the problems of women alive through her fiction. In real life she was campaigning for a seat in the Alberta Legislature and on 18 July 1921, at the age of forty-seven, she began a new career in government.

While women writers' delineations of town life generally focus on the "private" woman, not on the "public" one, the structures of signification emerging from the fiction emphasize that there was more to town life than silly teas and mediocre culture. Comparisons between town and country indicate that the country was not always the most desirable setting in which to live. Indeed, some inhabitants could take pride in identifying with their towns. Moreover, the town frequently offered women a larger sphere in which to exercise their talents and more options from which to choose. The town, clearly, is more than a cluster of false fronts that gradually evolve into a stable but mediocre business and cultural center on the prairie.

Michal Ward, taking her first excursion from the homestead to the new town, cries out indignantly at her first sight of the town: " 'Is that all?' " (Breneman/Thurston 96). This is an understandable response for a young girl with naive expectations. Yet her words have been repeated by visitors, historians, sociologists, and literary critics over the decades throughout the American and Canadian prairies. Admittedly, the prairie village, town, or city may be isolated and dull and mediocre. It may be—to use Canadian critic Dick Harrison's words—a false refuge from the hostilities of nature (*Unnamed Country* 128). Yet for others the prairie town represents better options, varied roles, stability, fellowship, and freedom.

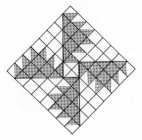

CHAPTER SEVEN

Prairie Born, Prairie Bred

In Edna Jaques's *Prairie Born, Prairie Bred: Poetic Reflections of a Pioneer*, the poem "To the Next Generation" poses this question:

> Will they, too, love these brown dear fields
> And call them home . . . and sing? (84)

A study of pioneer prairie women would not be complete without asking this question and looking for answers in the works about female heirs to the prairie. I have, therefore, selected works by over two dozen authors to discover the ways prairie women writers transformed their experiences and the lives of those around them into fiction. Most of these women were born on the prairie; others moved to the prairies and developed a strong sense of identity with the environment. In fact, many meet Hamlin Garland's criteria for western writers: "They must be born of the soil. They must be products of the environment. They must stand among the people, not above them, and then they can be true, and being true they will certainly succeed" ("The West" 676). I have selected works that are contemporaneous with the life of the writer and, at the same time, that focus on girls' and young women's experiences up to a threshold or turning point; from their experiences we can identify three central motifs—*Staying*, *Leaving*, and *Returning*. I have relied most heavily on those works that use the prairie landscape literally or symbolically in developing the characters;[1] the prairie is sometimes the child's Eden, sometimes her tutor.

---

1. In my interpretation of these works I have relied heavily on Yi-Fu Tuan's discussion of "home ground," "home place," and "homeland": "A homeland has its landmarks, which may be features of high visibility and public significance, such as monuments, shrines, a hallowed battlefield or cemetery. These visible signs serve to enhance a people's sense of identity; they

219

Over a hundred-year period, many writers have provided glimpses of childhood in the prairie garden; the fruitfulness, freedom, and innocence of certain settings strongly suggest that the garden is Edenic. In Mary Hartwell Catherwood's serial "Stephen Guthrie" (1882), a satire on the Indianapolis nouveau riche, the hero looks back on her childhood on the Illinois prairie:

> She stood again in the thick grove which was like an oasis in the prairie and saw the horizon-bounded plain sweeping off to the ends of the earth, now dipping to a "slew" and now rolling up to a ridge. Again she felt the plums rattle down about her sunbonneted head and gathered her apron full, shouting with the other children, who shook the trees or scrambled as she did. . . . In those days she was not groping around the world, full of self-dissatisfaction and half-understood desires. Her brown little paws were good enough to gather plums with, and the other children were wholesome companions, exhaling a spirit like the breath of flag-lilies. [29–30]

The prairie child enjoying life in Catherwood's garden is self-confident and secure.

In Margaret Lynn's *Stepdaughter of the Prairie* (1916), the Dakota land is still virgin sod. The twelve-year-old girl who rides across it grieves that she will be the last to feel its "wonderful emptiness" before the grasses give way to corn fields. To Lynn's narrator, the prairie garden is eternal; it never decays or dies like the farmer's crops: "For as its summer green passed away the coral tints at its roots would creep upward. All through the coming winter it would lie there rosy and rich, gleaming pink through the light, wind-tossed snow or glowing warmly under our clear western sun. It would never have a moment of real deadness until its

---

encourage awareness of and loyalty to place. But a strong attachment to the homeland can emerge quite apart from any explicit concept of sacredness; it can form without the memory of heroic battles won and lost, and without the bond of fear or of superiority vis-à-vis other people. Attachment of a deep though subconscious sort may come simply with familiarity and ease, with the assurance of nurture and security, with the memory of sounds and smells, of communal activities and homely pleasures accumulated over time" (*Space and Place*, 159). For some, home is where "real" life is lived (146). For others, as one Indian chief made clear in a nineteenth-century speech, "every part of this country is sacred to my people. Every hillside, every valley, every plain and grove has been hallowed by some fond memory or some sad experience of my tribe. Even the rocks, which seem to lie dumb as they swelter in the sun . . . thrill with memories of past events connected with the lives of my people" (155). In addition, home can be another person, as Sharon Riis illustrates in *The True Story of Ida Johnson*, in which two young women return home, find each other after several years' absence, and leave again, together. As Tuan says, "one human being can 'nest' in another" (139).

Fig. 20   MISS ELLA HARTT, *Little Girl Sitting on Doorstep*. Courtesy of Glenbow Archives, Calgary, Alberta.

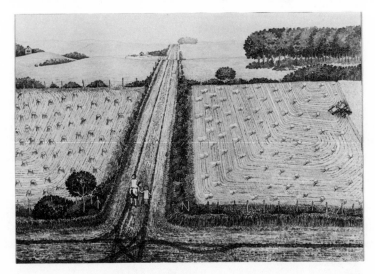

Fig. 21   HAZEL LITZGUS, *Walking Part Way*, 1972. Courtesy of the artist. "The paintings of Hazel Litzgus demonstrate how personal are the motivations which prompt artists who speak from their own hearts rather than as high art dictates. Many of her works recall her youth at Lloydminster, Alberta. During her childhood she and her mother would meander down a side road, flanked by her father's fields of freshly cut wheat. In this picture they go to meet her little friend whose home appears over the horizon" (Harper 80).

green appeared again in the early spring" (276–77). The narrator is reluctant to see her Eden—natural and unpopulated—turned into the world's breadbasket, plowed and planted by easterners. The image of the prairie as Eden hasn't completely died out. In Sharon Riis's *True Story of Ida Johnson* (1977), Ida concludes a description of her homeplace with this abrupt comment: "It's a children's paradise but," she adds, "time eats children" (15), thus reminding readers that no one can stay in the garden beyond childhood.

In other descriptions, the ability of children to physically see across vast expanses of plain becomes a symbol for their ability to know not only the land but self and life. In these instances, the prairie is a tutor. Space, instead of diminishing one's sense of self, actually enhances the self. This is suggested in Miriam Waddington's "Waiting in Alberta":

> And I think from
> my very remote
> corner of Alberta
> that after all this
> is a pretty clever
> and miraculous world
> where I can sit
> small as anything
> in such a big corner
> of it and the only
> archaic creatures
> are us people [Ricou, *Twelve Prairie Poets* 170]

In these lines there is no sense of being blotted out, of terror, of alienation, or of impotence. Oftentimes the girls demonstrate a strong confidence in their ability to figure things out. For example, in *Purple Springs*, Nellie McClung says that "Pearl, child of the prairie, never could think as clearly when her vision was bounded by walls. She had to have blue distance—the great, long look that swept away the little petty, trifling, hampering things, which so slavishly dominate our lives if we will let them" (245).

The poet Emily Dickinson explained that her preference for the robin and the buttercup resulted from having been "Orchard sprung"; she learned to see "New Englandly." Those born on the flat grasslands— the Prairie sprung—also value certain birds and flowers in the farmyards and the fields; but more importantly, they cherish the unimpeded view to the distant horizon. For many, powerful and penetrating physical sight is equated with intellectual and spiritual insight. When Ida Johnson can no longer tolerate bad jobs and selfish, mixed-up people on the West Coast, she knows that to survive she has to go back home: "All I could think was to get home out of the rain and low sky back to the prairie. I couldn't breathe and I put it down to there being no space in the air I could see" (101). Once she gets home where there is "all that sky" she is able to figure out what to do with her life.

Endless stretches of sky and long views to the horizon, rather than symbolizing emptiness, meaninglessness, or exposure, actually enable some of the prairie-born to make sense out of their lives and even assure them, in some cases, of having special abilities for seeing and understanding. For these reasons many are able, in Edna Jaques's words, to love those brown dear fields.

Staying

Females who have grown up on farms and remained on farms during the years of crop failures are a different sort. They emphasize in their stories other aspects of being prairie-born. These need not contradict the experiences just recounted, but they remind us that hunger and poverty place obstacles in the way of sight and understanding. The opening sentence of Meridel Le Sueur's story "Corn Village" (1931) introduces us to this kind of situation: "Like many Americans, I will never recover from my sparse childhood in Kansas. The blackness, weight and terror of childhood in mid-America strike deep into the stem of life. Like desert flowers we learned to crouch near the earth, fearful that we would die before the rains, cunning, waiting the season of good growth" (*Salute* 9).

Le Sueur describes the ability of the prairie to inflict what the narrator calls "mysterious wounds." Perhaps she chooses the word *mysterious* because the land sends forth contradictory signals, represented by an oxymoronic simile: the Kansas prairie is like a "strong raped virgin." The image of the raped virgin is intended to remind readers of the way farmers abused and exploited the land by poor farming methods; nevertheless, the land had the strength to renew itself. The prairie is also like "an idiotic lost peasant . . . scattering those incredibly tiny flowers" which will return after the winter's thaw (*Salute* 24). This image, too, carries connotations of renewal: both the "strong virgin" and the peasant's flowers suggest fertility. Le Sueur points out, however, that after the pioneer generation passed, there was nothing left for men to conquer, no spirit left in the people, no community to bind them together; all around, she observes, "the land lies desolate like a loved woman who has been forgotten. . . . misused through dreams of power and conquest" (12).

It is significant, however, that the narrator in "Corn Village" stays in Kansas although, as she tells the prairie, she has the option to leave: "Not going to Paris or Morocco or Venice, instead staying with you, trying to be in love with you, bent upon understanding you, bringing you to life. For your life is my life and your death is mine also" (*Salute* 25). Jaques's poem asked, "Will they love these dear brown fields?" Le Sueur says, finally, yes; but it is not easy. It will take time to come to terms with the prairie environment.

In "Corn Village" the young narrator has come to terms with the land and her relationship to it. In a second story about the 1930s, "Salute to Spring," Le Sueur demonstrates that one viable response to the situation is political activism. In a bleak farmhouse marked by years of drought, a woman watches her husband and knows his thoughts: What does a man do when the thaw comes and there's no seed for planting? She holds her ailing baby and makes a promise that has undoubtedly been made other springs with her other children. "If she'll live till spring . . . it will be all right, there will be food, carrots, tomatoes; I'll plant them myself" (146). Later that day, as this couple drives to town, Jim asks Mary, "'How we gonna live till spring?'" She replies, "'Is there ever a time when we haven't lived till spring?'" (148). Her determination gives him hope. In town he goes to the meeting on seed loans; she goes to the grocery store to talk with the other women.

Eventually, however, Mary slips into the meeting. Although she is intimidated by the presence of so many men and so few women, she is curious. Her apprehension increases when she sees Jim move forward to speak. He details each failure on his farm—things she never knew or only guessed. At the conclusion Jim calls for action, insisting that the farmers' need for seed on loan must be acknowledged by the authorities. He sits down. The chairman sets up a committee and says, "'I appoint Mary, Jim's wife, because there ought to be a woman on this here committee'" (154). Jim and Mary leave the meeting, arm in arm, close and moving together for the first time after a long, desperate winter. On the drive home she feels strong and secure. The isolation of each man, each woman, each family suffering alone on separate farms is coming to an end. People have spoken to each other about deeply felt human predicaments.

At the end of the story the baby dies, and Jim and Mary's sorrow, following so quickly after the hopeful meeting, is poignant. The title of the story becomes ironic because one form of the salute to spring will be the spade dug into the newly thawed soil as the earth is forced to receive the infant it failed to provide for. Nevertheless, images related to Jim and Mary's vigorous sexuality and their expectation of seed for planting symbolize another kind of salute—a defiant one. Spring comes and the indomitable human spirit moves forth to meet it. Where there is political action, a certain kind of woman can imagine surviving on the prairie.

Lorna Doone Beers also uses fiction to express her belief in the ability of farmers to unite against the bankers, businessmen, and grain monopolies that manipulate and control their lives during the 1920s. In *Prairie Fires* the main character, Christine, is a young woman, the daughter of a Danish pioneer. She imagines romantic escapes to faraway places like those described in her favorite romances. She finally settles for marriage with an ignorant, politically inept banker who symbolizes the materialism and insensitivity that the farmers are working against. A minor character, Christine's sister-in-law Lily, serves as a foil: Beers balances her gently satiric portrait of Christine with the portrait of Lily, the ideal farm woman. Christine, who had her stint at the capital as the wife of a state representative, is astonished when her brother is elected by the farmers' movement and her sister-in-law chooses to remain at home and run the farm. While Lily is doing not only what she wants to do but what she *ought* to do—a trait much admired by her father-in-law— Christine is wasting her young years dreaming:

> Was not her beauty fading? Was not every day making her doom more and more clear to her? Was she not meant to be a flaming figure, the mistress of a king, an actress, a model for a great picture, the source of inspiration to a genius! And this was happening to her, this! She was being made a placid wife, a woman whose whole interest was covered by the details of childbearing! And some day, out in the obscure prairie graveyard, naked to the winds, a tombstone: "Christine, wife of Christian Lovstad. She was born. She bore children. She died." O, it was awful! Terrible! [360]

The point is obvious: Christine describes what she regards as her obscure destiny in an insignificant farming community in mid-America; but women like her sister-in-law Lily remind us that some live meaningful and occasionally heroic lives because of their intellectual vigor and political commitment to set the prairie afire with new approaches to age-old problems.

Two novels describe success stories on the family farm: Sharon Butala's *Country of the Heart*, a contemporary story, and Edna Ferber's *So Big*, about farming in the early part of the century.

Country of the Heart, set in southern Alberta, describes the contentment of a woman who has grown up on a prosperous farm. Although Iris went away to college for a year, there was never any question about whether or not to return; essentially, she feels, she "had lived on the farm all her life. It never occurred to her that she might live anywhere else" (80). She marries Barney, a man who took over her father's farm; although he had been a rancher, Barney becomes an excellent farmer. Iris belongs to the farm and to the land: "The land lay before her, stretching out toward the sky. She could see the elevators of all the villages ten miles or more away in each direction. It always made her feel like she was flying. . . . Iris had lived all her life in this scene. She no longer even thought of it as home. It just was. It had entered her body and her heart" (80, 81). After years of planting gardens, she still gets excited over the miracle of planting seeds: "Can you imagine?" she says to her niece; "Each one of these will grow into a round red radish that's white as snow inside. . . . It's a miracle" (92).

Ferber's Pulitzer Prize–winning novel, *So Big*, tells a different kind of story about staying on the farm: Selina was not prairie-born, but from the age of nineteen she claimed that the prairie farm was the only place she belonged. Selina had grown up in cities—Denver, New York, San Francisco; in Chicago she had just completed her education at Miss Fister's finishing school when her gambler father was murdered. She gratefully accepted a teaching position arranged for her by a kind friend. Thus Selina moved to a small community of Dutch farmers ten miles from Chicago. After a year she marries one of those Dutch farmers and when he dies a few years later, she takes over the truck farming business.

The other truck farmers and their wives openly disapproved: "A woman—a High Prairie farmer's wife—driving to market like a man!" (160). Even Selina reprimands herself—not for driving to market like a man, but for feeling so *elated* about the prospect of doing business at Chicago's Haymarket (165). When a farmer criticizes her for selling vegetables at the market, she heatedly replies: " 'Don't talk to me like that, you great stupid! What good does it do a woman to stay home in her kitchen if she's going to starve there, and her boy with her!' " (178). Her boy, Dirk (Sobig), is the main reason she is able to break from traditional roles and at the same time maintain her pride and dignity. She is determined to give Dirk every opportunity he wants as he grows up.

Like Alexandra in *O Pioneers!* Selina manages the farm with imagination and farsightedness. She specializes in asparagus while the other farmers sell the usual cabbages and corn. A pound of her hothouse tomatoes brings as much as a bushel of the tomatoes her husband had grown. Success is not quick and easy, however. Ferber describes Selina's years of hard work: "a painful, grubbing, heart-breaking process. . . . She drove herself pitilessly. She literally tore a living out of the earth with her two bare hands." Ferber then describes Selina's heroic qualities: "There was nothing pitiable about this small energetic woman. . . . Rather, there was something splendid about her; something rich, prophetic. It was the splendour and richness that achievement imparts" (218).

Over the years Selina wins the town's respect: she serves on the board for the school where she once taught; she's a member of the Good Roads Commission and the Truck Farmer's Association. Her farm is "trim and neat." One of her son's friends observes that her face lights up "with the light that comes from inside; and the jaw-line like that of the woman who came over in the *Mayflower*; or crossed the continent in a covered wagon" (356).

Leaving

Le Sueur and Beers record various degrees of ambivalence and commitment to prairie farms. In contrast, Butala describes a Saskatchewan farm woman who has been able to love the prairie wholeheartedly because the farm on which she lives has been managed by capable farmers who have maintained stable incomes over several decades. Other writers demonstrate that some women, if they were given the opportunity, leave. Even these women, however, leave with regret. The narrator in Lois Phillips Hudson's *Reapers of the Dust* numbers the years of her childhood by the bad times: "On a suffocating summer day in 1937, the thirteenth year of drought and the seventh year of depression" (101). The narrator was born during the third year of the drought, and her childhood is represented by the image of "lost green fields," a line from a popular song which she had heard as a little girl. This same feeling dominates the reminiscences of the narrator in Nell Parson's *Upon a*

Sagebrush Harp. Parsons describes the situation on her father's farm near Yellow Grass: "Bumper crop expected. Prairie will-o-the-wisp! Year-to-year homesteaders lived on hope. Those wonderful prairie springs made you believe. They carried the conviction of invincibility" (140). For her, too, childhood was a time of lost green fields; the fantasies and expectations of the parents, especially of the fathers, were shared by the daughters, yet reality never reflected the dream.

Both Hudson and Parsons waited over three decades before describing their prairie childhoods. Hudson, writing in the early 1960s, begins her Dakota narration in the 1930s when she was four; Parsons, writing in the mid-1940s, goes back to 1907 when she was nine and homesteading thirty miles from Yellow Grass, Saskatchewan. In each case the narration ends, essentially, with departure from the prairie: at the age of seven, Hudson moves with her family to a location near Seattle; Parsons, at the conclusion of her narration, is eighteen and teaching a few miles from home when her mother writes that the farm is being sold—the parents plan to rent a better farm further north. Both Hudson and Parsons are removed from their childhoods by time; in addition, they seem to be well aware that many writers have distorted reality by writing romantic versions of childhood. Both seem to have sifted carefully through their personal experiences to get close to the real situation. They do not look away from difficult times and painful experiences.

At the same time, their accounts show that even life's hardest lessons on the prairie need not be entirely negative. The mothers are capable homemakers and educated women who enrich the lives of their daughters. The mother of Hudson's narrator has a college degree in mathematics. Nell Parsons says her own education as a prairie child was "catch-as-catch-can," but her mother came from an affluent, cultured English family; there were newspapers to read, an Edison phonograph, an old organ, and regular shipments of music and books from relatives in England.

More than "book" lessons are to be learned on the prairie. Nell was her father's "constant helper": "He had talked to me as to another adult as I helped sod the house walls, helped with the building of the barn, and with the well curbing. . . . Papa talked over a hundred, a thousand, common-sense subjects, stopping to comment on whatever project busied him at the moment—the correct way to mortise a wood joint, to angle a roof scantling, to lay a shingle" (138). There seems to be a wonderful lack of concern about gender roles in this father-daughter relationship.

While Parsons's father ignored gender and age in his relationship with Nell, thus allowing her an androgynous youth, Hudson became conscious at a very early age that females on the homestead were in a losing situation: "As a small girl on a North Dakota farm some thirty years ago, I probably resented the fate that made me female no more than did most of my contemporaries. There seemed to be nothing for us to look forward to except spending our lives as poor seconds to men" (16). She notes that some of her friends "achieved a resentful peace" by grudgingly admitting boys were superior. The narrator refused to give in; she intended to prove to her father that she could do anything a boy could do: drive the team of horses, feed the calves, herd the cattle, weed the garden, husk the corn, and haul the water. At the same time she wondered "what more a boy could do to please my father. In winter when he hunted jack rabbits over miles of snow-covered prairie, I plodded after him. . . . 'I swan, that child walks exactly like her father,' my grandmother would say disapprovingly. Her tone didn't bother me at all; I was proud of what she had said" (17). Hudson, as an adult looking back, concludes that the conflict may not have evolved entirely from gender-role expectations; the source of the conflict was, perhaps, generational, the child's sense of inadequacy in fulfilling the expectations of a parent.

Hudson speaks for many of the prairie-born when she says: "And in a way none of us ever really leaves those fields that made us. . . . It is from those fields, forever sealed against the trespasses of our grownup selves, forever splendid with light falling like trumpet salutes through the old heavy boughs of the world, that each of us keeps his long watch on the people who come to assume his face" (97). After moving from the homestead, Parsons writes: "I still felt tightly bound to that homestead where Mama and Papa lived. I had seen the fields carved out of raw prairie. I knew every stone on the land, knew where each remaining sagebrush grew" (141).

Hudson and Parsons do not gloss over problems and disadvantages, but their stories do represent fairly positive interpretations of female experiences. The fathers in both Hudson's and Parsons's works felt responsibility not only for the land but for the well-being of the family. Other men, however, in order to achieve their goals, exploit the land and their families. Even in relatively good times a prairie girlhood can be hellish rather than Edenic; a young woman who has undergone this experience may choose to leave. This point is illustrated in two Canadian novels, Vera Lysenko's *Yellow Boots* and Mary Ann Seitz's *Shelterbelt*.

Both works, although set in the 1930s, present pioneer homestead situations: old-fashioned farming techniques, isolation, and minimal social opportunities. As writers, both Lysenko and Seitz are, to a degree, outsiders; they record not their own lives as Hudson and Parsons did, but the lives of girls they observed while teaching school on the prairies.

In *Yellow Boots*, the father announces that he has arranged his daughter's marriage, insisting that as a female Lilli has no choices: "She must learn that life is work, hard work. Here in this country there is no room for ladies. The land takes before it gives" (195). In *Shelterbelt*, eight-year-old Francie feels inferior. Girls may work hard, but the results aren't valued. It is only when she listens to Mrs. Chorney's song that she realizes some women feel their lives in the New World are better than in eastern Europe: "In her song Mrs. Chorney . . . claimed that the Old Country was far worse than the new land of Canada. In the old land she worked as hard as an old mare. Besides, the men there drank too much and then beat their wives. . . . She'd had no fun, she sang, in the old land. She had just sat around there like an old hen. But here in Canada she had fun; she danced" (62).[2]

Lysenko believes otherwise; readers of *Yellow Boots* cannot forget the image of Lilli stumbling as she guides the plow, ignored by her father who walks ahead holding the horses' reins (41–42). Nor can Seitz's readers forget Francie, stripping feathers from geese at midnight, wishing she were a boy doing boy's work and winning her father's approval. As a Scot railroad sectionman says in *Yellow Boots*: "The land can't wait for them [the girls] to grow up. It takes away their childhood. Riding up and down this line, on these homesteads I've seen young girls doing tasks grown men would do among us" (5).

Both Francie and Liili escape from their fathers' farms. Francie's mother, pleased with Francie's success in school, intercedes and arranges for Francie to go to Normal School in Moose Jaw for teacher training: "All right," she tells Francie, "we send you. You doing good. No use for you to stay on da farm. Maybe you have easier life dat way" (171). During the story it becomes increasingly clear that the shelterbelt around the Polanski house should represent security, at least symbolically, but it fails to protect Francie. The shelterbelt is described as "holding the human and animal life in its arms, protecting them from winter gales and sum-

---

2. This kind of response of an immigrant woman is typical, according to Billington (*Land of Promise* 260).

mer storms" (5). The trees can protect the family from harsh weather; the shelterbelt symbolically marks off the Polanski territory and protects the family from a community that is frequently hostile toward foreigners. For both Francie and Lilli, however, the brutality of the father within the shelterbelt is the most difficult force to overcome.

In *Yellow Boots*, Lilli too, escapes. Her mother, unlike Francie's, is superstitious, conservative, and obedient to her husband; she is indifferent to her daughter's plight. Lilli finds an example of strength and independence in another woman, Tamara, a widow victimized by the Ukrainian community because she lives apart from it after her husband's death. Through Tamara, Lilli learns that her own people can be prejudiced, superstitious, and cruel. Tamara, rather than giving in to the will of the community, commits suicide by burning her home as the men from the community gather around to force entry into the house. This act of courage terrifies the men. More importantly, it shows Lilli that an individual has choices: one need not give way to the pressure of a group. Fortunately, Lilli never has to choose such a tragic option. She escapes to Winnipeg rather than marry the man her father has chosen for her. In the city she works as a domestic until she joins a choir and begins a modest career as a folksinger.

Both Francie and Lilli find freedom to develop as individuals in other Canadian communities—Francie among the French, Scot, and English communities where she teaches; Lilli among the factory workers and folksinging group in Winnipeg. Each returns home at the end of the novel to experience, finally, the approval of her father. These men, after years of hard work, have established their farms and feel financially secure; this affects their relationships with members of the families because they no longer feel compelled to drive themselves and others. They no longer need their daughters' labors and can appreciate the fact that the young women "have made something of themselves." Francie and Lilli also come to terms with their childhood homes, despite painful associations. Lilli is described walking into the countryside: "She wanted to establish contact with her childhood. Here were her roots; here, always, would be something of herself. . . . How beautiful the prairie spring! The wind running with light feet through the grass, the blue glass dome of prairie sky, the horizons where one could stretch one's soul after the confines of city streets!" (298). The prairie wind has been her teacher, she tells a young girl: " 'I heard songs all around me on the prairies, carried by the wind' " (288). Francie, on a visit home, walks beyond the shelterbelt, turns, and looks back on it: "Here she had grown up just enough so that she could go a little further by herself. . . . And the trees had grown. Little by little they had massed from scraggly seedlings into strong, mature trees that bent with the winds and bowed with the snow, growing despite the cycle of death and resurrection. She too had grown. Maybe even slower than the trees. She too could survive the wind and the snow. But she would no longer be afraid: there was always spring" (216).

Both novels end, symbolically, with spring. Both young women are on the threshold of careers, one as a singer preserving through song the myths and values of her own people and other groups, the other as a teacher moving among the children of many cultures on the prairie, sharing and preserving their cultures.

Francis Marion Beynon's novel *Aleta Dey* (1919) should also be mentioned, lest these stories imply that only girls in eastern European immigrant families suffered. Beynon's story about Aleta Dey includes the portrait of a narrow-minded, self-righteous father whose perverted Methodism dictates the cruel restrictions he imposes on his children. One day Aleta's town friends come to play in the haymow. Her father chases them out and intends to beat her. Aleta says, "I was sick with fear at the sight of this human creature, mad with lust for physical conquest over anything that stood in his way" (47–49). Fortunately her mother intervenes.

Aleta makes her escape from the Souris River Valley to Winnipeg, becoming a newspaperwoman. Like Le Sueur's farm woman, Aleta Dey sees political action as the means to survival. She works for women's suffrage and during World War I becomes a pacifist; after being jailed for her activities, she faces an angry crowd and dies from a blow she received while giving a speech. For Aleta Dey there was no return to the place of her youth; there was no reconciliation.

Growing up female in the prairie town has been presented by some women writers are a more secure experience than growing up on the farm. In an interview, Margaret Laurence talks about the sense of being protected in a very small town on the prairie: "It was both a stultifying experience and a very warm protective one too, because this was a place where no child could get lost: everybody knew who you were and who you belonged to" (quoted in Mitchell, *Horizon* 258). Even town girls, however, want to escape. Cather's Lucy considers herself "fortunate to have escaped from a little town to a city" (*Lucy Gayheart* 94). She tells a friend that "family life in a little town is pretty deadly. It's being planted in the earth, like one of your carrots there. I'd rather be pulled up and thrown away" (134). But another of Lucy's Chicago friends envies Lucy because she has roots in the Nebraska prairie: "He had missed the deepest of all companionships, a relation with the earth itself, with a countryside and a people. That relationship, he knew, cannot be gone after and found; it must be long and deliberate, unconscious. It must indeed be a way of living. Well, he had missed it, whatever it was, and he had begun to believe it the most satisfying tie men can have" (78).

Although Lucy rejects much of her Nebraska town heritage, it is while she is kneeling at the window of her old bedroom, looking over her father's yard, that she experiences a "flash of promise" and feels that life might still be holding out something to her, even after her lover's death. Unfortunately Lucy has lost touch with the ways of nature, fails to read its messages, and drowns in the river where she once skated.

In Nancy Stockwell's Kansas stories, *Out Somewhere and Back Again,* another narrator leaves the prairie to seek freedom. Returning home for a visit, she finds the town narrow-minded and frustrating. Several years before, Nancy had given up a secure teaching job in Kansas and moved to Boston so that she could write. Nancy's mother, like Lucy Gayheart's sister, cannot understand how a young woman can not only risk security but also make selfish demands on her family, all in pursuit of personal dreams. The nice irony of Stockwell's story is that Nancy represents a new type of pioneer: one hundred years before, women had left the narrow family and social confines of eastern towns in order to be free. William Wasserstrom made this point in his essay "The Lily and the Prairie Flower": wagonloads of young girls headed West with the hope that "life in the West would be freer and riper" (398–401). Now places like Myola, Kansas, have become (like mid nineteenth-century New England) virtuous and genteel. Nancy summarizes the conflict with her mother:

> My mother gets angry with me, . . . the way I will or will not live my life, the waste she imagines, about her fears, how she needs me, clutches, has tried to trap me, does not want me to go back to Boston, does not want to think about the woman there, wants me to get a good job as a school teacher, use my education, make a stable, secure life for myself, become something, write during a spring recess if I really have to write, or during the two summer months—isn't that what they give school teachers a vacation for she said— but write uplifting things, be good, have a nice apartment, don't dream, don't live in an imaginary world. [94]

Nancy's mother views the daughter's way of life with the same terror an eastern mother must have felt a century before when her pioneering daughter departed for the chaotic wilderness. Nancy tries to comfort her mother by telling her that although she has been living "out somewhere"—in Boston—for ten years, she has never truly left Kansas. This becomes clear in a scene where Nancy drives to John Brown's Lookout and experiences a oneness with the land and with the forces that formed the land.

In fact, Nancy discovers the parallels between the land and her experience of loving a woman:

> In the trauma of the land there is, finally, an evenness, a sameness which is like symmetry thought of differently, as if two bodies sharing similar parts are doubling, stretching, curling and folding in many mutual ecstasies. . . .
>
> I stand and look down—from the only hill southeast of Lawrence— imagining that I have inherited something here. I look at it, through it and at the distance it represents; that is all I can think of to know about it now, and as I stand here, it puts its arms around me, like a woman, like the only woman, I think, the one my life is saturated with, the idea of her, and the all I want and the all I see, all that is in every way precious, the land like a body lying changed in many positions and naked, always naked, and I hold her in my imagination, thinking of all she is. [85–86]

A strong sense of the land and her love relationship as an evolving, vital renewable resource permeates the story.

Also, the spirits of the past pioneers surround her. She identifies with the rebel "Osawatomi" Brown and, to an even greater degree, with the pioneer woman:

> I rise to a standing position like a hardened prairie woman standing on a hill facing the wind, the blowing skirt solidified in bronze like my arms, the patina green, clashing, fighting, withstanding everything just to stand there, arms stretched out wide, wild like the rebel waving a rifle and a book. I know it has been a great, long flight to reach her and another place, frantic, frenzied, wild, jaded, scratched, heaved up, battered, whirled, bruised, going faster than desire to move towards her and myself, always reaching, wanting more and more, and still more. [86]

For Nancy, the Kansas prairie contains spirits of women and men who struggled for survival and fought for freedom. They symbolize the kind of strength she needs to fight for the right to a life-style that clashes with the values of the dominant culture.

Stockwell is one of many writers who examine the relationship of the artist with the landscape and pioneer ancestors. In fact, artists make up an intriguing category among the prairie-born. By examining the stories, we gain further insights into the lives of women—the artist's life is Everywoman's life writ large. The artist may love the prairie and derive much of her inspiration from its landscape and its people, yet leave the homeplace and make her living elsewhere. The act of leaving, however, does not diminish the importance of her past associations.

One critic, Dick Harrison, observes that the artists in prairie fiction "usually fail, and when they succeed we suspect the authors themselves of dreaming." He says that the success of a musician and a fashion designer in Salverson's *Viking Heart* "are part of the obvious wish-fulfillment which so weakens the latter half of the book." He goes on to say that "Lilli Landash in [Lysenko's] *Yellow Boots* rises to fame as a singer, but again the purpose of her success is so obvious we cannot believe in it" (*Unnamed Country* 147). I would argue that we have the fact of the authors' own success to deal with. Both Salverson and Lysenko were born in Winnipeg of immigrant parents, yet they learned the English language and established careers as writers. Writers like Willa Cather, Gabrielle Roy, and Margaret Laurence—all prairie-bred—have received not only national but international recognition.

An American writer and critic, Ruth Suckow, points out in a 1926 essay entitled "Iowa" that "children of our Middle Western towns" become wanderers, without loyalty to the homeplace, in fact repudiating and "obliterating all traces of it" while seeking their identities in far places (613). Suckow herself studied in Boston and Colorado. Willa Cather left Nebraska in the late 1890s, like her character Lucy Gayheart; Meridel Le Sueur lived in Chicago, New York, and Hollywood before returning to the Midwest. Gabrielle Roy went to Montreal; Margaret Laurence went to England and Africa and settled, finally, in Ontario. From examples like these a pattern emerges, showing that the prairie-born artists indeed roamed abroad. But by the time they mature as writers, their alienation from and repudiation of homeplace has diminished—if it existed in the first place—while their appreciation has increased by enormous bounds.[3] Writers included in this study feel their identities were shaped by their prairie childhoods. They may return only in spirit or in memory; they may return physically, like Stockwell, for renewal. Wherever they live, however, they seem to belong in some way to the prairies.

Margaret Laurence and Gabrielle Roy, through autobiographical

3. For example, see the discussion of Cather's rejection, ambivalence toward, and gradual acceptance of the prairie as analyzed by Bruce Baker in "Nebraska Regionalism in Selected Works of Willa Cather," *Western American Literature* 3 (1968): 19–35.

essays and semiautobigraphical fiction, provide insight into the prairie writer and her relationship to her homeplace. As Laurence says, writing usually involves an attempt "to understand one's background and one's past, even sometimes a more distant past which one has not personally experienced" ("Sources" 80). She acknowledges that when she first began to write she was too close to her prairie town (Neepawa, Manitoba) and too prejudiced against it to present an accurate view of it. As a mature artist she recognizes two aspects of the writer-land relationship: "First, the physical presence itself—its geography, its appearance. Second, the people. For me, the second aspect of environment is the most important." She goes on to say that the people of the pioneer generation were difficult to live with: they were authoritarian, unbending, afraid to show love, and quick to anger ("Sources" 82). But—and this is a point made over and over in her fiction—many were survivors and their daughters and granddaughters were survivors: "The theme of survival—survival not just in the physical sense, but the survival of some human dignity and in the end the survival of some human warmth and ability to reach out and touch others—this is, I have come to think, an almost inevitable theme for a writer such as myself, who came from a Scots-Irish background of stern values and hard work and puritanism, and who grew up during the drought and depression of the thirties and then the war" ("Sources" 83).

In a semiautobigraphical short fiction collection, A Bird in the House, Laurence recounts her background and explores, through the narrator Vanessa, her movement toward acceptance of the Manitoba prairie town and of her pioneer grandfather. At one point Vanessa, who is about twelve, is writing an epic about pioneers in Manitoba; when her Aunt Edna mentions that Vanessa's grandfather was a pioneer, Vanessa loses interest: "If pioneers were like that, I had thought, my pen would be better employed elsewhere" (56). So she switches to writing a love story set in the Egyptian desert.

Vanessa is too young to appreciate her grandfather's stature as a pioneer. He built the first brick house of its kind in the new town—an "embattled fortress in a heathen wilderness" (1) and she has to live there after her father dies. She has to endure the grandfather's petty tyranny over her Aunt Edna, her mother, and her grandmother. She has to endure the retellings of an old boring tale: "To me," Vanessa insists, "there was nothing at all remarkable in the fact that he had come out west by sternwheeler and had walked the hundred-odd miles from Winnipeg to Manawaka. Unfortunately, he had not met up with any slit-eyed and treacherous Indians or any mad trappers, but only with ordinary farmers who had given him work shoeing their horses, for he was a blacksmith" (6–7). Her grandfather's adventures do not contain the necessary ingredients for this beginning writer's romances. As Vanessa grows in mind and spirit, however, her perceptions change. During her third year at the university she is called home for her grandfather's funeral, and as she hears her grandfather's story once again, she finds in it a story of meaning and substance for herself: he was a survivor, with dignity; she "had feared and fought the old man, yet he proclaimed himself in [her] veins" (6). She, too, it is suggested, will be a survivor.[4]

Christine, a character in Gabrielle Roy's semiautobiographical stories, presents an interesting contrast to Vanessa: she identifies strongly, from an early age, with her "trotting horse of a grandfather" and adventure-loving mother (Roy, *Road* 15–16) who, like artists, delight in exploring new territories, whether real or imaginary. Christine learns her most important lesson, however, from her grandmother, a reluctant immigrant who grumbles because she had to make a new home in Manitoba after having already made one back in Quebec. Christine observes that her grandmother, in the last months of her life, wants to remain in her own home on the edge of town—on what she has come to call "her prairie." The lesson Christine learns is that her career as a writer will undoubtedly take her away from the prairies, but she will put down roots and thrive in other places. In her essay "Mon héritage du Manitoba," Roy writes that she was happy in many places, including England, the Isle of Rhodes, and Quebec. Nevertheless, it is the prairie of her childhood with its level earth, domelike sky and shimmering sun that she loves most deeply: the limitless horizon beckons and challenges her imagination (Roy, *Fragiles lumières de la terre* 156–57). Roy suggests that her generation will never reach the horizon but that others will surely undertake the same adventure—"la même folle enterprise." Indeed, the horizon becomes, in Roy's mind, a symbol for the circle of humankind wherein all peoples are united (158).

Fascination with the horizon and its symbolic implications as a circle preoccupies two American writers, Lois Phillips Hudson and Margaret Lynn. Hudson, in describing her own life and role as a writer, articulates a process in which most prairie women writers participate—

4. See Laurence's discussion of survival in Kirkwood, "Revolution and Resolution" 17.

making "a loop in time." Drawing on a line from T. S. Eliot's *Family Reunion*,[5] Hudson describes a game children play in the snow: "Then one begins the circle—they call it a pie—and all follow, happy to be only feet weighted with boots and thick underwear and wet winter clothes: just feet following and followed by other feet making a narrow blue round ditch. Now comes the moment when the prairie is conquered; the wobbly loop meets its . . . end" (*Reapers* 149–50). Then Hudson moves from the concrete description of the game to comment on life. Children grow up believing that there is time to discover that place where the two ends of the loop meet—"the secret of the circle": "The circle seems small enough when you yourself are so small" and you believe that eventually "you will understand the secrets of the people who have tramped out the circle ahead of you, and so you will understand the circle." In fact, Hudson says, "it is the grandmothers who keep the secrets that prove we are not accidents but unique in the universe. They are the real past, upon which the only real future can be built. The grandmothers shade their foreheads with flat hands in a salute to some distant grandness we cannot see. When we first come to know them, we believe they are the set of boots that made the first track, the set that will close the circle" (*Reapers* 150–51). The circle of the horizon symbolizes human experience rich in possibilities; individuals are unique and faced with the exciting possibility of exploring the "distant grandness." Adventurous grandmothers have tramped out the first set of tracks, the set that has closed the circle. The granddaughter, therefore, feels that she can leave home and set out along the circle without fear of terrifying gaps opening into the unknown. Indeed, Hudson has the example of her "mountain grandmother": she was "transplanted from Tennessee to the North Dakota prairie, and though you would say that she was a prairie woman, still she was always different from the rest of us" (*Reapers* 151). In other words, she maintained her uniqueness. At the same time, Hudson adds, "her transplanting never faded or wilted." Hudson had her grandmother's example to assure her that people not only survive but even flourish in new places.

Margaret Lynn, in *A Stepdaughter of the Prairie* (1916), focuses primarily on the influence of the landscape itself, although she believes that her forebears are the keepers of the prairie. She reflects her father's

5. "When the loop in time comes—and it does come for everybody— / The hidden is revealed, and the spectres show themselves" (quoted in *Reapers* 147).

dismay that the prairie is to be broken up by "eastern owners . . . who held land not for homes, but for speculation" (280). One day as the narrator is horseback riding she meets on of these easterners and, although only twelve years old, she undergoes "a sort of rite, making a conscious farewell" (281). Eventually she will have to leave the prairie, but the landscape has left a permanent print on her psyche: it has taught her to treasure solitude and to recognize her own uniqueness within the circle formed by the horizon:

> I can't tell what strangeness lay in the line of wonder where the blue of the sky met the green of the hills. It was a mystery which far transcended in remoteness and promise any pot of gold of any childish tradition. That line itself held my attention. I had never before found myself where I could follow the full sweep of it all round. Now I revolved slowly, tracing the long ellipse which inclosed the narrow valley, lifting itself over the crest of a hill or dropping into a soft curve at the head of a draw. The completeness of the line fascinated me and I followed it round twice. I had never imagined it thus unbroken. . . . For once I had no wonder as to what lay beyond that line, either the green or the blue. The completeness and simplicity of what the horizon bounded set it off into a world by itself—a whole world, but so simple. And I was the only person in it. . . .
>
> Here was a real aloneness, a solitude that was almost tangible, and—I discovered—an exquisite, an adorable thing. It made everything mine in a way I had never known before and couldn't realize completely enough for my satisfaction now. Even my self seemed more mine than it ever had at those times when someone might break in at any moment. [153–55]

She, too, will eventually leave the prairie and explore the world beyond the line.

These works by Laurence, Roy, Hudson, and Lynn clearly demonstrate that some arts are positively molded and inspired by the prairie environment. In addition, these artists have relived in imagination the vivid and exciting immigration stories of parents and grandparents who created satisfying lives in a new setting. The message is, of course, that space is subjective; individuals can make of it what they will. These prairie women writers have inherited the attitudes of people who chose to view the spaces of the prairie in a positive way, thus ensuring survival of the spirit.

Margaret Atwood suggests in her study *Survival: A Thematic Guide to Canadian Literature* that the solution for the second generation of immigrants (those like Hudson, Roy, and Laurence) was to become a creator: a writer or artist sees herself as a person "with a vision communicable in words or images which [she] wishes to make accessible to others." Atwood goes on to say, "Take away the artist and the audience can never achieve self-knowledge. . . . [She] is us" (181). The writer, in redisovering and writing about her origins, illuminates a process and provides an example for the reader.

At this point Jaques's question—"Will they, too, love these brown dear fields?"—has to be interpreted metaphorically as well as literally; the brown fields represent more than a physical environment. They represent an entire way of life. The "brown" can be interpreted as the bad times—times of drought or economic failure—but also as times when the intellectual and creative climate seems dormant. Yet if we recall Margaret Lynn's image of the virgin prairie which never truly dies, we have a metaphor for explaining the artistic flowering of the grand-daughter of the prairie pioneers. As summer green passes away, coral tints from the roots creep upward; there is never, according to Lynn, a moment of real deadness. Although many were born during hard times when adults had become cautious and conservative, they listened to their parents' and grandparents' stories about tearing up roots in the old places. They heard them speak about turning optimistically toward the new land with the sense of freedom and possibility that comes with starting over. Rebelling against rigid patterns and limited options, they took risks; they tried something new. All these ingredients are as necessary to the artist's temperament as they are to the pioneer's. No wonder, then, that the pioneer spirit may lie dormant for a generation or two and then rise again in a writer or painter or singer whose new territories are the ever-changing and continuously challenging world of art.

Returning

The prairie-born artist may return on occasion to reestablish her roots, but she usually leaves again; her work and personality frequently require that she live in other settings. Others, as two recent novels show, return home "to get their bearings." In Byrna Barclay's *Summer of the Hungry Pup* (1982), Annika returns to her family homestead near North Battleford, Saskatchewan. She has two problems. First, she is grieving for her grandmother who has just died. As a child she had gone to live with her grandmother after her father died. Then, when her mother ran away with the Watkins salesman, her grandmother took complete responsibility for her. Second, she has just graduated from college, but is unable to decide what to do next. The months on the isolated homestead provide her with a quiet, peaceful environment for sorting out her feel-ings. During this period she also nurses her grandmother's friend, Old Woman, a Cree Indian, who is now in her nineties. While listening to Old Woman's stories, Annika learns that she has to "go backward before she can go forward": she must understand her grandmother's life and Old Woman's life, their friendship and the ordeals that each endured— Johanna as an immigrant from Sweden; Old Woman as a Cree displaced after the Riel Rebellion. Then, perhaps, Annika will be able to figure out who she is and what her values are.

Lannie, in Sharon Butala's *Country of the Heart* (1984), buys a one-way ticket to Chinook at the opening of the novel. As she ties the "Chinook" tag to her suitcase, she thinks, "Going home," although she has repeatedly denied that her aunt and uncle's home has also been her home since her mother died. At the end of the novel she leaves again, having decided to look for her father. The weeks at "home," however, have given her the time she has needed to find that she indeed *has* a home. One day when driving through the countryside, she realizes the effect that the land has on her: "Short patches of broken land were flanked now by long stretches of pale native grass. Here and there herds of cattle grazed peacefully. Now a sea of hills, the muted blue-green of early spring, lay beside her on each side of the road and ahead of her around the curves, as far as she could see. This landscape was calming, and she slowed down without even noticing" (105). When she leaves the farm at the end of the novel, she knows for the first time that she has a place to come back to whenever she wishes.

Returning to the prairie home is an emotional and sometimes painful experience, especially for Indian and Métis women. Many of their lives have been marked by poverty, alcoholism, prejudice, and rootlessness.[6] Experiences of these women are described by three writers: Margaret Laurence in *A Bird in the House* (1970) and *The Diviners* (1974); Beatrice Culleton in *In Search of April Raintree* (1983), and Louise Erdrich in *Love Medicine* (1984). Each writer includes a positive portrait of an Indian woman, showing that individuals are able to make choices that promise some kind of success—a place in society, a reintegration with their group, or a positive identity as an Indian.

In *The Diviners* Piquette Tonnerre symbolizes the alienation of the

6. For a discussion of native American female prototypes, see Bataille and Sands's essay on Maria Campbell (115–26).

Métis. Her ancestors once possessed the prairies; her grandfather had ridden with Louis Riel in the Rebellion of 1885. Yet Piquette grows up in a shack on the edge of the town, a victim of poverty and neglect. Her mother had abandoned her and the other children; her father had done his best to raise the children, but there was never enough money. At seventeen she escapes the prairie town that has repeatedly insulted and hurt her. In another Laurence story, "The Loons," Piquette quits high school and escapes to Winnipeg. When she returns for a visit, she boasts that "'all the old bitches an' biddies in this town will sure be surprised. I'm gettin' married this fall,'" she says, "'my boyfriend, he's an English fella.'" The narrator of the story, Vanessa, watches Piquette's eyes and finds in them "a terrifying hope" (*Bird in the House* 104). Within a few years, however, Piquette returns defeated, bringing her two babies with her. The return, she knows, is an admission of failure, a desperate act because she has no other options. She subsequently dies in a fire: "'One Saturday night last winter,'" Vanessa's mother tells her, "'during the coldest weather, Piquette was alone in the shack with the children. The Tonnerres made home brew all the time, so I've heard, and Lazarus said later she'd been drinking most of the day when he and the boys went out that evening. They had an old woodstove there—you know the kind, with exposed pipes. The shack caught fire. Piquette didn't get out, and neither did the children'" (*Bird in the House* 106).

This scene is also described in *The Diviners*. In this novel, Morag Gunn is the main character. Although white, she too is one of the dispossessed. Her parents died of poliomyelitis when she was small. She is adopted by a friend of her father's, Christie Logan, who is the town garbage collector. She recognizes at an early age that she can escape the "goddamned prairie town" if she gets a good education. She goes to college in Winnipeg and returns, one summer, to work as a reporter in Manawaka. She is sent to write up an account of the Tonnerre tragedy.

Several years later, Morag meets Piquette's brother, Jules, in Toronto. Morag and Jules had gone to school together; in fact, he was the first man to make love to her. They had gone their separate routes out of Manawaka: Morag, after graduating from college, had married a college professor; Jules had become a folksinger and, unlike Morag, he has achieved a degree of freedom and independence.[7] When Morag leaves

---

7. See Leslie Monkman's analysis, "The Tonnerre Family: Mirrors of Suffering." *Journal of Canadian Fiction* 27 (1980): 142–50.

her husband, she lives with Jules for a short time and, by choice, becomes pregnant with his child. She then leaves for Vancouver to try to establish herself as a writer. She names her baby after Jules's sister, Piquette.

This Piquette—Pique Gunn Tonnerre, goes "home," but not to the town where her mother and father, in their different ways, had experienced so much pain. Pique goes instead to Riding Mountain, where her father's people are trying to reestablish themselves in an environment where their traditional values can survive. There she can explore the past that she has heard about only through story and song. From her mother, Pique has heard Christie Logan's tales of Piper Gunn and the Scot rebels who settled in Manitoba—stories that are more fantasy than fact, but nevertheless meaningful to Morag and Pique. In these stories Morag tries to convey to Pique the same message Christie had intended for her: the hero, Piper Gunn, believed people could leave the old homeplace and make a new life for themselves in a new place. But Christie (perhaps unconsciously) and Morag (more consciously) told the story not only of Piper Gunn but of Piper's wife: "*Now Piper Gunn, he had a woman, and she had the courage of a falcon and the beauty of a deer, and the warmth of a home, and the faith of saints*" (italics in original, *Diviners* 368). A girl, as much as a boy, needs heroes.

Morag has also told Pique everything she remembers about the Tonnerre family, although Pique accuses her of not having told her enough. Supplementing Morag's stories are the songs written by Jules, Pique's folksinger father: "The Ballad of Jules Tonnerre" tells the story of the Tonnerre ancestor who fought with Louis Riel and Gabriel Dumont in the 1885 rebellion. Another song, "Lazarus," tells about Pique's grandfather who was "king of Nothing," who drank too much and lost his woman, but nevertheless managed to raise his children. Both songs are about failure but, more importantly, about survival. Thus the Gunn stories and the Tonnerre songs communicate the same message.

The novel concludes with Pique's own song expressing her sense of yearning for the mountain, the valley, and the prairie of Manitoba:

> I came to taste the dust out on a prairie road
> My childhood thoughts were heavy on me like a load
> But I left behind my fear
> When I found those ghosts were near
> Leadin' me back to that home I never knowed. [467]

Pique, raised by her mother in the white worlds of Vancouver, London, and Ontario, is compelled to go back to the home she has never known to discover and explore the Indian half of herself. Then, she hopes, she will know who she really is.

A pair of characters similar to Piquette and Pique appear in Beatrice Culleton's novel *In Search of April Raintree*. April tells the story of how she and her sister Cheryl were taken from their parents who were poor and alcoholic. The two girls grew up in a series of foster homes where some of the white families were kind and others were cruel and abusive toward the Indian children. At an early age April decides that the most expedient means to achieving security is to become as "white" as she possibly can:

> And when I grew up, I wouldn't be poor; I'd be rich. Being a half-breed meant being poor and dirty. It meant being weak and having to drink. It meant being ugly and stupid. It meant living off white people. And giving your children to white people to look after. It meant having to take all the crap white people gave. Well, I wasn't going to live like a half-breed. When I got free of this place, when I got free from being a foster child, then I would live just like a real white person. [49]

April is an obedient, conscientious student. She eventually goes to secretarial school, becomes a secretary in a law firm, and marries a white businessman from Toronto.

Cheryl, her sister, is an intelligent, lively child, but she refuses to conform to white expectations. She rebels against the textbook accounts which describe Louis Riel as a crazy, half-breed traitor. She has been fortunate in having one teacher who was herself Métis and who loaned Cheryl books about Canadian Indians. Therefore, when a teacher reads a book to Cheryl's class about Indians torturing and scalping "brave white explorers and missionaries," Cheryl objects loudly: " 'This is all a bunch of lies!' " The teachers replies, " 'I'm going to pretend I didn't hear that.' " So Cheryl says, " 'Then I'll say it again. I'm not going to learn this garbage about the Indian people. . . . Lies! Lies! Lies! Your history books don't say how the white people destroyed the Indian way of life. That's all you white people can do is teach a bunch of lies to cover your own tracks' " (57). Cheryl is, of course, punished and humiliated. She nevertheless remains loyal to her Indian blood and, as a young woman, makes a commitment to preserving her heritage and helping Indians and Métis. Her life revolves around Friendship Centre in Winnipeg; in addition, she takes courses at the university.

In the meantime, April's marriage fails. She realizes that her husband has probably married her to spite his mother. In addition, she doesn't fit in with upper-class society in Toronto; gradually she realizes she no longer *wants* to fit in with white society. She has just begun divorce procedures when she gets word that Cheryl has been hospitalized. She returns to Winnipeg and tries to piece together the events of her sister's life: Cheryl has quit school; she is an alcoholic; she is disillusioned about her work at Friendship Centre, where it seems impossible to help Indians and Métis youths change the destructive patterns of their lives.

At the end of the novel, Cheryl commits suicide. Ironically, it is April, the one who had denied her heritage, who finally achieves reintegration with her Indian culture and the Indian community along Main Street in Winnipeg. First, however, she undergoes a horrible ordeal. Mistaken for her sister Cheryl, she is subjected to a gang rape. The process of physical and psychic healing takes place slowly, but she has the help of Roger Madison, a young man who seems to understand when she tells him what it is like to be a person of mixed blood:

> "It would be better to be a full-blooded Indian or full-blooded Caucasian. But being a half-breed, well, there's just nothing there. You can admire Indian people for what they once were. They had a distinct heritage or is it culture? Anyway, you can see how much was taken from them. And white people, well, they've convinced each other they are the superior race and you can see they are responsible for the progress we have today. Cheryl once said, 'The meek shall inherit the Earth. Big deal, because who's going to want it once the whites are through with it?' So the progress is questionable. Even so, what was a luxury yesterday is a necessity today and I enjoy all the necessities. But what have the Métis people got? Nothing. Being a half-breed, you feel only the short-comings of both sides. You feel you're a part of the drunken Indians you see on Main Street. And if you inherit brown skin like Cheryl did, you identify with the Indian people more. In today's society, there isn't anything positive about them that I've seen. And when people say off-handedly, 'Oh, you shouldn't be ashamed of being Métis,' well, generally they haven't a clue as to what it's like being a native person." [156–57]

Fortunately, April is able to say these things to Roger without his getting defensive.

April is also helped toward reintegration with her people by an accidental meeting with one of the elders at the Friendship Centre. An old woman takes April's hand. At first April finds the woman's touch repulsive. Then she describes her transformation:

> I waited for her to take her hand away. I looked at her questioningly but she didn't say anything. Her gaze held mine for I saw in her eyes that deep simple

> wisdom of which Cheryl had spoken. And I no longer found her touch distasteful. Without speaking a word to me, the woman imparted her message with her eyes. She had seen something in me that was special, something that was deserving of her respect. I wondered what she could possibly have found in me that could have warranted her respect. I just stood there, humbled. At the same time I had this overwhelming feeling that a mystical spiritual occurrence had just taken place. [174–75]

Cheryl reinforces this experience, telling April that at the moment her "vision" is clouded; when it clears, however, she was sure April " 'would be a good person for the Métis people' " (175).

In the final section of the novel, April reads her dead sister's farewell letter. She discovers Cheryl has a little boy. April claims the baby, and the novel ends on a positive note. April remembers something Cheryl had said: " 'All life dies to give new life.' Cheryl had died. But for Henry Lee [Cheryl's baby] and me, there would be a tomorrow. And it would be better. I would strive for it. For my sister and her son. For my parents. For my people" (228). April's quest for identity has led her back to the city of her birth and to integration with her own people and, at the same time, to reintegration into the white community through her marriage to Roger.

The same pattern of one failed vision justaposed with one potentially fulfilled vision emerges in Louise Erdrich's novel about a North Dakota family from the Turtle Mountain Indian Reservation, *Love Medicine*. In the opening story of the collection, June King dies on the frozen prairie outside Williston. Earlier in the evening she had been about to board a bus for home, but when a man in the Rigger Bar motions for her to come in, she joins him. He is one of the men from the oil field and, when he pays for their drinks, she notes he has money:

> That roll helped. But what was more important, she had a feeling. . . . He had a good-natured slowness about him that seemed different. He could be different, she thought. The bus ticket would stay good, maybe forever. They weren't expecting her up home on the reservation. She didn't even have a man there, except the one she'd divorced. Gordie. If she got desperate he would still send her money. So she went on to the next bar with this man in the dark red vest. They drove down the street in his Silverado pickup. He was a mud engineer. Andy. She didn't tell him she'd known any mud engineers before. [3]

This passage shows how June has been drifting from man to man while hoping for something meaningful to happen in her life.

Later that night, after the mud engineer has fallen asleep, she "felt herself getting frail again. Her skin felt smooth and strange. And then she knew that if she lay there any longer she would crack wide open, not in one place but in many pieces that he would crush by moving in his sleep." She opened the door to the truck and fell out—her body had been wedged tightly between the man and the door. The fall, she thought, was "a shock like being born" (5). For June, however, there was imminent death, not rebirth; there was the final, irrevocable departure, not a return to home and family.

The outline of June's story is similar to the stories of Piquette in *The Diviners* and Cheryl in *In Search of April Raintree*: hope is quickly replaced by despair and a deadly passivity is accompanied by alcoholism and prostitution. Piquette died by fire; Cheryl died by drowning; June died by freezing in a prairie blizzard. But Erdrich, like Laurence and Culleton, believes that some women may return home and find themselves.

Why *does* a woman return home? To discover who she is. To rediscover her dreams. To find, possibly, love and support from family. When June got out of the truck and started walking in the direction of home, she had obviously rejected these possibilities. She was walking toward death. As her niece Albertine points out in the next story, June had grown up on the prairie; it wouldn't have mattered how drunk she was—she still would have known that the Chinook wind was deceptive and that she would die of exposure. With a bus ticket in her handbag, June chose death instead of home.

Erdrich's story about June King provides one prototype—the defeated woman. Her other stories describe four generations of women who are survivors: June's great-grandmother, Rushes Bear; her grandmother, Marie; her sisters, Aurelia and Zelda; and her niece, Albertine Johnson.

In the second story of the collection, Albertine returns home, but clearly her relations with her family are precarious. She is angry because her mother didn't immediately tell her about June's death. Nevertheless, she says, "I decided to go home. I wasn't crazy about the thought of seeing her, but our relationship was like a file we sharpened on, and necessary in that way" (10). Albertine has never known her father, called the Swede, who went AWOL when he discovered that Albertine's mother was pregnant with her. Her mother exclaims: "'I raised her Indian, and that's what she is'" (23). This positive attitude toward being an Indian has had a good effect on Albertine. She knows who she is, as well as the strengths and weaknesses of her family. After all, she's the granddaughter of Rushes Bear, a name which summons the image of a physically and spiritually powerful woman forcing a bear into retreat. Also, Albertine's grandfather has been active in tribal affairs, so she has grown up with a strong sense of political efficacy. One other factor has contributed to her sense of security. She has a homeplace—not just on the reservation itself, but in nature. She can lie on her back in the grass, beside her cousin Lipshen, and watch the Northern Lights:

> Everything seemed to be one piece. The air, our faces, all cool, moist, and dark, and the ghostly sky. . . . All of a piece. As if the sky were a pattern of nerves and our thought and memories traveled across it. As if the sky were one gigantic memory for us all. Or a dance hall. And all the world's wandering souls were dancing there. I thought of June. She would be dancing if there was a dance hall in space. She would be dancing the two-step for wandering souls. Her long legs lifting and falling. Her laugh an ace. Her sweet perfume the way all grown-up women were supposed to smell. Her amusement at both the bad and the good. Her defeat. Her reckless victory. Her sons. [34–35]

Albertine comes to terms with June's death at this time and, in fact, provides an entirely new perspective on June's death. The justaposition of the two phrases—"Her defeat. Her reckless victory"—emphasizes June's ability, finally, to control her life by choosing death.

In the last story of *Love Medicine*, Albertine has decided to go to medical school. Her decision is not only a sign of confidence in herself but a commitment to helping people. Certainly *love* is the best medicine, but all too often there is none available. Albertine cannot make up for all the lost, misplaced, or never-found loves in people's lives. The next best thing might be to help take care of their bodies.

In one episode Albertine's cousin and his wife have just had a fight, and when she walks into the kitchen she discovers they have ruined her mother's pies: "All the pies were smashed. Torn open. Black juice bleeding through the crusts. Bits of jagged shells were stuck to the wall and some were turned completely upside down." Albertine screams at them: "'The pies! . . . . You goddamn sonofabitch, you broke the pies!'" (38). Later Albertine returns to the kitchen: "I spooned the fillings back into the crusts, married slabs of dough, smoothed over edges of crusts with a wetted finger, fit crimps to crimps and even fluff to fluff on top of berries or pudding. I worked carefully for over an hour. But once they smash there is no way to put them right" (39). Albertine, as a doctor, will patiently try to piece people back together, fully conscious that the hearts and souls of the victims may be as fragmented as the bodies.

In Aritha Van Herk's novel *Judith* (1978), the main character also returns home in search of wholeness. Judith had been raised on a pig farm, where she enjoyed a secure childhood. Whe she pictures her child-hood, she sees herself walking between her parents, swinging from their strong arms and hands. Her alienation from home developed when she graduated from high school. At that time she rejected the farm and became a secretary in Edmonton. The novel opens with Judith's return to the country, but through flashbacks we observe the fragmentation that took place in Judith during her city years. The superficiality of city life is represented by her painted nails, ultra-feminine dress, awkward high heels, and intense but loveless relationship with her employer. In the urban setting her dislike for what she has become increases when her father asks her one last time to return and take over the farm. She refuses; the land is sold. It is not until after the deaths of her parents that she buys a farm similar to theirs and returns to the country.

The first scene occurs on a late November evening. Judith is working among her eight new pigs, shoveling "pig shit and wet greasy straw." She feels uncertain about herself, her pigs, her business venture and her place in the community. At the end of the novel, on the threshold of spring, she has become "her own father," making decisions for her own sake, not just to pacify her father's spirit. She is equally at ease in the house and in the barn. Her uneasy relationship with a neigh-boring farmer is resolved in a climactic scene when the young pigs are castrated. Jim intends to do the job, but after making the first clean cut, his hands become shaky; Judith insists on taking over. In this sensitive situation Judith becomes, literally, the castrating female, and both Judith and Jim are tested. Jim has been uncomfortable with her all along—she's an independent, self-possessed woman absorbed in suc-ceeding with the pig business, and thus intimidating. Judith's testing is related specifically to the castration process: she is finally experiencing the one aspect of pig-raising that her father had barred her from. She feels that her father had not been entirely honest with her. In trying to keep her innocent, as his little girl, he had kept power in his own hands. Once Judith comes to this realization, she sees her father in a new way. He was not a god whose powerful spirit must be placated; he was an ordinary man. Now she can live her own life, make choices for herself. And, free from her father but still loving his memory, she need no longer fear the control of other men. At the same time, Jim realizes he has two alter-natives: he can take a chance with Judith, make love to her and risk rejection; or he can go on fooling around with silly high school girls. Fortunately he chooses the former, accepting Judith's strength; the results are rewarding for both.

A reviewer of *Judith* observes that the novel is "spunky, if flawed"; the relationship with Jim is "done nicely," but the reviewer concludes that finally "there is only so much . . . one can do in describing a woman and her pigs" (Bilan 315). When *Judith* is placed within the tradition of prairie women's fiction, however, we realize that a great deal is being said in the novel and there are many things to say *about* the novel. The structures typical of the pioneer prairie novel persist. First, Judith's business venture represents a new beginning, "her lost chance" (114) to prove herself by starting over with a life-style that her parents would have approved. On another level, it represents a yearning for a simpler, more meaningful life according to the agrarian values to which many pioneers adhered. The old dilemma created by outside work continues to be a significant consideration for a woman. What *is* the effect of shoveling pig shit? Judith discovers, like her foremothers, that a woman can do a man's job and still enjoy—as the final scene shows—the dab of cologne behind the knee.

The ordeal of isolation persists in *Judith.* She is an outsider raising pigs in wheat country and trying to do by herself the work others do as couples. At first she has no desire to become a part of the community and reluctantly accepts a dinner invitation from the Stamby family. However, like many pioneer women, she unexpectedly experiences an intense female friendship with Mina Stamby, an aspect of the novel completely overlooked in Bilan's review, which mentions only Judith's relationship with the son. Mina Stamby, a lone female among four adult males, needs Judith's company. Judith discovers that she needs Mina. The most moving scene in the novel occurs when Mina asks Judith if one of the pigs can be given her name. Thus the pigs named Marie Antoinette, Josephine, Daisy Buchanan, Emily, Circe, Venus, Annie, and Lilith—who are named upon giving birth—are joined by the last two pigs, Mina and Judith (159–60).

In the epilogue to the novel, Judith makes her daily trip to the post office and asks for her mail. The postmaster stares at her, then asks, " 'You the lady with all those pigs?' " Judith replies that she is. He looks so "stubborn and reproving" that Judith can't help but laugh:

> In that instant she felt something snap, some high-tension wire spring into release.

"Well, Humphh."

She stopped laughing as suddenly as she had started. "I'd like my mail please." She said it deadly quiet.

"Yes, yes." He shuffled over to the General Delivery boxes and came back with a handful of letters. He held them on the counter and stared at her again. "You ought to get a box." [179]

When Judith asks him why, the postmaster replies that General Delivery is for folks passing through; those who stay rent boxes. "'You're not plannin' on leavin', are you?'" he asks. Judith rents a box (180).

The snap she hears represents her newly found security within the community and her willingness to make a permanent commitment to staying. It's the same kind of snap heard by pioneers as the old ties broke and new commitments were formed. Thus the novel ends on a note of reconciliation reminiscent of the pioneer prairie novels that traced the lives of women who emigrated, worked hard, survived, and finally affirmed the whole crazy business of starting over in a new territory. For Judith, however, the new territory is a symbolic one that represents a new state of mind, as she rediscovers the territory of her parents and claims it as her own.

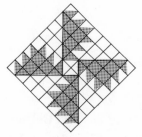

CHAPTER EIGHT

"Miyopayiwin"—The Unity of All Things under Sky

Prairie fiction reveals a remarkable consensus about the nature of female experiences on the tallgrass prairies of both Canada and the United States. Despite differences in geography and settlement patterns, the structures of signification are basically indistinguishable. Only one striking difference emerges: when we identify publication dates, it becomes apparent that Canadian writers have a more persisting sense of the prairie landscape, of prairie history, and of the prairie as home ground. Sixteen Canadian novels have been published since 1970 as compared with three American works. Over a hundred-year period, the structures of signification emerging from this corpus have remained consistent: the stories focus on females' responses to the land, the homestead or farm, and the town. Prairie women writers describe the nature of female work and the many varieties of gender roles. Women's prairie fiction also reveals a pervasive optimism rarely found in the works of men: many writers repeatedly insist that women can survive and frequently thrive on the prairies; at the very least, they acquire roots and lessons that sustain them in later life. I have argued in this book that females responded to the land emotionally and spiritually in positive ways and that these responses have naturally facilitated women's adjustments to the environment and difficult living conditions.

Northrop Frye has suggested the term "garrison mentality" to describe the response of Canadian settlers to what he calls a "huge, unthinking, menacing and formidable setting" (*The Bush Garden* 225). Thus people from Newfoundland to British Columbia clustered together in forts and small communities for protection against the unknown. Settlers, in order to survive a climate of extraordinary extremes and a

252

sparsely populated landscape, assented to the social and moral values of the group and submitted to the laws and institutions of the majority in return for protection; individual beliefs and customs were frequently relinquished in exchange for security.[1] Although most landscapes in women's prairie fiction are not as hostile as the one described by Frye, there is, nevertheless, evidence of a garrison mentality—but it is a more positive type. It is one that exists in American works, too.

Many critics have found the American western experience radically different from the Canadians'. In contrast to the emphasis placed on community in Canadian works, the prototype of the American westerner has been the individual (always male) who has cut himself off from the group and exists independently. His freedom is made possible in part by a state of mind that values individual freedom over group security; in fact, this state of mind has evolved from a national revolutionary response to outside control, and it contrasts sharply to the Anglo-Canadian compliance with British rule or the French-Canadian allegiance to the seigneury or the parish.[2]

Also, critics point out, the American response to nature has been radically different: Americans supposedly look on nature as a benign force. The possibilities for living harmoniously with nature are more promising than living within society. On the surface, it seems, Americans would have no need to develop a garrison mentality in order to survive. However, in an essay entitled "The 49th Parallel and the 98th Meridian: Some Lines for Thought," Frances W. Kaye makes some parallels that force us to reconsider the foregoing generalizations. I agree with Kaye's conclusion that *both* men and women east of the 98th meridian, Canadian *and* American, felt that membership in an organized community was essential for survival. Thus the male settler on the American prairie has more in common with the Canadian settler than with his

1. Margaret Atwood's poem "Progressive Insanitites of a Pioneer" explores the negative effects of the garrison mentality. For a discussion of the poem, see Jerome H. Rosenberg, *Margaret Atwood* (Boston: Twayne, 1984), 36–38.

2. For comparisons between the Canadian and American attitudes toward the West, see the following: Dick Harrison, "Across the Medicine Line: Problems in Comparing Canadian and American Western Fiction" in *The Westering Experience in American Literature: Bicentennial Essays* (Bellingham, Wash.: Bureau for Faculty Research, Western Washington University, 1977); Victor Howard and Edward Miles, "Canada and the United States: Some Paradoxes," *Journal of American Culture* 2 (1979): 660–69; Dick Harrison, "Fictions of the American and Canadian Wests," *Prairie Forum* 8 (1983): 89–97; Patricia Hunt, "North American Pastoral: Contrasting Images of the Garden in Canadian and American Literature," *American Studies* 23 (1982): 39–68.

counterpart in the fiction and history of the plains and the Far West who tried to escape from society. Both men and women east of the 98th meridian have, to varying degrees, a garrison mentality.[3]

Moreover, female pioneers established a more personal kind of garrison than that described by Frye. They located on their landscapes the neighbor (female or male) who could be called upon in emergencies—the midwife or the doctor, the woman adept with herbs, the place where shelter would be guaranteed or a horse offered for running errands. We can understand how crucial this kind of "garrison" was to an immigrant woman who, because of language, religion, or customs, was an outsider—unless, of course, she enjoyed the advantage of group immigration and settlement, which, occasionally, assured immediate and continuous garrisoning. Once a woman could accept the strengths and limitations of the garrison she had mapped out for mutual support and assistance, she was psychologically armed against a hostile environment. She knew where to turn for help; she knew when she would have to depend on her own resources, ingenuity, and perseverance. A woman without a garrison was vulnerable and more easily defeated by the new situation.

Within this context, the prairie woman's absorption with flowers, discussed above, takes on new significance: women on the prairie garrisoned themselves not only with shelterbelts but also with their flower gardens.[4] Margaret Wilson describes the process of erecting this symbolic garrison in *The Able McLaughlins*. Barbara McNair, on her excursion through town looking at women's flower gardens, hears the following story from a settler from eastern Iowa:

> That rose, the lady explained, she had brought with her from Davenport, in a little box with grape cuttings and the peony, which she had carried in her lap in a covered wagon long before there were railroads to the town. She had brought it to Davenport coming down the Ohio and up the Mississippi soon after she was married. A woman had given it to her when she left Ohio for the West. The peony her mother had brought from eastern to western Ohio many years ago, and when she died, her daughter had chosen

3. Harrison, in the articles listed in note 2, finds greater differences between American and Canadian responses to the West, but he does not distinguish as carefully as Kaye in separating the midwest from the Far West.

4. A plainswoman, Elinore Pruitt Stewart, eloquently describes the "garrison" provided by her flowers. "She wrote to a friend: 'The cattle died in piles and the horses died in other piles and I didn't want to write to anyone. But I can tell you, my dear, that it is a relief when things get to their worst. You know what the worst is then and can begin to plan better things. That's what I have done. I have planted flowers everywhere'" (quoted in Ferris xii–xiii).

the peony for her share of the estate. Her mother had got it from her mother, who came a bride to Ohio from western New York, clasping it against her noisy heart, out of the way of the high waters her husband had led her horse through, across the unbridged streams, cherishing it more resolutely than the household stuffs which had to be abandoned in the pathless woods. [162–63]

The fact that women cultivated flower gardens does not mean they did not love as well the wildflowers of the prairie. Harvey Dunn's painting *The Prairie Is My Garden* (see fig. 5 above) captures this relationship between a woman and the fields: a tall, handsome woman stands in the field, basket of flowers in one hand, scissors in the other. Her two daughters have accompanied her; one holds a bouquet, the other kneels to pick another flower. Their bouquets form bright clusters which stand out against the drab colors of the house and the barn in the background. Significantly, the faces of all three reflect the mood of the flowers, not of the buildings.

The most powerful description of the prairie woman and her flowers is found in Gabrielle Roy's "Garden in the Wind," already discussed in chapter two. Marta has witnessed the disintegration of the garrison, the town of Codessa, which had dreamed of becoming a little Ukrainian capital on the prairie. However, when the visions diminish after years of drought and the neighboring farmers and even her own children leave, having discovered that they cannot "tame" the prairie, Marta remains and finds the companionship she needs in the wildflowers, the frail aspen grove, and the flowers of her own personal garden. These and the onion-domed church across the fields are an adequate garrison.

Indeed, an extended analysis of women and their gardens in women's prairie fiction would reveal that the growing of flowers and vegetables symbolizes the ability of women to create and control their environments. This, I would argue, is one of the greatest adventures for prairie women. Their flowers and shrubs, sometimes linked in memory to former places and people, provide continuity and represent individual histories as well as buttresses against the unfamiliar. The vegetables, almost always the products of female labor, nourish the entire family, especially in the first year or two of homesteading when the fields are being prepared and remain unproductive. Women could control and protect their gardens, nestled as they were close to the front doorstep, in a way they could not control the fields they planted with the men. The tasks of digging, weeding, and hauling water were back-breaking and time-consuming, but their efforts were rewarded on a much more consistent basis than those expended in the fields.

Because women occupied and controlled a different space from men, their visions have differed. This conclusion brings us to an important generalization derived from prairie women's literature: female experiences are represented more positively in women's than in men's fiction. This difference relates directly to the socialization process of males and females in the nineteenth and early twentieth centuries. From an early age, many females have been reared to be passive, accommodating, adaptable, and obedient to the requirements and demands posed by the head of the household. Likewise, enormous pressures have been exerted on males to conform to a certain masculine type. Peter Gabriel Filene provides an insightful description of the Victorian male:

> Ideally, a man was self-reliant, strong, resolute, courageous, honest—traits that people summed up simply as *character*. At home he governed absolutely but justly, chivalrous toward wife and firm toward his children, defending them against all adversity. He provided a benevolent patriarchy. Outside the home, he worked to earn the income that would feed, clothe, and shelter his family in happy comfort. As breadwinner he must struggle against his fellow men and natural forces, but with enough determination he would succeed. [69]

This description illuminates our understanding of the prototypical male heroes in the novels by O. E. Rölvaag and Frederick Philip Grove, who devoted their lives to building mansions on the prairie and leaving their marks on the land. For both men, Per Hansa and Abe Spalding, the house was the most important element in their visions. The acreage or the livestock or the barns were important symbols of success, but the house is by far the most important because it announces the presence of a self-sufficient, strong, resolute, courageous, and benevolent patriarch—a statement to every passerby that the man of the house is financially successful and committed to his family.

The pressures on females to be successful wives and mothers was also intense, but in a different way. Most women could not control their economic situations directly; they could support, urge, or drive the men in their lives to acquire material wealth, they could spend frugally or liberally according to their individual situations, they could choose, sometimes, to marry the rich man or the poor man. Overall, however, their possibilities were limited. Thus their visions of future possibilities have taken a different shape than men's. When we adopt this perspective on women's roles and society's expectations, we can better understand the nature of the pioneer woman's response to the new land. The key difference between men and women is found in a phrase from Grove's novel, where Abe expresses his determination to "dominate" the prairie (23). Only the men, to prove their manhood, had to dominate, conquer, exploit, control, or possess the land.[5]

Women writers have recognized this attitude and applied it to their male characters. Bess Streeter Aldrich observes that for the men, "the wilderness was a giant with which to wrestle. It must be fought,—more, it must be overcome or it in turn would conquer them" (*Spring Came on Forever* 100). Tim Connor in Josephine Donovan's *Black Soil* tells his wife: "This country, me girl, is like Schwartzes' colt. It's high-spirited like all young things and must be broken, conquered. . . . But I wouldn't be back East today, Nell, for all the comforts in the world" (95). Tim thrives on this adversary relationship with the earth.

Not all men need to dominate the land, however, as a short story by Susan Glaspell implies. In "Pollen," Glaspell shows a somewhat different relationship. Ira Mead works *with* the soil—harmoniously and almost tenderly—to develop a better quality of corn:

> In planting his corn Ira would sometimes find himself thinking back to the Indians. As he did things over and over the movements made for themselves a sort of rhythm, and it was as if this rhythm swung him into all that was back of him. He was less awkward at such times; he seemed less a figure outside of other things. . . . Sometimes as he listened to his whispering field of corn he would think with a queer satisfaction that corn was American. It was here before we were; it was of the very soil of America—something bequeathed us which we carried along. He would think of all that corn did—things that could go on because of it. And then he would wonder, with a superiority in which there was a queer tinge of affection, what those Indians who had

---

5. Carol Pearson and Katherine Pope, in a study entitled *The Female Hero in American and British Literature,* point out that "the male central characters of contemporary literary works usually are anti-heroes in a hopeless and meaningless world. . . . In contrast, female characters in works by women are increasingly hopeful, sloughing off the victim role to reveal their true, powerful, and heroic identities" (9). Interestingly, Pearson and Pope support their thesis with a historical example: an article on women homesteaders argues that women's lives were frequently more hopeful and successful than the literature or history written by men has acknowledged. They quote the following figures: "An average of 11.9 percent . . . of homestead entrants were women. . . . 37 percent of the men succeeded in making final claim to the land, while 42.4 percent of the women succeeded, a percentage which discounts the [prevailing] theory of women as helpless, reluctant pioneers" (Sharon Patterson-Black quoted in Pearson and Pope 6).

> perhaps tended maize in this very field would say if they could see one of his
> ears of corn. Perhaps it was because he would like to have them see his corn
> that he sometimes had a feeling they were *there*. [448]

His experiments with the corn have brought him into an intimate relationship with the earth and with the Indians who planted before him.
While his relationship with the land is positive, one of his motives in
developing the corn was to demonstrate to all his neighbors his superiority as a farmer. He is angered and frustrated by the winds that carry his
good pollen to one farm and simultaneously bring inferior pollen from
another neighbor's field, which then fertilizes his corn and reduces its
quality. Eventually the corn forces him into a positive relationship with
his neighbors whom he has tried to ignore: he realizes his corn will never
be perfect unless he gives the neighboring farmer his good seed corn; that
is the only way to keep the winds from blowing inferior pollen from the
Balch farm.

In the last scene of the story, Ira Mead carries a pail of his good seed
corn to Joe Balch. As one of the lively young Balch girls opens the door to
let him in, there's a suggestion that his obsession with the corn will
diminish and the "instinct for fatherhood" (448) that has thus far been
spent on the corn may be redirected toward marriage and children. As
one critic notes. "he crosses the boundary line, like his pollen, and
rejoins the community" (Waterman 27). Ira Mead, like Abe Spalding
and Per Hansa, cannot, finally, control nature or use his power over
nature to establish his superiority over his neighbors. The story's main
significance, however, lies in its portrait of a man who is able to work in
harmony with the land; he is not very different from the Indians who had
planted before him. In fact, Ira is very much like Alexandra in Cather's
O Pioneers! or Dallas in Gates's *Plow-Woman*. As Carol Gilligan has
noted in her study *In a Different Voice*, "while men represent powerful
activity as assertion and aggression, women in contrast portray acts of
nurturance as acts of strength" (quoted in Ammons 84). What started
out as an act of assertion on Ira Mead's part became, by the end of the
story, an act of nurturance.[6]

The inordinate pressures on the American and Canadian male to
be successful also have influenced the interpretations of literature when
male critics compare the pioneer's dream with the reality. For example,

---

6. Other males with a nurturing relationship with the land have already been discussed:
Ivar Wingar in *O River, Remember!* and Nils Mattson in *Red Rust*.

critical articles by Michael A. Klug and James E. Miller, Jr., analyze the theme of despair, disillusionment, and unfulfilled dreams in Cather's works. Cather's characters, according to Klug, "find the ordinary world to be a deadly place for dreams and dreamers. The wild prairie of O Pioneers! is charged with life, but it is also malevolent—a 'stern frozen' land, a 'somber' waste, a dark country that swallows human desire" (289).[7] Yet we must take into account the fact that this response to the landscape is that of a young man, Carl Becker, on a bleak November evening during a period of bad crops on the Nebraska prairie—moreover, of a young man who leaves Nebraska to seek fame and fortune elsewhere as an artist, not a settler. Klug does not cite another passage from the same novel that modifies this view of the landscape: "Even Carl, never a very cheerful boy, and considerably darkened by these last two bitter years, loved the country on days like this, felt something strong and young and wild come out of it, that laughed at care" (49). (See fig. 22 for a typical landscape near Red Cloud, Nebraska. A painting by John Blake Bergers, The Divide, captures the same rolling landscape as Jones's photograph and shows the beauty of the prairie when the fields are green and glowing under a late afternoon sun.) At another point Klug refers to Alexandra's "indomitable will to conquer the land" (291), a characterization which seriously misrepresents Alexandra's attitude toward her farm and ignores the existence of the key passage in the novel: "For the first time, perhaps, since that land emerged from the waters of geologic ages, a human face was set toward it with love and yearning" (65).[8]

This passage is also ignored by David Lowenthal in his essay "The Pioneer Landscape: An American Dream." He argues that while the "pioneers enjoyed freedom from the dead weight of inherited structures that elsewhere impeded change and crippled progress," they paid the cost in loneliness. He then quotes from O Pioneers!: " 'Of all the bewildering things about a new country . . . the absence of human landmarks is one of the most depressing and disheartening.' " He goes on to say that "pioneer women, less engaged than men in the process of transforma-

7. Ronald Rees also misrepresents this passage in his article "In a Strange Land" (5).

8. Michael Peterman, in an essay on Cather and the Canadian prairie writer W. O. Mitchell, points out that these two authors "strive to create a vision of possibility and hope for mankind, based on the ministering power of the open prairie and the development in childhood of the fullest capacities of imagination and individuality" (104). In a footnote Peterman observes that David Stouck, in "Perspectives as Structure and Theme in My Ántonia" (Texas Studies in Literature and Language 92 [1970]: 285–94), "takes [James] Miller to task for over-emphasizing a 'fatalistic element in the novel'" (Peterman 106).

Fig. 22   ELEANOR JONES, *Prairie Landscape near Red Cloud, Nebraska.* Courtesy of the photographer.

tion, often found the solitude unbearable, as did Beret in Rölvaag's *Giants in the Earth*" (10). Lowenthal's conclusions are a serious distortion of Cather's work. The passage he quotes appears at the beginning of the novel when the prairie was still unmarked and unpeopled despite eleven years of hard work on the part of a man like John Bergson, who is dying without seeing his dream fulfilled. The passage was intended to show a dramatic contrast between John Bergson's unfulfilled dream and his daughter's fulfilled dream, which is described on the concluding pages of the novel. Alexandra tells Carl: " 'I've lived here a long time. There is great peace here, Carl, and freedom.' " Carl replies: " 'You belong to the land,' " and Alexandra says " 'Yes, now more than ever.' " Then she makes this point: " 'The land belongs to the future, Carl; that's the way it seems to me. How many of the names on the county clerk's plat will be there in fifty years? . . . We come and go, but the land is always here. And the people who love it and understand it are the people who own it—for a little while' " (307–08).

In "My Ántonia and the American Dream," James E. Miller, Jr., comes to the conclusion that My Ántonia embodies the "shattered" dreams of American pioneers; their lives, he claims, are "broken by the hardness of wilderness life. Even those who achieve, after long struggle, some kind of secure life, are diminished in the genuine stuff of life." He cites Tiny Soderball as one of the few examples of a success, but she seems to have lost her zest for life and has become a "thin, hard-faced woman" (Miller 117). We need to remember, however, that this is Jim's view of Tiny, not necessarily Cather's view. Certainly Cather chooses not to romanticize Tiny Soderball; she wants the reader to see her as Jim sees her. At the same time Cather would expect readers to recognize that Tiny could indeed be satisfied with her success, if not elated, especially as the daughter of an immigrant who had been able to escape the poverty and class restrictions of the Old World and the drudgery of her parents' large family on the prairie.

We need to keep in mind, therefore, the ways in which Cather's female characters have a sense of fulfillment rather than merely commenting on the deprivations of their ordinary lives. We need to focus less on the failures of the Carl Beckers and the Jim Burdens to fulfill their dreams. Instead, we need to focus on the ability of Cather's prairie women to find their secure and satisfying places in the order of things. If we refocus in this manner, we will come closer to Cather's understanding of prairie life and her value system. Two critics, Edward A. Bloom and Lillian D. Bloom, accurately represent Cather's position in their article "Willa Cather's Novels of the Frontier": "Miss Cather's philosophy is not one of despair. The seasons are merely tests of determination." They support this statement with a quotation from O Pioneers!: "And yet down under the frozen crusts, at the roots of the trees, the secret of life was still safe, warm as the blood in one's heart; and the spring would come again! Oh, it would come again" (Bloom and Bloom 86).

A sense of the secrets of life is at the heart of women's optimism. Belief in renewal and rebirth underlies the survival instinct in prairie women, as Joan Stradinger reveals in her drawing *Prairie Woman* (fig. 23). In an analysis of metaphors associated with the frontier, Ann-Janine Morey-Gaines explains why there are female heroes in prairie fiction: "It is no surprise that it is woman's uncompromised mutuality with earth that leaves her the transcendant figure closing each epic agrarian narrative. It is women who endure and triumph" (137). Men who have not developed this mutuality with earth (and thus far men writers have not been inspired to describe such a relationship) are doomed to disillusionment, mediocrity, or failure. Perhaps Richard Chadbourne is right when he says

Fig. 23   JOAN STRADINGER, *Prairie Woman.* Courtesy of the artist and *North Country Anvil.*

that women are tougher—Ántonia and Alexandra are certainly "tougher" than their fathers ("Two Visions" 101). Such characters abound in prairie fiction, making possible the generalization that *women* are tougher. They seem to know how to respond to a situation in a way that insures their survival.[9] A similar point has been made by Margaret Laurence. In an interview she says of her Manawaka women (from the "Manawaka novels"—*The Stone Angel, The Fire Dwellers, A Jest of God,* and *The Diviners*): "What they do have for the most part is the ability ultimately to come to some kind of understanding of themselves. They are *not* victims. They may be victims for a time, but they are certainly not incapable of action" (quoted in Kirkwood 17).[10]

Seventy years after Cather wrote *O Pioneers!* Jessica Lange produced and directed the film *Country.* As a cultural artifact, this film reminds us that the people who love the land must be kept on the land. Jewell and Gil Ivy are told that they are not making enough from their wheat to live decently; the Farmers Home Administration tells them they should "work toward voluntary liquidation." The banker tells them that he knows there's no better land or better cared for land than their 180 acres; nevertheless, he can't lend them the money they need to prepare for another year of crops. Gil reacts emotionally, shouting "I've never been on any damn list my whole life!" Feeling that the situation is hopeless, he begins drinking. Jewell's first response to liquidation is a rational one: "What exactly are we supposed to do?" When the auctioneer calls for an appointment, Gil says, "It's coming—might as well

---

9. Notice that Henry Commager arrives at a dramatically different conclusion in his essay "The Literature of the Pioneer West." He concludes with a very emotional reaction to the immigrant experience in America, with quotations from Rölvaag's novel: "'Not for them the triumphant song of 'Pioneers! O pioneers,' but the silence 'on the border of utter darkness.' . . . 'The Great Plain drinks the blood of Christian men'—it is the handwriting on the wall of American history" (327–28).

10. Harrison, in *Unnamed Country,* says that "all of Laurence's prairie heroines are in some way imprisoned by pride and guilt, and they are seeking the absolution that could free them. At the same time they are victims of the prairie's Manawaka culture—its bigotry, its Calvinist self-repression, its dedication to a few limited and life-denying truths which may have sustained the pioneers but which stifle the next generation and isolate them from the life which should be accessible to them. What Laurence finds most consistently in her search through the past is confirmation of a need to be freed from that past and the burden of guilt it has left" (197). Laurence herself, however, sees another side of the Manawaka-Neepawa experience: "My writing, then, has been my own attempt to come to terms with the past. I see this process as the gradual one of freeing oneself from the stultifying aspect of the past, while at the same time beginning to see its true value—which, in the case of my own people (by which I mean the total community, not just my particular family), was a determination to survive against whatever odds" (*Heart* 17).

get it over with." Jewell takes a stand. She says she and her family belong on the land. They won't "just walk away . . . like a bunch of sheep." Determined to fight, she organizes the farmers. Some reluctantly, others wholeheartedly support her plan to frustrate the liquidation process. On the day of the auction, the farmers come, but they refuse to buy anything. When the FmHA man calls off the auction, he assures Jewell that he'll use other procedures to get her off the farm. She replies that he can take the equipment, "but when you try to get *us* off, you'll need more than a piece of paper." The message of *Country* insists that the American dream associated with the family farm is still not a failed dream. [11]

Two pioneer women have written down what survival means to them. Jennie Osborn doesn't talk about "triumph" or victimization; but she does talk about endurance. At the age of 87 when she wrote down her memories, she wonders what their meaning is, finally, for her children and grandchildren who will read them. She concludes that her purpose has been "to show that, with good health and energy, we can conquer most any hardship if we have the stick-to-it-iveness in our constitution. This is required. Well, we stuck" (42). Charlotte Ouisconsin Van Cleve, born at Prairie du Chien in 1819 while her parents were traveling from Connecticut to Fort Snelling, has a similar message in her reminiscences. Referring to her years in the pioneer community of Long Prairie, Minnesota, Van Cleve says that life there had taught her much: "We felt our hearts stronger and richer for its lessons, and we all look back on that memorable time as something we would not willingly have missed out of our lives, for we learned that one may be reduced to great straits, may have few or no external comforts, and yet be very happy, with that satisfying, independent happiness which outward circumstances cannot affect" (92). Underlying Osborn's and Van Cleve's messages is an additional characteristic that I would call human dignity—dignity that comes from hard work and from endurance in spite of adversity.

A definition of heroism gradually emerges from the characters of prairie women's fiction, from the philosophy of the writers themselves, and from the optimistic interpretations of numerous critics. Chadbourne says women are "tough." Two pioneer women emphasize "stick-to-it-

---

11. Some interesting statistics indicate a trend by women either to stay in farming or to become farmers. Over 2,000 Minnesota farmers are women, according to *Agaware*, the publication of Minnesota Women for Agriculture: "Since the census of 1978, farm women in Minnesota have increased by fifteen percent; they are three percent of all farm operators." Male farm operators have dropped by five percent (*Plainswoman* 8.3 [1984]: 17).

iveness" and an ability to find contentment without material comforts. Laurence emphasizes the ability of individuals to act in positive ways against victimization. Morey-Gaines proclaims women's ability to "endure and triumph"—primarily because of their "mutuality with the earth." While all these qualities characterize the female heroes of the literature we've studied, it is women's association with the land and the cycles of nature that seems to receive the most emphasis.

Chapter two outlined the positive images of the prairie that many women carried with them into the West and the ways in which other characters came to accept and love the prairie. Cather, in an essay entitled "Nebraska," said that "the splendid story of the pioneers is finished, and . . . no new story worthy to take its place has yet begun" (625). Nevertheless, novels published since Cather's *My Ántonia* show that there indeed have been other stories to tell. They may not be completely new stories, but they explore new—or at least different—relationships with the prairie: the prairie is rich in associations with home ground, erotic experiences, imagination and creativity; it is a sacred place, sometimes linked with psychic healing, a place of oneness with nature.

Ellen Moers, in her classic work *Literary Women,* concludes that a study of women and the landscape produces "no simple answers." However, "that certain lands have been good for women is clear—open lands, harsh and upswelling, high-lying and undulating" (60)—clearly these are lands like Willa Cather's Nebraska, Margaret Laurence's Manitoba, Edna Ferber's Illinois, Louise Erdrich's North Dakota.[12]

No one has felt more strongly about home ground than Meridel Le Sueur. The midwestern prairies, the people, the farms, the towns, and the history have formed everything she has written. In the concluding lines of *North Star Country* she expresses faith in people and their relationships with nature: "The people are a story that is a long incessant coming alive from the earth in better wheat, Percherons, babies, and engines, persistent and inevitable. The people always know that some of the grain will be good, some of the crop will be saved, some will return and bear the strength of the kernel, that from the bloodiest year some survive to outfox the frost" (321). If, after reading these lines, we turn to reexamine John Weaver's statue *Madonna of the Wheat* (see fig. 9 above),

12. Moers's sources for this interpretation of women and landscape include examples from American, English, South African, and Australian literature.

we better understand its powerful symbolism: the woman's life and purpose are rooted in the prairie soil, which has frustrated and challenged her but also rewarded her with fruits of the earth—with the wheat that she cradles in her arms, the wheat that feeds the world. As Neala J. Y. Schleuning has observed, the prairie, for Meridel Le Sueur, "is that space in which she has centered her entire world view. Her vision of a global consciousness is an image born directly from the great open spaces of the Midwest. Perhaps the experience of the land does have a different feeling in the Midwest, creating a broader vision of expansiveness and spaciousness. Meridel has succeeded in translating that sense of wholeness and circularity and all-inclusiveness that bridges the religion of the prairie tribes and the early pioneer sense of awe for the great land spaces" (38). Le Sueur's inclusive vision is captured in these lines from her poem "Dòan Kêt"[13]:

> I saw the women of the earth rising on horizons of nitrogen.
> I saw the women of the earth coming toward each other
>> with praise and heat
>> without reservations of space.
> All shining and alight in solidarity.
> Transforming the wound into bread and children
> In a new abundance, a global summer.
> Tall and crying out in song we arise
>> in mass meadows. [Rites 54]

One need not be born in a particular place for it to be home ground. An eastern European immigrant, a French-Canadian immigrant, a European and an easterner all discover, during the course of their stories, that the prairie is home ground—not their former homes. In "Garden in the Wind," Marta wonders, as she walks to the little Ukrainian church with her scarlet lilies, where she belongs:

> Marta contemplated the sky, so wide, and the horizon, so patient, and her own life, buried in so much silence that it seemed to have dissolved in it.
> "What kind of life did you have anyway, Marta Yaramko?" she asked herself as candidly as if she had been talking to a mere acquaintance. But she didn't know what kind of life she'd had. . . .
> But seeing herself underway on this long, long road . . . she felt drawn onward, carried toward a human family, a murmur of voices. . . . It seemed to her that she was travelling toward Canada.
> She was a part of Canada, of course; somewhere, carefully tucked

---

13. Le Sueur says "dòan kêt" means "solidarity" in Vietnamese (Rites 51).

Fig. 24   MICHAEL HILGER, *Ukrainian Church near Tolstoi, Manitoba,* 1979. Courtesy
of the photographer.

> away, she even kept her naturalization certificate. . . . But Canada seemed
> to her less a country than an immense map with strange cutouts, especially in
> the North; or was it no more than a sky, a deep and dream-filled waiting, a
> future in suspense? Sometimes it seemed her life had been spent on the edge
> of the country, in some vague zone of wind and loneliness that Canada might
> yet embrace. [Roy 139–40]

She accuses the sky of always posing questions and never providing
answers. As she looks around her, however, her "heart melted in a
mysterious way, as if in this eternal play of wind and grass and sunlight
there was for her an inexhaustible consolation" (141). Marta doesn't
understand her place in Canada or in the universe, but she is secure in
her sense of home ground.

Gabrielle Roy's "almighty grandmother" also has ambivalent feelings about her home ground. She railed most of her adult life about having to leave Quebec and her beloved mountains. But when her daughter wants her to move into St. Boniface, the grandmother puts her off, saying, "we'll see, we'll see." Her granddaughter Christine watches her standing in the doorway: "From the threshold she looked ahead of her at the naked prairie about which she has complained so bitterly all her life, saying that it wearied her to death, that she would never get used to it, that it would never be her country . . . and yet I wonder if it isn't the same prairie that holds her there so strongly today—her old enemy, or what she believed was her enemy" (ellipses in original; *Road* 20).

In *Crinoline to Calico*, Berta, a German immigrant, talks about her feelings for her new home: "'Ach! Is happy place, this country. But my country too . . . was happy there'" (ellipses in original). When asked if she gets homesick, Berta says no. "'My Axel and boys is here. Is my home, this. Old country, my Mudder's home.'" Castle Gayle, the easterner, insists that the prairie "was not *her* home, nor ever would be" (Heacock 60). Yet by the end of the novel she does not even want to return to visit family in Pennsylvania, the place she thought would always be her home. She, too, has found a new home ground to replace the old.

Land has erotic associations for women, as well as for men. Nancy, the narrator in Stockwell's *Out Somewhere and Back Again*, discovers an analogy between the land and her female lover. Abbie Lane, in Aldrich's *A Lantern in Her Hand*, watches her husband turn the first furrow in their virgin fields and finds a much more conventional analogy: "The first loam turned back, clean-cut with the sharp knife of the plowshare, mellow, black as a crow's wing. A fringe of coarse grass held fast to the heavy soil, as though the two could not be parted after all these wild free centuries together,—the grass maiden clinging to the breast of her prairie lover" (58). One of the best-known examples of woman's erotic associations with the land is found in Martha Ostenso's *Wild Geese*: "Judith took off all her clothing and lay flat on the damp ground with the waxy feeling of new, sunless vegetation under her. . . . Oh, how knowing the bare earth was, as if it might have a heart and mind hidden here in the woods. . . . Here was something forbiddenly beautiful, secret as one's own body. And there was something beyond this. She could feel it in the freeness of the air, in the depth of the earth" (53). Although Judith rejects her father's cultivated fields, she responds intuitively to the fecundity of the soil in the woods, a place which has not been violated by the plow.

For others, the prairie is a source of imagination and creativity; it offers a sense of possibilities. The narrator in O Pioneers! says "that a pioneer should have imagination, should be able to enjoy the idea of things more than the things themselves" (48). As Richard Chadbourne observes, this imagination extends beyond Alexandra's corn fields; her imagination engages in other subjects than her agricultural ventures ("Two Visions" 101). Christine, the narrator in Roy's Road Past Altamont, describes the way the prairie stimulates the imagination—once in her childhood "an entire city rose from the ground at the end of the prairie especially for me, a strange city with cupolas" (116). Her imagination creates a personality for the prairies and, as a result, readers of the story see the prairie landscape in a new way. One day as Christine drives toward Pembina, she personifies the prairie, saying that after lying "level and submissive" since the beginning of time, it rebelled and began swelling, then erupting to put forth the hills of Pembina. The road, too, becomes personified: "The dirt road was perceptibly climbing, without pretense, with a sort of elation, in joyous little bounds, in leaps like a young dog straining at the leash" (116–17).

In "Mon héritage du Manitoba," Roy says that the prairie was "an inexhaustible source of dreams," "endlessly calling, endlessly slipping away"; she goes on to say that in this way the prairies symbolize our lives: "the image in our lives of the ideal, or of the future, which appears to us, when we are young, to be a generous source of ever abundant and renewed promises" (quoted in Chadbourne, "Two Visions" 112). In Heart of a Stranger, Margaret Laurence says this about the prairie: "Stultifying to the mind it certainly could be, and sometimes was, but not to the imagination. It was many things, but it was never dull" (217). In The Diviners, Morag Gunn describes the prairie's potential: "People who'd never lived hereabouts always imagined it was dull, bleak, hundreds of miles of nothing. They didn't know. They didn't know the renewal that came out of the dead cold" (Laurence 282).

Lois Phillips Hudson also emphasizes the ability of prairie people to see things that outsiders miss: "All prairie people, like desert people, can recognize from a great distance the elongated dots of their kind" (Reapers of the Dust 152). At the end of the story, the narrator describes the time her mother took her "to look up into the space over the prairie and count the dots in Pleiades. If I could see the seventh dot, the papoose on the squaw's back, then according to those people who came before us on the plains, I would grow up to have the keen eyes of the great hunter" (171–72). Keen sight, for the narrator, represents imagination, the ability to see into others' lives and write about them.

The prairie is also a sacred place. In "O Prairie Girl Be Lonely" by Meridel Le Sueur, the girl leaves the body of her lover on a spot of prairie in northern Iowa after he dies of gunshot wounds (71). In Breneman/Thurston's *Land They Possessed* Michal has her "place of rocks" where she goes for renewal. In Beynon's *Aleta Dey* the child discovers that at Sunday school God always seems angry at someone; out in the pasture, however, she experiences what for her is the real God one day when a breeze passes by (29). In *Summer of the Hungry Pup*, Annika listens to Old Woman's stories and through her is carried into a sacred place—"a memory that didn't belong to me but was full of promises for me" (Barclay 43). Old Woman takes Annika, through imagination, out of the garrison, beyond the shelterbelt of caragana and northern spruce which surrounds the homestead, and into Deer's Rump Hill: "She carried us both through frosted glass and true barriers to her place of belonging" (43). At the end of the novel Annika follows Old Woman's funeral procession part of the way, and then breaks away to seek Old Woman's true place of belonging: " '*Waskicosihk!*' " I cry. It is Deer's Rump Hill. It does touch sky. It stretches from the east, across the horizon, to the west; links two homes of sun. I am crying. I have followed the words of Old Woman, and they have led me to the place of belonging" (301).

The healing qualities of the prairie are described in Joy Kogawa's *Obasan*. Naomi, a third generation Japanese-Canadian, has come home for her uncle's funeral. After the burial service, her two aunts and the minister decide it is time to tell Naomi and her brother why their mother never returned from a visit to Japan. The mother had gone to Japan in the late 1930s to visit her dying mother; she failed to return after the war because she had been disfigured by the atomic explosion and had to choose between separation from her children or returning and thereby exposing them to the horrors she had experienced. For thirty years, therefore, Naomi has had to endure the "not knowing" resulting from her mother's silence: not knowing what happened to her, not knowing whether her mother had loved her. After she learns the truth, she goes out into the predawn morning and walks through the coulee grass, the wild rose bushes, the wildflowers, along the river. She goes to the spot where she and her uncle have returned year after year. Now she understands that each visit has been in remembrance of her mother and the ordeal she underwent: they always made the visit about the ninth of August. Here on the prairie the memories are "potent and pervasive as a prairie dust storm," but it is also a place of silence and healing (247).

A discussion by Carol P. Christ in *Diving Deep and Surfacing: Women Writers on Spiritual Quest* illuminates the relationship between females and nature. First, Christ points out, women who have been excluded from culture tend to experience transcendence in nature. The very fact that women have been limited to the sphere of children, home, and garden has "encouraged women to be open to mystical experiences in nature. In almost all cultures women's bodily experiences of menstruation, pregnancy, childbirth, and lactation, combined with their cultural roles in caring for children, the sick, the dying and the dead have led to the cultural association of women with the body and nature, and men with culture, the spirit, and transcendence" (22). Thus, Christ argues, "whether or not women really are closer to nature than men, cultural attitudes and cultural roles have encouraged women to develop a sense of their own affinity with nature" (23).

Historian Susan H. Armitage says that the major question dominating the field of western women's history is the following: "Did the frontier liberate women?" ("Western Women" 71). In answering that question, we usually search for examples of women with several choices of roles. Christ's discussion suggests that we should instead be attentive to spiritual forms of liberation. Christ says: "Women's experiences in nature are extremely significant because they can occur in solitude when a woman feels isolated from other people and has nowhere to turn. When in the depths of despair and loneliness many women are rescued by sensing their grounding in nature" (23).

One of the most extended descriptions of a mystical experience in nature is provided by Margaret Lynn in *A Stepdaughter of the Prairie.* The narrator has roamed the prairie throughout her childhood years; one day is different—she finally *sees* the prairie: "I scarcely breathed or consciously felt. I only looked. A long, long, irregular valley lay before me, with hillslopes cutting down onto it occasionally from each side. It all spread out in gentle curves, with soft risings and slow descents, and it was all, all clothed in the rare full green of the prairie-grass" (151). She goes on to describe the "aloneness" which for her was "an exquisite, an adorable thing" (155).

This was a landscape, for the moment at least, completely satisfying. . . .
The wind seemed to be bringing the grass toward me, in a constant motion, and I ran to meet it. I ran and ran, in a sort of ecstasy, of all I realized of the place, the prairie wind in my hair, the prairie-grass about my feet, the prairie sun in my eyes. Every minute was an adventure in life. [157]

No contemporary novelist has caught the sense of oneness with the cycles of nature better than Aritha Van Herk in her novel *Judith.* When Judith goes to the barn to feed her pigs, she notices the new snowfall and remembers being a child and rising one morning, dressing, and entering the snowy world of the farmyard. She remembers how she "flung herself into it, heedless, flat on her back, arms flailing and legs scissoring. . . . Again and again, jumping from one angel to create another, she pressed them into the mold of the snow with her body. . . . Angels, robed and winged, lifting themselves magically in the smooth bluish layer" (62). Later Judith returns from the barn, having just witnessed one of her sows giving birth. She walks the slope to the house, stops, and views the scene:

She stood still, looking around her glowing world: the white, self-effacing house, the vibrant red barn, the jewelled celebration of the snow.
Carefully she walked to a smooth patch, flopped down on her back and swung her arms through the snow high above her head and down to her sides, then spread her legs and brought them together, again and again in a convulsive act of love. [72][14]

Nature can also provide links between generations. In Kristjana Gunnars's *Axe's Edge*, Sveinborg Sigfúsdóttir sits with the scrapbook in which her mother had attentively, perhaps lovingly, pressed the grasses—witch grass, wild rye, bluebunch fescue, bluegrass, foxtail, four-leaf clover, thief-root, and, finally, the rare creeping bent (62). Her mother had died when she was born, so Sveinborg tries to discover or recreate her mother through the collection of grasses: "I look for mother's thoughts in the way she bent the blades and situated the joints. Did you also use these

14. In an article entitled "'A Kingdom and a Place of Exile': Women Writers and the World of Nature," Dorothy Jons points out that "identification of the female body with natural landscape is a very ancient literary motif which, with its associated imagery of expropriation, conquest and domination, is frequently used to describe a lover's triumph. . . . But for women writers, identification of woman with landscape and the world of nature does not as a rule generate imagery of a male lover's subjugation. Rather it opens up possibilities whereby a woman character may learn to command a space of her own—a space which represents her own life and in particular her body and her sexuality" (269). Jones then illustrates this statement with reference to Van Herk's novel *Judith.*

weeds to calm down with, Margret Sveinborg?" (66). She draws several conclusions from the grasses and, in the process, understands her mother. She discerns the symbolic implications of the collection. The past, she realizes, like the grasses, is "pressed, dried and labelled. Our job," she decides, "is to imagine the soft, moist life that must have been there," referring to the lives of her parents when they were young. "I do not know what associations mother's grasses had for her. They must have seemed unfamiliar. Prairie weeds meant for dry hot summers, dust storms and spring floods, grasshoppers and blackflies, have nothing in common with the moss and lyng [heather] she grew up with [in Iceland]. More than that, they have no stories or beliefs in them. They carry no possibility of hope" (63). This negative view of the grasses, however, quickly gives way to a new understanding as she looks at the Kentucky bluegrass:

> It covers the entire page in one long slender line with delicate tufts at the head. The tip is shaped like a boat and the veins stand out. The collar is yellow, almost green, and it fades out of sight almost where it begins. She could have found it anywhere among the crops, even on the lawn. They say it is introduced from Europe, but it seems so native here.
>
> That is how it is with people. We adapt to circumstances. When our luck changes or chance gives us a blow, we accept it. [63]

Finally, she declares, she understands her mother: "It is in the grasses. Even the strange ones communicate a certain feeling, a sense of open-mindedness about time and history." She points to the witch grass. "It grows in lonely places where no one normally goes and you notice the fringes of hair at the base of the plant immediately. . . . It does not seem dead on the page" (64–65). Nor is her mother completely dead to her, but sends her a message through the grasses, a message that says people can survive transplanting.

Nor are the prairie stories addressed in the present study dead words on a page, but messages of import to absorb into our personal lives. The universe represented by the prairie is far from being denuded, nor does it denude those within its broad expanse. Rather, the individual may be "garmented with space," to use the phrase that describes the relationship between the Hindu goddess and surrounding space. I borrow this expression from an Eastern culture to describe the relationship between females and space on the American and Canadian prairies, but indeed we need not look beyond the grasslands of our own continent for a model. Roberta Hill Whiteman suggests one way of existing in the contemporary world:

> Let us survive
> Inside a sacred space.
> Look at the Earth.
> She feels us. She feeds us.
>
> Look to the West.
> Look to the North.
> Look to the East.
> Look to the South.
>
> Look at the Sky.
> He feeds us. He heals us.
> Inside a sacred space
> Let us survive. [*Star Quilt* i]

This sacred space—*miyopayiwin*—is interpreted by Susan J. Scar-berry in an article entitled "Land into Flesh: Images of Intimacy": "Rela-tionships between living beings and the land and the sky are experienced as cyclic and enduring. . . . where intimacy is a shared sense of closeness made possible because the world is not objectified or abstracted: the world is connected through physical and spiritual comprehension of relationships. Land and flesh are two expressions of the same reality" (24). Roberta Hill Whiteman, a member of the Oneida tribe, has not had to *learn* to recognize this relationship with the land; she inherited it through her culture. For most of us, however, whether nineteenth-century immigrants or contemporary women, it is a learned experience.

Annika, in *Summer of the Hungry Pup*, recalls the day she began learning about the intimacy of space. She was seven years old and had been to her first fair in North Battleford. Uncle has just put gas in his truck for the return home. Auntie is leaning against the truck door. Old Woman and Annika have settled in the back of the truck between the cream cans. Suddenly Johanna, Annika's grandmother, runs across the highway: "Head down, she plunged through the open gate onto a sum-merfallowed field. Beyond that, prairie stretched away forever. My grandmother ran forth and back, holding her head" (Barclay 187). Then Old Woman (at that time called Medicine Woman) leaps from the back of the truck and catches her friend Johanna. Annika describes the scene as she recalls it:

> Thick brown arms wrapped around Johanna's shoulders and arms; the Indian woman held her still. Slowly, she turned them both in a circle, her smooth cheek pressed against Johanna's. . . .

The hefty, tall Indian woman suddenly thrust my grandmother down to the ground, face down, and pinned her arms above her head. She spoke in Cree, voice low and deep, and I couldn't hear what she said. Then she let my grandmother go, stood back, still talking, but pointing to east and north and west and south.

My grandmother pulled herself up, smoothed her skirt and brushed it with her hands. She lifted her head, wrapped her arms around herself; slowly turned in a circle.

The Indian woman pointed at fixed places on the horizon. "Where earth meets sky," she said.

The grandmothers stretched out their arms, together turned, drawing the long line in a circle around them: the protective circle of prairie. [188]

Most prairie women have had to come to terms with the prairie without the aid of a friend. They have, so to speak, come naked and vulnerable into the prairie landscape. Some remain naked and exposed; many, however, like the Swedish-born Johanna and her prairie-born granddaughter Annika become garmented with space, protected and defined, yet at the same time free and unhampered in their view of the universe.

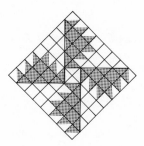

Bibliography

Many of the following works have been annotated in *Farm Women on the Prairie Frontier: A Sourcebook for Canada and the United States* by Carol Fairbanks and Sara Brooks Sundberg (Metuchen, N.J.: Scarecrow Press, 1983).

THE FICTION

American

Aldrich, Bess Streeter. *A Lantern in Her Hand.* New York: D. Appleton, 1928.
———. *The Rim of the Prairie.* 1925. Reprint. Lincoln: Univ. of Nebraska Press, 1966.
———. *Song of Years.* New York: D. Appleton-Century, 1939.
———. *Spring Came on Forever.* New York: D. Appleton-Century, 1941.
Aydelotte, Dora. *Across the Prairie.* New York: D. Appleton-Century, 1941.
———. *Full Harvest.* New York: D. Appleton-Century, 1939.
———. *Trumpets Calling.* New York: D. Appleton-Century, 1938.
Beers, Lorna Doone. *Prairie Fires.* New York: E. P. Dutton, 1925.
Breneman, Muriel, and Mary Worthy Thurston [Mary Worthy Breneman, pseud.]. *The Land They Possessed.* New York: Macmillan, 1956.
Cannon, Cornelia James. *Red Rust.* Boston: Little, Brown, 1928.
Cather, Willa. *Lucy Gayheart.* 1935. Reprint. New York: Vintage Books, 1976.
———. *My Ántonia.* Boston: Houghton Mifflin, 1917.
———. *O Pioneers!* Boston: Houghton Mifflin, 1913.
———. "A Wagner Matinee." 1905. In *Willa Cather's Collected Short Fiction, 1892–1912.* Intro. Mildred R. Bennett. Lincoln: Univ. of Nebraska Press, 1965.

Catherwood, Mary Hartwell. "The Apples on the Crane." *Wide Awake,* June 1886, 13–17.

————. "The Bride of Arne Sandstrom." In *The Queen of the Swamp and Other Plain Americans.* 1899. Reprint. New York: Garrett Press, 1969.

————. "The Career of a Prairie Farmer." .iLippincott's Magazine 25 (1880): 706–13.

————. "A Little God." *Weekly Dispatch* (Kokomo, Indiana), 19 December 1878; 26 December 1878; 2 January 1879; 9 January 1879.

————. "The Little Renault." *Century Magazine,* August 1891, 557–66.

————. "The Monument to the First Mrs. Smith. A True Story of Today by 'Lewtrahl.'" *Weekly Dispatch* (Kokomo, Indiana), 7 November 1878.

————. *Old Caravan Days.* 1880. Reprint. Boston: D. Lothrop, 1884.

————. "The Old Colony House," *Lippincott's Magazine* 32 (1883): 578–95.

————. "The Spirit of an Illinois Town." *Atlantic Monthly* 78 (August-September-October 1896): 168–74; 338–47; 480–91.

————. "Stephen Guthrie." *Lippincott's Magazine* 29 (1882): 21–38, 122–38, 231–54, 329–46, 436–49, 540–54.

————. *The Story of Tonty.* Chicago: A. C. McClurg, 1890.

Chambers, Mrs. C. R. *See* Beers, Lorna Doone

Donovan, Josephine. *Black Soil.* Boston: Stratford, 1930.

Erdman, Loula Grace. *The Edge of Time.* New York: Dodd, Mead, 1950.

Erdrich, Louise. *Love Medicine.* New York: Holt Rinehart & Winston, 1984.

Fairbank, Janet Ayer. *Rich Man Poor Man.* Boston: Houghton Mifflin, 1936.

Faralla, Dana. *A Circle of Trees.* Philadelphia: J. B. Lippincott, 1955.

Ferber, Edna. *So Big.* Garden City, N.Y.: Doubleday, Page, 1924.

Fernald, Helen Clark. *Plow the Dew Under.* New York: Longmans, Green, 1952.

Ford, Elisabeth. *Amy Ferraby's Daughter.* New York: Coward-McCann, 1944.

————. *No Hour of History.* New York: I. Washburn, 1940.

French, Alice [Octave Thanet, pseud.]. "Mrs. Finlay's Elizabethan Chair." In *Knitters in the Sun.* 1887. Reprint. New York: Garrett Press, 1969.

————. *Stories of a Western Town.* 1893. Reprint. New York: Charles Scribner's Sons, 1897.

Gale, Zona. "The Night of the Storm." In *Old-Fashioned Tales.* New York: D. Appleton-Century, 1933.

Gates, Eleanor. *The Biography of a Prairie Girl.* New York: Century, 1902.

————. *The Plow-Woman.* New York: Grossett & Dunlap, 1906.

Glaspell, Susan. *Judd Rankin's Daughter.* Philadelphia: J. B. Lippincott, 1945. Also published as *Prodigal Giver.* London: Victor Gollancz, 1945.

————. "A Jury of Her Peers." In *The Best Stories of 1917.* Ed. E. U. O'Brien. Boston: Small, Maynard, 1918.

————. *Norma Ashe.* Philadelphia: J. B. Lippincott, 1942.

———. "Pollen." *Harper's Magazine*, March 1919, 446–51.

Heacock, Nan. *Crinoline to Calico*. Ames: Iowa State Univ. Press, 1977.

Hudson, Lois Phillips. *The Bones of Plenty*. Boston: Atlantic-Little, Brown, 1957.

———. *Reapers of the Dust: A Prairie Chronicle*. Boston: Little, Brown, 1957.

Lane, Rose Wilder. *Free Land*. New York: Longmans, Green, 1938.

———. *Let the Hurricane Roar*. New York: Longmans, Green, 1933.

Le Sueur, Meridel. "Corn Village." *Scribner's Magazine*, August 1931, 133–40. Reprinted in *Corn Village*. Sauk City, Wisc.: Stanton & Lee, 1970. Also reprinted in *Salute to Spring*. New York: International Publishers, 1977.

———. *I Hear Men Talking: Stories of the Early Decades*. Edited with an afterword by Linda Ray Pratt. Minneapolis: West End Press, 1984.

———. "O Prairie Girl Be Lonely." In *Cross Section 1947*. Ed. Edwin Seaver. New York: Simon & Schuster, 1947.

———. "Salute to Spring." In *Salute to Spring*. New York: International Publishers, 1977.

Lovelace, Maud Hart. *Early Candelight*. New York: John Day, 1929.

Lynn, Margaret. *Free Soil*. New York: Macmillan, 1920.

———. *A Stepdaughter of the Prairie*. New York: Macmillan, 1916.

McCarter, Margaret Hill. *The Price of the Prairie: A Story of Kansas*. Chicago: A. C. McClurg, 1910.

McDonald, Julie. *Amalie's Story*. New York: Simon & Schuster, 1970.

North, Jessica Nelson [Mrs. Reed Inness MacDonald]. *Morning in the Land*. New York: Greystone Press, 1941.

Stockwell, Nancy. *Out Somewhere and Back Again (The Kansas Stories)*. Washington, D.C.: Women in Distribution, 1978.

Suckow, Ruth. *Country People*. New York: Knopf, 1924.

———. *The Odyssey of a Nice Girl*. New York: Knopf, 1925.

Thanet, Octave. *See* French, Alice

Thurston, Mary Worthy. *See* Breneman, Muriel, and Mary Worthy Thurston

Wilder, Laura Ingalls. *By the Shores of Silver Lake*. 1939. Reprint. New York: Harper & Row, 1953.

———. *The First Four Years*. New York: Harper & Row, 1971.

———. *Little House on the Prairie*. 1935. Reprint. New York: Harper & Row, 1953.

———. *Little Town on the Prairie*. 1941. Reprint. New York: Harper & Row, 1953.

———. *The Long Winter*. 1940. Reprint. New York: Harper & Row, 1953.

———. *On the Banks of Plum Creek*. 1937. Reprint. New York: Harper & Row, 1953.

Wilson, Margaret. *The Able McLaughlins*. New York: Grosset & Dunlap, 1923.

Canadian

Barclay, Byrna. *Summer of the Hungry Pup*. Edmonton: NeWest Press, 1982.
Beynon, Francis Marion. *Aleta Dey*. London: C. W. Daniel, 1919.
Blondal, Patricia. *A Candle to Light the Sun*. 1960. Reprint. Toronto: McClelland & Stewart, 1976.
Butala, Sharon. *Country of the Heart*. Saskatoon, Sask.: Fifth House, 1984.
Campbell, Maria. *Halfbreed*. 1973. Reprint. Toronto: McClelland & Stewart-Bantam, 1979.
Chapman, Ethel. *The Homesteaders*. Toronto: Ryerson, 1936.
Cormack, Barbara Villy. *The House*. Toronto: Ryerson, 1955.
_____. *Local Rag*. Toronto: Ryerson, 1951.
Culleton, Beatrice. *In Search of April Raintree*. Winnipeg: Pemmican, 1983.
Elston, Miriam. "A Mess of Things." *Westminster:* 437–43. (Miriam Elston mss., Provincial Archives of Alberta.)
Gunnars, Kristjana. *The Axe's Edge*. Toronto: Press Porcepic, 1983.
Haas, Maara. *The Street Where I Live*. Toronto: McGraw-Hill Ryerson, 1976.
Hayes, Catherine E. (Simpson) [Mary Markwell, pseud.]. *"Aweena": An Indian Story of a Christmas Tryst in the Early Days*. Winnipeg: John A. Hart, 1906.
_____. *Prairie Pot-Pourri*. Winnipeg: Stovel Co., 1895.
_____. "Rough Ben." *Derby Days and Other Poems of the 'Northland' by Yukon Bill*. Toronto: Musson, n.d.
_____. *The Legend of the West*. Victoria, B.C.: n.p., 1908.
Knox, Olive. *Red River Shadows*. Toronto: Macmillan, 1948.
Kogawa, Joy. *Obasan*. 1981. Reprint. Ontario: Penguin, 1983.
Laurence, Margaret. *A Bird in the House*. 1970. Reprint. Toronto: McClelland & Stewart-Bantam, 1974.
_____. *The Diviners*. 1974. Reprint. Toronto: McClelland & Stewart, 1978.
_____. *The Fire-Dwellers*. 1969. Reprint. Toronto: McClelland & Stewart, 1973.
_____. *A Jest of God*. 1966. Reprint. Toronto: McClelland & Stewart-Bantam, 1974.
_____. *The Stone Angel*. 1964. Reprint. Toronto: McClelland & Stewart, 1968.
Laut, Agnes C. *Lords of the North*. Toronto: William Briggs, 1900.
Lysenko, Vera. *Westerly Wild*. Toronto: Ryerson, 1956.
_____. *Yellow Boots*. Toronto: Ryerson, 1954.
McClung, Nellie L. *The Black Creek Stopping-House and Other Stories*. Toronto: William Briggs, 1912.
_____. *Painted Fires*. Toronto: Thomas Allen, 1925.
_____. *Purple Springs*. Toronto: Thomas Allen, 1921.
_____. *The Second Chance*. New York: Doubleday, Page, 1910.

————. *Sowing Seeds in Danny*. Toronto: William Briggs, 1908.

McDougall, E. Jean. *See* Rolyat, Jane

Macmillan, Ann. *Levko*. Toronto: Longmans, Green, 1956.

Markwell, Mary. *See* Hayes, Catherine E.

Ostenso, Martha. *O River, Remember!* New York: Dodd, Mead, 1943.

————. *Wild Geese*. 1925. Reprint. Toronto: McClelland & Stewart, 1961.

Parsons, Nell W. *The Curlew Cried: A Love Story of the Canadian Prairie*. Seattle: Frank McCaffrey, 1947.

————. *Upon a Sagebrush Harp*. Saskatoon, Sask.: Western Producer Prairie Books, 1969.

Riis, Sharon. *The True Story of Ida Johnson*. Toronto: Women's Educational Press, 1977.

Riley, W. L. "Pies." *Stories from Saskatchewan*. Ed. Robert Kroetsch. Moose Jaw: Thunder Creek Publishing Cooperative, 1980.

Rolyat, Jane [E. Jean McDougall]. *The Lily of Fort Garry*. Reprint. Toronto: J. M. Dent & Sons, 1933.

Roy, Gabrielle. *Children of My Heart (Ces enfant de ma vie, 1977)*. Trans. Alan Brown. Toronto: McClelland & Stewart, 1979.

————. *Garden in the Wind (Un jardin au bout du monde, 1975)*. Trans. Alan Brown. Toronto: McClelland & Stewart, 1977.

————. *The Road Past Altamont (La Route D'Altamont, 1966)*. Trans. Joyce Marshall. Toronto: McClelland & Stewart, 1976.

————. *Street of Riches (Rue Deschambault, 1955)*. Trans. Harry Binsse. Toronto: McClelland & Stewart, 1967.

Salverson, Laura G. *The Dark Weaver*. Toronto: Ryerson, 1937.

————. *The Viking Heart*. 1947. Reprint. Toronto: McClelland & Stewart, 1975.

Sapergia, Barbara. *Foreigners*. Moose Jaw, Sask.: Coteau Books, 1984.

Seitz, Mary Ann. *Shelterbelt*. Saskatoon, Sask.: Western Producer Prairie Books, 1979.

Simpson, Kate B. *See* Hayes, Catherine E.

Sluman, Norma. *Poundmaker*. Scarborough, Ont.: McGraw–Hill Ryerson, 1967.

Truss, Jan. *Bird at the Window*. Toronto: Macmillan, 1974.

van der Mark, Christine. *Honey in the Rock*. Toronto: McClelland & Stewart, 1966.

————. *In Due Season*. 1947. Reprint. Vancouver: New Star Books, 1979.

Van Herk, Aritha. *Judith*. 1978. Reprint. Toronto: McClelland & Stewart-Bantam, 1979.

Wiseman, Adele. *Crackpot*. 1974. Reprint. Toronto: McClelland & Stewart, 1978.

————. *The Sacrifice*. 1956. Reprint. Toronto: Macmillan, 1977.

SECONDARY SOURCES

Adamson, Arthur. "Identity through Metaphor: An Approach to the Question of Regionalism in Canadian Literature." *Studies in Canadian Literature* 5.1 (1980): 83–99.

Aldrich, Bess Streeter. "The Story behind *A Lantern in Her Hand.*" *Nebraska History Magazine* 56.2 (1975): 237–41.

Allen, Paula Gunn. "Who Is Your Mother? Red Roots of White Feminism." *Sinister Wisdom* 25 (1984): 34–46.

Ammons, Elizabeth. "Going in Circles: The Female Geography of Jewett's *Country of the Pointed Firs.*" *Studies in the Literary Imagination* 16 (1983): 83–92.

Anderson, William T. "The Literary Apprenticeship of Laura Ingalls Wilder." *South Dakota History* 13.4 (1983): 285–331.

Andrews, Clarence. *A Literary History of Iowa.* Iowa City: Univ. of Iowa Press, 1972.

Angus, Terry, ed. *The Prairie Experience.* Toronto: Macmillan, 1975.

Armitage, Susan H. "Reluctant Pioneers." In *Women and Western American Literature,* ed. Stauffer and Rosowski, 40–51. Troy, N.Y.: Whitston, 1982.

————. "Western Women Writers: A Review Essay." *Frontiers* 5.3 (1981): 71–74.

————. "Women's Literature and the American Frontier: A New Perspective on the Frontier Myth." In *Women, Women Writers, and the West,* ed. Lee and Lewis, 5–13. Troy, N.Y.: Whitston, 1979.

Artibise, Alan. *Winnipeg: An Illustrated History.* Toronto: James Lorimer National Museum of Man, National Museums of Canada, 1977.

Atherton, Stanley S. "Ostenso Revisited." In *Modern Times: A Critical Anthology,* ed. John Moss, 57–65. Toronto: NC Press, 1982.

Atkins, Annette. "Women on the Farming Frontier: The View from Fiction." *Midwest Review* ns 3 (1981): 1–10.

Atwood, Margaret. *Survival: A Thematic Approach to Canadian Literature.* Toronto: Anansi, 1972.

Bataille, Gretchen, and Kathleen Mullen Sands. *American Indian Women: Telling Their Lives.* Lincoln: Univ. of Nebraska Press, 1984.

Baym, Nina. "Melodramas of Beset Manhood: How Theories of American Fiction Exclude Women Authors." *American Quarterly* 33.2 (1981): 123–39.

The Beaver. Special issue. Autumn 1983.

Beecher, Catherine. "On Female Health in America." In *Root of Bitterness,* ed. Nancy F. Cott, 263–76. New York: E. P. Dutton, 1972.

Bennett, Mildred R. "Willa Cather and the Prairie." *Nebraska History Magazine* 2.2 (1975): 231–35.

_____. *The World of Willa Cather*. New York: Dodd, Mead, 1951.

Bercovitch, Sacvan. "The Ritual of American Consensus." *Canadian Review of American Studies* 10 (1979): 272–73.

Berry, Michael W. "Documenting the 19th-Century Quilt." *American Craft*, February/March 1985, 23–27.

Bilan, R. P. Review of *Judith*, by Aritha Van Herk. *University of Toronto Quarterly* 48 (1979): 315.

Billington, Ray. *Land of Savagery, Land of Promise*. New York: W. W. Norton, 1981.

_____. *Westward Expansion*. New York: Macmillan, 1949.

Binnie-Clark, Georgina. *Wheat and Woman*. 1914. Reprint. Toronto: Univ. of Toronto Press, 1979.

Bloom, Edward A., and Lillian D. Bloom. "Willa Cather's Novels of the Frontier: A Study in Thematic Symbolism." *American Literature* 21 (1949): 71–93.

Bogue, Allan G. *From Prairie to Cornbelt*. Chicago: Univ. of Chicago Press, 1963.

Booher, Edwin R. "The Garden Myth in 'The Prairies.' " *Western Illinois Regional Studies* 1.1 (1978): 15–26.

Brinkley, Alan. Review of *Culture as History*, by Warren I. Susman. *New Republic*, 1 April 1985, 36–38.

Brooks, Van Wyck. *The World of Washington Irving*. Philadelphia: Blakiston, 1944.

Brown, Russell M. "The Canadian Eve." *Journal of Canadian Fiction* 3.3 (1974): 89–93.

Brown, Samuel R. *The Western Gazetteer; or Emigrant's Directory*. Auburn, N.Y.: H. C. Southwick, 1817.

Bunkers, Suzanne L. "Strong Women Grow from Black Soil." *Plainswoman* 8.5 (1985): 4–6.

Burlend, Rebecca, and Edward Burlend. *A True Picture of Emigration*. 1848. Reprint. Chicago: Lakeside Press, 1936.

Carp, Roger E. "Hamlin Garland and the Cult of True Womanhood." In *Women, Women Writers, and the West*, ed. Lee and Lewis, 83–99. Troy, N.Y.: Whitston, 1979.

Cather, Willa. "Nebraska." In *America Is West: An Anthology of Middlewestern Life and Literature*, ed. John T. Flanagan. Minneapolis: Univ. of Minnesota Press, 1954.

Catherwood, Mary Hartwell. *Heroes of the Middle West: The French*. Boston: Ginn, 1898.

Chadbourne, Richard. "Two Visions of the Prairies: Willa Cather and Gabrielle Roy." In *The New Land*, ed. Chadbourne and Dahlie, 93–120. Waterloo: Wilfred Laurier Univ. Press, 1978.

Chadbourne, Richard, and Hallvard Dahlie, eds. *The New Land: Studies in a Literary Theme.* Waterloo: Wilfrid Laurier Univ. Press, 1978.

Christ, Carol P. *Diving Deep and Surfacing: Women Writers on Spiritual Quest.* Boston: Beacon Press, 1980.

Colt, Miriam. *Went to Kansas.* 1862. Ann Arbor: University Microfilms, 1966.

Comeau, Paul. "Sinclair Ross's Pioneer Fiction." *Canadian Literature* 103 (1984): 174–84.

Commager, Henry Steele. "The Literature of the Pioneer West." *Minnesota History,* December 1927, 319–28.

Cook, Ramsay. "Imagining a North American Garden: Some Parallels & Differences in Canadian & American Culture." *Canadian Literature* 103 (1984): 10–26.

Cooper, James Fenimore. *The Prairie: A Tale.* 1827. Reprint. New York: Signet, 1964.

Crèvecoeur, J. Hector St. John de. *Letters from an American Farmer.* New York: E. P. Dutton, 1957.

Drake, Earl G. "Regina in 1895: The Fair and the Fair Sex." *Saskatchewan History* 8 (1955): 56–63.

Duncan, Patricia D. *Tallgrass Prairie: The Inland Sea.* Kansas City: Lowell, 1978.

Dyrud, David L. "Varieties of Marginality: Treatment of the European Immigrant in the Middlewestern Frontier Novel." Ph.D. diss., Purdue Univ., 1979.

Fairbanks, Carol, and Sara Brooks Sundberg. *Farm Women on the Prairie Frontier: A Sourcebook for Canada and the United States.* Metuchen, N.J.: Scarecrow Press, 1983.

Faragher, John Mack. *Women and Men on the Overland Trail.* New Haven: Yale Univ. Press, 1979.

Farmer, Catherine D. "Beret as the Norse Mythological Goddess Freya/Gerthr." In *Women and Western American Literature,* ed. Stauffer and Rosowski, 179–93. Troy, N.Y.: Whitston, 1982.

Faulkner, Virginia, and Frederick C. Luebke, eds. *Vision and Refuge: Essays on the Literature of the Great Plains.* Lincoln: Univ. of Nebraska Press for the Center for Great Plains Studies, 1982.

Ferber, Edna. *Cimarron.* New York: Grossett & Dunlap, 1929.

Ferris, Elizabeth Fuller. Foreword to *Letters on an Elk Hunt by a Woman Homesteader,* by Elinore Pruitt Stewart. 1915. Reprint. Lincoln: Univ. of Nebraska Press, 1979.

Filene, Peter Gabriel. *Him/Her/Self: Sex Roles in Modern America.* New York: New American Library, 1976.

Flanagan, Thomas. "Louis Riel and Métis Literature." *World Literature Written in English* 24.1 (1984): 136–44.

Fowler, Marian. *The Embroidered Tent: Five Gentlewomen in Early Canada.*
    Toronto: Anansi, 1982.
Francis, R. Douglas. "Changing Images of the West." *Revue d'études cana-*
    diennes/Journal of Canadian Studies 17 (1982): 5–19.
Frye, Northrop. *The Bush Garden: Essays on the Canadian Imagination.* Toronto:
    Anansi, 1971.
Fuller, Margaret. *Summer on the Lakes* (1844). In *The Writings of Margaret Fuller,*
    ed. Mason Wade, 3–104. Clifton, N.J.: Augustus M. Kelley, 1973.
Garland, Hamlin. *A Daughter of the Middle Border.* 1921. Reprint. New York:
    Sagamore, 1957.
———. *A Pioneer Mother.* Chicago: The Bookfellows, 1922.
———. *A Son of the Middle Border.* 1917. Reprint. New York: Macmillan, 1961.
———. *Trail-makers of the Middle Border.* 1926. Reprint. New York: Grosset &
    Dunlap, 1927.
———. "The West in Literature." *Arena,* November 1892, 669–76.
Geertz, Clifford. *The Interpretation of Cultures: Selected Essays.* New York: Basic
    Books, 1973.
Glaspell, Susan. *The Inheritors.* Boston: Small, Maynard, 1921.
Gom, Leona. *The Land of the Peace.* Saskatoon, Sask.: Thistledown, 1980.
Grove, Frederick Philip. *Fruits of the Earth.* 1933. Reprint. Toronto: Mc-
    Clelland & Stewart, 1965.
———. *Over Prairie Trails.* 1922. Reprint. Toronto: McClelland & Stewart,
    1970.
Gunn, Giles. *The Interpretation of Otherness.* New York: Oxford Univ. Press,
    1979.
Hampsten, Elizabeth. *Read This Only to Yourself: The Private Writings of Mid-*
    western Women, 1880–1910. Bloomington: Indiana Univ. Press, 1982.
Hancock, Geoff. "Interview: Sharon Butala on Prairie Writing." *Books in Cana-*
    da, June/July 1984, 22–23.
Hand, Gail. "Native Daughter: Author Louise Erdrich Comes Home." *Plains-*
    woman 8.4 (1984): 3–5.
Harper, J. Russell. *A People's Art.* Toronto: Univ. of Toronto Press, 1974.
Harrison, Dick. "Rölvaag, Grove and Pioneering on the American and Canadi-
    an Plains." *Great Plains Quarterly* 1 (1981): 252–62.
———. *Unnamed Country: The Struggle for a Canadian Prairie Fiction.* Edmonton:
    Univ. of Alberta Press, 1977.
Haugen, Einar. *Ole Edvart Rölvaag.* Boston: Twayne, 1983.
Healy, W. J. *Women of Red River.* Winnipeg: Women's Canadian Club, 1923.
Henson, Clyde E. *Joseph Kirkland.* New York: Twayne, 1962.
Heriot, George. *Travels through the Canadas.* London: 1807.
Holtz, William. "Closing the Circle: The American Optimism of Laura Ingalls
    Wilder." *Great Plains Quarterly* 4.2 (1984): 79–90.

Hough, Emerson. *The Passing of the Frontier.* New Haven: Yale Univ. Press, 1918.

Inderwich, Mary E. "A Lady and Her Ranch." *Alberta Historical Review* 15 (1967): 1–9.

Jahner, Elaine. "A Laddered, Rain-bearing Rug: Paula Gunn Allen's Poetry." In *Women and Western American Literature,* ed. Stauffer and Rosowski, 312–26. Troy, N.Y.: Whitston, 1982.

James, Stuart B. "Western American Space and Human Imagination." *Western Humanities Review* 24 (1970): 150.

Jameson, Elizabeth. "Women as Workers, Women as Civilizers: True Womanhood in the American West." *Frontiers* 7 (1984): 1–8.

Jaques, Edna. *Prairie Born, Prairie Bred: Poetic Reflections of a Pioneer.* Saskatoon, Sask.: Western Producer Prairie Books, 1979.

Jeffrey, Julie Roy. *Frontier Women: The Trans-Mississippi West, 1840–1880.* New York: Hill & Wang, 1979.

Johnson, E. Pauline. *The White Wampum.* London: John Lane, 1895.

Jones, Dorothy. "'A Kingdom and a Place of Exile': Women Writers and the World of Nature." *World Literature Written in English* 24 (1984): 257–73.

Kane, Paul. *Wanderings of an Artist.* Toronto: The Radisson Society of Canada, 1925.

Karolides, Nicholas J. *The Pioneer in the American Novel, 1900–1950.* Norman: Univ. of Oklahoma Press, 1964.

Kaufman, Polly Welts. *Women Teachers on the Frontier.* New Haven: Yale Univ. Press, 1984.

Kaye, Frances W. "The 49th Parallel and the 98th Meridian: Some Lines for Thought." *Mosaic* 14.2 (1981): 165–75.

———. "Hamlin Garland's Feminism." In *Women and Western American Literature,* ed. Stauffer and Rosowski, 135–61. Troy, N.Y.: Whitston, 1982.

Kirland, Caroline M. *A New Home—Who'll Follow?* 1839. Reprint. Edited with an introduction by William S. Osborne. New Haven: College & University Press, 1965.

———. *Western Border Life; or, What Fanny Hunter Saw and Heard in Kanzas and Missouri.* New York: Derby & Jackson, 1856.

Kirkland, Joseph. *Zury: The Meanest Man in Spring County.* 1887. Reprint. Urbana: Univ. of Illinois Press, 1956.

Kirkwood, Hilda. "Revolution and Resolution: An Interview with Margaret Laurence." *Canadian Forum,* March 1980, 15–18.

Klinck, Carl. Introduction to *The Backwoods of Canada,* by Catherine Parr Traill. Toronto: McClelland & Stewart, 1966.

Klooss, Wolfgang. "Canada's Forgotten People: The Métis in Nineteenth-century Fiction and Drama." *World Literature Written in English* 24.1 (1984): 144–57.

Klug, Michael A. "Willa Cather: Between Red Cloud and Byzantium." *Canadian Review of American Studies* 12.3 (1981): 287–99.

Kolodny, Annette. *The Land before Her: Fantasy and Experience of the American Frontiers, 1630–1860.* Chapel Hill: Univ. of North Carolina Press, 1984.

Kriesel, Henry. "The Prairie: A State of Mind." In *Contexts of Canadian Criticism,* ed. Eli Mandel, 254–66. Chicago: Univ. of Chicago Press, 1971.

Kroetsch, Robert. "The Harvester." In *Wild Rose Country: Stories from Alberta,* ed. David Carpenter, 79–90. Ottawa: Oberon Press, 1977.

_____, ed. *Creation.* Toronto: New Press, 1970.

Lander, Dawn. "Eve among the Indians." In *The Authority of Experience,* ed. Arlyn Diamond and Lee R. Edwards, 194–213. Amherst: Univ. of Massachusetts Press, 1977.

Lang, Andrea. "Sculptor Leo Mol." *Alberta Magazine,* November/December 1980, 8–9.

Laurence, Margaret. *Heart of a Stranger.* Toronto: McClelland & Stewart, 1976.

_____. "Sources." *Mosaic* 3 (Spring 1970): 80–84.

Lauter, Estella. *Women as Mythmakers: Poetry and Visual Art by Twentieth-Century Women.* Bloomington: Indiana Univ. Press, 1984.

Lee, L. L., and Merrill Lewis, eds. *Women, Women Writers, and the West.* Troy, N.Y.: Whitston, 1979.

Le Sueur, Meridel. *North Star Country.* New York: Book Find Club, 1945.

_____. *Rites of Ancient Ripening.* Minneapolis: Vanilla Press, 1975.

Livesay, Dorothy. "Matrona." In *For Openers: Conversations with 24 Canadian Writers,* ed. Alan Twig, 127–37. Madiera Park: Harbour, 1981.

Lowenthal, David. "The Pioneer Landscape: An American Dream." *Great Plains Quarterly* 2.2 (1982): 5–19.

McClung, Nellie L. *Clearing in the West: My Own Story.* New York: Fleming H. Revell, 1936.

McCourt, Edward. *Saskatchewan.* Toronto: Macmillan, 1968.

MacEwan, Grant. *. . . And Mighty Women Too: Stories of Notable Western Canadian Women.* Saskatoon, Sask.: Western Producer Prairie Books, 1975.

McKenna, Isobel. "As They Really Were: Women in the Novels of Grove." *English Studies in Canada* 2 (1976): 109–16.

McKnight, Jeannie. "American Dream, Nightmare Underside: Diaries, Letters and Fiction of Women on the American Frontier." In *Women, Women Writers, and the West,* ed. Lee and Lewis, 25–44. Troy, N.Y.: Whitston, 1979.

McQuin, Susan C. "Alice French's View of Women." *Books at Iowa* 20 (1974): 34–42.

Maclellan, W. E. "Real 'Canadian Literature.'" *Dalhousie Review* 6 (1926): 18–23.

Meier, A. Mabel. "Bess Streeter Aldrich: A Literary Portrait." *Nebraska History Magazine* 50 (1969): 67–100.

Melendy, Mary H. *Perfect Womanood for Maidens—Wives—Mothers.* Chicago: Monarch, 1901.

Mihalyi, Martha. "The Locusts Return." Unpublished poem, 1979.

Miller, James E., Jr. "My *Ántonia* and the American Dream." *Prairie Schooner* 48 (1974): 112–23.

Mitcham, Allison. "Roy's West." *Canadian Literature* 88 (1981): 161–63.

Mitchell, Ken, ed. *Horizon: An Anthology of the Canadian Prairie.* Don Mills: Oxford Univ. Press, 1977.

Moers, Ellen. *Literary Women: The Great Writers.* Garden City: Doubleday Anchor, 1977.

Monk, Janice. "Approaches to the Study of Women and Landscape." *Environmental Review* 8 (1984): 23–33.

Morey-Gaines, Ann-Janine. "On Menace and Men: The Sexual Tensions of the American Frontier Metaphor." *Soundings* 64 (1981): 132–49.

Morris, Wright. *Plains Song: For Female Voices.* 1980. Reprint. New York: Penguin, 1981.

Myres, Sandra L. *Westering Women: The Frontier Experience, 1800–1915.* Albuquerque: Univ. of New Mexico Press, 1982.

Nelson, Frank C. "The Norwegian-American's Image of America." *Illinois Quarterly* 36 (1974): 6.

Nevins, Allan. "A Hero in the Wheatfields." *Saturday Review of Literature,* 25 February 1928, 63.

New York Times Book Review. Review of *The Plow-Woman,* by Eleanor Gates. 13 October 1906: 674.

Nimmo, Dan, and James E. Combs. *Mediated Political Realities.* New York: Longman, 1983.

Norwood, Vera L. "Heroines of Nature: Four Women Respond to the American Landscape." *Environmental Review* 8 (1984): 34–56.

Nute, Grace Lee, ed. "Journey for Frances." *The Beaver,* December 1953, 50–54; March 1954, 12–17; June 1954, 12–18.

Nye, Russel B. "History and Literature: Branches of the Same Tree." In *Essays on History and Literature,* ed. Robert H. Bremner, 123–59. Columbus: Ohio State Univ. Press, 1966.

O'Connor, John J. "Saskatchewan Sirens: The Prairie as Sea in Western Canadian Literature." *Journal of Canadian Fiction* 28/29 (1980): 157–71.

O'Hagan, Thomas. "Some Canadian Women Writers." *Catholic World* 63 (September 1896): 779–95.

Olson, Paul A. "The Epic and Great Plains Literature: Rølvaag, Cather, and Neihardt." *Prairie Schooner* 55 (1981): 263–85.

Osborn, Jennie Stoughton. *Memories.* Medicine Lodge, Kans.: Barber County Index, 1935.

Osborne, William S. *Caroline M. Kirkland.* New York: Twayne, 1972.

Owram, Doug. *Promise of Eden: The Canadian Expansionist Movement and the Idea of the West, 1856–1900.* Toronto: Univ. of Toronto Press, 1980.

Parks, M. G. Introduction to *Fruits of the Earth,* by Frederick Philip Grove. Toronto: McClelland & Stewart, 1965.

Pearson, Carol, and Katherine Pope. *The Female Hero in American and British Literature.* New York: R. R. Bowker, 1981.

Peck, J. M. *Guide for Emigrants, Containing Sketches of Illinois, Missouri, and the Adjacent Parts.* Boston: Lincoln & Edmands, 1831.

Peterman, Michael. "'The Good Game': The Charm of Willa Cather's My Ántonia and W. O. Mitchell's Who Has Seen the Wind." *Mosaic* 14.2 (1981): 93–106.

Pocock, Douglas C. D. "Introduction: Imaginative Literature and the Geographer." In *Humanistic Geography and Literature: Essays on the Experience of Place,* 9–19. London: Croom Helm, 1981.

Powell, Kirsten H. "Cowboy Knights and Prairie Madonnas: American Illustrations of the Plains and Pre-Raphaelite Art." *Great Plains Quarterly* 5 (1985): 39–52.

Price, Robert. "Mrs. Catherwood's Early Experiments with Critical Realism." *American Literature* 17 (1945): 140–51.

_____. "A Critical Biography of Mrs. Mary Hartwell Catherwood: A Study in Middle Western Regional Authorship, 1847–1902." Ph.D. diss., Ohio State Univ., 1943.

Quantic, Diane Dufva. "The Ambivalence of Rural Life in Prairie Literature." *Kansas Quarterly* 12 (1980): 109–19.

Rasmussen, Linda, Lorna Rasmussen, Candace Savage, and Anne Wheeler. *A Harvest Yet to Reap: A History of Prairie Women.* Toronto: Women's Press, 1976.

Rees, Ronald. "In a Strange Land . . . Homesick Pioneers on the Canadian Prairie." *Landscape* 26.3 (1982): 1–9.

_____. "Nostalgic Reaction and the Canadian Prairie Landscape." *Great Plains Quarterly* 2 (1982): 157–67.

Reid, Mary J. "The Theories of Octave Thanet and Other Western Realists." *Midland Monthly* 9.2 (1898): 99–108.

Reigstad, Paul. *Rölvaag: His Life and Art.* Lincoln: Univ. of Nebraska Press, 1972.

Rich, Adrienne. *On Lies, Secrets and Silence.* New York: W. W. Norton, 1979.

Ricou, Laurence. "Empty as Nightmare: Man and Landscape in Recent Canadian Prairie Fiction." *Mosaic* 6.2 (1973): 143–60.

———. *Twelve Prairie Poets.* Ottawa: Oberon, 1976.

———. *Vertical Man/Horizontal World: Man and Landscape in Canadian Prairie Fiction.* Vancouver: Univ. of British Columbia Press, 1973.

Riley, Glenda. *Frontierswomen: The Iowa Experience.* Ames: Iowa State Univ. Press, 1981.

———. *Women and Indians on the Frontier, 1825–1915.* Albuquerque: Univ. of New Mexico Press, 1984.

———. "Women on the Great Plains: Recent Developments Research." *Great Plains Quarterly* 5.2 (1985): 81–92.

Robbins, Frances Lamont. "An Epic Unachieved." *Outlook,* 21 May 1928, 475.

Rölvaag, Ole. *Giants in the Earth: A Saga of the Prairie.* Trans. Lincoln Colcord and the author. 1927. Reprint. New York: Perennial Library, 1955.

———. *Peder Victorious.* Trans. Nora O. Solum and the author. New York: Harper, 1929.

Ross, Sinclair. *Sawbones Memorial.* 1974. Reprint. Toronto: McClelland & Stewart, 1978.

Roy, Gabrielle. "Mon héritage du Manitoba." *Mosaic,* 3 (1970): 69–79.

———. *Fragiles lumières de la terre.* Montreal: Les éditions quinze, 1978. *The Fragile Lights of Earth: Articles and Memories 1942–1970.* Trans. Alan Brown. Toronto: McClelland & Stewart, 1982.

Sallquist, Sylvia Lea. "The Image of the Hired Girl in Literature: The Great Plains, 1860 to World War I." *Great Plains Quarterly* 4 (1984): 166–77.

Salverson, Laura Goodman. "An Autobiographical Sketch." *Ontario Library Review* 14 (1930): 69–73.

———. *Confessions of an Immigrant's Daughter.* London: Faber & Faber, 1939.

Savage, Candace. *Foremothers.* N.p., n.d.

———. *Our Nell: A Scrapbook Biography of Nellie L. McClung.* Saskatoon, Sask.: Western Producer Prairie Books, 1979.

Scarberry, Susan J. "Land into Flesh: Images of Intimacy." *Frontiers* 6 (1982): 24–28.

Schleuning, Neala J. Y. "Meridel Le Sueur: Toward a New Regionalism." *Books at Iowa* 33 (1980): 22–41.

Scholes, Robert. "The Fictional Heart of the Country: From Rølvaag to Gass." In *Ole Rølvaag: Artist and Cultural Leader,* ed. Gerald Thorson, 1–13. Northfield, Minn.: St. Olaf College Press, 1975.

Sears, Sue. "Louise Erdrich's Family Tree Has Deep Roots." *Plainswoman* 8.4 (1984): 5, 7.

Shanks, William F. G. "The Great American Desert." *Lippincott's Magazine* 49 (1892): 735–42.

Simpson, Frances. *See* Nute, Grace Lee

Skårdal, Dorothy Burton. *The Divided Heart: Scandinavian Immigrant Experience through Literary Sources.* Lincoln: Univ. of Nebraska Press, 1974.

Smith, Henry Nash. *Virgin Land: The American West as Symbol and Myth.* Cambridge: Harvard Univ. Press, 1950.

Smith-Rosenberg, Carroll. "The Female World of Love and Ritual: Relations between Women in Nineteenth-Century America." *Signs* 1 (1975): 1–29.

Smith-Steffen, Pamela S. "Quilt Making in Fort Atkinson, Wisconsin: A View of the Personal Aspects, 1830–1900." M.S. thesis, Univ. of Wisconsin-Madison, 1975.

Socken, Paul. "Art and the Artist in Gabrielle Roy's Works." *Revue de l'Université d'Ottawa* 45 (1975): 344–50.

Soule, Caroline A. *The Pet of the Settlement: A Story of Prairie-Land.* Boston: A. Tompkins, 1860.

Spence, Thomas. *The Prairie Lands of Canada.* Montreal: Gazette Printing House, 1880.

Stauffer, Helen Winter, and Sandra J. Rosowski, eds. *Women and Western American Literature.* Troy, N.Y.: Whitston, 1982.

Steele, Charles, ed. *Taking Stock: The Calgary Conference on the Canadian Novel.* Toronto: ECW Press, 1982.

Stewart, Catherine. *New Homes in the West.* 1843. Ann Arbor: University Microfilms, 1966.

Stratton, Joanna L. *Pioneer Women: Voices from the Kansas Frontier.* New York: Simon & Schuster, 1981.

Suckow, Ruth. "Iowa." In *America Is West: An Anthology of Middlewestern Life and Literature,* ed. John T. Flanagan, 609–18. Minneapolis: Univ. of Minnesota Press, 1954.

Sundberg, Sara Brooks. "A Study of Farmwomen on the Minnesota Prairie Frontier: 1850–1900." M.A. thesis, Univ. of Wisconsin–Eau Claire, 1984.

Svendsen, Gro. *Frontier Mother: The Letters of Gro Svendsen.* Northfield, Minn.: Norwegian-American Historical Association, 1950.

Thomas, Clara. "Women Writers and the New Land." In *The New Land,* ed. Chadbourne and Dahlie, 45–59. Waterloo: Wilfrid Laurier Univ. Press, 1978.

Thomas, Mrs. Henry J. *The Prairie Bride; or The Squatter's Triumph.* New York: Beadle, 1869.

Thomas, Lewis G. "Western Responses in History and Fiction: Social Structures in a Canadian Hinterland." In *Crossing Frontiers: Papers in American and Canadian Western Literature,* ed. Dick Harrison, 59–72. Edmonton: Univ. of Alberta Press, 1979.

Thompson, Eric Callum. "The Prairie Novel in Canada: A Study in Changing Form and Perception." Ph.D. diss., Univ. of New Brunswick, 1974.

Thomson, Gladys Scott. *A Pioneer Family: The Birkbecks in Illinois, 1818–1827.* London: Jonathan Cape, 1953.

de Tocqueville, Alexis. *Democracy in America.* Trans. George Lawrence. Garden City: Doubleday Anchor, 1969.

Traill, Catherine Parr. *The Backwoods of Canada.* 1836. Reprint. Toronto: McClelland & Stewart, 1966.

Tuan, Yi-Fu. "Literature and Geography: Implications for Geographical Research." In *Humanistic Geography: Prospects and Problems,* ed. David Ley and Marwyn S. Samuels, 194–206. London: Croom Helm, 1978.

———. *Space and Place: The Perspective of Experience.* Minneapolis: Univ. of Minnesota Press, 1977.

———. *Topophilia: A Study of Environmental Perception, Attitudes, and Values.* Englewood Cliffs: Prentice-Hall, 1974.

Underwood, June O. "The Civilizers: Women's Organizations and Western American Literature." In *Women and Western American Literature,* ed. Stauffer and Rosowski, 3–16. Troy, N.Y.: Whitston, 1982.

Van Cleve, Charlotte Ouisconsin. *"Three Score Years and Ten": Life-Long Memories of Fort Snelling, Minnesota, and Other Parts of the West.* Minneapolis: Harrison & Smith, 1888.

Van Kirk, Sylvia. *Many Tender Ties: Women in Fur-Trade Society, 1670–1870.* Norman: Univ. of Oklahoma Press, 1980.

Victor, Frances Fuller. *Alicia Newsome; or The Land Claim: A Tale of the Upper Missouri.* New York: Beadle, 1862.

Victor, Metta Victoria. *Myrtle, the Child of the Prairie.* New York: Beadle, 1863?

———. *Uncle Ezekial and His Exploits on Two Continents.* New York: Beadle, 1861?

Wasserstrom, William. "The Lily and the Prairie Flower." *American Quarterly* 9 (1957): 398–411.

Waterman, Arthur E. *Susan Glaspell.* New York: Twayne, 1966.

Waterston, Elizabeth. *Survey: A Short History of Canadian Literature.* Toronto: Methuen, 1973.

Webb, Walter Prescott. *The Great Plains.* Boston: Ginn, 1931.

Westfall, William. "On the Concept of Region in Canadian History and Literature. *Journal of Canadian Studies* 15 (1980): 3–15.

Whiteman, Roberta Hill. *Star Quilt.* Minneapolis: Holy Cow! Press, 1984.

Wood, Susan. "God's Doormats: Women in Canadian Prairie Fiction." *Journal of Popular Culture* 14.2 (1980): 350–59.

Woodcock, George. *Canada and the Canadians.* Harrisburg, Pa.: Stackpole Books, 1973.

———. *The Canadians.* Cambridge: Harvard Univ. Press, 1979.

Wright, John S. *Letters from the West; or A Caution to Emigrants:* 1819. Ann Arbor: University Microfilms, 1966.

Wydeven, Joseph J. "Wright Morris, Women, and American Culture." In *Women and Western American Literature,* ed. Stauffer and Rosowski, 212–29. Troy, N.Y.: Whitston, 1982.

Zieman, Margaret. "Nellie Was a Lady Terror." *Maclean's,* 1 October 1953, 20–21, 62–66.

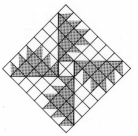

Index